International
Accounting
Standards
Explained

INTERNATIONAL ACCOUNTING STANDARDS EXPLAINED

International
Accounting Standards
Committee®

JOHN WILEY & SONS, LTD
New York • Chichester • Weinheim • Brisbane • Singapore • Toronto

Published in 2000 by   John Wiley & Sons Ltd.,
                            Baffins Lane, Chichester,
                            West Sussex PO19 1UD, England

                            National   01243 779777
                            International   (+44) 1243 779777
                            e-mail (for orders and customer service enquiries): cs-books@wiley.co.uk
                            Visit our Home Page on http://www.wiley.co.uk
                            or http://www.wiley.com

Other Wiley Editorial Offices

John Wiley & Sons, Inc., 605 Third Avenue,
New York, NY 10158-0012, USA

Wiley-VCH Verlag GmbH, Pappelallee 3,
D-69469 Weinheim, Germany

Jacaranda Wiley Ltd, 33 Park Road, Milton,
Queensland 4064, Australia

John Wiley & Sons (Asia) Pte Ltd, 2 Clementi Loop #02-01,
Jin Xing Distripark, Singapore 129809

John Wiley & Sons (Canada) Ltd, 22 Worcester Road,
Rexdale, Ontario M9W 1L1, Canada

British Library Cataloguing in Publication Data

A catalogue record for this book is available from the British Library.

ISBN 0-471-72037-2

Typeset in 10pt Palatino by Nick Battley, London, England (http://www.nickbattley.com).
Printed and bound in Great Britain by Antony Rowe Ltd., Chippenham, Wiltshire.
This book is printed on acid-free paper responsibly manufactured from sustainable forestation, for which at least two trees are planted for each one used for paper production.

Contents

Preface

Increasingly, there are two accepted global financial reporting languages: US Generally Accepted Accounting Principles (US GAAP) and International Accounting Standards (IAS). IAS are increasingly recognised as having reached a level of maturity and rigour that they are used in the preparation of the financial statements of many global companies and accepted by securities markets in many countries of the world.

The International Accounting Standards Committee – a private organisation with members from all over the world who work in the accounting field – is responsible for the development, approval and constant improvement of IAS.

This book is an introduction to IASC and to the requirements of IAS. It outlines how the standards are used on a daily basis by companies in the preparation of their financial statements. However, the book is also written for students. Fundamental knowledge of IASC Standards is getting more and more relevant during the time at university as well as an advantage in the labour market.

Part One of this book offers a detailed description of the International Accounting Standards Committee, how it is structured, its various standard-setting bodies and the process it follows in developing IAS. The remainder of the book examines the use of IAS from a practice orientation, and looks at the main components of the financial statements, including questions of recognition and measurement of key financial statement items.

There is also a discussion of the IASC *Framework for the Preparation and Presentation of Financial Statements*. The Framework provides a foundation for the development of new standards and is used as a reference for applying IAS in the absence of detailed application guidance.

Individual paragraphs in an IAS are referenced by numbers in brackets after each paragraph in the text. The reason for this is twofold: it is important to know where a requirement referred to in the text comes from; but, more importantly, the IASC Standards have a great deal of background material which provides important context for the requirements.

This book is, necessarily, a summary of the IASC Standards and may not be suitable for all purposes. Where a particular fact pattern is being assessed, reference to the actual Standards is recommended.

London, September 2000

Kurt P. Ramin
IASC Commercial Director

An Important Note about IASC Standards

Throughout this book, references are made to specific numbered IASC Standards. If readers wish to consult the full text of any such Standard, they should obtain a copy of the current *Bound Volume of International Accounting Standards*, an annual publication which may be ordered through the IASC's website: www.iasc.org.uk.

For the convenience of readers who consult specific IASC Standards in the *Bound Volume* or elsewhere, the following article may clarify certain issues concerning typography:

It's all Black and White[1]

Paul Pacter, IASC International Accounting Fellow, gives his opinion on the continuing controversy about whether there is any difference between what is written in bold type and in normal type in IASC Standards.

At IASC we recently received this inquiry from one of the large accounting firms on the use of bold faced type in International Accounting Standards:

> *Do you know how the concept of black letter v. grey letter guidance originated in IASC standards? Is there an "official description" of the difference? It's never been quite clear to me. Some people believe strongly that the grey is "guidance" which may be applied versus the black-letter standard which must be applied (though I'm not sure how anyone would ever apply a standard with only benefit of the black letter). Others, as I'm sure you're aware – like the SEC – assert that the whole thing is standard and don't distinguish. I'm just trying to figure out what the "official" version is.*

At the beginning of each IAS the following statement is made:

> *The standards, which have been set in bold italic type, should be read in the context of the background material and implementation guidance in this Standard, and in the context of the Preface to International Accounting Standards.*

Neither the IASC Constitution nor the Preface to International Accounting Standards prescribes how an IAS should be formatted. Neither of those documents refers to black letter (bold type) paragraphs and grey letter (normal type) paragraphs in an IAS. Since the IASC Standards were reformatted in the early 1990s, the Board has used bold type to express matters of general principle (what IASC calls standards, lowercase "s"). Normal type has been used to express finer points of detail. Both, however, are part of the International Accounting Standard. (Standard with an uppercase "s" means a numbered IASC pronouncement.)

The grey letter paragraphs are intended to elaborate on the standards – to provide guidance on how to apply the general principles. They do not require accounting

---

[1] *This article appeared originally in 'World Accounting Report', May 2000. Reprinted with permission.*

treatments or disclosures that do not flow directly from the standards. And, of course, they do not contradict the standards.

By convention, IASC uses the word "should" in drafting the standards in the bold type paragraphs ("revenue from the sale of goods should be recognised when all the following conditions have been satisfied..."). We avoid using the word "should" in the guidance paragraphs because it might suggest a new accounting treatment or disclosure additional to those prescribed by the standards.

IAS 1, *Presentation of Financial Statements*, requires compliance "with all the requirements of each applicable Standard [note the uppercase 's'] and each applicable Interpretation" if financial statements are to be described as conforming to IAS. IAS 1 makes no distinction between black and grey letter typefaces in the Standard. It is the view of the IASC Secretariat that:

• the standards, the background material, and the implementation guidance, taken together, form the Standards to which IAS 1 requires compliance; and

• the bold type and normal type paragraphs are equally authoritative under IAS 1.

None of us would support a mandatory versus optional distinction.

Incidentally, in voting to approve an International Accounting Standard, the IASC Board votes on the Standard in its entirety. The Board does not vote only on the bold type paragraphs or on them separately from the grey.

Some IAS include appendixes with illustrative disclosures (see, for instance, IAS 35, *Discontinuing Operations*) or examples of applying the principles in the Standard (see, for instance, IAS 34, *Interim Reporting*, and IAS 37, *Provisions, Contingent Liabilities and Contingent Assets*). These appendixes begin with a commentary similar to the following:

> *This appendix is illustrative only and does not form part of the standards. The purpose of the appendix is to illustrate the application of the standards to assist in clarifying their meaning.*

The illustrative appendixes are included in the draft that is before the Board when it votes to approve a Standard, as well as in the exposure draft on which public comment was sought before the Standard was issued. While the illustrations do not form part of the standards (lowercase "s"), they do represent guidance that has been subjected to thorough due process and review by the IASC Board.

The Board has published the basis for its conclusions with some Standards. Bases for conclusions are not intended to contain any new standards or, for that matter, any new guidance. Rather, they are intended to provide background information that may be useful to understanding the reasons for the standards and the guidance in the IAS.

The bottom line, as we at the IASC Secretariat see it, is that the black letter paragraphs and grey letter paragraphs in an IASC pronouncement together, and with equal authoritativeness, constitute an International Accounting Standard.

Part I:

General Description of IASC

Introduction

The International Accounting Standards Committee (IASC) is an independent private sector body, formed with the objective of achieving uniformity in the accounting principles which are used by businesses and other organisations for financial reporting around the world. It was formed in 1973 through an agreement made by professional accountancy bodies from Australia, Canada, France, Germany, Japan, Mexico, the Netherlands, the United Kingdom and Ireland and the United States of America. Since 1983, IASC's members have included all the professional accountancy bodies that are members of the International Federation of Accountants (IFAC). At present, 153 members in 112 countries represent over two million accountants. Many other organisations are now involved in the work of IASC and many countries that are not members of IASC make use of International Accounting Standards.

In addition to the accountancy profession, IASC's work has the worldwide support and involvement of the business community, financial executives, financial analysts, stock exchanges, securities regulators, lawyers, and bankers.

IASC also works closely with the national standard setting bodies, securities regulatory agencies and stock exchanges in individual countries, intergovernmental organisations—such as the European Commission, the OECD, and the UN—and development agencies such as the World Bank.

The work of IASC is made possible by financial support from the professional accountancy bodies and other organisations on its Board, by IFAC, and by contributions from companies, financial institutions, accounting firms and other organisations. IASC also generates revenue from the sale of its publications.

As this book is being written (March 2000), the structure of IASC is being changed. These changes are discussed in the section 'A New Structure for IASC', on page 22, with further details provided in the Appendix on pages 23-27.

Use of International Accounting Standards

International Accounting Standards have done a great deal to improve, harmonise and encourage convergence in financial reporting standards around the world. They are used:

(a) as a basis for national accounting requirements in many countries;

(b) as an international benchmark by certain countries that develop their own requirements (including major industrialised countries as well as an increasing number of emerging markets such as China and many other countries in Asia, Central Europe and the former Soviet Union);

(c) by stock exchanges and regulatory authorities that allow or require foreign or domestic companies to present financial statements in accordance with IAS;

(d)   by supranational bodies such as the European Commission, which announced that it is relying heavily on IASC to produce standards that meet the needs of capital markets; and

(e)   by a growing number of companies, even in countries that do not require IAS.

IOSCO "Core Standards" Programme

The International Organization of Securities Commissions (IOSCO) is looking to IASC to provide acceptable International Accounting Standards for use in multinational securities offerings and other international offerings. Already, many stock exchanges require or permit foreign issuers to present financial statements in accordance with International Accounting Standards. As a result, a growing number of companies disclose the fact that their financial statements conform with International Accounting Standards.

In 1995, IASC agreed with IOSCO to develop a set of "core standards", as identified in a list developed by IOSCO in 1993. If the completed core standards satisfy IOSCO, it will consider endorsing International Accounting Standards for cross-border capital raising and listing purposes in all global markets.

By March 2000, IASC had completed work on the projects in the agreed work programme. IASC believes that the body of IAS now provides a comprehensive basis of accounting. The Standards are of high quality — that is, they will result in transparency and comparability and they provide for full disclosure.

Along with other commentators, IOSCO has responded to IASC Invitations to Comment on each of those projects as they progressed. IOSCO is nearing the completion of its assessment of whether the core standards will enable it to endorse the set of core standards as a whole. In February 2000, the United States Securities and Exchange Commission issued a *Concept Release* on the acceptance of International Accounting Standards as a basis of registering securities in the US markets. In light of the IOSCO assessment, this action by the SEC is seen as additional evidence that IASC will have achieved its goal when it undertook the 'core standards' project.

Objectives of IASC

The objectives of IASC, as stated in its 1992 Constitution, are:

- "to formulate and publish in the public interest accounting standards to be observed in the presentation of financial statements and to promote their worldwide acceptance and observance; and

- to work generally for the improvement and harmonisation of regulations, accounting standards and procedures relating to the presentation of financial statements."(Paragraph 2)

At present, financial reports prepared for shareholders and other users involve principles and procedures that can vary widely from country to country, and sometimes even within a country. Accounting reports, therefore, can lack comparability. This is highly unsatisfactory because investment analysts and other users incur extra costs of analysis when the reports are prepared according to different standards. They may be confused in their interpretation of the reports. Effective competition among the capital markets of the world may be impaired and companies may have to bear higher costs of capital because of the difficulties involved in financial analysis. Accounting reports lose credibility if a company reports different profit numbers in different countries for given transactions. Also, international diversity may cause:

- preparation costs for financial reports that are much higher than necessary — a multinational company may have to prepare different reports on its operations for use in different countries; and

- businesses to want a uniform system for assessing financial performance in their operations in different countries. They may also want their external reports to be consistent with internal assessments of performance. These two objectives are not achievable if accounting standards vary from country to country.

International Accounting Standards are also of great usefulness for developing countries or other countries which do not have a national standard setting body or do not have the resources to undertake the full process of preparing accounting standards. The preparation of accounting standards involves considerable cost and, quite apart from the advantages of uniformity, it would not be economic for each country to have a separate process.

The magnitude of cross-border financing transactions, securities trading, and direct foreign investment is enormous, often in smaller as well as larger countries. To support cross-border and financing decisions, the world needs a single, uniform, globally-applied and enforced set of standards of financial accounting and reporting. The statistics below about cross-border financing transactions provide clear evidence of that need.

Most stock exchanges around the world have foreign listings, in many cases a relatively large percentage of total listings.

Exchange	Total Number of Companies	% Foreign Companies
North America		
Amex	705	8.9
Nasdaq	4,894	8.5
NYSE	2,652	14.5
Toronto	1,412	3.5
South America		
Lima	249	1.2
Rio de Janeiro	531	0.2
Sao Paulo	492	0.2
Europe, Africa, Middle East		
Amsterdam	377	38.2
Barcelona	413	1.0
Bilbao	264	0.8
Brussels	269	43.5
Copenhagen	250	4.4
Germany	3,872	80.5
Helsinki	137	1.5
Ireland	104	21.2
Italy	241	0.8
Johannesburg	686	2.6
London	2,863	17.5
Luxemburg	270	81.5
Madrid	551	0.7
Oslo	232	9.5
Paris	1,121	15.6
Stockholm	288	6.6
Switzerland	411	44.3
Vienna	123	22.8
Asia Pacific		
Australian	1,218	5.0
Hong Kong	685	2.0
Kuala Lumpur	737	0.4
New Zealand	177	33.3
Osaka	1.272	0.1
Singapore	298	12.4
Tokyo	1,901	2.5

Figure A **Number of domestic and foreign companies with shares listed on major Stock Exchanges and Parallel Markets, 1998, excluding investment funds**

Source: Table 5, Website of the Fédération Internationale des Bourses de Valuers (FIBV, the International Federation of Stock Exchanges) – www.fibv.com

Some bond markets also have a relatively large percentage of foreign listings.

Exchange	Total Issuers	% of Foreign Bond Issuers
NYSE	533	10.9
Amsterdam	204	35.3
Germany	653	53.0
London	1,686	41.9
Madrid	125	21.6
Paris	498	22.5
Tokyo	568	4.8

Figure B   **Number of domestic and foreign bond issuers with bonds listed on selected major exchanges, 1998**

Source: Table II.1.1, Web Site of the Fédération Internationale des Bourses de Valuers (FIBV, the International Federation of Stock Exchanges) – www.fibv.com

Cross-border securities sales in five of the six major countries below exceed the country's gross domestic product.

	1980	1985	1990	1995	1996	1997	1998
United States	9	35	89	135	160	213	230
Japan	8	62	119	65	79	96	91
Germany	7	33	57	172	199	253	334
France	5	21	54	187	258	313	415
Italy	1	4	27	253	470	672	640
Canada	9	27	65	189	251	358	331

Figure C   **Cross-border transactions in bond equities as a percentage of gross domestic product (GDP) (Gross purchases and sales of securities between residents and non-residents)**

Source: Table VI.1, Bank for International Settlements, 68th Annual Report (1998)

Organisation

This section describes the structure of the IASC as at 1 July 2000 (see Figure D). This structure will likely be replaced in 2001. The proposed new structure is described at the end of this section.

The basic structural Framework for the IASC is set out by the IASC's Constitution. A new IASC Constitution was approved by the Members of IASC in May 2000. The new Constitution provides the necessary Framework for the transition from the current structure to the new structure, especially with respect to the powers and responsibilities of the IASC Trustees appointed in May 2000 (see page 24). The Trustees have the duty, under the Constitution, to make preparatory arrangements for bringing into effect the new structure set out in the Constitution. The duties of the Trustees include determining and creating a new legal entity as a vehicle for the operations of IASC and that legal entity must confer limited liability on its members. The new Constitution requires the Trustees to incorporate its provisions in the Constitution of the new legal entity, *mutatis mutandis*, and the authoritative statement of the Constitution will therefore be given in the documents of the new entity in due course.

IASC Board

The Members of IASC are all those professional accountancy bodies that are Members of IFAC. A meeting of the Members is held every two-and-a-half years in conjunction with each General Assembly of IFAC. Under IASC's Constitution, the Members have no direct role in the approval of International Accounting Standards or the appointment of the IASC Board.

Under the IASC Constitution, the Members of IASC have delegated the responsibility for all IASC's activities to the IASC Board. The Board has the power to:

(a)   co-opt up to four organisations having an interest in financial reporting on to the Board;

(b)   remove from membership of the Board any Board Member whose financial contribution is more than one year in arrears or which fails to be represented at two successive Board meetings;

(c)   publish documents relating to international accounting issues for discussion and comment provided a majority of the Board votes in favour of publication;

(d)   issue documents in the form of exposure drafts for comment (including amendments to existing standards) in the name of the International Accounting Standards Committee provided that at least two-thirds of the Board votes in favour of publication;

(e)   issue International Accounting Standards provided that at least three-quarters of the Board votes in favour of publication;

IASC – Current Structure (as at 1 July 2000)

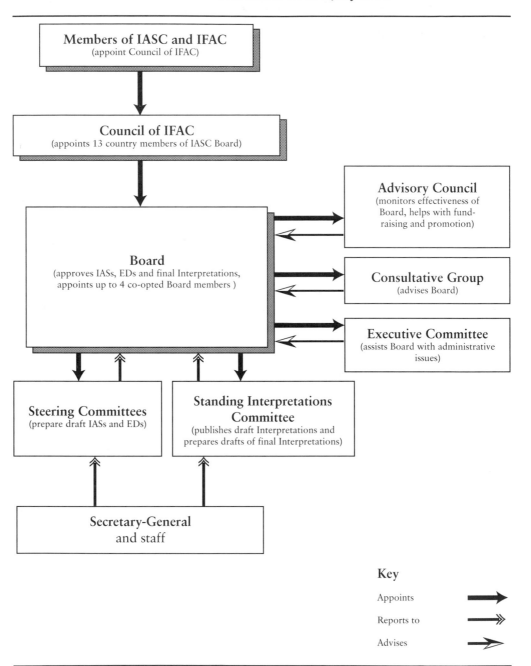

Figure D

(f)   establish operating procedures, so long as they are not inconsistent with the provisions of IASC's Constitution;

(g)   enter into discussions, negotiations or associations with outside bodies and generally promote the world-wide improvement and harmonisation of accounting standards; and

(h)   seek and obtain funds from Members of IASC and non-members which are interested in supporting the objectives of IASC provided that such funding is organised in such a way that it does not impair the independence, or the appearance of independence, of IASC.

It follows from the powers granted to the Board that it is, at present, solely responsible for, among other things:

(a)   determining the due process used to develop International Accounting Standards;

(b)   choosing topics on its work programme and the priorities attached to those topics; and

(c)   appointing Steering Committees, the Consultative Group, the Advisory Council and the Executive Committee.

The Board comprises:

(a)   thirteen country Members, appointed by the Council of IFAC after seeking the advice of the outgoing Board; and

(b)   up to four co-opted Members, appointed by the Board itself.

The thirteen country Members represent Members of IASC. To widen the membership of the Board, the Council of IFAC has appointed more than one country to share certain seats. Under the Constitution, the thirteen country Members are appointed by the Council of IFAC for up to five years, although recent appointments have been for two and a half years. Board Members may be re-appointed without limit.

Under Mutual Commitments agreed between IFAC and IASC, the Council of IFAC nominates to the IASC Board, after seeking the advice of the outgoing Board:

(a)   at least nine of the most significant countries in terms of the status and development of the accountancy profession or that are of significant importance to international commerce and trade; and

(b)   preferably, not less than three developing countries.

The Council of IFAC must satisfy itself that the nominees have standards and resources which would enable them to contribute to the work of the Board and are willing on the invitation of the Board to nominate persons to carry out assignments or to join Steering Committees or groups constituted to undertake tasks allotted by the Board.

The co-opted Members are organisations with an interest in financial reporting. The terms of the co-opted Board Members are determined by the Board itself, with no upper limit.

Each Board Member has one vote. Decisions are taken on a simple majority of the Board, except that a positive vote by two-thirds of all Board Members is required to approve an Exposure Draft and a positive vote by three-quarters of all Board Members is required to approve an International Accounting Standard, or, subject to the ratification of IASC's Members, to approve changes to the Constitution.

Each Board Member may nominate up to two representatives and a technical adviser to attend Board meetings. Neither the Board nor IASC can compel Board Members to nominate particular individuals, or individuals with particular characteristics. However, the Board encourages each Board Member to include in its delegation at least one person working in business and one person who is directly involved in the work of the national standard setting body.

The IASC Constitution states that Board Representatives shall not regard themselves as representing sectional interests, but shall be guided by the need to act in the public interest.

In addition to the Board Members, four organisations have observer status at IASC Board meetings. They have the right of the floor (i.e. to participate in the deliberations), but do not have a vote.

The IASC Board used to meet three times a year for three or four days at a time. In 1996 the Board agreed to accelerate its work programme under an agreement with IOSCO. As a result, the Board now meets four times a year for five or six days at a time. This imposes heavy demands on the Board and it would be difficult for a Board made up of volunteers to continue meeting so often once the IOSCO work programme is completed.

IASC Board meetings are open to the public. IASC announces administrative details on its website (www.iasc.org.uk).

Figure E shows the IASC Board Members (Board Representatives and Technical Advisors) for the two-and-a-half year term ending 30 June 2000, as well as organisations with observer status.

The IASC Chairman is elected by the Board Representatives from among their number and serves a non-renewable term of two-and-a-half years. The Board has applied an informal policy that the Chairmanship should rotate between different regions.

The Board agreed in November 1997 to appoint two Vice-Chairmen for the next term, instead of a Deputy Chairman. The main reasons for this are to:

(a)   avoid the need to identify a Chairman-elect at a time when, because of the current strategy review, the Chairman's role was under review; and

(b)   spread the increasing burden of speaking commitments and other promotional and representational duties more widely.

In July 2000, Thomas E. Jones, International Association of Financial Executives Institutes (IAFEI) became Chairman of the Board of the IASC. Patricia A. McConnell, International Council of Investment Associations (ICIA) is the Vice Chairman of the IASC. They will continue in office until the new IASC structure becomes operational.

Board Representatives and *Technical Advisers (1 July 2000)

- *Australia*
  Brian Morris, Edwards, Marshall & Co, Adelaide
  Ken Spencer, Accounting Standards Board, Melbourne
  Angus Thomson*, Australian Accounting Standards Board, Melbourne

- *Canada*
  Paul Cherry, PricewaterhouseCoopers, Toronto
  James C. Gaa, University of Alberta, Edmonton
  Robert Rutherford*, The Canadian Institute of Chartered Accountants, Toronto

- *France*
  Gilbert Gélard, KPMG Audit, Paris
  Jean Keller, Lafarge, St. Cloud
  Christophe Patrier*, Conseil Supérieur de l'Ordre des Experts Comptables, Paris

- *Germany*
  Helmut Berndt, Henkel KGaA, Düsseldorf
  Jochen H. Pape, PricewaterhouseCoopers, Düsseldorf
  Klaus-Peter Naumann*, Institut der Wirtschaftsprüfer, Düsseldorf

- *India and Sri Lanka*
  Thekkiam Sitaram Vishwanath, New Delhi
  Reyaz Mihular, KPMG Ford, Rhodes, Thornton & Co., Colombo, Sri Lanka

- *Japan*
  Tatsumi Yamada, Chuo Audit Corporation, Tokyo
  Shozo Yamazaki, Tohmatsu & Co., Tokyo

- *Malaysia*
  Katharene Expedit, Malaysian Institute of Accountants, Kuala Lumpur
  Tony Seah, Malaysian Institute of Accountants, Kuala Lumpur

- *Mexico*
  Luis Moiron, PricewaterhouseCoopers, Mexico D.F.
  Carlos Buenfil*, Ruíz Urquiza y Cia, SC, Mexico D.F.

- *Netherlands*
  Jean den Hoed, Akzo Nobel NV, Arnhem
  Jan Klaassen, KPMG Accountants NV, and Vrije Universiteit, Amsterdam
  Ruud G. A. Vergoossen*, Koninklijk Nederlands Instituut van Registeraccountants, Amsterdam

- *Nordic Federation of Public Accountants (Denmark, Finland, Iceland, Norway, and Sweden)*
  Per Gunslev, KPMG, Copenhagen
  Sigvard Heurlin, PricewaterhouseCoopers, Stockholm
  Erik Mamelund, Arthur Andersen, Oslo

- *South Africa and Zimbabwe*
  Rosanne Blumberg, The South African Institute of Chartered Accountants, Johannesburg
  Peter Wilmot, Deloitte & Touche, Gallo Manor
  W. Leslie Anderson*, Deloitte & Touche, Harare, Zimbabwe
  Erna Swart*, South African Institute of Chartered Accountants, Johannesburg

Cont.

(cont.)

- *United Kingdom*
  Christopher W. Nobes, University of Reading, Reading
  Sir David Tweedie, Accounting Standards Board, London
  David A. Perry*, Institute of Chartered Accountants in England and Wales, London

- *United States of America*
  Mitchell A. Danaher, General Electric Company, Fairfield, CT
  Elizabeth A. Fender*, American Institute of Certified Public Accountants, New York
  Fred Gill*, American Institute of Certified Public Accountants, New York

- *International Council of Investment Associations*
  David C. Damant, The European Federation of Financial Analysts' Societies, London
  Patricia A. McConnell, Bear, Stearns & Co. Inc., New York (IASC Vice Chairman)
  Rolf Rundfelt, KPMG AB, Stockholm
  Patricia Doran Walters*, Association for Investment Management and Research, Charlottesville
  Toshihiko Amano (Observer), Security Analysts Association of Japan

- *Federation of Swiss Industrial Holding Companies*
  Harry Schmid, Nestlé, Vevey
  Malcolm Cheetham, Novartis, Basel
  Philipp M. Hallauer*, KPMG Fides Peat, Zurich

- *International Association of Financial Executives Institutes (IAFEI)*
  Thomas E. Jones, Citigroup, New York (IASC Chairman)
  David C. Potter, British American Tobacco PLC, London

Board Observers

- *European Commission*
  Karel van Hulle
  Allister Wilson*

- *U.S. Financial Accounting Standards Board (FASB)*
  Anthony Cope

- *International Organization of Securities Commissions (IOSCO)*
  Francis Desmarchelier, France
  D J Gannon, Unites States of America
  Toshiyuki Kenmochi, Japan

- *People's Republic of China*
  Feng Shuping
  Shen Xiaonan
  Chen Yugui

Figure E

Executive Committee

The Board appoints an Executive Committee to address administrative matters. It does not have power with respect to setting International Accounting Standards. Normally, it studies a matter and makes a recommendation to the Board. For certain urgent matters, the Executive Committee reaches decisions subject to ratification by the Board. Among the kinds of administrative matters dealt with by the Executive Committee are:

- organisation, plans, and structure of the IASC
- promotional activities
- budgets and finance
- appointment and membership of steering committees
- dates and locations of Board meetings
- appointment of the Secretary-General
- IASC due process
- relationships with Member Bodies and IFAC.

Members of the Executive Committee

- Thomas E. Jones, IASC Chairman
- Patricia McConnell, IASC Vice Chairman
- David Damant, Financial Analysts
- Gilbert Gélard, France
- Jan Klaassen, Netherlands
- Jochen Pape, Germany
- Thekkiam Sitaram Vishwanath, India
- Peter Wilmot, South Africa
- Tatsumi Yamada, Japan
- Sir Bryan Carsberg, IASC Secretary-General

Figure F

Consultative Group

In 1981, the IASC Board established a Consultative Group that includes representatives of international organisations of preparers and users of financial statements, stock exchanges, securities regulators, development agencies, standard setting bodies, and intergovernmental organisations.

The Consultative Group advises the Board on technical issues in specific projects, on the plans and priorities as set out in the work programme, on the likely acceptability of IASC's standards and on the strategy. This group plays a helpful part in IASC's due process for the setting of International Accounting Standards and in gaining acceptance for them.

The Consultative Group used to meet the full Board twice a year, for one day at a time. With the increasing numbers of participants, these meetings became less productive and the Consultative Group now meets selected Board Representatives, once a year for two days at a time.

Current Members of the Consultative Group

- European Commission*
- Fédération Internationale des Bourses de Valeurs (FIBV)
- Financial Accounting Standards Board (FASB)*
- International Association for Accounting Education and Research (IAAER)
- International Banking Associations
- International Bar Association (IBA)
- International Chamber of Commerce (ICC)
- International Confederation of Free Trade Unions (ICFTU), and World Confederation of Labour
- International Finance Corporation (IFC)
- International Valuation Standards Committee (IVSC)
- The World Bank
- Organisation for Economic Co-operation and Development (OECD)*
- United Nations Division on Transnational Corporations and Investment*

*Observers

Figure G

Advisory Council

In 1995, IASC established a high-level international Advisory Council to promote generally the acceptability of International Accounting Standards and enhance the credibility of IASC's work by, among other things:

- reviewing and commenting on the Board's strategy and plans so as to satisfy itself that the needs of IASC's constituencies are being met;
- preparing an annual report on the effectiveness of the Board in achieving its objectives and in carrying out its due process;
- promoting participation in, and acceptance of, the work of IASC by the accountancy profession, the business community, the users of financial statements and other interested parties;
- seeking and obtaining funding for IASC's work in a way that it does not impair IASC's independence; and
- reviewing IASC's budget and financial statements.

Among other things, the Advisory Council ensures that the independence and objectivity of the Board in making technical decisions on proposed International Accounting Standards are not impaired. The Advisory Council does not participate in, or seek to influence, those decisions.

The members of the Advisory Council are outstanding individuals in senior positions from the accountancy profession, business and other users of financial statements from different backgrounds. The Advisory Council does not include representatives of national standard setters. The Chairman, Deputy-Chairmen and Secretary-General of IASC are invited to, and expected to attend, all meetings of the Advisory Council, but the Council is free to meet without them. The members of the Advisory Council are appointed by the IASC Board and serve two-year terms and they can be re-elected. Currently, the Council has 11 members. The Advisory Council elects its own Chairman. It meets at least annually.

Members of Advisory Council

- Stephen D. Eccles (Chairman), Former Vice President, The World Bank

- James Cochrane, United States, New York Stock Exchange

- Michael Cook, United States,
        Deloitte & Touche, Former Chairman, US Financial Accounting Foundation

- Thomas E. Jones, IASC Chairman

- Frank Harding, United Kingdom, President of IFAC

- Dr. Jürgen Krumnow, Germany,
        Member of the Board of Managing Directors, Deutsche Bank AG

- Kimiaki Nakajima, Japan, Corporation Finance Research Institute (COFRI)

- Linda Quinn, United States, Shearman & Sterling

- Michael Sharpe, Australia, Former Chairman of IASC

- Gerard Worms, France, Partner, Rothschild Bank

- Antonio Zoido, Spain, President, Madrid Stock Exchange

Figure H

Steering Committees

For its technical projects, the Board normally appoints a Steering Committee to:

(a)   direct the preliminary research carried out by the staff;

(b)   submit a Point Outline to the Board, in order to clarify the scope of the project;

(c)   in the light of the Board's comments on the Point Outline, prepare and publish a Draft Statement of Principles;

(d)   in the light of public comments on the Draft Statement of Principles, prepare and submit a Statement of Principles to the Board;

(e)   based on the Statement of Principles approved by the Board, prepare and submit a draft Exposure Draft to the Board; and

(f)   in the light of public comments on the Exposure Draft, prepare and submit a draft of the final International Accounting Standard to the Board.

For certain projects, the Board may permit Steering Committees to omit one or more of stages (b), (c) and (d).

Steering Committees are chaired by a Board Representative and usually have around six to eight members (four from Board Member countries, one from a Consultative Group organisation, and one or more members from other organisations). Most Steering Committee members are neither Board Representatives nor members of their national standard setter.

The candidates for membership of a Steering Committee may be nominated by Members of IASC, other organisations that are represented on the Board or the Consultative Group and other organisations that are expert in the particular topic. In appointing Steering Committees, the Board seeks both a geographical balance and a mix of accountants in public practice, preparers and users. The Board also aims to ensure that the Steering Committee has sufficient specialist knowledge of the topic.

The Constitution states that members of Steering Committees shall not regard themselves as representing sectional interests but shall be guided by the need to act in the public interest.

The Board's current policy is to ask IOSCO to nominate an observer to attend each Steering Committee in which IOSCO has a special interest. Steering Committee meetings are not open to the public.

Standing Interpretations Committee

The Standing Interpretations Committee (SIC) was formed by the IASC Board in 1997 to consider, on a timely basis, accounting issues that are likely to receive divergent or unacceptable treatment in the absence of authoritative guidance. Its review will be within the context of existing International Accounting Standards and the IASC Framework. In developing interpretations, the SIC will work closely with similar national committees. The SIC meets four times each year.

The SIC deals with issues of reasonably widespread importance, and not issues of concern to only a small set of enterprises. The interpretations will cover both:

• mature issues (unsatisfactory practice within the scope of existing International Accounting Standards); and

• emerging issues (new topics relating to an existing International Accounting Standard but not considered when the Standard was developed).

The SIC has twelve voting members from various countries, including individuals from the accountancy profession, preparer groups and user groups. Some current members of the SIC are members of similar national bodies. IOSCO and the European Commission are observers. Because of the required time commitment, only two current members of the SIC are also Board Representatives. To ensure adequate liaison with the Board, two Board Representatives will attend SIC meetings as non-voting Board Liaison Members.

The SIC publishes a draft interpretation, if no more than three of its voting members have voted against the draft. The public comment period for draft interpretations is two months. After considering comments received, the SIC amends the draft as it considers necessary. If no more than three of its voting members have voted against the final interpretation, the SIC will ask the Board to approve the interpretation for formal publication; as for International Accounting Standards, this requires three-quarters of the Board to vote in favour.

Members of the SIC (as at 1 July 2000)

- Paul Cherry, Chairman, Canada

- Junichi Akiyama, Professor of Accounting, Japan

- Yves Bernheim, Mazars and Guérard, France

- Mary Keegan, PricewaterhouseCoopers, United Kingdom

- Domingo Marchese, Marchese Grandi Meson, Argentina

- Harry Schmid, Switzerland

- Wienand Schruff , KPMG, Germany

- John Smith, Deloitte & Touche, United States

- Kevin Stevenson, Stevenson McGregor, Australia

- Leo van der Tas, Ernst & Young, The Netherlands

- Patricia Doran Walters,
    Association for Investment Management and Research, United States

IASC Board Member Liaison

- Peter Wilmot, Deloitte & Touche, South Africa

Observers

- IOSCO

- European Commission

Secretary to SIC

- Susan Harding – sharding@iasc.org.uk

Figure I

IASC Staff

The IASC Board is supported by a staff based in London, headed by a Secretary-General. The staff currently comprises:

(a)   the Secretary-General (Sir Bryan Carsberg from the UK);

(b)   a Technical Director (James Saloman from Canada), and six other full-time technical staff. Current and recent past technical staff have been from Australia, Bermuda, China, France, Germany, Japan, Malaysia, New Zealand, South Africa, the UK and the USA. The technical staff are generally on secondments for one to two years, although some are employed on a longer-term basis; and

(c)   a Commercial Director (Kurt P. Ramin from the United States) and nine other support staff.

Two recent IASC projects have been carried out jointly with national standard setters who have supplied project managers at no cost to IASC (other than direct travel costs).

The Role of IFAC

Under the current structure of IASC, the accountancy profession plays a major part in supporting and funding the work of IASC. Professional accountancy bodies took the lead in establishing IASC because of the accountancy profession's important role at that time in the setting of national accounting standards in many countries. The support of the national and accountancy bodies and IFAC has contributed greatly to the acceptance of International Accounting Standards. IASC's relationship with IFAC is set out in Mutual Commitments signed in 1982. In summary these are:

(a)   all Members of IFAC are automatically also Members of IASC;

(b)   after seeking the advice of the outgoing Board, the Council of IFAC nominates the thirteen country Members of the IASC Board;

(c)   the IASC Board is required to discuss with the Council of IFAC any proposed changes to the constitution of IASC. However, IFAC or IASC may amend their respective constitutions without the approval of the other body provided that such amendment is not in conflict with the substance of the Mutual Commitments (amendments to IASC's Constitution require a three-quarters majority of the IASC Board and approval by the Members of IASC as expressed by a simple majority of those voting);

(d)   the President of IFAC or his designate is entitled to attend, and speak at, IASC Board meetings and the IASC Chairman may attend, and speak at, meetings of the Council of IFAC;

(e)   IFAC recognises IASC as the sole body having responsibility and authority to issue, in its own name, pronouncements on international accounting standards with full authority in so doing to negotiate and associate with outside bodies and to promote the worldwide acceptance and observance of those standards. IFAC shall not appoint or support any other body for this purpose and shall not itself formulate or consider or publish any other such standards but shall support the standards promulgated by IASC and shall require its Members to support the work of IASC by publishing in their respective countries every International Accounting Standard approved for issue by the Board of IASC and by using their best endeavours:

(i)   to ensure that published financial statements comply with International Accounting Standards in all material respects and disclose the fact of such compliance;

(ii)   to persuade governments and standard-setting bodies that published financial statements should comply with International Accounting Standards in all material respects;

(iii)   to persuade authorities controlling securities markets and the industrial and business community that published financial statements should comply with International Accounting Standards in all material respects and disclose the fact of such compliance;

(iv)   to ensure that the auditors satisfy themselves that the financial statements comply with International Accounting Standards in all material respects; and

(v)   to foster acceptance and observance of International Accounting Standards internationally;

(f) IFAC contributes one ninth of the budgeted net expenditure that the Board determines should be borne by Board members. Also, IFAC currently reimburses the cost of one Board seat. This subsidy is shared equally by India, Sri Lanka and Zimbabwe; and

(g) changes to the Mutual Commitments require both the approval of the Council of IFAC and three-quarters of the total of the votes of the Board of IASC.

Funding of IASC

IASC is a non-profit organisation that depends primarily on financial contributions from its constituents for its operating expenses. The work of IASC is made possible by financial support from the professional accountancy bodies and other organisations on its Board, by IFAC, and by contributions from companies, financial institutions, accounting firms, and other organisations. IASC also generates revenue from the sale of its publications. IASC's 1999 budget was approximately £2 million.

A New Structure for IASC

The IASC completed the last review of its strategy and structure in 1994. However, the experience gained while completing the IOSCO 'Core Standards' work programme prompted the IASC Board to instigate a review of its structure, operating procedures and funding arrangements.

In 1997, the IASC Board formed the Strategy Working Party, which was charged (among other things) with the task of reviewing *"the strategy of IASC generally for the period following completion of the current work programme in 1998."* In particular, the working party was to *"consider whether a major focus of the work of IASC after 1998 should be to narrow further the differences between national standards and international standards. It should consider what procedures would be appropriate for this task and, in particular, whether some new form of association, agreement or working arrangement between IASC and national standard setters is desirable."*

The Working Party prepared a discussion document, "Shaping IASC for the Future", for comment in December 1998, which noted that while work on the IOSCO 'Core Standards' was nearly complete, challenging work faced IASC. Of primary importance was the need to bring about convergence between national accounting standards and practices and high-quality global accounting standards. To this end, the Working Party believed that IASC needed an effective infrastructure that will bring its experience and current work together with those of national standard setters.

The Working Party's original plans for change were subsequently revised, and its final recommendations were presented in its Final Report, "Recommendations on Shaping IASC for the Future", to the IASC Board in November 1999. The IASC Board subsequently adopted the Working Party's recommendations (which are discussed overleaf) in December 1999 and began implementing them immediately.

Appendix

IASC – New Structure

A New Governing Body

Under the recommendations, the IASC will be reorganised as a separate body, such as a Foundation, and be governed by Trustees.

In December 1999, the Board appointed a **Nominating Committee**. The sole responsibility of the Nominating Committee is to appoint the initial Trustees under the new structure. The members of the Nominating Committee were:

IASC – Nominating Committee

- Dr. Karl H. Baumann, Chairman of the Supervisory Board, Siemens AG, and Deputy Chairman of DRSC (the German national accounting standard setter)

- Mr James Copeland, Jr, Chief Executive Officer, Deloitte Touche Tohmatsu

- Mr Howard Davies, Chairman, UK Financial Services Authority

- Mr Arthur Levitt, Jr, Chairman, US Securities and Exchange Commission (Chairman)

- Mr Michel Prada, Chairman, French Commission des Opérations de Bourse

- Mr Andrew Sheng, Chairman, Hong Kong Securities and Futures Commission

- Mr James Wolfensohn, President, The World Bank

Figure J

The Nominating Committee appointed the Initial Trustees in May 2000. Having completed its work, the Nominating Committee has disbanded.

The **Trustees** will appoint the Members of the Board, SIC and Standards Advisory Council. The Trustees will also monitor IASC's effectiveness, raise funds for IASC, approve IASC's budget and have responsibility for constitutional changes. The Trustees will be nineteen individuals of diverse geographic and functional backgrounds. Trustees will be appointed so that, initially, there will be six from North America, six from Europe, four from Asia Pacific, and three others from any area, as long as geographic balance is maintained. IFAC will suggest candidates to fill five of the nineteen Trustee seats and international organisations of preparers, users, and academics will each suggest one candidate. The remaining eleven Trustees will be "at-large", in that they will not be selected through the constituency nomination process. The existing Trustees will follow similar procedures in selecting subsequent Trustees to fill vacancies.

Figure K

The Standard Setting Function

The current Board will be replaced by a new **Board** of fourteen individuals (twelve full-time Members and two part-time Members). The Board will have sole responsibility for setting accounting standards. The foremost qualification for Board membership will be technical expertise and the Trustees will exercise their best judgement to ensure that the Board is not dominated by any particular constituency or regional interest. At least five Board Members will have a background as practising auditors, at least three will have a background in the preparation of financial statements, at least three will have a background as users of financial statements, and at least one will have an academic background. Several (but no more than seven) of the fourteen Board Members will be expected to have direct responsibility for liaison with one or more national standard setters. The publication of a Standard, Exposure Draft, or final SIC Interpretation will require approval by eight of the Board's fourteen Members.

IASC – New Structure

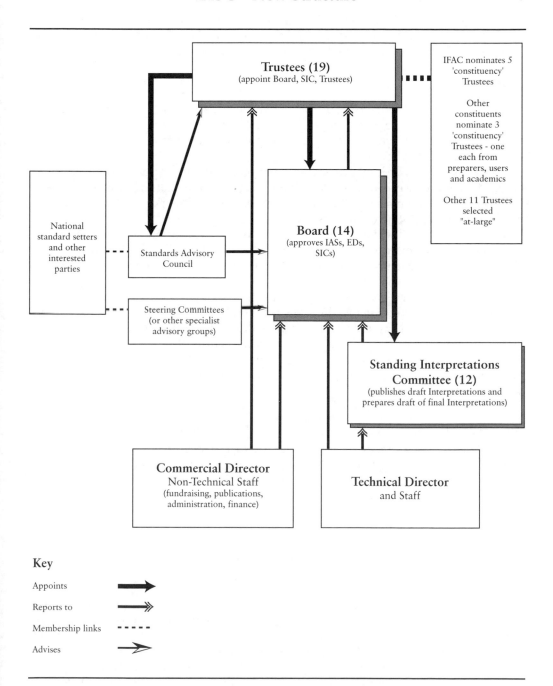

Figure L

Standards Advisory Council

A new **Standards Advisory Council** will provide a formal vehicle for further groups and individuals having diverse geographic and functional backgrounds to give advice to the Board and, at times, to advise the Trustees.

Staff

The Report stressed that IASC must be self-sufficient as regards having the staff to carry out its technical agenda. The technical staff will support the Board, Standards Advisory Council, and SIC. A high quality technical staff of fifteen was considered to be a 'reasonable starting number'.

Some projects may be joint projects with national standard setters and the national standard setter concerned may contribute some of the staff resources needed. However, IASC's own staff will need to monitor the staff work on these projects to ensure that the output meets IASC's needs.

Technical functions will be headed by a Technical Director who will be appointed by the Board Chairman in consultation with the Trustees. The Technical Director, while not a Board Member, will be entitled to participate in the debate at Board meetings.

A Commercial Director will manage publications and copyright, communications, fundraising, administrative and finance staff. The Board Chairman, in consultation with the Trustees, will appoint an individual to the position of Commercial Director.

The function of chief executive officer, currently performed by the Secretary-General, should pass to the Chairman of the Board. However, to ensure continuity, the current position of Secretary-General will probably be maintained in the transitional period.

Due Process

To secure IASC's legitimacy, IASC's due process must ensure the development of International Accounting Standards that are of high quality, requiring transparent and comparable information that will enable participants in capital markets to make sound economic decisions. Users and preparers of financial statements are more likely to accept the Standards if they have extensive opportunities to contribute to their development. Given IASC's higher profile today, the greatly increased interest in its work and a changing role, it is appropriate to seek improvement of IASC's due process. Commentators responding to the December 1998 Discussion Paper expressed strong support for its recommendations in relation to strengthening IASC's due process.

In general, the Board would work in whatever way it considers most effective and cost efficient. It would normally form Steering Committees or other forms of specialist advisory groups to give advice on major projects. The Board may also wish to outsource detailed research or other work to national standard setters.

The Board would determine the scope of any projects formally added to its agenda. The process for the development of a Standard would involve the following steps:

(a)   during the early stages of a project, the Board would normally establish a Steering Committee to give advice on the issues arising in the project. Consultation with the Steering Committee and the Standards Advisory Council would occur throughout the project;

(b)   the Board would normally develop and publish a Draft Statement of Principles or similar discussion document for public comment;

(c)   following the receipt and review of comments, the Board would develop and publish an Exposure Draft for public comment; and

(d)   following the receipt and review of comments, the Board would issue a final Standard.

The following passages address additional elements of the due process that would be followed in the development of an International Accounting Standard.

Voting

Each Board Member would have one vote on technical and other matters. The publication of a Standard, Exposure Draft, or final SIC Interpretation would require approval by eight of the Board's fourteen Members. Other decisions, including the issuance of a Draft Statement of Principles or a Discussion Paper and agenda decisions, would require a simple majority of the Board Members present at a meeting attended by 50% or more of the Board Members. The Board would have full control over its technical agenda.

Each SIC Member would have one vote on a SIC Interpretation. Eight voting Members of the SIC would represent a quorum. Approval of SIC Interpretations would require no more than three Members of the SIC present at the meeting voting against the proposal.

Openness of Meetings

Board meetings would continue to be open to public observation, as has been the case from March 1999. SIC meetings would be opened to public observation as soon as is practical. However, certain discussions (primarily selection, appointment and other personnel issues) would need, at the Board's and SIC's discretion, to be held in private. Portions of the Trustees' meetings would also be open to the public, at the discretion of the Trustees.

IASC could make more use of new technology (such as the Internet, the website, electronic observation of meetings), to overcome geographical barriers and the logistical problems for members of the public in attending open meetings.

IASC would publish in advance the agenda for each meeting of the Standing Interpretations Committee, Board and Trustees and would publish promptly a summary of the technical decisions made at Board and SIC meetings and, where appropriate, decisions of the Trustees.

When IASC publishes a Standard, it would publish a Basis for Conclusions to explain publicly how it reached its conclusions and to give background information that may help users of IASC standards to apply them in practice. IASC would also publish dissenting opinions (IASC's current Constitution prohibits this).

Comment Periods

IASC would continue its practice of issuing each Exposure Draft of a Standard, Discussion Paper, and Draft SIC Interpretation for public comment. The Working Party believes that there is now a case for IASC to extend its comment periods for Exposure Drafts and other discussion documents relating to a proposed Standard. A minimum of four to six months would be appropriate. Draft Interpretations would continue to be exposed for a 60-day comment period.

Public Hearings and Field Tests

The Working Party believes that the Board should make appropriate use of the following, although there would be no requirement to do so for every project:

(a)   'public hearings' to discuss proposed standards; and

(b)   field tests (both in developed countries and in emerging markets) to ensure that proposals are practical and workable around the world.

Where practical, public hearings and field tests should be coordinated with national standard setters.

The IASC Board approved the resolutions necessary for formal amendment of its constitution at its meeting in March 2000. The changes were also approved by the member bodies of IASC in May 2000. It is expected that the proposed structure will come into effect on 1 January 2001.

Development of International Accounting Standards and Interpretations

The following discussion about the development of IAS is based on the existing due process, not on the proposed one in connection with IASC's new structure.

IASC's due process tries to ensure that International Accounting Standards are of high quality in that they require appropriate accounting practices in particular economic circumstances. The due process also ensures, through consultation with the Consultative Group, IASC's Member Bodies, standard setting bodies and other interested groups and individuals on a worldwide basis, that International Accounting Standards are acceptable to the users and preparers of financial statements.

The due process for an International Accounting Standard is as follows:

Procedures for issuing an IASC Standard

- Agenda Decision
- Steering Committee appointed by the Board
- Point Outline

  Defines the scope of the project.

  Steering Committee prepares, Board approves.

- Draft Statement of Principles

  Issued by Steering Committee for comment.

- Final Statement of Principles

  Prepared by Steering Committee.

  Approved by Board (simple majority).

- Exposure Draft

  Prepared by Steering Committee.

  Approved by Board (two-thirds vote).

  Published for public comment.

  On some projects, the Board proceeds directly to an Exposure Draft without first publishing a Draft Statement of Principles. Occasionally, if significant changes are made as a result of public comments on an Exposure Draft, a revised Exposure Draft is published for comment before a final IAS is issued.

- Final International Accounting Standard

  Approved by Board (three-quarters vote).

Figure M

Detailed Steps of the Due Process

- Board Representatives, Member Bodies, members of the Consultative Group, other organisations and individuals, and the IASC staff are encouraged to submit suggestions for new topics which might be dealt with in IAS.

- The Steering Committee identifies and reviews all the accounting issues associated with the topic. The Steering Committee considers the application of IASC's Framework for the Preparation and Presentation of Financial Statements to those accounting issues. The Steering Committee also studies national and regional accounting requirements and practice, including the different accounting treatments that may be appropriate in different circumstances. Having considered the issues involved, the Steering Committee may submit a Point Outline to the Board, in order to clarify the scope of the project.

- After receiving comments from the Board on the Point Outline, if any, the Steering Committee normally prepares and publishes a Draft Statement of Principles (DSOP) or other discussion document. The purpose of this Statement is to set out the underlying accounting principles that will form the basis for the preparation of an Exposure Draft. It also describes the alternative solutions considered and the reasons for recommending their acceptance or rejection. Board approval is not required for the Draft Statement of Principles. Comments are invited from all interested parties during the exposure period, usually around three months. The Board may instruct the Steering Committee to prepare an Exposure Draft without first publishing a Draft Statement of Principles.

- The Steering Committee reviews the comments on the Draft Statement of Principles and normally agrees a final Statement of Principles, which is submitted to the Board for approval and used as the basis for preparing an Exposure Draft of a proposed International Accounting Standard. The final Statement of Principles is available to the public on request, but is not formally published.

- The Steering Committee prepares a draft Exposure Draft for approval by the Board. After revision, and with the approval of at least two-thirds of the Board, the Exposure Draft is published. Comments are invited from all interested parties during the exposure period, a minimum of one month and usually at least three months.

- The Steering Committee reviews the comments and prepares a draft International Accounting Standard for review by the Board. After revision, and with the approval of at least three-quarters of the Board, the standard is published.

During this process, the Board may decide that the needs of the subject under consideration warrant additional consultation or would be better served by issuing a Discussion Paper for comment. Under the IASC Constitution, the Board has the power to publish documents relating to international accounting issues for discussion and comment provided that a majority of the Board votes in favour. In some cases, Steering Committees or the staff have issued Discussion Papers or Issues Papers without formal Board approval.

Standing Interpretations Committee Procedures

Suggestions for an SIC issue may be put forward by any individual or organisation for consideration by SIC. However, someone who wishes to have an issue added to the agenda should take into consideration the following criteria:

- the issue should involve an interpretation of an existing Standard within the context of the IASC Framework (i.e. "parallel standard setting" or interfering with current projects is not within SIC's mandate);

- the issue should have practical and widespread relevance (i.e. priority is given to issues that are important to the accounting practice of many companies, usually across countries and industries; issues that are merely of theoretical interest are not dealt with);

- the issue relates to a specific fact pattern (i.e. broad or politically highly contentious areas where no guidance exists so far will be transferred to the Board; for example, the measurement of equity compensation); and

- significantly divergent interpretations are emerging or exist already in practice (i.e. divergence or even abuse have been observed).

If no more than three of its twelve voting members have voted against an interpretation, the SIC will ask the Board to approve the interpretation for issue; as for International Accounting Standards, this will require three-quarters of the Board to vote in favour.

The public is invited to comment on Draft Interpretations. Interpretations will be formally published after approval by the Board.

IASC's Operating Procedures do not allow IASC staff to give private advice on the meaning of International Accounting Standards.

Authoritative Pronouncements

The IASC has three basic categories of authoritative pronouncements:

- The Framework for the Preparation and Presentation of Financial Statements
- International Accounting Standards
- Interpretations

Framework

The IASC "Framework for the Preparation and Presentation of Financial Statements" (often called the Framework) sets out the concepts that underlie the preparation and presentation of financial statements for external users.

The Framework assists the Board:

(a)   in the development of future International Accounting Standards and in its review of existing International Accounting Standards; and

(b)   in promoting the harmonisation of regulations, accounting standards and procedures relating to the presentation of financial statements by providing a basis for reducing the number of alternative accounting treatments permitted by International Accounting Standards.

International Accounting Standards (IAS)

Outstanding IAS

IASC publishes its Standards in a series of pronouncements called International Accounting Standards (often abbreviated as "IAS"). Standards are numbered sequentially IAS 1, IAS 2, etc. When an IAS is revised, it may retain its old number, with the revision date shown parenthetically, for example, IAS 12 (revised 1996). IASC publishes and prints individual Standards, usually within 30 days after the Board approves them. IASC publishes a Bound Volume of all Standards and Interpretations annually, usually in March, as well as a CD-ROM of all Standards and Interpretations and certain other due process documents (updated three times a year).

Proposed Standards, known as Exposure Drafts, are numbered sequentially: E51, E52, E53, and so on. These are published individually.

Outstanding IAS

IAS	Title / Content
IAS 1	Presentation of Financial Statements
IAS 2	Inventories
IAS 7	Cash Flow Statements
IAS 8	Profit or Loss for the Period, Fundamental Errors and Changes in Accounting Policies
IAS 10	Events After the Balance Sheet Date
IAS 11	Construction Contracts
IAS 12	Income Taxes
IAS 14	Segment Reporting
IAS 15	Information Reflecting the Effects of Changing Prices
IAS 16	Property, Plant and Equipment
IAS 17	Leases
IAS 18	Revenue
IAS 19	Employee Benefits
IAS 20	Accounting for Government Grants and Disclosure of Government Assistance
IAS 21	The Effects of Changes in Foreign Exchange Rates
IAS 22	Business Combinations
IAS 23	Borrowing Costs
IAS 24	Related Party Disclosures
IAS 26	Accounting and Reporting by Retirement Benefit Plans
IAS 27	Consolidated Financial Statements and Accounting for Investments in Subsidiaries
IAS 28	Accounting for Investments in Associates
IAS 29	Financial Reporting in Hyperinflationary Economies
IAS 30	Disclosures in the Financial Statements of Banks and Similar Financial Institutions
IAS 31	Financial Reporting of Interests In Joint Ventures
IAS 32	Financial Instruments: Disclosures and Presentation
IAS 33	Earnings Per Share
IAS 34	Interim Financial Reporting
IAS 35	Discontinuing Operations
IAS 36	Impairment of Assets
IAS 37	Provisions, Contingent Liabilities and Contingent Assets
IAS 38	Intangible Assets
IAS 39	Financial Instruments: Recognition and Measurement
IAS 40	Investment Property

Figure N

Outstanding Exposure Drafts

E	Comment Deadline	Title / Content
E65	31 January 2000	Agriculture
E66	10 September 2000	Financial Instruments: Recognition and Measurement - Limited Revision to IAS 39
E67	10 September 2000	Pension Plan Assets – Limited Revision to IAS 19
E68	10 September 2000	Income Tax Consequences of Dividends – Limited Revision to IAS 12

Figure O

Benchmark and Allowed Alternative Treatments

In some cases, where International Accounting Standards permit two accounting treatments for like transactions and events, one treatment is designated as the *benchmark treatment* and the other as the *allowed alternative treatment*.

The Board's 1990 Statement of Intent on the Comparability of Financial Statements gave the following explanation: *"The Board has concluded that it should use the term 'benchmark' instead of the proposed term 'preferred' [the term proposed in E32, Comparability of Financial Statements] in those few cases where it continues to allow a choice of accounting treatment for like transactions and events. The term 'benchmark' more closely reflects the Board's intention of identifying a point of reference when making its choice between alternatives."*

Interpretations

Outstanding and Draft Interpretations

In 1997, IASC began publishing a series of Interpretations of International Accounting Standards developed by the Standing Interpretations Committee (SIC) and approved by the IASC Board.

- Final Interpretations are numbered sequentially: SIC-1, SIC-2, and so on.

- Draft Interpretations are numbered sequentially: D1, D2, D3, and so on.

Outstanding Interpretations

SIC	Title / Content
SIC–1	Consistency – Different Cost Formulas for Inventories
SIC–2	Consistency – Capitalisation of Borrowing Costs
SIC–3	Elimination of Unrealised Profits and Losses on Transactions with Associates
SIC–5	Classification of Financial Instruments – Contingent Settlement Provisions
SIC–6	Costs of Modifying Existing Software
SIC–7	Introduction of the Euro
SIC–8	First-Time Application of IASs as the Primary Basis of Accounting
SIC–9	Business Combinations – Classification either as Acquisitions or Uniting of Interests
SIC–10	Government Assistance – No Specific Relation to Operating Activities
SIC–11	Foreign Exchange – Capitalisation of Losses Resulting from Severe Currency Devaluations
SIC–12	Consolidation – Special Purpose Entities
SIC–13	Jointly Controlled Entities – Non-Monetary Contributions by Venturers
SIC–14	Property, Plant and Equipment – Compensation for the Impairment or Loss of Items
SIC–15	Operating Leases – Incentives
SIC–16	Presentation of Treasury Shares
SIC–17	Equity – Costs of an Equity Transaction
SIC–18	Consistency – Alternative Methods
SIC–20	Equity Accounting Method – Recognition of Losses
SIC–21	Income Taxes – Recovery of Revalued Non-Depreciable Assets
SIC–22	Business Combinations – Subsequent Adjustment of Fair Values and Goodwill Initially Reported
SIC–23	Property, Plant and Equipment – Major Inspection or Overhaul Costs
SIC–25	Income Taxes – Changes in the Tax Status of an Enterprise or its Shareholders

---

Figure P

Draft Interpretations

- D19, Reporting Currency – Hyperinflationary Economies *(see D19R)*

- Revised D19, Reporting Currency – Measurement and Presentation of Financial Statements Under IAS 21 and IAS 29 – *12 July 00*

- D24, Earnings Per Share – Financial Instruments that May Be Settled in Shares – *12 July 00*

Figure Q

Projects

At any point in time, the IASC Board normally has several projects on its agenda. Some deal with accounting matters not currently addressed in IASC Standards. Others involve revising existing Standards.

Projects for New IAS

IASC's current work plan is summarised below. IASC reports on its technical projects in its quarterly newsletter, *IASC Insight* and on its website. IASC publishes a report on Board decisions immediately after each Board meeting in its newsletter *IASC Update*.

List of IASC current projects in 2000 / 2001:

- Agriculture
- Business Combinations
- Business Reporting on the Internet
- Disclosure by Banks and Similar Financial Institutions
- Discounting
- Emerging Markets (*formerly Developing Countries and Economies in Transition*)
- Extractive Industries
- Financial Instruments: Limited Revisions to IAS 39
- Financial Instruments: IAS 39 Implementation Guidance
- Financial Instruments Comprehensive Project (*International Joint Working Group*)
- Income Tax Consequences of Dividends
- Insurance
- Pension Plan Assets
- Present Value (*formerly Discounting*)
- Reporting Financial Performance

Figure R

Agriculture

- Point outline approved.
- World Bank is providing funding.
- Draft Statement of Principles – December 1996.
- Exposure Draft E65 – July 1999.

Summary of Exposure Draft

❑ *Definition of Agriculture:* The managed transformation of biological assets (living animals and plants) to yield agricultural produce awaiting further processing, sale, or consumption.

❑ *Measurement:* All biological assets are measured at fair value.

   Agricultural produce is measured at fair value at the point of harvest (thereafter, inventory accounting standards apply.

   The change in fair value of biological assets during a period is reported in net profit or loss.

   Fair value is the highest price obtainable, net of costs, in any available market. Market price in the intended location of sale is starting point to determine fair value.

   The change in fair value of biological assets is part physical change (growth, etc.) and part unit price change.

   Fair value measurement stops at harvest.

   IAS 2, *Inventories*, applies after harvest.

❑ *Disclosure:* Separate disclosure of the two components should be encouraged, not required.

❑ *Non-biological assets used in agricultural activity:* follow other existing IASC Standards.

❑ *Agricultural land:* follow IAS 16.

❑ *Grants:* Unconditional government grants received in respect of biological assets measured at fair value are reported as income when the grant becomes receivable.

When the new standard is adopted, any adjustments to previous carrying amounts of biological assets and agricultural produce to remeasure them to fair value are adjustments of the balance of retained earnings.

Next steps

- Field test of Exposure Draft proposals.
- Final IAS – late 2000.

Steering Committee

- Reyaz Mihular, Sri Lanka (Chairman)
- Jean Allimant, France
- J. A. Atkinson, Zimbabwe
- Sandra Dedman, United Kingdom
- Jan van Ham, The Netherlands
- Bronwyn Monopoli, New Zealand
- Kesree Narongdej, Thailand
- Angkarat Priebjrivat, Thailand
- George Russell, The World Bank
- Narendra Sarda, India

Project Manager

- Rieko Yanou – ryanou@iasc.org.uk

Business Combinations

Status

- This project was added to the Board's agenda in November 1998. It will involve a review of IAS 22 with respect to the use of acquisition accounting vs. unitings of interests.
- Discussion Paper – December 1998.

Progress to Date

The IASC staff have published, and invited comments on, a Discussion Paper entitled *Convergence on the Methods of Accounting for Business Combinations* developed by the G4+1 group of standard setters. The G4+1 comprises standard setters from Australia, Canada, New Zealand, the UK and the USA. Representatives of IASC attend G4+1 meetings as observers. The paper considers:

- whether a single method of accounting for business combinations is preferable to two (or more) methods;
- if so, which method should be applied to all business combinations; and
- if not, which methods should be applied, and to which combinations they should be applied.

The IASC Board has appointed a Steering Committee to review responses to the G4+1 paper and to consider whether changes are needed to IAS 22's requirements in this area.

Steering Committee

Members:

- Sigvard Heurlin, Sweden, Chairman
- Malcolm Cheetham, Switzerland
- Enrique Fowler Newton, Argentina
- Claude Lopater, France
- Jörg Baetge, Germany
- Masaru Sato, Japan
- Ronald Paterson, United Kingdom
- Michael Tambosso, Canada

Observers:

- Todd Johnson, FASB, United States
- J. H. Escamila, European Commission
- Paul Leder, IOSCO

Project Manager

- Susan Harding – sharding@iasc.org.uk

Business Reporting on the Internet

Status

- Staff Discussion Paper *Business Reporting on the Internet* – **November 1999.**
- Project adopted – March 2000.

Fundamental Issues Facing IASC

- What are the current technologies available for electronic business reporting?
- What are companies around the world actually doing?
- What kind of standards for electronic business reporting are needed now, within the constraint of today's technologies?
- What are the shortcomings of business reporting on the Internet within current technologies?
- What technological changes are on the horizon and how can they improve electronic business reporting (particularly the ability to go beyond the Internet as "electronic paper" to facilitate downloading and analysis of financial data)?

Outline of the Discussion Paper

- *Chapter 1* reviews some of the impetuses behind the proliferation of web-based business reporting. It also provides background information on the increasing types and number of corporate websites, and the increasing number of online traders.

- *Chapter* 2 explores and summarises the multitude of different electronic reporting technologies that can be used by web designers. These technologies are not mutually exclusive, which means that a designer can use any mix of these technologies to develop a website.
- *Chapter* 3 summarises the findings of the existing literature on web-based financial reporting and adds further findings from a survey of 660 corporations in 22 countries conducted by the authors. The chapter also discusses electronic reporting environments within national disclosure and regulatory regimes such as EDGAR and SEDAR in the USA and Canada, respectively.
- *Chapter* 4 examines the information presented in the prior chapters and proposes that the IASC should seriously consider the development of a "code of conduct" that would cover both the form and content aspects of Web-based business reporting.
- *Chapter* 5 addresses issues raised by pending and future technologies, which are evolving at a rapid rate. The chapter suggests that to add value to information consumers, it is critical that international standard setters and other organisations respond to these new technologies, which can greatly improve business reporting and subsequent Internet searches. This chapter highlights the significant need for a universal Business Reporting Language (BRL) to facilitate the electronic dissemination and use of business information. This chapter suggests a consortia approach that will help ensure the development of standards that provide both certainty in reporting and flexibility for future innovations.
- *Chapter* 6 synthesises the information provided in the prior chapters to discuss the opportunities, challenges, and implications for the accounting profession and the IASC, its international standard setter.

Project Manager

- Colin Fleming – cfleming@iasc.org.uk

Disclosures by Banks and Similar Financial Institutions

Status

- IAS 30 – 1990.
- Project adopted – July 1999.

Project Description

To consider the need to revise the presentation and disclosure requirements of IAS 30, particularly in light of developments in the industry and the issuance of IAS 1 (revised 1997), *Presentation of Financial Statements*, and IAS 39, *Financial Instruments: Recognition and Measurement*.

Project Manager

- Magnus Orrell – morrell@iasc.org.uk

Discounting

Status

- Project adopted – April 1998.
- Point outline approved – November 1998.

Key Issues

- When should assets and liabilities be discounted (measured at present value)?
- How should present value be determined?

Possible Outcomes of the Project

- Amendments to existing International Accounting Standards. Such amendments may make existing requirements more detailed, amend existing requirements, or remove explicit or implicit choices.
- A general Standard on discounting to supplement specific requirements in individual IAS.
- Material for the Framework for the Preparation and Presentation of Financial Statements, to guide the Board in future projects that involve discounting.

Next Steps

- Issues Paper – first half of 2000.

Steering Committee

Members:
- Patricia Doran Walters, International Council of Investment Associations, Chair
- Jörg Baetge, Germany
- Nelson Carvalho, International Association of Financial Executives Institutes
- Malcolm Cheetham, Switzerland
- Sam Gutterman, International Actuarial Association
- Eric Phipps, United Kingdom
- Shinichi Tanimoto, Japan
- Dominique Thouvenin, France

Observers:
- Ulf Linder, European Commission
- Bengt-Allan Mettinger, Basel Committee
- Richard Thorpe, IOSCO
- Wayne S. Upton, FASB

Project Manager

- Peter Clark – pclark@iasc.org.uk

Emerging Markets

[*Formerly* Developing Countries and Economies in Transition]

Status

- Project adopted – April 1998.
- Preparatory Committee appointed 1999.

Possible Issues

- Should IASC develop a basic procedural standards and guidelines for accounting for developing countries?
- Should there be different accounting standards or different disclosure standards for enterprises in developing countries and economies in transition?
- Should IASC develop standards or guidelines on bartering?

Preparatory Committee

Members:
- Mr Tony Seah, Malaysia, Chairman
- Mr Serge Castillon, France
- Mr Chen Yugui, China
- Mr David Damant, Financial Analysts
- Mr Gerard Ee, Singapore
- Ms Larissa Gorbatova, Russian Federation
- Mr K Abdel-Aziz Hegazy, Egypt
- Mr Charles Muchene, Kenya
- Mr David Perry, United Kingdom
- Ms Lorraine Ruffing, UNCTAD
- Mr Mark Smith, Brazil
- Mr Francisco Vasquez, Venezuela
- Mr Peter Walton, Academic

Observers:
- Mr Christian Grossmann, IFC
- Mr Ulf Linder, European Commission

Project Manager

- Colin Fleming – cfleming@iasc.org.uk

Extractive Industries

Status

- Project Adopted – April 1998.
- Steering Committee is developing an Issues Paper, to be published 3rd quarter 2000.

Definition of Extractive Industries

At its October 1999 meeting, the Steering Committee tentatively approved the following definition of extractive industries:

> Extractive industries are those industries involved in finding and removing wasting natural resources from the earth. Wasting natural resources are those natural resources that cannot be replaced in their original state by human beings. Examples of those minerals include sand, gravel, stone, coal, salt, sulphur, metal ores (such as copper, gold, iron, nickel, lead, zinc, silver, tin, and platinum), oil (including natural gas liquids), natural gas, and other gaseous substances.

Thus, in short, the extractive industries comprise the petroleum (oil and gas) and mining industries. Mining of some types of minerals at the earth's surface, such as sand, gravel, and stone, is often called quarrying.

Although other industries are sometimes referred to as extractive industries, for example, the harvesting of timber in its natural state, the IASC project uses that term to mean the petroleum and mining industries.

By defining extractive industries as "removing wasting natural resources from the earth", the project excludes extraction of minerals from the sea or from the air. However, the principles set out in a final Standard on the extractive industries may provide guidance in accounting for extraction of minerals from the sea and air.

Scope of Project

The project is restricted to the upstream activities in the petroleum and mining industries. Upstream activities are exploring for, finding, acquiring, developing, and producing mineral up to the point that the minerals are removed from the earth and are capable of being sold (even if the enterprise intends to process them further). The Standard will not deal with the so-called downstream activities – the refining or processing of the petroleum, natural gas, or mined mineral (beyond that necessary to make the minerals that have been removed from the earth capable of being sold), or the marketing and distributing of those commodities. Existing IASC Standards apply to such activities. Conceptually, the point at which upstream activities end and downstream activities begin is the point at which the company's principal risk changes from that of a producer of minerals to that of a manufacturer and marketer of commodities.

Next Steps

- Issues Paper: 3rd quarter 2000
- Draft Statement of Principles: 2nd quarter 2001

- Exposure Draft: 1st quarter 2002
- Either a single final IAS or separate Standards for the petroleum and mining industries: 4th quarter 2002

Steering Committee

Members:

- Ken Spencer, Australia, Chairman (KPMG, Australia)
- Keith Cameron, Switzerland (Holderbank)
- Robert Garnett, South Africa (Anglo-American)
- Peter Goeth, Germany (RWE)
- John Gordon, Canada (KPMG)
- Keith Klaver, USA (PricewaterhouseCoopers)
- Alfredo Mazzoni, IAFEI (Eni-Agip)
- Rahul Roy, India (Institute of CAs of India)
- Fred Wellings, ICIA (Financial Analysts)

Observers:

- Angelo Apponi, IOSCO
- John Franke, UK Oil Industry Accounting Committee

Project Staff

- Paul Pacter – ppacter@iasc.org.uk, Project Manager
- Horace Brock – hbrock@pdi.org, Project Consultant

Financial Instruments – Comprehensive Project

Although IAS 39, *Financial Instruments: Recognition and Measurement*, should bring about a substantial improvement in accounting for financial instruments, the Board recognises the need for further development.

IASC is participating in an international Joint Working Group on Financial Instruments. This Group was established during 1997 to explore the feasibility of moving to comprehensive fair value accounting requirements for Financial Instruments over the medium term. The Joint Working Group is chaired by the IASC representative and has members representing 13 national standard setters or other national administrations. The Group was formed because several standard setters felt that fair value measurement would be the only satisfactory long-term solution for all financial instruments. They also recognised, however, that more work was needed to confirm or refute this point of view and to deal with the many practical difficulties that must be resolved before any such requirement could be introduced. There can, at present, be no certainty regarding the outcome of the work, but the members of the Joint Working Group regard it as a matter of urgency to establish whether or not further developments in accounting for financial instruments are desirable.

Status

- IAS 32, *Financial Instruments: Disclosure and Presentation* (1995).
- Discussion Paper published 1st Quarter 1997.
- At its meeting in November 1997, the Board decided to pursue both a Comprehensive Standard and an interim Standard on Recognition and Measurement.
- IAS 39, *Recognition and Measurement,* was published December 1998.

Comprehensive Standard

The IASC Board has established an international Joint Working Group (JWG) with a number of national accounting standard setters to develop an integrated and harmonised standard on financial instruments. Completion is targeted for the end of 2000. This project will build on the March 1997 IASC Discussion Paper and the work of national standard setters. For information about this project, see below.

Standard on Recognition and Measurement

At the same time, recognising the urgency of the need for guidance worldwide, IASC developed a Standard (IAS 39) on recognition and measurement that was completed in December 1998.

Standard Setters Participating in Joint Working Group

- International Accounting Standards Committee
- Australia
- Canada
- France
- Germany
- Japan
- New Zealand
- Nordic Countries
- United Kingdom
- United States

Members of the Joint Working Group

- Alex Milburn, IASC, Chairman
- Wayne Longergan, Australia
- Patricia Stebbens, Australia
- Tricia O'Malley, Canada
- Gerard Gil, France
- Etienne Boris, France
- Jochen Pape, Germany

- Norbert Breker, Germany
- Shigeo Ogi, Japan
- Mike Bradbury, New Zealand
- Warwick Hunt, New Zealand
- Erik Mamelund, Nordic Countries
- Allan Cook, United Kingdom
- Sandra Thompson, United Kingdom
- James Leisenring, Financial Accounting Standards Board, USA
- Halsey Bullen, Financial Accounting Standards Board, USA

Discussion Paper Proposals

- Recognise a financial asset or financial liability when the enterprise becomes a party to its contractual provisions.
- Remove a financial asset (or part) when the rights are realised, expired, or surrendered.
- Remove a financial liability (or part) when extinguished, discharged, cancelled, or expired.
- Initial measurement of financial asset or liability: fair value of consideration given or received for it.
- Subsequent measurement: At fair value.
- All gains and losses arising from fair valuation should be recognised as income immediately. However, "income" does not mean net profit or loss.
- Gains/losses on designated hedges of anticipated transactions to acquire an asset or incur a liability that will be measured at fair value subsequent to acquisition or incurrence should be recognised in profit or loss immediately.
- Gains/losses on other financial assets designated as hedges of anticipated transactions should be in "other comprehensive income" (part of equity) and transferred to the statement of profit and loss in future periods when the hedged transactions affect income.

Next Steps

- Agreement of the Joint Working Group on an Issues Paper – 2000.

IASC Manager

- Magnus Orrell – morrell@iasc.org.uk

JWG Project Managers

- Alex Milburn – alex.milburn@cica.ca
- Ian Hague – ian.hague@cica.ca

Financial Instruments – Recognition and Measurement – Limited Revision to IAS 39

Status

As a result of its work developing guidance on IAS 39, *Financial Instruments, Recognition and Measurement*, the IAS 39 Implementation Guidance Committee (see next section) recommended five limited revisions to IAS 39. In June 2000, the IASC Board approved Exposure Draft E66 on five limited revisions to IAS 39, *Financial Instruments: Recognition and Measurement*, and related Standards. None of the proposed revisions represents a change to a fundamental principle in IAS 39. Instead, the purpose of the proposed changes is primarily to address technical application issues that have been identified following the approval of IAS 39 in December 1998. The Board's assessment is that the proposed changes will assist enterprises preparing to implement IAS 39 for the first time in 2001 and help ensure a consistent application of the Standard. No further changes to IAS 39 are contemplated.

E66 proposes:

- consistent accounting for purchases and sales of financial assets using either trade date accounting or settlement date accounting. IAS 39 currently requires settlement date accounting for sales of financial assets, but permits both trade date and settlement date accounting for purchases.
- elimination of a requirement for a lender to recognise collateral received from a borrower in its balance sheet. IAS 39 currently requires a lender to recognise certain collateral in its balance sheet.
- improvement of the wording on impairment recognition.
- consistent accounting for temporary investments in equity securities between IAS 39 and other International Accounting Standards.
- elimination of redundant disclosure requirements for hedges in IAS 32, *Financial Instruments: Disclosure and Presentation*.

It is the Board's intention to have the proposed changes to IAS 39 in place when IAS 39 becomes effective, that is, for financial years beginning on or after 1 January 2001.

Staff

- Magnus Orrell – morrell@iasc.org.uk

IAS 39 Implementation Guidance

When the IASC Board voted to approve IAS 39 in December 1998, the Board instructed its staff to monitor implementation issues and to consider how IASC can best respond to such issues and thereby help financial statement preparers, auditors, financial analysts, and others understand IAS 39 and those preparing to apply it for the first time. In March 2000, the Board approved an approach to publish implementation guidance on IAS 39 in the form of Questions and Answers (Q&A) and appointed an IAS 39 Implementation Guidance Committee (IGC) to review and approve the draft Q&A and to seek public comment before final publication. Also, the IAS 39 Implementation Guidance Committee may refer some issues either to the Standing Interpretations Committee (SIC) or to the IASC Board.

The IGC approved a first set of proposed Q&A to be posted on the IASC Web Site for public comment in early May 2000, with subsequent sets approved in June and July 2000. The Q&A are based largely on inquiries received by IASC or by national standard-setters. The IGC recognises that IAS 39 takes effect for financial years beginning on or after 1 January 2001 and intends to have as many of the Q&A as possible published in final form before that date.

IAS 1, *Presentation of Financial Statements*, requires compliance "with all the requirements of each applicable Standard and each applicable Interpretation" if financial statements are to be described as conforming to IAS. The final Q&A will not have the status of a Standard or an Interpretation. However, the Q&A are intended to provide best practice guidance on the appropriate interpretation and practical application of IAS 39 in a range of circumstances. Since the Q&A have been developed to be consistent with the requirements and guidance provided in IAS 39, other IASC Standards, and Interpretations of the Standing Interpretations Committee, and the IASC Framework, enterprises should consider this guidance as they select and apply accounting policies in accordance with IAS 1 paragraphs 20-22.

The IGC has ten members (all experts in financial instruments with backgrounds as accounting standard-setters, auditors, bankers, and corporate treasury officers, from seven countries) and observers from the Basel Committee, IOSCO, and the European Commission.

Implementation Guidance Committee

Members:

- John T. Smith, Deloitte & Touche, USA, Chairman
- Andreas Bezold, Dresdner Bank, Germany
- Sigvard Heurlin, Öhrlings PricewaterhouseCoopers, Sweden
- Petri Hofste, KPMG Accountants, Netherlands
- James J. Leisenring, Financial Accounting Standards Board, USA
- J. Alex Milburn, Joint Working Group on Financial Instruments, Canada
- Ralph Odermatt, UBS, Switzerland
- Robert Swan, Tetra Laval, Switzerland
- Pauline Wallace, Arthur Andersen, United Kingdom
- Tatsumi Yamada, ChuoAoyama Audit Corporation, Japan

Observers:

- Jerry Edwards, Basel Committee on Banking Supervision
- David Swanney, International Organization of Securities Commissions(IOSCO)
- Allister Wilson, European Commission

Project Staff:

- Magnus Orrell – morrell@iasc.org.uk

Income Tax Consequences of Dividends

Status

- Added to the Board's agenda March 2000.

- Exposure Draft, *Income Tax Consequences of Dividends* (E68) – Comments due 10 September 2000

Project Description

- In this limited scope project the issues associated with how an enterprise should account for the income tax consequences of dividends by the reporting enterprise will be considered. IAS 12 (revised 1996), *Income Taxes* does not give guidance on such income tax consequences.

- This limited project does not intend to change the Standard in respect of discounting of deferred tax assets and liabilities. Currently the IASC considers in the project on discounting whether to require or permit discounting of all deferred tax assets and liabilities.

Income Tax Consequences of Dividends (E68)

- In June 2000, the IASC Board approved Exposure Draft E68, Income Tax Consequences of Dividends, which proposes limited changes to IAS 12, *Income Taxes*.

- In some jurisdictions, income taxes are payable at a higher or lower rate if part or all of the net profit or retained earnings is paid out as a dividend. In some other jurisdictions, income taxes may be refundable if part or all of the net profit or retained earnings is paid out as a dividend. E68 proposed that current and deferred tax assets and liabilities would be measured using the tax rate applicable to undistributed profits.

- IAS 12, paragraph 51, indicates that measurement is based on the carrying amounts of its assets and liabilities. As a result, the income tax consequences of dividends would be recognised when dividends are recognised as a liability. The income tax consequences of dividends would, in most cases, be included in net profit or loss for the period because they are more directly linked to past transactions or events than to distributions to owners.

- E68 also includes disclosure requirements regarding the potential income tax consequences of dividends.

Project Staff

- Martin Faarborg – mfaarborg@iasc.org.uk

Insurance

Status

- Project adopted April 1997.
- Issues Paper – December 1999

Tentative Steering Committee Views

❏ *Scope*

The project addresses accounting for insurance contracts (or groups of contracts), rather than all aspects of accounting by insurance enterprises.

❏ *Definition of Insurance Contracts*

An insurance contract is a contract under which one party (the insurer) accepts an insurance risk by agreeing with another party (the policyholder) to make payment if a specified uncertain future event occurs (other than an event that is only a change in a specified interest rate, security price, commodity price, foreign exchange rate, index of prices or rates, a credit rating or credit index, or similar variable).

❏ *Recognition and Measurement*

- The objective should be to measure the assets and liabilities that arise from insurance contracts (an asset-and-liability measurement approach), rather than to defer income and expense so that they can be matched with each other (a deferral-and matching approach).

- Insurance liabilities (both general insurance and life insurance) should be discounted.

- The measurement of insurance liabilities should be based on current estimates of future cash flows from the current contract. Estimated future cash flows from renewals are:

  (a) included if the current contract commits the insurer to pricing for those renewals; and

  (b) excluded if the insurer retains full discretion to change pricing.

- In the view of a majority of the Steering Committee, catastrophe and equalisation reserves are not liabilities under IASC's Framework. There may be a need for specific disclosures about low-frequency, high-severity risks — perhaps by segregating a separate component of equity.

- The measurement of insurance liabilities should reflect risk to the extent that risk would be reflected in the price of an arm's length transaction between knowledgeable, willing parties. It follows that the sale of a long-term insurance contract may lead in some cases to the immediate recognition of income. The Steering Committee recognises that some may have reservations about changing current practice in this way.

- Overstatement of insurance liabilities should not be used to impose implicit solvency or capital adequacy requirements.
- Acquisition costs should not be deferred as an asset.
- All changes in the carrying amount of insurance liabilities should be recognised as they arise. In deciding what components of these changes should be presented or disclosed separately, the Steering Committee will monitor progress by the Joint Working Group on Financial Instruments.
- The Steering Committee is working on the assumption that IAS 39 will be replaced, before the end of the Insurance project, by a new International Accounting Standard that will require full fair value accounting for the substantial majority of financial assets and liabilities. The Steering Committee believes that:

    (a)   if such a standard exists, portfolios of insurance contracts should also be measured at fair value. IASC defines fair value as "*the amount for which an asset could be exchanged or a liability settled between knowledgeable, willing parties in an arm's length transaction*";

    (b)   in a fair value accounting model, the liability under a life insurance contract that has an explicit or implicit account balance may be less than the account balance; and

    (c)   determining the fair value of insurance liabilities on a reliable, objective and verifiable basis poses difficult conceptual and practical issues, because there is generally no liquid and active secondary market in liabilities and assets arising from insurance contracts. To avoid excessive detail, the Issues Paper discusses measurement issues in fairly general terms. The Steering Committee will develop more specific guidance on measurement issues at a later stage in the project.

- Pending further discussion, the Steering Committee is evenly divided on the effect of future investment margins. Some members believe that future investment margins should be reflected in determining the fair value of insurance liabilities. Other members believe that they should not.
- For participating and with-profits policies:

    (a)   where the insurer does not control allocation of the surplus, unallocated surplus should be classified as a liability; and

    (b)   where the insurer controls allocation of the surplus, unallocated surplus should be classified as equity (except to the extent that the insurer has a legal or constructive obligation to allocate part of the surplus to policyholders). Liability classification is the default, to be used unless there is clear evidence that the insurer controls allocation of the surplus

- For investment-linked insurance contracts, premiums received may need to be split into a risk component (revenue) and an investment component (deposit).
- The accounting for reinsurance by a reinsurer should be the same as the accounting for direct insurance by a direct insurer.

Presentation and Disclosure

- Amounts due from reinsurers should not be offset against related insurance liabilities.

- Most of the disclosures required by IAS 32 and IAS 37 are likely to be relevant for insurance contracts. Some of the disclosures required by IAS 39 may not be needed in a fair value context.

- Other items that may require disclosure are regulatory solvency margins, key performance indicators (such as sum insured in life, retention/lapse rates, level of new business) information about risk adjustments and information about value-at-risk and sensitivity.

Next Steps

- Draft Statement of Principles – 2000/2001.

Steering Committee

Members:

- Warren McGregor, Australia, Chair
- David Allvey, United Kingdom
- Adrian Cowell, International Council of Investment Associations
- Howard E. Dalton, United States
- William Freda, United States
- Dr. Gerd Geib, Germany
- Jacques le Douit, France
- Drs. Hans Schoen, The Netherlands
- Eiichi Tachibana, Japan

Observers:

- John Carchrae, IOSCO
- Ulf Linder, European Commission
- Florence Lustman, International Association of Insurance Supervisors
- W. Paul McCrossan, International Actuarial Association
- Wayne Upton, US Financial Accounting Standards Board

Project Manager

- Peter Clark – pclark@iasc.org.uk

Pension Plan Assets

Status

• Project Adopted – July 1999.

Project Description

To consider whether a revision to IAS 19 is desirable to address certain pension fund arrangements which are not 'plan assets' as defined in IAS 19 because the employer retains an obligation to pay the benefits directly. This issue has arisen in Sweden, Germany, and perhaps other countries, due to certain legal requirements.

IAS 19 defines plan assets as assets held by an entity (a fund) that satisfy all of the following three conditions: the entity is legally separate from the reporting enterprise; the assets of the fund are to be used only to settle the employee benefit obligations, are not available to the enterprise's own creditors, and cannot be returned to the enterprise (or can be returned to the enterprise only if the remaining assets of the fund are sufficient to meet the plan's obligations; and to pay the related employee benefits directly.

This limited scope project will consider how an enterprise should account for assets that satisfy the first two, but not the third, of those conditions.

Pension Plan Assets (E67)

In June 2000, the Board approved Exposure Draft E67, *Pension Plan Assets*, which proposed limited changes to IAS 19, *Employee Benefits*.

E67 proposed to change the definition of plan assets in IAS 19. E67 defines plan assets as assets (other than non-transferable financial instruments issued by the reporting enterprise) that:

• are held by an entity (a fund) that is legally separate from the reporting enterprise and was established solely to pay or fund employee benefits; and

• are available to be used only to pay or fund employee benefits, are not available to the enterprise's own creditors (even in bankruptcy), and cannot be returned to the reporting enterprise, unless either:

(i) the remaining assets of the fund are sufficient to meet all the related employee benefit obligations of the plan or the reporting enterprise; or

(ii) the assets are returned to the reporting enterprise to reimburse it for paying employee benefits.

E67 also proposed recognition and measurement requirements for certain reimbursements of employee benefits – for example, reimbursements under insurance policies that an enterprise holds directly (rather than through a fund) in order to fund employee benefits. E67 proposed that an enterprise should recognise its rights under the policies as a separate asset, rather than as a deduction from the related obligations. In all other respects (for example, the use of the "corridor"), E67 proposed that an enterprise should treat such reimbursements in the same way as plan assets.

Project Manager

- Peter Clark – pclark@iasc.org.uk

Present Value (*formerly* Discounting)

Status

- Added to Agenda April 1998
- Point Outline approved November 1999 (unpublished)

Key Issues

- When should assets and liabilities be measured at their present value (discounted)?
- How should present value be determined in those International Accounting Standards that require or permit discounting?
- How should the effect of using discounting be presented and disclosed in financial statements?

Discounting issues have arisen in several recent IASC projects, including Income Taxes, Employee Benefits, Impairment of Assets, Provisions, and Financial Instruments. This project aims to develop a general Framework so that IASC's requirements on discounting are conceptually valid, consistent from Standard to Standard, and capable of practical implementation.

Steering Committee Tentative Conclusions to Date

Possible Outcomes of the Project

- Material for the Framework for the Preparation and Presentation of Financial Statements, to guide the Board in future projects that could involve discounting.
- A separate Standard on discounting to describe how discounting should be applied in Standards that require present value measurements.
- Amendments to existing International Accounting Standards. Such amendments may move existing requirements to the new Standard on discounting, eliminate inconsistencies, expand application guidance, and remove explicit or implicit choices

Scope

- Present value principles should be used in all measurements based on future cash flows, except where the time value of money and uncertainty do not have a material effect. Among other things, this conclusion implies that present value principles should be applied to:
    - deferred tax (Under IAS 12, deferred tax represents the incremental income taxes that an enterprise will pay or receive when it recovers/settles the carrying amount of its assets/liabilities); and

- determining recoverable amount, for impairment testing, of assets not covered by IAS 36 (notably inventories, construction contract balances and deferred tax assets).

- For assets and liabilities that, currently, are not measured solely on the basis of future cash flows, present value concepts should:

  - in principle, be applied to prepayments and revenue in advance, in the rare cases when the effect is material;

  - be applied to construction contracts, to allow a more meaningful aggregation of cash flows that occur in different periods (under IAS 11, measurement partly reflects past cash flows, and partly reflects undiscounted future, cash flows); and

  - not be applied in determining depreciation and amortisation, as the cost of applying present value concepts would exceed the benefits.

Measurement Objectives

- Discounting is currently used in International Accounting Standards to meet three main measurement objectives. The Steering Committee does not intend to recommend when each objective should be used, as the Steering Committee believes that the Board of IASC should decide in individual projects whether the measurement objective is:

  - to estimate the **fair value** (FV) of an item when the fair value cannot be observed directly in the market. Fair value is *"the amount for which an asset could be exchanged or a liability settled between knowledgeable, willing parties in an arm's length transaction"*. It is a permitted or required measurement objective in several IASC standards;

  - to determine the **entity-specific value** (ESV) of an asset or liability. Entity-specific value represents the value of an asset or liability to the enterprise that holds it, and may reflect factors that are not available (or not relevant) to other market participants. One form of entity-specific value is value in use, as used in IAS 36, *Impairment of Assets*; or

  - to determine the **amortised cost** (AC) of a financial asset or financial liability using the effective interest rate. This is the rate that exactly discounts a stream of future cash payments through maturity or the next market-based repricing date to the current net carrying amount of the asset or liability. IAS 39 requires the effective interest method for some financial assets and financial liabilities.

- Except where otherwise specified below, the summary that follows applies to both FV and ESV. A separate summary for AC follows later.

Consistency

- For assets and liabilities that generate cash flows defined by contract, two approaches are possible:

  - traditional approach – use nominal cash flows and a discount rate that reflects expected credit losses; or

– expected cash flows approach – use expected cash flows (probability-weighted average across scenarios) and exclude the effect of expected credit losses from the discount rate.

- Conceptually, the two approaches are often equivalent. Practical factors may favour one approach in particular cases. For example, the expected cash flows approach should be used where there is uncertainty about the timing of future cash flows.

- Cash flows and the discount rate should both be expressed consistently in either real terms (excluding general inflation) or nominal terms.

Estimating Future Cash Flows

- Cash flows should reflect all future events that would affect the cash flows arising for:
    - a typical market participant that holds the asset or liability (FV);
    - the enterprise that holds the asset or liability (ESV)

- Cash flows should reflect:
    - information that is available without undue cost or effort about the market's assessment of the future cash flows (FV). If there is contrary data indicating that market participants would not use the same assumptions as the enterprise, the enterprise should adjust its assumptions to incorporate that market information;
    - the enterprise's assessment of the cash flows (ESV).

- Market-based assumptions should be based on current market data, except where reliable evidence indicates current experience will not continue.

- Cash flows include overheads that are directly attributable, or can be allocated on a reasonable and consistent basis (reflecting market assessment for FV and reflecting the enterprise's own assessment for ESV). Administrative costs should be included in cash flows (not in the discount rate).

- Cash flows exclude cash flows that will be capitalised and, if practical to exclude them, cash flows that will affect internally generated goodwill.

- FV includes the profit margin that the market would require for consumption of internal resources. ESV excludes such profit margins (except to the extent that a risk adjustment is required – see below). Similarly, FV reflects goods or services to be transferred to or from related parties at fair value, whereas ESV reflects them at estimated actual transaction prices.

- FV includes reflects the undiscounted amount of transaction costs that would be incurred at the reporting date in disposing of an asset or settling a liability. ESV includes the discounted amount of transaction costs if, and only if, disposal is expected.

- The Joint Working Group on Financial Instruments is likely to propose that the measurement of liabilities should reflect an issuer's own credit standing. The Steering Committee has not yet developed a position on this issue.

Risk and Uncertainty

- FV and ESV should reflect risk and uncertainty to the extent that these would be reflected in the price of an arm's length transaction between knowledgeable, willing parties. For FV, the adjustment for risk reflects the market's assessment of the amount of risk and the risk is priced using the market's risk and time preferences. For ESV, the adjustment for risk reflects the enterprise's own assessment of risk, priced using the market's risk and time preferences.

- Risk may be reflected by adjusting either the cash flows or the discount rate. In principle, both approaches often give the same answer. Practical considerations may suggest one approach in particular cases. For example, if risk-adjusted discount rates are observable in the market, it may be best to use these rates directly; conversely, if risk does not decline evenly over time, it may be best to reflect risk in the cash flows.

- Both FV and ESV should reflect only undiversifiable risk, unless there is persuasive empirical evidence that market prices would also reflect diversifiable risk.

- In principle, both FV and ESV should reflect risk of imperfect information, illiquidity and market imperfections, although it may often impractical to quantify the necessary adjustment.

- Asset/liability management techniques should not affect the FV or ESV of individual assets and liabilities. It is beyond the scope of this project to consider whether it is appropriate to adjust FV or ESV using hedge accounting.

- The FV or ESV of an uncertain liability is always more than FV or ESV of a fixed liability with the same expected cash flows.

- The FV or ESV of a portfolio of assets or liabilities is not necessarily the same as the sum of the individual FVs or ESVs. Similarly, the FV or ESV of a large block of divisible assets (such as a large shareholding) is not necessarily proportionate to the FV or ESV of a smaller block. However, it may often be impractical to quantify adjustments for such factors.

Discount Rate

- The discount rate should reflect:
    - current market interest rates;
    - the characteristics of the asset or liability being measured, rather than the enterprise's incremental borrowing rate or cost of capital. Thus, regulatory capital requirements may affect the FV or ESV of an asset or liability, but not significantly. Similarly, the FV or ESV of a liability should not reflect returns on assets (unless the terms of the liability require specific investments);
    - the term (maturity) of the asset or liability. Conceptually, a different discount rate should be used for each future period to reflect yield curve effects, although in practice a single rate may be a reasonable approximation. In principle, interest should be compounded quarterly, if the effect is material.

Real Options

- The implicit managerial and operating flexibilities that are embedded (inherent) in many non-financial assets and liabilities are known as real options. They represent management's ability to delay an irreversible decision until after some uncertainty has been resolved. For example:
  - the owner of a factory has various options – to continue operating the factory, change the way that the factory is used, stop using the factory and leave it idle or empty, or sell the factory;
  - the holder of a patent has options to use the patent, sell the patent, cease or suspend the use of the patent or conduct further research and development activities using the knowledge embedded in the assets;
  - the owner of a gold mine has options to increase, decrease, suspend, delay or cease production in the light of changes in gold prices and production costs;
  - an enterprise that owns several factories has the option to switch production between the factories. It may also have an option to change production methods or the level of output;
  - the owner of an investment property has options to lease part or all of the property out, to sell the property, to occupy it for the owner's operating activities, to demolish the property and either sell or redevelop the land, or to leave the property vacant temporarily in the hope that market conditions will change; and
  - a manufacturer that issues an explicit or implicit product warranty may have an option to subcontract the remedial work or to carry out the corrective work itself.

- Both FV and ESV should reflect any real options that are available to all holders of the asset or liability. ESV (but not FV) should also reflect any further real options that are available only to the current holder.

- Widely used techniques, such as the Black-Scholes model, exist for valuing financial options. Such techniques may give some insight into the valuation of real options.

Changes in Fair Value or Entity-Specific Value

- If FV or ESV are used for subsequent measurement, an enterprise should recognise immediately experience adjustments and the effect of changes in (1) assumptions (2) the discount rate and (3) risk adjustments.

- The increase in FV or ESV that arises from the passage of time ("unwinding of the discount") should be presented as finance income or expense. IAS 37 already requires this for provisions. IAS 19 permits it for defined benefit employee benefits.

The Joint Working Group on Financial Instruments is likely to propose that interest income and interest expense should be based on current interest rates and current fair values. The Steering Committee has not yet developed a position on this issue.

Amortised Cost

- Amortised cost uses:
  - the original assumptions and estimates of cash flows as reflected in the original transaction price. These are not updated over time (but unfavourable changes may lead to recognition of an impairment loss); and
  - the original discount rate implicit in the asset or liability at inception.

- Further issues may arise if amortised cost is used for non-monetary assets and non-monetary liabilities (assets and liabilities that are not to be received or paid in fixed or determinable amounts of money).

Other Measurement Issues

- Foreign currency cash flows should be discounted using discount rate(s) appropriate for that currency and then converted into the reporting currency at the period-end spot rate. No adjustment should be made to reflect foreign exchange risk (although repatriation risk should be reflected).
- FV, ESV and AC should be determined using pre-tax cash flows and pre-tax discount rate(s). Future tax effects should continue to be recognised separately as "deferred" tax, but present value principles should be introduced into deferred tax.

Disclosure

- Disclosures should:
  - explain the discounted amounts included in the financial statements;
  - give information that will help users estimate the amount, timing and uncertainty of future cash flows. Such information is likely to focus on cash flows and risks from individual assets and liabilities, rather than enterprise-wide cash flows and risks and will probably be developed in individual projects, rather than this project.

Next Steps

- Steering Committee Issues Paper – target date for publication: late October 2000.

Steering Committee

Members:

- Patricia Doran Walters, International Council of Investment Associations, Chair
- Jörg Baetge, Germany
- Nelson Carvalho, International Association of Financial Executives Institutes
- Malcolm Cheetham, Switzerland
- Sam Gutterman, International Actuarial Association
- Eric Phipps, United Kingdom
- Shinichi Tanimoto, Japan
- Dominique Thouvenin, France

Observers:

- Ulf Linder, European Commission
- Bengt-Allan Mettinger, Basel Committee
- Richard Thorpe, IOSCO
- Wayne S. Upton, FASB
- Paul Sharma, International Association of Insurance Supervisors

Project Staff

- Peter Clark – pclark@iasc.org.uk

Reporting Financial Performance

Status

- G4+1 Discussion Paper, *Reporting Future Performance: Current Developments and Future Directions* – January 1998.
- Project Adopted – July 1999.
- G4+1 Discussion Paper, *Reporting Financial Performance: Proposals for Change* – August 1999.

Project Description

- To consider whether further developments should now be made in reporting financial performance, beyond the requirements of IAS 1, *Presentation of Financial Statements*, to report all changes in equity.
- IAS 1 requires presentation of a statement showing changes in equity. Various formats are allowed:

    1. The statement shows (a) each item of income and expense, gain or loss, which, as required by other IASC Standards, is recognised directly in equity, and the total of these items (examples include property revaluations (IAS 16, *Property, Plant and Equipment*), certain foreign currency translation gains and losses (IAS 21, *The Effects of Changes in Foreign Exchange Rates*), and changes in fair values of financial instruments (IAS 39, *Financial Instruments: Recognition and Measurement*)) and (b) net profit or loss for the period, but no total of (a) and (b). Owners' investments and withdrawals of capital and other movements in retained earnings and equity capital are shown in the notes.

    2. Same as above, but with a total of (a) and (b) (sometimes called 'comprehensive income'). Again, owners' investments and withdrawals of capital and other movements in retained earnings and equity capital are shown in the notes.

    3. The statement shows both the recognised gains and losses that are not reported in the income statement and owners' investments and

withdrawals of capital and other movements in retained earnings and equity capital. An example of this would be the traditional multicolumn statement of changes in shareholders' equity.

Main Proposals in the G4+1 Paper

- Financial performance should be presented in one financial statement rather than two or more statements;
- The single statement of financial performance should be divided into three components:

    (a)   the results of operating (or trading) activities;

    (b)   the results of financing and other treasury activities; and

    (c)   other gains and losses.

- Recycling should not generally be permitted (recycling is reporting the same item of income, expense, gain, or loss in two different periods in two different types of performance measures, for example, first in "other gains and losses" and subsequently in the results of operating activities);
- The category of extraordinary items should be abolished, and abnormal or exceptional items should not be reported as a separate category of revenue or expenses;
- Results of continuing and discontinued operations should be segregated; and
- Changes in accounting policy should be reported by retrospectively applying the new policy with restatement of prior periods.

Steering Committee

Members:

- Patricia McConnell, International Association of Investment Analysts, Chair
- Anthony Cope, Financial Accounting Standards Board
- Egbert Eeftink, Netherlands
- Adir Inbarr, Israel
- Jean Keller, France
- Kwon-fung Kim, Korea
- Tricia O'Malley, Canada
- John Spencer, New Zealand

Observers

- Francis Desmarchellier, IOSCO
- Kavel van Hulle, European Commission

Project Manager

- Colin Fleming – cfleming@iasc.org.uk

Acceptability of IAS

IASC Standards are gaining widespread use and recognition throughout the world. Many countries endorse IASC Standards as their own, either without amendment or else with minor additions or deletions. In addition, hundreds of companies, mainly large multinational companies and international financial institutions, state that they prepare their financial reports in accordance with International Accounting Standards. And many stock exchanges accept International Accounting Standards for cross-border listing purposes, though there are some important exceptions.

Broadening Acceptance

The broadening acceptance of IAS is shown by comments about IASC Standards by various regulators. Examples are shown below.

International Organization of Securities Commissions (IOSCO)

Of special importance for the widespread use and recognition of International Accounting Standards is their acceptance for cross-border listings by the International Organization of Securities Commissions (IOSCO).

In 1995, IASC adopted a work programme to produce a comprehensive core set of high quality standards that has been reviewed with IOSCO. In July 1995, the Technical Committee of IOSCO said that successful completion of this work plan would allow IOSCO to consider recommending endorsement of International Accounting Standards for cross-border capital raising and listing purposes in all global markets. The Chairman of IOSCO's Technical Committee said that IOSCO was committed to working with IASC to ensure a successful completion of its work plan on a timely basis.

Aware of the strong demand for early completion of its work programme and recognising that delay would cause inconvenience and cost to international companies, IASC decided in March 1996 to adopt fast track procedures for completing its programme of core standards. In December 1998, the IASC Board approved IAS 39, *Financial Instruments: Recognition and Measurement*, completing the core set of standards as agreed with IOSCO.

In its Final Communiqué of the XXIVth Annual Conference held in Lisbon, 22-28 May 1999, IOSCO stated:

"An important component of IOSCO's overall commitment to facilitating cross-border offerings and listings by multinational issuers is the Technical Committee's participation in the International Accounting Standards Committee (IASC) project to develop a "core" set of international accounting standards. In 1995, the IASC Board and the Technical Committee announced a work program and agreed that, once the IASC completed that work program, the Technical Committee would consider recommending that its members accept financial statements prepared on the basis of the resulting standards in documents used for cross-border offerings and listings. An important

milestone was achieved in March 1999 when the IASC published its interim standard on financial instruments, thereby substantially completing the key components of the core standards work program.

The Technical Committee now has begun its assessment of the IASC's core standards. This assessment is focused on whether the core standards are of sufficiently high quality to warrant permitting foreign issuers to use them to access a country's capital markets as an alternative to domestic standards.[1]..."

In May 2000, the Technical Committee presented its Report and the Presidents Committee adopted the following Resolution:

"In order to respond to the significant growth in cross-border capital flows, IOSCO has sought to facilitate cross-border offerings and listings. IOSCO believes that cross-border offerings and listings would be facilitated by high quality, internationally accepted accounting standards that could be used by incoming multinational issuers in cross-border offerings and listings. Therefore, IOSCO has worked with the International Accounting Standards Committee (IASC) as it sought to develop a reasonably complete set of accounting standards through the IASC core standards work program.

IOSCO has assessed 30 IASC standards, including their related interpretations ("the IASC 2000 standards"),[2] considering their suitability for use in cross-border offerings and listings. IOSCO has identified outstanding substantive issues relating to the IASC 2000 standards in a report that includes an analysis of those issues and specifies supplemental treatments that may be required in a particular jurisdiction to address each of these concerns.

The Presidents' Committee congratulates the IASC for its hard work and contribution to raising the quality of financial reporting worldwide. The IASC's work to date has succeeded in effecting significant improvements in the quality of the IASC standards. Accordingly, the Presidents' Committee recommends that IOSCO members permit incoming multinational issuers to use the 30 IASC 2000 standards to prepare their financial statements for cross-border offerings and listings, as supplemented in the manner described below (the "supplemental treatments") where necessary to address outstanding substantive issues at a national or regional level.[3]

---

[1] *IOSCO's work on the core standards project is focused on cross-border offerings and listings and is not intended to address jurisdictions' domestic standards, particularly since domestic standards usually apply to a much broader range of companies than would be expected to engage in cross-border offerings and listings.*

[2] *All current IASC Standards other than IAS 15, Information Reflecting the Effects of Changing Prices, which is not mandatory; IAS 26, Accounting and Reporting by Retirement Benefit Plans and IAS 30, Disclosures in the Financial Statements of Banks and Similar Financial Institutions, which have more limited application to specific types of enterprises; and IAS 40, Investment Property, which was issued in May 2000.*

[3] *This recommendation is made without prejudice to the treatments or measures that would be adopted regionally as part of a specific legal framework and / or mutual recognition agreements.*

Those supplemental treatments are:

- **reconciliation**: *requiring reconciliation of certain items to show the effect of applying a different accounting method, in contrast with the method applied under IASC standards;*

- **disclosure**: *requiring additional disclosures, either in the presentation of the financial statements or in the footnotes; and*

- **interpretation**: *specifying use of a particular alternative provided in an IASC standard, or a particular interpretation in cases where the IASC standard is unclear or silent.*

In addition, as part of national or regional specific requirements, waivers may be envisaged of particular aspects of an IASC standard, without requiring that the effect of the accounting method used be reconciled to the effect of applying the IASC method. The use of waivers should be restricted to exceptional circumstances such as issues identified by a domestic regulator when a specific IASC standard is contrary to domestic or regional regulation.

The concerns identified and the expected supplemental treatments are described in the Assessment Report

IOSCO notes that a body of accounting standards like the IASC standards must continue to evolve in order to address existing and emerging issues. IOSCO's recommendation assumes that IOSCO will continue to be involved in the IASC work and structure and that the IASC will continue to develop its body of standards. IOSCO strongly urges the IASC in its future work program to address the concerns identified in the Assessment Report, in particular, future projects.

IOSCO expects to survey its membership by the end of 2001 in order to determine the extent to which members have taken steps to permit incoming multinational issuers to use the IASC 2000 standards, subject to the supplemental treatments described above. At the same time IOSCO expects to continue to work with the IASC, and will determine the extent to which IOSCO's outstanding substantive issues, including proposals for future projects, have been addressed appropriately."

European Commission (EC)

The European Commission also attaches great importance to international uniformity of accounting as a contribution to its objective of fair and effective competition throughout the European Union. International Accounting Standards are important to even-handed competition among the capital markets of Europe as well as, more generally, to all markets for goods and services. In an official statement of policy, *Accounting Harmonisation: A New Strategy vis-à-vis International Harmonisation*, adopted in November 1995, the Commission said that only IASC was producing results which had a clear prospect of recognition within a time scale which corresponds to the urgency of the problem.

"Rather than amend existing Directives, the proposal is to improve the present situation by associating the EU with the efforts undertaken by IASC and IOSCO towards a broader international harmonisation of accounting standards.

The European Commission will achieve progress partly by encouraging appropriate developments at the national level. Recently, the governments of France and Germany have indicated that multinational companies in their countries should be able to use International Accounting Standards in preparing group accounts for both domestic and international purposes."[1]

In May 1999, the European Commission adopted an Action Plan to improve the Single Market for Financial Services over the next five years. With respect to financial reporting, the Action Plan states:

"Comparable, transparent and reliable financial information is fundamental for an efficient and integrated capital market. Lack of comparability will discourage cross-border investment because of uncertainty as regards the credibility of financial statements. FSPG [Financial Services Policy Group] discussions pinpointed the urgent need for solutions which give companies the option of raising capital throughout the EU using financial statements prepared on the basis of a single set of financial reporting requirements. Capital-raising does not stop at the Union's frontiers: our companies may also need to raise finance on international capital markets. Solutions to enhance comparability within the EU market must mirror developments in internationally accepted best practice. At the present juncture, International Accounting Standards (IAS) seem the most appropriate bench-mark for a single set of financial reporting requirements which will enable companies (which wish to do so) to raise capital on international markets. In the same way, International Standards on Auditing appear to be the minimum which should be satisfied in order to give credibility to published financial statements."[2]

In June 2000, the Commission issued a Communication, *EU Financial Reporting Strategy: The Way Forward[3]*, which proposed that all EU companies listed on a regulated market (including banks and other financial institutions) should be required to prepare consolidated accounts in accordance with IAS. It is intended that this requirement will be effective by 2005 at the latest. The Commission proposed also that Member States be permitted either to require or to allow unlisted companies to publish financial statements in accordance with the same set of standards as those for listed companies. The requirement to use IAS relates to the consolidated accounts of listed companies.

The Commission recognised that it is not able to influence the elaboration of US GAAP. On the other hand, it considered that IAS provides a comprehensive and conceptually robust set of standards for financial reporting that is able serve the needs of the international business community. IAS also has the advantage also of being

---

[1] *Communication From the Commission COM 95 (508), November 1995, page 13.*

[2] *Financial Services – Implementing the Framework for Financial Markets: Action Plan, Commission Communication of 11 May 1999, COM (1999) 232.*

[3] *EU Financial Reporting Strategy: The Way Forward, Commission Communication of 14 June 2000, COM(2000) 359*

developed with an international perspective, rather than being tailored to any one business environment. In addition, through its Observer status at the IASC Board and on steering committees, the Commission has participated in IASC deliberations.

However, the Commission believed that the EU could not 'delegate responsibility for setting financial reporting requirements for listed EU companies to a non-governmental third party' and that, within the EU's legislative structure it was appropriate to exercise oversight. It therefore proposed a two-tier mechanism to give legislative weight to IAS in Europe.

There would be a committee at the EU level that will facilitate the adoption of IAS in Member States. In addition, there would be a technical level of review, supported by the private sector. The Commission means to establish a constructive, dedicated and continuous dialogue with the IASC, in particular with the IASC's Standing Interpretations Committee, when implementation guidance is required. The endorsement mechanism would also advise the Commission whether or not an amendment to the EU Accounting Directives was recommended in the light of international accounting developments.

Enforcement of IAS was also addressed in the Communication. The Commission will be looking to strengthen the statutory audit function and improve oversight by securities regulators. Finally, it wants to ensure that there are effective sanctions in place. This will involve the co-operation of the accounting profession and the Forum of European Securities Commissions.

US Securities and Exchange Commission (SEC)

On April 11, 1996, the United States Securities and Exchange Commission issued a statement which noted that:

"The Commission is pleased that the IASC has undertaken a plan to accelerate its development efforts with a view toward completion of the requisite core set of standards by March 1998. The Commission supports the IASC's objective to develop, as expeditiously as possible, accounting standards that could be used for preparing financial statements used in cross-border offerings. From the Commission's perspective, there are three key elements to this program and the Commission's acceptance of its results:

- *The standards must include a core set of accounting pronouncements that constitutes a comprehensive, generally accepted basis of accounting;*
- *The standards must be of high quality — they must result in comparability and transparency, and they must provide for full disclosure; and*
- *The standards must be rigorously interpreted and applied.*

The Commission is committed to working with its securities regulatory colleagues, through IOSCO, and with the IASC to provide the necessary input to achieve the goal of establishing a comprehensive set of international accounting standards. As soon as the IASC completes its project, accomplishing each of the noted key elements, it is the Commission's intention to consider allowing the utilization of the resulting standards by foreign issuers offering securities in the U.S."

In March 1997, the Chairman of the SEC, Arthur Levitt, reported to the US Congress that:

> *"The Commission, through the International Organization of Securities Commissions (IOSCO), continues to provide active support to the efforts of the International Accounting Standards Committee (IASC) to develop a core set of high-quality, comprehensive, international accounting standards. The development of a single set of standards that can be used in securities markets around the world would allow companies more readily to cross borders to raise capital in markets that offer favorable financing conditions. The IASC has set a goal of completing these standards by March 1998. The Commission will report to Congress on progress in the development of international standards in October 1997, as required by NSMIA."*

On 16 February 2000, the SEC unanimously approved and issued for public comment a concept release regarding the use of international accounting standards. The release:

- sought feedback from domestic and foreign parties regarding both acceptance of IASC standards and the broader issue of shaping a global financial structure for increasingly globalised capital markets;

- solicited comment regarding the quality of the IASC standards and raised questions regarding what supporting infrastructure would be necessary in an environment where issuers and auditors often are multinational organizations, providing financial information in many countries;

- sought to identify what important concerns would be raised by acceptance of IASC standards; and then asked for comment on whether the SEC should modify its current requirement for all financial statements to be reconciled to US GAAP; and

- emphasised the SEC's desire to gain knowledge of first hand experience that issuers have had with applying IASC standards when preparing financial statements, public accountants have had with auditing the application of IASC standards and investors have had with using financial statements prepared using IASC standards.

The Concept Release represented the SEC's first rule-making step towards accepting those standards in the US market. IAS 7, Cash Flow Statements has already been accepted by the SEC for use by foreign registrants. The Background Note accompanying the Concept Release stated clearly that the quality of IASC standards was only part of the SEC's concerns, questions of the 'supporting infrastructure', including the quality of the external audit, also needed to be addressed.

The comment period on the Concept Release ended in May 2000, and the SEC has not made any further announcements about future rule-making activities.

Conformity of IAS with EC Directives

In 1999, the European Community issued a Report on Conformity between IAS and the European Accounting Directives.

The 1999 Report followed an earlier document issued by the Contact Committee in 1996[1] and in order to facilitate the application of IAS by European companies for the 1998 financial reporting term, the Contact Committee has examined the conformity between all applicable IAS and the European Accounting Directives. The examination covered all IAS and interpretations of the SIC in issue and applicable to accounting periods beginning before 1 July 1998.

However, the EU's examinations did not include the requirements of those revised standards which were applicable to accounting periods beginning after 1 July 1998, including:

- IAS 1, *Presentation of Financial Statements*

- IAS 14, *Segment Reporting*

- IAS 17, *Leases*

- IAS 19, *Employee Benefits*

This examination also did not address the following standards issued in 1998 and 1999:

- IAS 35, *Discontinuing Operations*

- IAS 36, *Impairment of Assets*

- IAS 37, *Provisions, Contingent Liabilities and Contingent Assets*

- IAS 38, *Intangible Assets*, and

- IAS 39, *Financial Instruments: Recognition and Measurement*, as well as

- the amendments to IASs 16, 22, 28 and 31 which were consequential to the adoption of IASs 37 and 38,

- IAS 10 (revised 1999), *Events after the Balance Sheet Date*,

- the amendments to IASs 1, 2, 11, 12, 18, 19, 20, 28, 30, 31 and 35 which were consequential to the adoption of IAS 10 (revised 1999), and

- IAS 40.

---

[1] *Contact Committee on the Accounting Directives: An Examination of the Conformity Between the International Accounting Standards and the European Accounting Directives, European Commission, Office for Official Publications of the European Communities. Luxembourg 1996.*

The disclosure standard IAS 32, *Financial Instruments: Disclosure and Presentation*, was not included in the examination.

The interpretations of the Standing Interpretations Committee in issue and applicable to accounting periods beginning before 1 July 1998 are as follows:

- SIC-2: *Consistency – Capitalisation of Borrowing Costs;*
- SIC-3: *Elimination of Unrealised Profits and Losses on Transactions with Associates;*
- SIC-5: *Classification of Financial Instruments – Contingent Settlement Provisions;*
- SIC-6: *Costs of Modifying Existing Software;*
- SIC-7: *Introduction of the Euro;* and
- SIC-8: *First-Time Application of IASs as the Primary Basis of Accounting.*

Objective and Scope of the Examination

The analysis in the 1999 Report was restricted to the relationship between IAS and the Accounting Directives. Within the EU, the competence of the Contact Committee is restricted to matters relating to EU accounting legislation, and therefore the Committee was not in a position to express any opinion relating to the relationship between IAS and any other rules (most notably, national legislation or national accounting standards) which are not based on the Accounting Directives themselves.

The objective of the examination was to determine whether – and if so, to what extent – conflicts existed between the EU Accounting Directives and the IAS applicable to accounting periods beginning before 1 July 1998, so that European companies wishing and able to apply IAS in their consolidated accounts could do so without conflicting with European legislation.

This examination did not address IAS that were published, but that were not yet in force on the effective date of the study. If companies adopted some or all of these standards on a voluntary basis or before the Standard's effective date, they were cautioned that further conformity problems could occur. The European Commission expects to publish conformity examinations covering these standards.

The Application of IAS Options

European companies wishing to prepare and present their financial statements in accordance with IAS must at the same time, comply with European accounting legislation. In such cases, since the Accounting Directives have overriding effect, it is assumed that any company wishing to comply with both Frameworks:

- will select the appropriate accounting treatment which conforms with the Accounting Directives in cases where IAS lay down both a *Benchmark Treatment* and an *Allowed Alternative Treatment;*
- is ready to accept all additional requirements imposed by IAS that do not conflict with the Accounting Directives;

- will select the appropriate accounting treatment that conforms with IAS in cases where the Accounting Directives allow either companies or Member States the option of choosing between two accounting treatments; and

- will apply the presentational requirements of IAS in such a way so as to be in conformity with the balance sheet and profit and loss account layouts prescribed respectively by Articles 9/10 and Articles 23 to 26 of the Fourth Directive.

Conclusions

The 1999 Report concluded that, in general, there were no significant conflicts between the Directives and those International Accounting Standards and interpretations of the Standing Interpretations Committee (SIC) that were addressed by the study. However, one minor conflict between IAS and the Directives remains.

IAS 27, *Consolidated Financial Statements and Accounting for Investments in Subsidiaries*, with respect to the exclusion of an undertaking from consolidated accounts. IAS 27 only provides for exclusion from consolidation when control is intended to be temporary or where the subsidiary operates under severe long-term restrictions. In contrast, Article 14(1) of the Seventh Directive states that an undertaking must be excluded from the consolidated accounts when its inclusion would be incompatible with the true and fair view.

The Contact Committee saw no case where Article 14 would require the exclusion of any undertaking from consolidation.[1] Whilst there seemed to be a textual conflict between IAS 27 and the Directive, whether or not this would have any effect in practice was a debatable point. For example, whilst IAS 27 does not allow for the exclusion from consolidation of a subsidiary on the grounds of different activities, it is a matter of judgement as to whether the consolidation of enterprises which undertake different activities would be incompatible with the true and fair view. The current thinking is that such undertakings should be consolidated, with the appropriate segmental information being given in the notes to the accounts in order to explain the performance of the individual operations.

---

[1] *The considerations expressed in this paragraph do not apply to those mixed groups comprising banks and insurance undertakings which are often referred to as "financial conglomerates", because this matter has not been specifically examined by the Contact Committee.*

IASC Chronology:

Significant Dates in IASC's History

1973

❏ IASC formed by accountancy bodies from 9 countries – inaugural meeting 29 June, London.

1974

❏ First Exposure Draft published.

❏ First associate members admitted (Belgium, India, Israel, New Zealand, Pakistan and Zimbabwe).

❏ IAS 1, *Disclosure of Accounting Policies*.

1976

❏ Group of Ten Bank Governors decides to work with IASC, and fund an IASC project on bank financial statements.

1977

❏ Revised constitution adopted – Board expanded to 11 countries – 'associate' members become members – reference to 'basic' standards removed.

❏ IFAC formed – IASC continues to be autonomous, but with close relationship with IFAC.

1978

❏ South Africa and Nigeria join Board.

1979

❏ IASC meets OECD working group on accounting standards.

1980

❏ Discussion papers on bank disclosures published.

❏ United Nations Intergovernmental Working Group on Accounting and Reporting meets for first time – IASC presents position paper on co-operation.

1981

❏ Consultative Group formed.

❏ IASC starts visits to national standard setters.

1982

❏   IASC/IFAC mutual commitments – Board expanded to 13 countries plus four 'other organisations with an interest in financial reporting'.

1983

❏   Italy joins Board.

1984

❏   Taiwan joins Board.
❏   Formal meeting with US SEC.

1985

❏   OECD forum on accounting harmonisation.
❏   IASC responds to SEC multinational prospectus proposals.

1986

❏   Financial analysts join Board.
❏   Joint conference with New York Stock Exchange and International Bar Association on the globalisation of financial markets.

1987

❏   Comparability project started.
❏   IOSCO joins Consultative Group and supports Comparability project.
❏   First IASC Bound Volume of International Accounting Standards.

1988

❏   Jordan, Korea and Nordic Federation replace Mexico, Nigeria and Taiwan on the Board.
❏   Financial instruments project started in conjunction with Canadian Accounting Standards Board.
❏   IASC publishes survey on the use of IASs.
❏   FASB joins Consultative Group and joins Board as observer.
❏   E32, *Comparability of Financial Statements*.

1989

❏   FEE president Hermann Nordemann argues that Europe's best interests are served by international harmonisation and greater involvement in IASC.
❏   Framework for the Preparation and Presentation of Financial Statements approved.
❏   IFAC public sector guideline requires government business enterprise to follow IASs.

1990

❏ Statement of Intent on Comparability of Financial Statements.
❏ European Commission joins Consultative Group and joins Board as observer.
❏ External funding launched.
❏ Bishop committee confirms relationship between IASC and IFAC.

1991

❏ First IASC conference of standard setters (organised in conjunction with FEE and FASB).
❏ *IASC Insight*, *IASC Update* and publications subscription scheme launched.
❏ FASB plan supports international standards.

1992

❏ First delegation to People's Republic of China.

1993

❏ India replaces Korea on Board.
❏ IOSCO agrees list of core standards and endorses IAS 7, *Cash Flow Statements*.
❏ Comparability and Improvements project completed with approval of ten revised IASs.

1994

❏ SEC accepts three IAS treatments plus IAS 7.
❏ Board meets standard setters to discuss E48, *Financial Instruments*.
❏ World Bank agrees to fund Agriculture project.
❏ Establishment of Advisory Council approved.
❏ IOSCO accepts 14 IASs but rejects step-by-step endorsement of IAS.
❏ FASB agrees to work with IASC on earnings per share.
❏ *Future Events* – first joint publication of G4+1.

1995

❏ Agreement with IOSCO to complete core standards by 1999 – on successful completion IOSCO will consider endorsing IAS for cross-border offerings.
❏ First German companies report under IAS.
❏ Swiss holding companies join Board.
❏ Malaysia and Mexico replace Italy and Jordan on Board – India and South Africa agree to share Board seats with Sri Lanka and Zimbabwe.
❏ European Commission supports IASC/IOSCO agreement and use of IAS by EU multinationals.

1996

❑ Core standards programme accelerated, target 1998.

❑ Financial executives join Board and IOSCO joins Board as observer.

❑ Board starts joint project on Provisions with UK Accounting Standards Board.

❑ EU Contact Committee finds IAS compatible with EU directives, with minor exceptions.

❑ US Congress calls for 'a high-quality comprehensive set of generally accepted international accounting standards'.

❑ Australian Stock Exchange supports programme to harmonise Australian standards with IAS.

❑ Ministers at World Trade Organization encourage successful completion of international standards.

1997

❑ Standing Interpretations Committee formed.

❑ IASC and FASB issue similar EPS standards. IASC, FASB and CICA issue new Segments standards with relatively minor differences.

❑ Discussion paper proposes fair value for all Financial Assets and Financial Liabilities – IASC holds 45 consultation meetings in 16 countries.

❑ Joint Working Group on financial instruments formed with national standard setters.

❑ People's Republic of China becomes a member of IASC and IFAC and joins IASC Board as observer.

❑ FEE calls on Europe to use IASC's Framework.

❑ Strategy Working Party formed.

❑ IASC sets up its Internet website.

1998

❑ New laws in Belgium, France, Germany and Italy allow large companies to use IASs domestically.

❑ First official translation of IAS (German).

❑ IFAC Public Sector Committee publishes draft Guideline for Governmental Financial Reporting as a platform for a set of International Public Sector Accounting Standards, to be based on IAS.

❑ Number of countries with IASC members passes 100.

❑ Strategy Working Party proposes structural changes, closer ties to national standard setters.

❑ Core standards completed with approval of IAS 39 in December.

1999

❑ IASC Board meetings opened to public observation.

❏ G7 finance ministers and IMF urge support for IAS to 'strengthen the international financial architecture'.

❏ IFAC forum of international financial institutions, development agencies, and accounting firms commits to 'support the use of International Accounting Standards as the minimum benchmark' worldwide.

❏ Proposed EC single market plan for financial services includes use of IAS.

❏ FEE urges allowing European listed companies to use IASs without EC Directives and phase-out of US GAAP.

❏ Eurasian Federation of Accountants and Auditors plans adoption of IAS in CIS countries.

❏ IASC Board accepts Strategy Working Party's proposals for reform; also endorsed by World Bank, SEC, etc. Nominating Committee members appointed.

❏ Over 300,000 visitors to IASC website view nearly two million web pages during 1999.

❏ IASC Board unanimously approves restructuring into 14-member board (12 full-time) under independent trustees.

2000

❏ Basel Committee expresses support for IAS and for efforts to harmonise accounting internationally.

❏ SEC concept release regarding the use of international accounting standards in the USA.

❏ As part of restructuring programme, IASC Board approves a new Constitution.

❏ IOSCO recommends that its members allow multinational issuers to use 30 IASC standards in cross-border offerings and listings.

❏ Nominating Committee announces initial Trustees of the restructured IASC.

❏ IASC Member Bodies approve IASC's restructuring and the new IASC Constitution.

❏ European Commission announces plans to require IASC standards for all EU listed companies from no later than 2005.

Part II:

International Accounting Standards

Chapter 1

Fundamentals of International Accounting Standards

This chapter introduces IASC's "Framework for the Preparation and Presentation of Financial Statements" and discusses the application of International Accounting Standards in financial statements and reporting generally.

1.1 Framework for the Preparation and Presentation of Financial Statements

Introduction

Purpose and Status

The Framework sets out the concepts that underlie the preparation and presentation of financial statements for external users. The purpose of the Framework is to:

(a) assist the Board of IASC in the development of future International Accounting Standards and in its review of existing International Accounting Standards;

(b) assist the Board of IASC in promoting harmonisation of regulations, accounting standards and procedures relating to the presentation of financial statements by providing a basis for reducing the number of alternative accounting treatments permitted by International Accounting Standards;

(c) assist national standard-setting bodies in developing national standards;

(d) assist preparers of financial statements in applying International Accounting Standards and in dealing with topics that have yet to form the subject of an International Accounting Standard;

(e) assist auditors in forming an opinion as to whether financial statements conform with International Accounting Standards;

(f) assist users of financial statements in interpreting the information contained in financial statements prepared in conformity with International Accounting Standards; and

(g) provide those who are interested in the work of IASC with information about its approach to the formulation of International Accounting Standards. *(1.)*

The Framework is not an International Accounting Standard and hence does not define standards for any particular measurement or disclosure issue. Nothing in the Framework overrides any specific International Accounting Standard. *(2.)*

The Board of IASC recognises that in a limited number of cases there may be a conflict between the Framework and an International Accounting Standard. In those cases where there is a conflict, the requirements of the International Accounting Standard prevail over those of the Framework. However, the Board of IASC will be guided by the Framework in the development of future Standards and in its review of existing Standards, and the number of cases of conflict between the Framework and International Accounting Standards is expected to diminish through time. *(3.)*

Scope

The Framework addresses:

(a)   the objective of financial statements;

(b)   the qualitative characteristics that determine the usefulness of information in financial statements;

(c)   the definition, recognition and measurement of the elements from which financial statements are constructed; and

(d)   concepts of capital and capital maintenance. *(5.)*

Financial statements form part of the process of financial reporting. A complete set of financial statements normally includes a balance sheet, an income statement, a statement of changes in financial position (which may be presented in a variety of ways, for example, as a statement of cash flows or a statement of funds flow), and those notes and other statements and explanatory material that are an integral part of the financial statements. They may also include supplementary schedules and information based on or derived from, and expected to be read with, such statements. Such schedules and supplementary information may deal, for example, with financial information about industrial and geographical segments and disclosures about the effects of changing prices. Financial statements do not, however, include such items as reports by directors, statements by the chairman, discussion and analysis by management and similar items that may be included in a financial or annual report. *(7.)*

The Framework applies to the financial statements of all commercial, industrial and business reporting enterprises, whether in the public or the private sectors. A reporting enterprise is an enterprise for which there are users who rely on the financial statements as their major source of financial information about the enterprise. *(8.)*

Users and Their Information Needs

The users of financial statements include present and potential investors, employees, lenders, suppliers and other trade creditors, customers, governments and their agencies and the public. They use financial statements in order to satisfy some of their different needs for information. *(9.)*

While all of the information needs of these users cannot be met by financial statements, there are needs which are common to all users. As investors are providers of risk capital to the enterprise, the provision of financial statements that meet their needs will also meet most of the needs of other users that financial statements can satisfy. *(10.)*

The management of an enterprise has the primary responsibility for the preparation and presentation of the financial statements of the enterprise. Management is also interested in the information contained in the financial statements even though it has access to additional management and financial information that helps it carry out its planning, decision-making and control responsibilities. Management has the ability to determine the form and content of such additional information in order to meet its own needs. The reporting of such information, however, is beyond the scope of the Framework. Nevertheless, published financial statements are based on the information used by management about the financial position, performance and changes in financial position of the enterprise. *(11.)*

The Objective of Financial Statements

The Framework states that the objective of financial statements is to provide information about the financial position, performance and changes in financial position of an enterprise that is useful to a wide range of users in making economic decisions. *(12.)*

Financial statements also show the results of the stewardship of management, or the accountability of management for the resources entrusted to it. Those users who wish to assess the stewardship or accountability of management do so in order that they may make economic decisions; these decisions may include, for example, whether to hold or sell their investment in the enterprise or whether to reappoint or replace the management. *(14.)*

Financial Position, Performance and Changes in Financial Position

The financial position of an enterprise is affected by the economic resources it controls, its financial structure, its liquidity and solvency, and its capacity to adapt to changes in the environment in which it operates.

- Information about the *economic resources* controlled by the enterprise and its capacity in the past to modify these resources is useful in predicting the ability of the enterprise to generate cash and cash equivalents in the future.

- Information about *financial structure* is useful in predicting future borrowing needs and how future profits and cash flows will be distributed among those with an interest in the enterprise; it is also useful in predicting how successful the enterprise is likely to be in raising further finance.

- Information about *liquidity and solvency* is useful in predicting the ability of the enterprise to meet its financial commitments as they fall due.

  - *Liquidity* refers to the availability of cash in the near future after taking account of financial commitments over this period.

– *Solvency* refers to the availability of cash over the longer term to meet financial commitments as they fall due. *(16.)*

Information about the performance of an enterprise, in particular its profitability, is required in order to assess potential changes in the economic resources that it is likely to control in the future. Information about variability of performance is important in this respect. Information about performance is useful in predicting the capacity of the enterprise to generate cash flows from its existing resource base. It is also useful in forming judgements about the effectiveness with which the enterprise might employ additional resources. *(17.)*

Information concerning changes in the financial position of an enterprise is useful in order to assess its investing, financing and operating activities during the reporting period. This information is useful in providing the user with a basis to assess the ability of the enterprise to generate cash and cash equivalents and the needs of the enterprise to utilise those cash flows. *(18.)*

Information about financial position is primarily provided in a balance sheet. Information about financial performance is primarily provided in the income statement and information about cash flows is provided in the statement of cash flows. *(19.)*

Notes and Supplementary Schedules

The financial statements also contain notes and supplementary schedules and other information. For example, they may contain additional information that is relevant to the needs of users about the items in the balance sheet and income statement. They may include disclosures about the risks and uncertainties affecting the enterprise and any resources and obligations not recognised in the balance sheet (such as mineral reserves). Information about geographical and industry segments and the effect on the enterprise of changing prices may also be provided in the form of supplementary information. *(21.)*

Underlying Assumptions

Accrual Basis

In order to meet their objectives, financial statements are prepared on the accrual basis of accounting. Under this basis, the effects of transactions and other events are recognised when they occur (and not as cash or its equivalent is received or paid) and they are recorded in the accounting records and reported in the financial statements of the periods to which they relate. Financial statements prepared on the accrual basis inform users not only of past transactions involving the payment and receipt of cash but also of obligations to pay cash in the future and of resources that represent cash to be received in the future. Hence, they provide the type of information about past transactions and other events that is most useful to users in making economic decisions. *(22.)*

Going Concern

The financial statements are normally prepared on the assumption that an enterprise is a going concern and will continue in operation for the foreseeable future. Hence, it is assumed that the enterprise has neither the intention nor the need to liquidate or curtail materially the scale of its operations; if such an intention or need exists, the financial statements may have to be prepared on a different basis and, if so, the basis used is disclosed. *(23.)*

Qualitative Characteristics of Financial Statements

Qualitative characteristics are the attributes that make the information provided in financial statements useful to users. The four principal qualitative characteristics are understandability, relevance, reliability and comparability. *(24.)*

Understandability

An essential quality of the information provided in financial statements is that it is readily understandable by users. For this purpose, users are assumed to have a reasonable knowledge of business and economic activities and accounting and a willingness to study the information with reasonable diligence. However, information about complex matters that should be included in the financial statements because of its relevance to the economic decision-making needs of users should not be excluded merely on the grounds that it may be too difficult for certain users to understand. *(25.)*

Relevance

To be useful, information must be relevant to the decision-making needs of users. Information has the quality of relevance when it influences the economic decisions of users by helping them evaluate past, present or future events or confirming, or correcting, their past evaluations. *(26.)*

Materiality

The relevance of information is affected by its nature and materiality. In some cases, the nature of information alone is sufficient to determine its relevance. For example, the reporting of a new segment may affect the assessment of the risks and opportunities facing the enterprise irrespective of the materiality of the results achieved by the new segment in the reporting period. In other cases, both the nature and materiality are important, for example, the amounts of inventories held in each of the main categories that are appropriate to the business. *(29.)*

Information is material if its omission or misstatement could influence the economic decisions of users taken on the basis of the financial statements. Materiality depends on the size of the item or error judged in the particular circumstances of its omission or misstatement. Thus, materiality provides a threshold or cut-off point rather than being a primary qualitative characteristic which information must have if it is to be useful. *(30.)*

Reliability

To be useful, information must also be reliable. Information has the quality of reliability when it is free from material error and bias and can be depended upon by users to represent faithfully that which it either purports to represent or could reasonably be expected to represent. *(31.)*

Information may be relevant but so unreliable in nature or representation that its recognition may be potentially misleading. For example, if the validity and amount of a claim for damages under a legal action are disputed, it may be inappropriate for the enterprise to recognise the full amount of the claim in the balance sheet, although it may be appropriate to disclose the amount and circumstances of the claim. *(32.)*

Faithful Representation

To be reliable, information must represent faithfully the transactions and other events it either purports to represent or could reasonably be expected to represent. Thus, for example, a balance sheet should represent faithfully the transactions and other events that result in assets, liabilities and equity of the enterprise at the reporting date which meet the recognition criteria. *(33.)*

Substance Over Form

If information is to represent faithfully the transactions and other events that it purports to represent, it is necessary that they are accounted for and presented in accordance with their substance and economic reality and not merely their legal form. The substance of transactions or other events is not always consistent with that which is apparent from their legal or contrived form. For example, an enterprise may dispose of an asset to another party in such a way that the documentation purports to pass legal ownership to that party; nevertheless, agreements may exist that ensure that the enterprise continues to enjoy the future economic benefits embodied in the asset. In such circumstances, the reporting of a sale would not represent faithfully the transaction entered into (if indeed there was a transaction). *(35.)*

Neutrality

To be reliable, the information contained in financial statements must be neutral, that is, free from bias. Financial statements are not neutral if, by the selection or presentation of information, they influence the making of a decision or judgement in order to achieve a predetermined result or outcome. *(36.)*

Prudence

The preparers of financial statements do, however, have to contend with the uncertainties that inevitably surround many events and circumstances, such as the collectability of doubtful receivables, the probable useful life of plant and equipment and the number of warranty claims that may occur. Such uncertainties are recognised by the disclosure of their nature and extent and by the exercise of prudence in the preparation of the financial statements. Prudence is the inclusion of a degree of caution in the exercise of the judgements needed in making the estimates required under conditions of uncertainty, such that assets or income are not overstated and liabilities or expenses are not understated. However, the exercise of prudence does not allow, for example, the creation of hidden reserves or excessive provisions, the deliberate understatement of assets or income, or the deliberate overstatement of liabilities or expenses, because the financial statements would not be neutral and, therefore, not have the quality of reliability. *(37.)*

Completeness

To be reliable, the information in financial statements must be complete within the bounds of materiality and cost. An omission can cause information to be false or misleading and thus unreliable and deficient in terms of its relevance. *(38.)*

Comparability

Users must be able to compare the financial statements of an enterprise through time in order to identify trends in its financial position and performance. Users must also be able to compare the financial statements of different enterprises in order to evaluate their relative financial position, performance and changes in financial position. Hence, the measurement and display of the financial effect of like transactions and other events must be carried out in a consistent way throughout an enterprise and over time for that enterprise and in a consistent way for different enterprises. *(39.)*

Because users wish to compare the financial position, performance and changes in financial position of an enterprise over time, it is important that the financial statements show corresponding information for the preceding periods. *(42.)*

Constraints on Relevant and Reliable Information

Timeliness

If there is undue delay in the reporting of information it may lose its relevance. Management may need to balance the relative merits of timely reporting and the provision of reliable information. To provide information on a timely basis it may often be necessary to report before all aspects of a transaction or other event are known, thus impairing reliability. Conversely, if reporting is delayed until all aspects are known, the information may be highly reliable but of little use to users who have had to make decisions in the interim. In achieving a balance between relevance and reliability, the overriding consideration is how best to satisfy the economic decision-making needs of users. *(43.)*

Balance between Benefit and Cost

The balance between benefit and cost is a pervasive constraint rather than a qualitative characteristic. The benefits derived from information should exceed the cost of providing it. The evaluation of benefits and costs is, however, substantially a judgemental process. Furthermore, the costs do not necessarily fall on those users who enjoy the benefits. Benefits may also be enjoyed by users other than those for whom the information is prepared; for example, the provision of further information to lenders may reduce the borrowing costs of an enterprise. For these reasons, it is difficult to apply a cost-benefit test in any particular case. Nevertheless, standard setters in particular, as well as the preparers and users of financial statements, should be aware of this constraint. *(44.)*

Balance between Qualitative Characteristics

In practice a balancing, or trade-off, between qualitative characteristics is often necessary. Generally the aim is to achieve an appropriate balance among the characteristics in order to meet the objective of financial statements. The relative importance of the characteristics in different cases is a matter of professional judgement. *(45.)*

True and Fair View / Fair Presentation

Financial statements are frequently described as showing a true and fair view of, or as presenting fairly, the financial position, performance and changes in financial position of an enterprise. Although the Framework does not deal directly with such concepts, the application of the principal qualitative characteristics and of appropriate accounting standards normally results in financial statements that convey what is generally understood as a true and fair view of, or as presenting fairly, such information. *(46.)*

The Elements of Financial Statements

Financial statements portray the financial effects of transactions and other events by grouping them into broad classes according to their economic characteristics. These broad classes are termed the elements of financial statements. The elements directly related to the measurement of financial position in the balance sheet are assets, liabilities and equity. The elements directly related to the measurement of performance in the income statement are income and expenses. The statement of changes in financial position usually reflects income statement elements and changes in balance sheet elements; accordingly, the Framework identifies no elements that are unique to this statement. *(47.)*

Financial Position

The elements directly related to the measurement of financial position are assets, liabilities and equity. These are defined as follows:

(a)　An asset is a resource controlled by the enterprise as a result of past events and from which future economic benefits are expected to flow to the enterprise.

(b)　A liability is a present obligation of the enterprise arising from past events, the settlement of which is expected to result in an outflow from the enterprise of resources embodying economic benefits.

(c)　Equity is the residual interest in the assets of the enterprise after deducting all its liabilities. *(49.)*

The definitions of an asset and a liability identify their essential features but do not attempt to specify the criteria that need to be met before they are recognised in the balance sheet. Thus, the definitions embrace items that are not recognised as assets or liabilities in the balance sheet because they do not satisfy the criteria for recognition discussed in paragraphs 82 to 98. In particular, the expectation that future economic benefits will flow to or from an enterprise must be sufficiently certain to meet the probability criterion in paragraph 83 before an asset or liability is recognised. *(50.)*

Assets

The future economic benefit embodied in an asset is the potential to contribute, directly or indirectly, to the flow of cash and cash equivalents to the enterprise. The potential may be a productive one that is part of the operating activities of the enterprise. It may also take the form of convertibility into cash or cash equivalents or a capability to reduce cash outflows, such as when an alternative manufacturing process lowers the costs of production. *(53.)*

An enterprise usually employs its assets to produce goods or services capable of satisfying the wants or needs of customers; because these goods or services can satisfy these wants or needs, customers are prepared to pay for them and hence contribute to the cash flow of the enterprise. Cash itself renders a service to the enterprise because of its command over other resources. *(54.)*

Many assets, for example, property, plant and equipment, have a physical form. However, physical form is not essential to the existence of an asset; hence patents and copyrights, for example, are assets if future economic benefits are expected to flow from them to the enterprise and if they are controlled by the enterprise. *(56.)*

Many assets, for example, receivables and property, are associated with legal rights, including the right of ownership. In determining the existence of an asset, the right of ownership is not essential; thus, for example, property held on a lease is an asset if the enterprise controls the benefits which are expected to flow from the property. Although the capacity of an enterprise to control benefits is usually the result of legal rights, an item may nonetheless satisfy the definition of an asset even when there is no legal control. For example, know-how obtained from a development activity may meet the definition of an asset when, by keeping that know-how secret, an enterprise controls the benefits that are expected to flow from it. *(57.)*

The assets of an enterprise result from past transactions or other past events. Enterprises normally obtain assets by purchasing or producing them, but other transactions or events may generate assets; examples include property received by an enterprise from government as part of a programme to encourage economic growth in an area and the discovery of mineral deposits. Transactions or events expected to occur in the future do not in themselves give rise to assets; hence, for example, an intention to purchase inventory does not, of itself, meet the definition of an asset. *(58.)*

Liabilities

An essential characteristic of a liability is that the enterprise has a present obligation. An obligation is a duty or responsibility to act or perform in a certain way. Obligations may be legally enforceable as a consequence of a binding contract or statutory requirement. This is normally the case, for example, with amounts payable for goods and services received. Obligations also arise, however, from normal business practice, custom and a desire to maintain good business relations or act in an equitable manner. If, for example, an enterprise decides as a matter of policy to rectify faults in its products even when these become apparent after the warranty period has expired, the amounts that are expected to be expended in respect of goods already sold are liabilities. *(60.)*

A distinction needs to be drawn between a present obligation and a future commitment. A decision by the management of an enterprise to acquire assets in the future does not, of itself, give rise to a present obligation. An obligation normally arises only when the asset is delivered or the enterprise enters into an irrevocable agreement to acquire the asset. In the latter case, the irrevocable nature of the agreement means that the economic consequences of failing to honour the obligation, for example, because of the existence of a substantial penalty, leave the enterprise with little, if any, discretion to avoid the outflow of resources to another party. *(61.)*

Liabilities result from past transactions or other past events. Thus, for example, the acquisition of goods and the use of services give rise to trade payables (unless paid for in advance or on delivery) and the receipt of a bank loan results in an obligation to repay the loan. An enterprise may also recognise future rebates based on annual purchases by customers as liabilities; in this case, the sale of the goods in the past is the transaction that gives rise to the liability. *(63.)*

Equity

Although equity is defined in paragraph 49 as a residual, it may be sub-classified in the balance sheet. For example, in a corporate enterprise, funds contributed by shareholders, retained earnings, reserves representing appropriations of retained earnings and reserves representing capital maintenance adjustments may be shown separately. Such classifications can be relevant to the decision-making needs of the users of financial statements when they indicate legal or other restrictions on the ability of the enterprise to distribute or otherwise apply its equity. They may also reflect the fact that parties with ownership interests in an enterprise have differing rights in relation to the receipt of dividends or the repayment of capital. *(65.)*

The creation of reserves is sometimes required by statute or other law in order to give the enterprise and its creditors an added measure of protection from the effects of losses. Other reserves may be established if national tax law grants exemptions from, or reductions in, taxation liabilities when transfers to such reserves are made. The existence and size of these legal, statutory and tax reserves is information that can be relevant to the decision-making needs of users. Transfers to such reserves are appropriations of retained earnings rather than expenses. *(66.)*

The amount at which equity is shown in the balance sheet is dependent on the measurement of assets and liabilities. Normally, the aggregate amount of equity only by coincidence corresponds with the aggregate market value of the shares of the enterprise or the sum that could be raised by disposing of either the net assets on a piecemeal basis or the enterprise as a whole on a going-concern basis. *(67.)*

Performance

Profit is frequently used as a measure of performance or as the basis for other measures, such as return on investment or earnings per share. The elements directly related to the measurement of profit are income and expenses. The recognition and measurement of income and expenses, and hence profit, depends in part on the concepts of capital and capital maintenance used by the enterprise in preparing its financial statements. These concepts are discussed in paragraphs 102 to 110. *(69.)*

The elements of income and expenses are defined as follows:

(a)   Income is an increase in economic benefits during the accounting period in the form of inflows or enhancements of assets or decreases of liabilities that result in increases in equity, other than those relating to contributions from equity participants.

(b)   Expenses are decreases in economic benefits during the accounting period in the form of outflows or depletions of assets or incurrences of liabilities that result in decreases in equity, other than those relating to distributions to equity participants. *(70.)*

Income

The definition of income encompasses both revenue and gains. Revenue arises in the course of the ordinary activities of an enterprise and is referred to by a variety of different names including sales, fees, interest, dividends, royalties and rent. *(74.)*

Gains represent other items that meet the definition of income and may, or may not, arise in the course of the ordinary activities of an enterprise. Gains represent increases in economic benefits and as such are no different in nature from revenue. Hence, they are not regarded as constituting a separate element in this Framework. *(75.)*

Gains include, for example, those arising on the disposal of non-current assets. The definition of income also includes unrealised gains; for example, those arising on the revaluation of marketable securities and those resulting from increases in the carrying amount of long term assets. When gains are recognised in the income statement, they are usually displayed separately because knowledge of them is useful for the purpose of making economic decisions. Gains are often reported net of related expenses. *(76.)*

Expenses

The definition of expenses encompasses losses as well as those expenses that arise in the course of the ordinary activities of the enterprise. Expenses that arise in the course of the ordinary activities of the enterprise include, for example, cost of sales, wages and depreciation. They usually take the form of an outflow or depletion of assets such as cash and cash equivalents, inventory, property, plant and equipment. *(78.)*

Losses represent other items that meet the definition of expenses and may, or may not, arise in the course of the ordinary activities of the enterprise. Losses represent decreases in economic benefits and as such they are no different in nature from other expenses. Hence, they are not regarded as a separate element in the Framework. *(79.)*

Capital Maintenance Adjustments

The revaluation or restatement of assets and liabilities gives rise to increases or decreases in equity. While these increases or decreases meet the definition of income and expenses, they are not included in the income statement under certain concepts of capital maintenance. Instead these items are included in equity as capital maintenance adjustments or revaluation reserves. These concepts of capital maintenance are discussed in paragraphs 102 to 110 of the Framework. *(81.)*

Recognition of the Elements of Financial Statements

An item that meets the definition of an element should be recognised if:

(a)   it is probable that any future economic benefit associated with the item will flow to or from the enterprise; and

(b)   the item has a cost or value that can be measured with reliability. *(83.)*

The Probability of Future Economic Benefit

The concept of probability is used in the recognition criteria to refer to the degree of uncertainty that the future economic benefits associated with the item will flow to or from the enterprise. The concept is in keeping with the uncertainty that characterises the environment in which an enterprise operates. Assessments of the degree of uncertainty attaching to the flow of future economic benefits are made on the basis of the evidence available when the financial statements are prepared. For example, when it is probable that a receivable owed by an enterprise will be paid, it is then justifiable, in the absence of any evidence to the contrary, to recognise the receivable as an asset. For a large population of receivables, however, some degree of non-payment is normally considered probable; hence an expense representing the expected reduction in economic benefits is recognised. *(85.)*

Reliability of Measurement

The second criterion for the recognition of an item is that it possesses a cost or value that can be measured with reliability as discussed in paragraphs 31 to 38 of this Framework. In many cases, cost or value must be estimated; the use of reasonable estimates is an essential part of the preparation of financial statements and does not undermine their reliability. When, however, a reasonable estimate cannot be made the item is not recognised in the balance sheet or income statement. For example, the expected proceeds from a lawsuit may meet the definitions of both an asset and income as well as the probability criterion for recognition; however, if it is not possible for the claim to be measured reliably, it should not be recognised as an asset or as income; the existence of the claim, however, would be disclosed in the notes, explanatory material or supplementary schedules. *(86.)*

Recognition of Assets

An asset is recognised in the balance sheet when it is probable that the future economic benefits will flow to the enterprise and the asset has a cost or value that can be measured reliably. *(89.)*

An asset is not recognised in the balance sheet when expenditure has been incurred for which it is considered improbable that economic benefits will flow to the enterprise beyond the current accounting period. Instead such a transaction results in the recognition of an expense in the income statement. This treatment does not imply either that the intention of management in incurring expenditure was other than to generate future economic benefits for the enterprise or that management was misguided. The only implication is that the degree of certainty that economic benefits will flow to the enterprise beyond the current accounting period is insufficient to warrant the recognition of an asset. *(90.)*

Recognition of Liabilities

A liability is recognised in the balance sheet when it is probable that an outflow of resources embodying economic benefits will result from the settlement of a present obligation and the amount at which the settlement will take place can be measured reliably. In practice, obligations under contracts that are equally proportionately unperformed (for example, liabilities for inventory ordered but not yet received) are generally not recognised as liabilities in the financial statements. However, such obligations may meet the definition of liabilities and, provided the recognition criteria are met in the particular circumstances, may qualify for recognition. In such circumstances, recognition of liabilities entails recognition of related assets or expenses. *(91.)*

Recognition of Income

Income is recognised in the income statement when an increase in future economic benefits related to an increase in an asset or a decrease of a liability has arisen that can be measured reliably. This means, in effect, that recognition of income occurs simultaneously with the recognition of increases in assets or decreases in liabilities (for example, the net increase in assets arising on a sale of goods or services or the decrease in liabilities arising from the waiver of a debt payable). *(92.)*

Recognition of Expenses

Expenses are recognised in the income statement when a decrease in future economic benefits related to a decrease in an asset or an increase of a liability has arisen that can be measured reliably. This means, in effect, that recognition of expenses occurs simultaneously with the recognition of an increase in liabilities or a decrease in assets (for example, the accrual of employee entitlements or the depreciation of equipment). *(94.)*

Expenses are recognised in the income statement on the basis of a direct association between the costs incurred and the earning of specific items of income. This process, commonly referred to as the matching of costs with revenues, involves the simultaneous or combined recognition of revenues and expenses that result directly and jointly from the same transactions or other events; for example, the various components of expense making up the cost of goods sold are recognised at the same time as the income derived from the sale of the goods. However, the application of the matching concept under the Framework does not allow the recognition of items in the balance sheet which do not meet the definition of assets or liabilities. *(95.)*

When economic benefits are expected to arise over several accounting periods and the association with income can only be broadly or indirectly determined, expenses are recognised in the income statement on the basis of systematic and rational allocation procedures. This is often necessary in recognising the expenses associated with the using up of assets such as property, plant, equipment, goodwill, patents and trademarks; in such cases the expense is referred to as depreciation or amortisation. These allocation procedures are intended to recognise expenses in the accounting periods in which the economic benefits associated with these items are consumed or expire. *(96.)*

An expense is recognised immediately in the income statement when an expenditure produces no future economic benefits or when, and to the extent that, future economic benefits do not qualify, or cease to qualify, for recognition in the balance sheet as an asset. *(97.)*

An expense is also recognised in the income statement in those cases when a liability is incurred without the recognition of an asset, as when a liability under a product warranty arises. *(98.)*

Measurement of the Elements of Financial Statements

A number of different measurement bases are employed to different degrees and in varying combinations in financial statements. They include the following:

(a) *Historical cost.* Assets are recorded at the amount of cash or cash equivalents paid or the fair value of the consideration given to acquire them at the time of their acquisition. Liabilities are recorded at the amount of proceeds received in exchange for the obligation, or in some circumstances (for example, income taxes), at the amounts of cash or cash equivalents expected to be paid to satisfy the liability in the normal course of business.

(b) *Current cost.* Assets are carried at the amount of cash or cash equivalents that would have to be paid if the same or an equivalent asset was acquired currently. Liabilities are carried at the undiscounted amount of cash or cash equivalents that would be required to settle the obligation currently.

(c) *Realisable (settlement) value.* Assets are carried at the amount of cash or cash equivalents that could currently be obtained by selling the asset in an orderly disposal. Liabilities are carried at their settlement values; that is, the undiscounted amounts of cash or cash equivalents expected to be paid to satisfy the liabilities in the normal course of business.

(d) *Present value.* Assets are carried at the present discounted value of the future net cash inflows that the item is expected to generate in the normal course of business. Liabilities are carried at the present discounted value of the future net cash outflows that are expected to be required to settle the liabilities in the normal course of business. *(100.)*

Concepts of Capital and Capital Maintenance

Concepts of Capital

A financial concept of capital is adopted by most enterprises in preparing their financial statements. Under a financial concept of capital, such as invested money or invested purchasing power, capital is synonymous with the net assets or equity of the enterprise. Under a physical concept of capital, such as operating capability, capital is regarded as the productive capacity of the enterprise based on, for example, units of output per day. *(102.)*

The selection of the appropriate concept of capital by an enterprise should be based on the needs of the users of its financial statements. Thus, a financial concept of capital should be adopted if the users of financial statements are primarily concerned with the maintenance of nominal invested capital or the purchasing power of invested capital. If, however, the main concern of users is with the operating capability of the enterprise, a physical concept of capital should be used. The concept chosen indicates the goal to be attained in determining profit, even though there may be some measurement difficulties in making the concept operational. *(103.)*

Concepts of Capital Maintenance and the Determination of Profit

The concepts of capital in paragraph 102 give rise to the following concepts of capital maintenance:

(a) *Financial capital maintenance.* Under this concept a profit is earned only if the financial (or money) amount of the net assets at the end of the period exceeds the financial (or money) amount of net assets at the beginning of the period, after excluding any distributions to, and contributions from, owners during the period. Financial capital maintenance can be measured in either nominal monetary units or units of constant purchasing power.

(b) *Physical capital maintenance.* Under this concept a profit is earned only if the physical productive capacity (or operating capability) of the enterprise (or the resources or funds needed to achieve that capacity) at the end of the period exceeds the physical productive capacity at the beginning of the period, after excluding any distributions to, and contributions from, owners during the period. *(104.)*

Under the concept of financial capital maintenance where capital is defined in terms of nominal monetary units, profit represents the increase in nominal money capital over the period. Thus, increases in the prices of assets held over the period, conventionally referred to as holding gains, are, conceptually, profits. They may not be recognised as such, however, until the assets are disposed of in an exchange transaction. When the concept of financial capital maintenance is defined in terms of constant purchasing power units, profit represents the increase in invested purchasing power over the period. Thus, only that part of the increase in the prices of assets that exceeds the increase in the general level of prices is regarded as profit. The rest of the increase is treated as a capital maintenance adjustment and, hence, as part of equity. *(108.)*

Under the concept of physical capital maintenance when capital is defined in terms of the physical productive capacity, profit represents the increase in that capital over the period. All price changes affecting the assets and liabilities of the enterprise are viewed as changes in the measurement of the physical productive capacity of the enterprise; hence, they are treated as capital maintenance adjustments that are part of equity and not as profit. *(109.)*

Chapter 2

Financial Statement Presentation

The presentation (including structure and content) of financial statements is addressed specifically in several International Accounting Standards (IAS), particularly:

- **IAS 1** prescribes the presentation of general purpose financial statements in order to ensure comparability both with the enterprise's own financial statements of previous periods and with those of other enterprises.

- **IAS 8** (in part) addresses the presentation of items included in net profit or loss for the period. This Standard requires the classification and disclosure of extraordinary items and the disclosure of certain items within profit or loss from ordinary activities.

- **IAS 7** prescribes the structure and presentation of the statement of cash flows which is a required basic financial statement.

Other International Accounting Standards address certain components of general purpose financial statements:

- **IAS 24** requires special disclosures where the enterprise has participated in related party transactions.

- **IAS 14** addresses reporting financial information by segment—information about the different types of products and services an enterprise produces and the different geographical areas in which it operates—to help users of financial statements to understand the enterprise's past performance better, to assess the enterprise's risks and returns better as well as to make more informed judgements about the enterprise as a whole.

- **IAS 35** deals with the recognition and presentation of discontinuing operations.

- **IAS 10** prescribes when an enterprise should adjust its financial statements for events after the balance sheet date and the disclosures that an enterprise should give about the date when the financial statements were authorised for issue.

- **IAS 8** also specifies the accounting treatment for changes in accounting estimates, changes in accounting policies and the correction of fundamental errors.

- **IAS 21** addresses the principal issues in accounting for foreign currency transactions and foreign operations, including deciding which exchange rate to use and how to recognise in the financial statements deciding the financial effect of changes in exchange rates.

- **IAS 33** prescribes principles for the determination and presentation of earnings per share.

The effects of changing prices as well as the financial reporting in hyperinflationary economies are part of **IAS 15** and **IAS 29**.

In addition, specialised financial statements are addressed by:

- **IAS 26** with respect to accounting and reporting by retirement benefit plans.
- **IAS 30** with respect to financial statements of banks and similar financial institutions.
- **IAS 34** prescribes the minimum content of an interim financial report and describes the principles for recognition and measurement in complete or condensed financial statements for an interim period.

2.1   General Considerations Applicable to All Financial Statements

Fair Presentation and Compliance with International Accounting Standards

IAS 1 sets out overall considerations for the presentation of financial statements, guidelines for their structure and minimum requirements for the content of financial statements. IAS 1 should be applied in the presentation of all general purpose financial statements prepared and presented in accordance with IAS. *(1.1)*

General purpose financial statements are those intended to meet the needs of users who are not in a position to demand reports tailored to meet their specific information needs and include those that are presented separately or within another public document such as an annual report or a prospectus. IAS 1 does not apply to condensed interim financial information (see IAS 34), but does apply to the financial statements of an individual enterprise and to consolidated financial statements for a group of enterprises. However, it does not preclude the presentation of consolidated financial statements complying with IAS and financial statements of the parent company under national requirements within the same document, as long as the basis of preparation of each is clearly disclosed in the statement of accounting policies. *(1.2)*

IAS 1 applies to all types of enterprises including banks and insurance enterprises and uses terminology that is suitable for enterprises with a profit objective. Public sector business enterprises may apply the requirements of the Standard. Not-for-profit, government and other public sector enterprises seeking to apply the Standard may need to amend the descriptions used for certain line items in the financial statements and for the financial statements themselves. Such enterprises may also present additional components *(1.3, 1.4)*

The financial statements should present fairly the financial position, financial performance and cash flows of an enterprise. It is presumed that the appropriate application of IAS, with additional disclosure when necessary, results, in virtually all circumstances, in financial statements that are presented fairly. *(1.10)*

An enterprise whose financial statements comply with International Accounting Standards should disclose that fact. Financial statements should not be described as complying with International Accounting Standards unless they comply with all the requirements of each applicable Standard and each applicable Interpretation of the Standing Interpretations Committee. *(1.11)*

Inappropriate accounting treatments are not rectified either by disclosure of the accounting policies used or by notes or explanatory material. *(1.12)*

In the extremely rare circumstances when management concludes that compliance with a requirement in a Standard would be misleading, and therefore that departure from a requirement is necessary to achieve a fair presentation, an enterprise should disclose:

(a)   that management has concluded that the financial statements fairly present the enterprise's financial position, financial performance and cash flows;

(b)   that it has complied in all material respects with applicable International Accounting Standards except that it has departed from a Standard in order to achieve a fair presentation;

(c)   the Standard from which the enterprise has departed, the nature of the departure, including the treatment that the Standard would require, the reason why that treatment would be misleading in the circumstances and the treatment adopted; and

(d)   the financial impact of the departure on the enterprise's net profit or loss, assets, liabilities, equity and cash flows for each period presented. *(1.13)*

When, in accordance with specific provisions in that Standard, an International Accounting Standard is applied before its effective date, that fact should be disclosed. *(1.19)*

Accounting Policies

Management should select and apply an enterprise's accounting policies so that the financial statements comply with all the requirements of each applicable International Accounting Standard and Interpretation of the Standing Interpretations Committee. Where there is no specific requirement, management should develop policies to ensure that the financial statements provide relevant and reliable information. *(1.20)*

Going Concern

When preparing financial statements, management should make an assessment of an enterprise's ability to continue as a going concern. Financial statements should be prepared on a going concern basis unless management either intends to liquidate the enterprise or to cease trading, or has no realistic alternative but to do so (see also IAS 10, paragraph 10.13, p. 144). When management is aware, in making its assessment, of material uncertainties related to events or conditions which may cast significant doubt upon the enterprise's ability to continue as a going concern, those uncertainties should be disclosed. When the financial statements are not prepared on a going concern basis, that fact should be disclosed, together with the basis on which the financial statements are prepared and the reason why the enterprise is not considered to be a going concern. *(1.23)*

Accrual Basis of Accounting

An enterprise should prepare its financial statements, except for cash flow information, under the accrual basis of accounting. *(1.25)*

Consistency of Presentation

The presentation and classification of items in the financial statements should be retained from one period to the next unless:

(a)   a significant change in the nature of the operations of the enterprise or a review of its financial statement presentation demonstrates that the change will result in a more appropriate presentation of events or transactions; or

(b)   a change in presentation is required by an International Accounting Standard or an Interpretation of the Standing Interpretations Committee. *(1.27)*

SIC-18, *Consistency – Alternative Methods*, requires that, where more than one accounting policy is available under a Standard or Interpretation, an enterprise should choose and apply consistently one of those policies. Where a Standard or Interpretation specifically requires or permits categorisation of items for which different policies are appropriate, the most appropriate accounting policy should be selected and applied consistently to each category. *(SIC-18)*

Materiality and Aggregation

Each material item should be presented separately in the financial statements. Immaterial amounts should be aggregated with amounts of a similar nature or function and need not be presented separately. *(1.29)*

In this context, information is material if its non-disclosure could influence the economic decisions of users taken on the basis of the financial statements. Materiality depends on the size and nature of the item judged in the particular circumstances of its omission. In deciding whether an item or an aggregate of items is material, the nature and the size of the item are evaluated together. Depending on the circumstances, either the nature or the size of the item could be the determining factor. For example, individual assets with the same nature and function are aggregated even if the individual amounts are large. However, large items which differ in nature or function are presented separately. *(1.31)*

Offsetting

Assets and liabilities should not be offset except when offsetting is required or permitted by another International Accounting Standard. *(1.33)*

Items of income and expense should be offset when, and only when:

(a)   an International Accounting Standard requires or permits it; or

(b)   gains, losses and related expenses arising from the same or similar transactions and events are not material. Such amounts should be aggregated in accordance with 1.29. *(1.34)*

Comparative Information

Unless a Standard permits or requires otherwise, comparative information should be disclosed in respect of the previous period for all numerical information in the financial statements. Comparative information should be included in narrative and descriptive information when it is relevant to an understanding of the current period's financial statements. *(1.38)*

When the presentation or classification of items in the financial statements is amended, comparative amounts should be reclassified, unless it is impractical to do so, to ensure comparability with the current period, and the nature, amount of, and reason for any reclassification should be disclosed. When it is impractical to reclassify comparative amounts, an enterprise should disclose the reason for not reclassifying and the nature of the changes that would have been made if amounts were reclassified. *(1.40)*

2.2	**Structure and Content**

Identification of Financial Statements

Financial statements should be clearly identified and distinguished from other information in the same published document. *(1.44)*

Each component of the financial statements should be clearly identified. In addition, the following information should be prominently displayed, and repeated when it is necessary for a proper understanding of the information presented:

(a)   the name of the reporting enterprise or other means of identification;

(b)   whether the financial statements cover the individual enterprise or a group of enterprises;

(c)   the balance sheet date or the period covered by the financial statements, whichever is appropriate to the related component of the financial statements;

(d)   the reporting currency; and

(e)   the level of precision used in the presentation of figures in the financial statements. *(1.46)*

Reporting Period

Financial statements should be presented at least annually. When, in exceptional circumstances, an enterprise's balance sheet date changes and annual financial statements are presented for a period longer or shorter than one year, an enterprise should disclose, in addition to the period covered by the financial statements:

(a)   the reason for a period other than one year being used; and

(b)   the fact that comparative amounts for the income statement, changes in equity, cash flows and related notes are not comparable. *(1.49)*

Timeliness

The usefulness of financial statements is impaired if they are not made available to users within a reasonable period after the balance sheet date. An enterprise should be in a position to issue its financial statements within six months of the balance sheet date. Ongoing factors such as the complexity of an enterprise's operations are not sufficient reason for failing to report on a timely basis. More specific deadlines are dealt with by legislation and market regulation in many jurisdictions. *(1.52)*

2.2.1 Balance Sheet

The Current/Non-current Distinction

IAS does not require enterprises to distinguish between current and non-current assets and liabilities when presenting a balance sheet. However, enterprises should determine, based on the nature of its operations, whether or not to present current and non-current assets and current and non-current liabilities as separate classifications on the face of the balance sheet. When an enterprise chooses not to make this classification, assets and liabilities should be presented broadly in order of their liquidity. *(1.53)*

Whichever method of presentation is adopted, an enterprise should disclose, for each asset and liability item that combines amounts expected to be recovered or settled both before and after twelve months from the balance sheet date, the amount expected to be recovered or settled after more than twelve months. *(1.54)*

Current Assets

When an enterprise chooses to make the current/non-current distinction, the following guidance should be followed.

An asset should be classified as a current asset when it:

(a)   is expected to be realised in, or is held for sale or consumption in, the normal course of the enterprise's operating cycle; or

(b)   is held primarily for trading purposes or for the short-term and expected to be realised within twelve months of the balance sheet date; or

(c)   is cash or a cash equivalent asset which is not restricted in its use.

All other assets should be classified as non-current assets. *(1.57)*

The operating cycle of an enterprise is the time between the acquisition of materials entering into a process and its realisation in cash or an instrument that is readily convertible into cash. Current assets include inventories and trade receivables that are sold, consumed and realised as part of the normal operating cycle even when they are not expected to be realised within twelve months of the balance sheet date. Marketable securities are classified as current assets if they are expected to be realised within twelve months of the balance sheet date; otherwise they are classified as non-current assets. The proper classification of such securities is further influenced by their classification under IAS 39. *(1.59)*

Current Liabilities

A liability should be classified as a current liability when it:

(a)   is expected to be settled in the normal course of the enterprise's operating cycle; or

(b)   is due to be settled within twelve months of the balance sheet date.

All other liabilities should be classified as non-current liabilities. *(1.60)*

An enterprise should continue to classify its long-term interest-bearing liabilities as non-current, even when they are due to be settled within twelve months of the balance sheet date if:

(a)   the original term was for a period of more than twelve months;

(b)   the enterprise intends to refinance the obligation on a long-term basis; and

(c)   that intention is supported by an agreement to refinance, or to reschedule payments, which is completed before the financial statements are approved.

The amount of any liability that has been excluded from current liabilities in accordance with this paragraph, together with information in support of this presentation, should be disclosed in the notes to the balance sheet. *(1.63)*

Information to be Presented on the Face of the Balance Sheet

As a minimum, the face of the balance sheet should include line items which present the following amounts:

(a)   property, plant and equipment;

(b)   intangible assets;

(c)   financial assets (excluding amounts shown under (d), (f) and (g));

(d)   investments accounted for using the equity method;

(e)   inventories;

(f)   trade and other receivables;

(g)   cash and cash equivalents;

(h)   trade and other payables;

(i)   tax liabilities and assets;

(j)   provisions;

(k)   non-current interest-bearing liabilities;

(l)   minority interest; and

(m)   issued capital and reserves. *(1.66)*

Additional line items, headings and sub-totals should be presented on the face of the balance sheet when a Standard requires it, or when such presentation is necessary to present fairly the enterprise's financial position. *(1.67)*

IAS 1 does not prescribe the order or format in which items are to be presented. Paragraph 1.66 simply provides a list of items that are so different in nature or function that they deserve separate presentation on the face of the balance sheet. Adjustments to the line items above include the following:

(a)   line items are added when another Standard requires separate presentation on the face of the balance sheet, or when the size, nature or function of an item is such that separate presentation would assist in presenting fairly the enterprise's financial position; and

(b)   the descriptions used and the ordering of items may be amended according to the nature of the enterprise and its transactions, to provide information that is necessary for an overall understanding of the enterprise's financial position. *(1.68)*

Information to be Presented Either on the Face of the Balance Sheet or in the Notes

An enterprise should disclose, either on the face of the balance sheet or in the notes to the balance sheet, further sub-classifications of the line items presented, classified in a manner appropriate to the enterprise's operations. Each item should be sub-classified, when appropriate, by its nature and, amounts payable to and receivable from the parent enterprise, fellow subsidiaries and associates and other related parties should be disclosed separately. *(1.72)*

An enterprise should disclose the following, either on the face of the balance sheet or in the notes:

(a)   for each class of share capital:

   (i)   the number of shares authorised;

   (ii)   the number of shares issued and fully paid, and issued but not fully paid;

   (iii)   par value per share, or that the shares have no par value;

Balance Sheet – Example of IAS Presentation

(DM million)	Dec. 31, 1998	Dec. 31, 1997
Assets		
Non-current assets		
Intangible assets	3,733	2,056
Property, plant and equipment	21,177	20,158
Investments	2,156	1,706
	27,066	23,920
Current assets		
Inventories	11,306	10,608
Receivables and other assets		
Trade accounts receivable	10,899	10,686
Other receivables and other assets	3,249	2,816
	14,148	13,502
Liquid assets	3,366	4,802
	28,820	28,912
Deferred taxes	754	872
Deferred charges	576	466
	57,216	54,170
Stockholders' Equity and Liabilities		
Stockholders' equity		
Capital stock of Bayer AG	3,652	3,652
Capital reserves of Bayer AG	5,760	5,760
Retained earnings	13,923	12,276
Net income	3,157	2,941
Translation differences	(1,914)	(1,143)
Minority stockholders' interest	413	437
	24,991	23,923
Provisions		
Provisions for pensions and other post-employment benefits	9,225	9,144
Other provisions	4,996	5,085
	14,221	14,229
Other liabilities		
Financial obligations	9,012	7,620
Trade accounts payable	3,155	3,134
Miscellaneous liabilities	3,962	3,726
	16,129	14,480
Deferred taxes	1,534	1,208
Deferred income	341	330
	57,216	54,170

Figure 1   **Bayer AG: Extract from the Financial Statement 1998**

(iv) a reconciliation of the number of shares outstanding at the beginning and at the end of the year;

(v)   the rights, preferences and restrictions attaching to that class including restrictions on the distribution of dividends and the repayment of capital;

(vi) shares in the enterprise held by the enterprise itself or by subsidiaries or associates of the enterprise; and

(vii) shares reserved for issuance under options and sales contracts, including the terms and amounts;

(b) a description of the nature and purpose of each reserve within owners' equity;

(c) when dividends have been proposed but not formally approved for payment, the amount included (or not included) in liabilities; and

(d) the amount of any cumulative preference dividends not recognised.

An enterprise without share capital, such as a partnership, should disclose information equivalent to that required above, showing movements during the period in each category of equity interest and the rights, preferences and restrictions attaching to each category of equity interest. *(1.74)*

2.2.2	**Income Statement**

Information to be Presented on the Face of the Income Statement

As a minimum, the face of the income statement should include line items which present the following amounts:

(a) revenue;

(b) the results of operating activities;

(c) finance costs;

(d) share of profits and losses of associates and joint ventures accounted for using the equity method;

(e) tax expense;

(f) profit or loss from ordinary activities;

(g) extraordinary items;

(h) minority interest; and

(i) net profit or loss for the period.

Additional line items, headings and sub-totals should be presented on the face of the income statement when required by an International Accounting Standard, or when such presentation is necessary to present fairly the enterprise's financial performance. *(1.75)*

Information to be Presented Either on the Face of the Income Statement or in the Notes

An enterprise should present, either on the face of the income statement or in the notes to the income statement, an analysis of expenses using a classification based on either the nature of expenses or their function within the enterprise. *(1.77)*

The method of analysis of expenses most simple to apply is 'by nature'. Expenses are aggregated in the income statement according to their nature (e.g. wages and benefits, advertising, transport cost, depreciation and amortisation, etc.) without any allocation to functions within the enterprise *(1.80)*

Expenses are analysed 'by function' when they are allocated to the various functions within the enterprise (e.g. distribution, administration, cost of sales, development, etc.). This presentation may provide users with more relevant information, but can also involve arbitrary allocation of expenses and the exercise of judgement. *(1.82)*

Enterprises classifying expenses by function should disclose additional information on the nature of expenses, including depreciation and amortisation expense and staff costs. *(1.83)*

An enterprise should disclose, either on the face of the income statement or in the notes, the amount of dividends per share, declared or proposed, for the period covered by the financial statements. *(1.85)*

Net Profit or Loss for the Period

IAS require that all items of income and expense recognised in a period should be included in the determination of the net profit or loss for the period unless a Standard requires or permits otherwise. *(8.7)*

The net profit or loss for the period comprises the following components, each of which should be disclosed on the face of the income statement:

- profit or loss from ordinary activities, including the effects of changes in accounting estimates; and
- extraordinary items. *(8.10)*

Profit or Loss from Ordinary Activities

Ordinary activities are any activities which are undertaken by an enterprise as part of its business and such related activities in which the enterprise engages in furtherance of, incidental to, or arising from these activities. *(8.6)*

When items of income and expense within profit or loss from ordinary activities are of such size, nature or incidence that their disclosure is relevant to explain the performance of the enterprise for the period, the nature and amount of such items should be disclosed separately. *(8.16)*

Income Statement – Example of Presentation*

(DM million)	1998	1997
Net sales	54,884	55,005
Cost of goods sold	(30,269)	(30,999)
Gross profit	24,615	24,006
Selling expenses	(12,404)	(11,989)
Research and development expenses	(3,920)	(3,878)
General administration expenses	(1,910)	(1,737)
Other operating income	1,585	1,351
Other operating expenses	(1,815)	(1,737)
Operating result	6,151	6,018
Income from investments in affiliated companies – net	41	39
Interest expense – net	(350)	(308)
Other non-operating expense – net	(506)	(641)
Non-operating result	(815)	(910)
Income before income taxes	5,336	5,108
Income taxes	(2,177)	(2,156)
Income after taxes	3,159	2,952
Minority stockholders' interest	(2)	(11)
Net income	3,157	2,941
Earnings per share	DM 4,32	DM 4,05

Figure 2   **Bayer AG: Extract from the Financial Statements 1998**

* *Expenses classified by function*

Changes in Accounting Estimates

As a result of the uncertainties inherent in business activities, many financial statement items cannot be measured with precision but can only be estimated. The estimation process involves judgements based on the latest information available. *(8.23)*

When management changes its estimates of an amount included in the financial statements, the effect of a change in an accounting estimate should be included in the determination of net profit or loss in:

- the period of the change, if the change affects the period only; or

- the period of the change and future periods, if the change affects both. *(8.26)*

The effect of a change in an accounting estimate should be included in the same income statement classification as was used previously for the estimate. *(8.28)*

The nature and amount of a change in an accounting estimate that has a material effect in the current period or which is expected to have a material effect in subsequent periods should be disclosed. If it is impractical to quantify the amount, this fact should be disclosed. *(8.30)*

Extraordinary Items

Extraordinary items are income or expenses that arise from events or transactions that are clearly distinct from the ordinary activities of the enterprise and therefore are not expected to recur frequently or regularly.

The nature and the amount of each extraordinary item should be disclosed separately. *(8.11)*

2.2.3   Changes in Equity

IAS requires, as a primary financial statement, a statement of changes in equity. An enterprise should present a statement showing:

(a)   the net profit or loss for the period;

(b)   each item of income and expense, gain or loss which, as required by other Standards, is recognised directly in equity, and the total of these items; and

(c)   the cumulative effect of changes in accounting policy and the correction of fundamental errors dealt with under the benchmark treatments in IAS 8.

In addition, an enterprise should present, either within this statement or in the notes:

(d)   capital transactions with owners and distributions to owners;

(e)   the balance of accumulated profit or loss at the beginning of the period and at the balance sheet date, and the movements for the period; and

(f)   a reconciliation between the carrying amount of each class of equity capital, share premium and each reserve at the beginning and the end of the period, separately disclosing each movement. *(1.86)*

Statement of Equity Changes – Example of Presentation

DM (million)	Capital stock of Bayer AG	Capital reserves of Bayer AG	Retained earnings	Net income	Bayer stockholders' interest	Minority stockholders interest	Translation differences	Total
31/12/96	3,621	5,589	10,571	2,725	22,506	457	(1,907)	21,056
Changes in stockholders' equity resulting from capital contributions and dividend payments								
Capital contributions	31	171			202			202
Dividend payments				(1,231)	(1,231)	(9)		(1,240)
	31	**171**		**(1,231)**	**(1,029)**	**(9)**		**(1,038)**
Other changes in stockholders' equity not recognised in income								
Exchange differences							932	932
Other differences			211		211	(22)	(168)	21
			211		**211**	**(22)**	**764**	**953**
Changes in stockholders' equity recognised in income								
Allocation to retained earnings			1,494	(1,494)	0			0
Income after taxes for 1997				2,941	2,941	11		2,952
			1,494	**1,447**	**2,941**	**11**		**2,952**
31/12/1997	3,652	5,760	12,276	2,941	24,629	437	(1,143)	23,923
Changes in stockholders' equity resulting from capital contributions and dividend payments								
Capital contributions								
Dividend payments				(1,388)	(1,388)	(5)		(1,393)
				(1,388)	**(1,388)**	**(5)**		**(1,393)**
Other changes in stockholders' equity not recognised in income								
Exchange differences							(771)	(771)
Other differences			94		94	(21)		73
			94		**94**	**(21)**	**(771)**	**(698)**
Changes in stockholders' equity not recognised in income								
Allocation to retained earnings			1,553	(1,553)	0			0
Income after taxes for 1998				3,157	3,157	2		3,159
			1,553	**1,604**	**3,157**	**2**		**3,159**
31/12/1998	**3,652**	**5,760**	**13,923**	**3,157**	**26,492**	**413**	**(1,914)**	**24,991**

Figure 3   Bayer AG: Extract from the Financial Statements 1998

The requirements in paragraph 1.86 may be met in a number of ways. The approach adopted in many jurisdictions follows a columnar format which reconciles between the opening and closing balances of each element within shareholders' equity, including items (a) to (f). An alternative is to present a separate component of the financial statements which presents only items (a) to (c). Under this approach, the items described in (d) to (f) are shown in the notes to the financial statements. Whichever approach is adopted, paragraph 1.86 requires a sub-total of the items in (b) to enable users to derive the total gains and losses arising from the enterprise's activities during the period. *(1.89)*

2.2.4	**Cash Flow Statements**

All enterprises are required to prepare a cash flow statement in accordance with the requirements of IAS 7 and should present it as an integral part of its financial statements for each period for which financial statements are presented *(7.1)*. IAS incorporates the requirements of IAS 7 by reference. *(1.90)*

The cash flow statement, when used in conjunction with the rest of the financial statements, provides information that enables users to evaluate the changes in net assets of an enterprise, its financial structure (including its liquidity and solvency) and its ability to affect the amounts and timing of cash flows in order to adapt to changing circumstances and opportunities. Cash flow information is useful in assessing the ability of the enterprise to generate cash and cash equivalents and enables users to develop models to assess and compare the present value of the future cash flows of different enterprises. It also enhances the comparability of the reporting of operating performance by different enterprises because it eliminates the effects of using different accounting treatments for the same transactions and events. *(7.4)*

Historical cash flow information is often used as an indicator of the amount, timing and certainty of future cash flows. It is also useful in checking the accuracy of past assessments of future cash flows and in examining the relationship between profitability and net cash flow and the impact of changing prices. *(7.5)*

The following terms are used in IAS 7:

- *Cash* comprises cash on hand and demand deposits.
- *Cash equivalents* are short-term, highly liquid investments that are readily convertible to known amounts of cash and which are subject to an insignificant risk of changes in value.
- *Cash flows* are inflows and outflows of cash and cash equivalents.
- *Operating activities* are the principal revenue-producing activities of the enterprise and other activities that are not investing or financing activities.
- *Investing activities* are the acquisition and disposal of long-term assets and other investments not included in cash equivalents.

- *Financing activities* are activities that result in changes in the size and composition of the equity capital and borrowings of the enterprise. *(7.6)*

Cash equivalents are held for the purpose of meeting short-term cash commitments rather than for investment or other purposes. For an investment to qualify as a cash equivalent it must be readily convertible to a known amount of cash and be subject to an insignificant risk of changes in value. Therefore, an investment normally qualifies as a cash equivalent only when it has a short maturity of, say, three months or less from the date of acquisition. Equity investments are excluded from cash equivalents unless they are, in substance, cash equivalents, for example, in the case of preferred shares acquired within a short period of their maturity and with a specified redemption date. *(7.7)*

Bank borrowings are generally considered to be financing activities. However, in some countries, bank overdrafts which are repayable on demand form an integral part of an enterprise's cash management. In these circumstances, bank overdrafts are included as a component of cash and cash equivalents. A characteristic of such banking arrangements is that the bank balance often fluctuates from being positive to overdrawn. *(7.8)*

Cash flows exclude movements between items that constitute cash or cash equivalents because these components are part of the cash management of an enterprise rather than part of its operating, investing and financing activities. Cash management includes the investment of excess cash in cash equivalents. *(7.9)*

Presentation of a Cash Flow Statement

The cash flow statement should report cash flows during the period classified by operating, investing and financing activities. *(7.10)*

Operating Activities

Cash flows from operating activities are primarily derived from the principal revenue-producing activities of the enterprise. Therefore, they generally result from the transactions and other events that enter into the determination of net profit or loss.

Some transactions, such as the sale of an item of plant, may give rise to a gain or loss which is included in the determination of net profit or loss. However, the cash flows relating to such transactions are cash flows from investing activities. *(7.14)*

An enterprise may hold securities and loans for dealing or trading purposes, in which case they are similar to inventory acquired specifically for resale. Therefore, cash flows arising from the purchase and sale of dealing or trading securities are classified as operating activities. Similarly, cash advances and loans made by financial institutions are usually classified as operating activities since they relate to the main revenue-producing activity of that enterprise. *(7.15)*

Investing Activities

The separate disclosure of cash flows arising from investing activities is important because the cash flows represent the extent to which expenditures have been made for resources intended to generate future income and cash flows. Examples of cash flows arising from investing activities are:

(a)   cash flows (payments and receipts) from the acquisition and disposition of payments, property, plant and equipment, intangibles and other long-term assets. These payments include those relating to capitalised development costs and self-constructed property, plant and equipment;

(b)   cash payments to acquire equity or debt instruments of other enterprises and interests in joint ventures (other than payments for those instruments considered to be cash equivalents or those held for dealing or trading purposes); and

(c)   cash receipts from sales of equity or debt instruments of other enterprises and interests in joint ventures (other than receipts for those instruments considered to be cash equivalents and those held for dealing or trading purposes).

When a contract is accounted for as a hedge of an identifiable position, the cash flows of the contract are classified in the same manner as the cash flows of the position being hedged. *(7.16)*

Financing Activities

The separate disclosure of cash flows arising from financing activities is important because it is useful in predicting claims on future cash flows by providers of capital to the enterprise. Examples of cash flows arising from financing activities are:

(a)   cash proceeds from issuing shares or other equity instruments;

(b)   cash payments to owners to acquire or redeem the enterprise's shares;

(c)   cash proceeds from issuing debentures, loans, notes, bonds, mortgages and other short or long-term borrowings;

(d)   cash repayments of amounts borrowed; and

(e)   cash payments by a lessee for the reduction of the outstanding liability relating to a finance lease. *(7.17)*

Reporting Cash Flows from Operating Activities

An enterprise should report cash flows from operating activities using either:

(a)   the direct method, whereby major classes of gross cash receipts and gross cash payments are disclosed; or

(b)   the indirect method, whereby net profit or loss is adjusted for the effects of transactions of a non-cash nature, any deferrals or accruals of past or future operating cash receipts or payments, and items of income or expense associated with investing or financing cash flows. *(7.18)*

Enterprises are encouraged but not required to report cash flows from operating activities using the direct method. *(7.19)*

Reporting Cash Flows from Investing and Financing Activities

An enterprise should report separately major classes of gross cash receipts and gross cash payments arising from investing and financing activities, except to the extent that cash flows described in paragraphs 7.22 and 7.24 are reported on a net basis. *(7.21)*

Reporting Cash Flows on a Net Basis

Cash flows arising from the following operating, investing or financing activities may be reported on a net basis:

(a)   cash receipts and payments on behalf of customers when the cash flows reflect the activities of the customer rather than those of the enterprise; and

(b)   cash receipts and payments for items in which the turnover is quick, the amounts are large, and the maturities are short. *(7.22)*

Cash flows arising from each of the following activities of a financial institution may be reported on a net basis:

(a)   cash receipts and payments for the acceptance and repayment of deposits with a fixed maturity date;

(b)   the placement of deposits with and withdrawal of deposits from other financial institutions; and

(c)   cash advances and loans made to customers and the repayment of those advances and loans. *(7.24)*

Foreign Currency Cash Flows

Cash flows arising from transactions in a foreign currency should be recorded in an enterprise's reporting currency by applying to the foreign currency amount the exchange rate between the reporting currency and the foreign currency at the date of the cash flow. *(7.25)*

The cash flows of a foreign subsidiary should be translated at the exchange rates between the reporting currency and the foreign currency at the dates of the cash flows. *(7.26)*

Extraordinary Items

The cash flows associated with extraordinary items should be classified as arising from operating, investing or financing activities as appropriate and disclosed separately. *(7.29)*

Interest and Dividends

Cash flows from interest and dividends received and paid should each be disclosed separately. Each should be classified in a consistent manner from period to period as either operating, investing or financing activities. *(7.31)*

Interest paid and interest and dividends received are usually classified as operating cash flows for a financial institution. However, there is no consensus on the classification of these cash flows for other enterprises. Interest paid and interest and dividends received may be classified as operating cash flows because they enter into the determination of net profit or loss. Alternatively, interest paid and interest and dividends received may be classified as financing cash flows and investing cash flows respectively, because they are costs of obtaining financial resources or returns on investments. *(7.33)*

Dividends paid may be classified as a financing cash flow because they are a cost of obtaining financial resources. Alternatively, dividends paid may be classified as a component of cash flows from operating activities in order to assist users to determine the ability of an enterprise to pay dividends out of operating cash flows. *(7.34)*

Taxes on Income

Cash flows arising from taxes on income should be disclosed separately and should be classified as cash flows from operating activities unless they can be specifically identified with financing and investing activities. *(7.35)*

Investments in Subsidiaries, Associates and Joint Ventures

When accounting for an investment in an associate or a subsidiary accounted for by use of the equity or cost method, an investor restricts its reporting in the cash flow statement to the cash flows between itself and the investee, for example, to dividends and advances. *(7.37)*

An enterprise which reports its interest in a jointly-controlled entity (see IAS 31, *Financial Reporting of Interests in Joint Ventures*, under section 7.4, p. 411) using proportionate consolidation, includes in its consolidated cash flow statement its proportionate share of the jointly-controlled entity's cash flows. An enterprise which reports such an interest using the equity method includes in its cash flow statement the cash flows in respect of its investments in the jointly-controlled entity, and distributions and other payments or receipts between it and the jointly-controlled entity. *(7.38)*

Acquisitions and Disposals of Subsidiaries and Other Business Units

The aggregate cash flows arising from acquisitions and from disposals of subsidiaries or other business units should be presented separately and classified as investing activities. *(7.39)*

An enterprise should disclose, in aggregate, in respect of both acquisitions and disposals of subsidiaries or other business units during the period each of the following:

(a)   the total purchase or disposal consideration;

(b)   the portion of the purchase or disposal consideration discharged by means of cash and cash equivalents;

(c)   the amount of cash and cash equivalents in the subsidiary or business unit acquired or disposed of; and

(d)   the amount of the assets and liabilities other than cash or cash equivalents in the subsidiary or business unit acquired or disposed of, summarised by each major category. (7.40)

Non-cash Transactions

Investing and financing transactions that do not require the use of cash or cash equivalents should be excluded from a cash flow statement. Such transactions should be disclosed elsewhere in the financial statements in a way that provides all the relevant information about these investing and financing activities. (7.43)

Components of Cash and Cash Equivalents

An enterprise should disclose the components of cash and cash equivalents and should present a reconciliation of the amounts in its cash flow statement with the equivalent items reported in the balance sheet. (7.45)

Other Disclosures

An enterprise should disclose, together with a commentary by management, the amount of significant cash and cash equivalent balances held by the enterprise that are not available for use by the group. (7.48)

The disclosure of segmental cash flows enables users to obtain a better understanding of the relationship between the cash flows of the business as a whole and those of its component parts and the availability and variability of segmental cash flows. (7.52)

Cash Flow Statement – Example of Presentation*

DM (million)	1998	1997
Cash and cash equivalent at beginning of year	3,414	3,015
Operating result	6,151	6,018
Income taxes currently payable	(1,687)	(1,941)
Depreciation and amortisation	3,001	3,050
Change in long-term provisions	(655)	(622)
Gains (losses) on retirements of non-current assets	(208)	(25)
Gross cash provided by operating activities	6,602	6,480
Increase in inventories	(735)	(43)
Increase in trade accounts receivable	(265)	(623)
Increase in trade accounts payable	99	419
Changes in other working capital	(185)	474
Net cash provided by operating activities	5,516	6,707
Cash outflows for additions to property, plans and equipment	(5,232)	(4,615)
Cash outflows from sales of property, plans and equipment	993	276
Cash outflows for additions to investments	(33)	(337)
Cash outflows for acquisitions	(2,825)	(748)
Interest and dividends received	484	445
Cash inflows from marketable securities	386	332
Net cash used in investing activities	(6,227)	(4,647)
Capital contributions	0	226
Bayer AG dividend and dividend payments to minority stockholders	(1,393)	(1,240)
Issuances of debts	3,319	2,398
Retirements of debt	(1,608)	(2,488)
Interest paid	(674)	(669)
Net cash used in financing activities	(356)	(1,773)
Change in cash and cash equivalents due to business activities	(1,067)	287
Change in cash and cash equivalents due to changes in companies consolidated	(36)	67
Change in cash and cash equivalents due to exchange rate movements	4	45
Cash and cash equivalent at end of year	2,315	3,414
Marketable securities and other instruments	1,051	1,388
Liquid assets as per balance sheets	3,366	4,802

Figure 4   **Bayer AG: Extract from the Financial Statement 1998**

Prepared using the 'indirect' method of reporting cash flows from operating activities.

2.2.5 | Notes to the Financial Statements

Notes to the financial statements include narrative descriptions or more detailed analyses of amounts shown on the face of the balance sheet, income statement, cash flow statement and statement of changes in equity, as well as additional information such as contingent liabilities and commitments. They include information required and encouraged to be disclosed by International Accounting Standards, and other disclosures necessary to achieve a fair presentation. *(1.93)*

Structure

The notes to the financial statements of an enterprise should:

(a) present information about the basis of preparation of the financial statements and the specific accounting policies selected and applied for significant transactions and events;

(b) disclose the information required by International Accounting Standards that is not presented elsewhere in the financial statements; and

(c) provide additional information which is not presented on the face of the financial statements but that is necessary for a fair presentation. *(1.91)*

Notes to the financial statements should be presented in a systematic manner. Each item on the face of the balance sheet, income statement and cash flow statement should be cross-referenced to any related information in the notes. Notes are normally presented in the following order which assists users in understanding the financial statements and comparing them with those of other enterprises:

(a) statement of compliance with International Accounting Standards;

(b) statement of the measurement basis (bases) and accounting policies applied;

(c) supporting information for items presented on the face of each financial statement in the order in which each line item and each financial statement is presented; and

(d) other disclosures, including:

(i) contingencies, commitments and other financial disclosures; and

(ii) non-financial disclosures. *(1.92, 1.94)*

Accounting Policies

The accounting policies section of the notes to the financial statements should describe the following:

(a) the measurement basis (or bases) used in preparing the financial statements; and

(b)   each specific accounting policy that is necessary for a proper understanding of the financial statements. *(1.97)*

Other Disclosures

An enterprise should disclose the following if not disclosed elsewhere in information published with the financial statements:

(a)   the domicile and legal form of the enterprise, its country of incorporation and the address of the registered office (or principal place of business, if different from the registered office);

(b)   a description of the nature of the enterprise's operations and its principal activities;

(c)   the name of the parent enterprise and the ultimate parent enterprise of the group; and

(d)   either the number of employees at the end of the period or the average for the period. *(1.102)*

2.3   Segment Disclosures

Many enterprises provide groups of products and services or operate in geographical areas that are subject to differing rates of profitability, opportunities for growth, future prospects, and risks. Information about an enterprise's different types of products and services and its operations in different geographical areas – often called segment information – is relevant to assessing the risks and returns of a diversified or multinational enterprise but may not be determinable from the aggregated data. Therefore, segment information is widely regarded as necessary to meeting the needs of users of financial statements.

IAS 14 addresses segment disclosures which should be applied in complete sets of published financial statements that comply with International Accounting Standards. *(14.1)*

IAS 14 should be applied by enterprises whose equity or debt securities are publicly traded and by enterprises that are in the process of issuing equity or debt securities in public securities markets. If an enterprise whose securities are not publicly traded chooses to disclose segment information voluntarily in financial statements that comply with International Accounting Standards, that enterprise should comply fully with the requirements of this Standard. *(14.3, 14.5)*

If a single financial report contains both consolidated financial statements of an enterprise whose securities are publicly traded and the separate financial statements of the parent or one or more subsidiaries, segment information need be presented only on the basis of the consolidated financial statements. If a subsidiary is itself an enterprise whose securities are publicly traded, it will present segment information in its own separate financial report. *(14.6)*

Similarly, if a single financial report contains both the financial statements of an enterprise whose securities are publicly traded and the separate financial statements of an equity method associate or joint venture in which the enterprise has a financial interest, segment information need be presented only on the basis of the enterprise's financial statements. If the equity method associate or joint venture is itself an enterprise whose securities are publicly traded, it will present segment information in its own separate financial report. *(14.7)*

IAS 14 defines segments as follows:

- A *business segment* is a distinguishable component of an enterprise that is engaged in providing an individual product or service or a group of related products or services and that is subject to risks and returns that are different from those of other business segments.

- A *geographical segment* is a distinguishable component of an enterprise that is engaged in providing products or services within a particular economic environment and that is subject to risks and returns that are different from those of components operating in other economic environments.

- A *reportable segment* is a business segment or a geographical segment identified based on the foregoing definitions for which segment information is required to be disclosed by IAS 14. *(14.9)*

IAS 14 also uses the following additional terms:

- *Segment revenue* is revenue reported in the enterprise's income statement that is directly attributable to a segment and the relevant portion of enterprise revenue that can be allocated on a reasonable basis to a segment, whether from sales to external customers or from transactions with other segments of the same enterprise. Segment revenue does not include:

    (a)   extraordinary items;

    (b)   interest or dividend income, including interest earned on advances or loans to other segments, unless the segment's operations are primarily of a financial nature; or

    (c)   gains on sales of investments or gains on extinguishment of debt unless the segment's operations are primarily of a financial nature.

Segment revenue includes an enterprise's share of profits or losses of associates, joint ventures, or other investments accounted for under the equity method only if those items are included in consolidated or total enterprise revenue.

Segment revenue includes a joint venturer's share of the revenue of a jointly-controlled entity that is accounted for by proportionate consolidation in accordance with IAS 31, *Financial Reporting of Interests in Joint Ventures* which is described in section 7.4, p. 411.

- *Segment expense* is expense resulting from the operating activities of a segment that is directly attributable to the segment and the relevant portion of an expense that can be allocated on a reasonable basis to the segment, including expenses relating to sales to external customers and expenses relating to transactions with other segments of the same enterprise. Segment expense does not include:

(a)   extraordinary items;

(b)   interest, including interest incurred on advances or loans from other segments, unless the segment's operations are primarily of a financial nature;

(c)   losses on sales of investments or losses on extinguishment of debt unless the segment's operations are primarily of a financial nature;

(d)   an enterprise's share of losses of associates, joint ventures, or other investments accounted for under the equity method;

(e)   income tax expense; or

(f)   general administrative expenses, head-office expenses, and other expenses that arise at the enterprise level and relate to the enterprise as a whole. However, costs are sometimes incurred at the enterprise level on behalf of a segment. Such costs are segment expenses if they relate to the segment's operating activities and they can be directly attributed or allocated to the segment on a reasonable basis.

Segment expense includes a joint venturer's share of the expenses of a jointly-controlled entity that is accounted for by proportionate consolidation in accordance with IAS 31. For a segment's operations that are primarily of a financial nature, interest income and interest expense may be reported as a single net amount for segment reporting purposes only if those items are netted in the consolidated or enterprise financial statements.

• *Segment result* is segment revenue less segment expense. Segment result is determined before any adjustments for minority interest.

• *Segment assets* are those operating assets that are employed by a segment in its operating activities and that either are directly attributable to the segment or can be allocated to the segment on a reasonable basis.

If a segment's segment result includes interest or dividend income, its segment assets include the related receivables, loans, investments, or other income-producing assets.

Segment assets do not include income tax assets.

Segment assets include investments accounted for under the equity method only if the profit or loss from such investments is included in segment revenue. Segment assets include a joint venturer's share of the operating assets of a jointly-controlled entity that is accounted for by proportionate consolidation in accordance with IAS 31.

Segment assets are determined after deducting related allowances that are reported as direct offsets in the enterprise's balance sheet.

- *Segment liabilities* are those operating liabilities that result from the operating activities of a segment and that either are directly attributable to the segment or can be allocated to the segment on a reasonable basis.

  If a segment's segment result includes interest expense, its segment liabilities include the related interest-bearing liabilities.

  Segment liabilities include a joint venturer's share of the liabilities of a jointly-controlled entity that is accounted for by proportionate consolidation in accordance with IAS 31.

  Segment liabilities do not include income tax liabilities.

- *Segment accounting policies* are the accounting policies adopted for preparing and presenting the financial statements of the consolidated group or enterprise as well as those accounting policies that relate specifically to segment reporting. *(14.16)*

Identifying Reportable Segments

Primary and Secondary Segment Reporting Formats

The dominant source and nature of an enterprise's risks and returns should govern whether its primary segment reporting format will be business segments or geographical segments. If the enterprise's risks and rates of return are affected predominantly by differences in the products and services it produces, its primary format for reporting segment information should be business segments, with secondary information reported geographically. Similarly, if the enterprise's risks and rates of return are affected predominantly by the fact that it operates in different countries or other geographical areas, its primary format for reporting segment information should be geographical segments, with secondary information reported for groups of related products and services. *(14.26)*

An enterprise's internal organisational and management structure and its system of internal financial reporting to the board of directors and the chief executive officer should normally be the basis for identifying the predominant source and nature of risks and differing rates of return facing the enterprise and, therefore, for determining which reporting format is primary and which is secondary, except as provided in (a) and (b) below:

(a) if an enterprise's risks and rates of return are strongly affected both by differences in the products and services it produces and by differences in the geographical areas in which it operates, as evidenced by a "matrix approach" to managing the company and to reporting internally to the board of directors and the chief executive officer, then the enterprise should use business segments as its primary segment reporting format and geographical segments as its secondary reporting format; and

(b) if an enterprise's internal organisational and management structure and its system of internal financial reporting to the board of directors and the chief executive officer are based neither on individual products or services or on groups of related products/services nor on geography, the directors and management of the enterprise should determine whether the enterprise's risks and returns are related more to the products and services it produces or more to the geographical areas in which it operates and, as a consequence, should choose either business segments or geographical segments as the enterprise's primary segment reporting format, with the other as its secondary reporting format. *(14.27)*

Business and Geographical Segments

An enterprise's business and geographical segments for external reporting purposes should be those organisational units for which information is reported to the board of directors and to the chief executive officer for the purpose of evaluating the unit's past performance and for making decisions about future allocations of resources, except as provided in paragraph 14.32. *(14.31)*

If an enterprise's internal organisational and management structure and its system of internal financial reporting to the board of directors and the chief executive officer are based neither on individual products or services or on groups of related products/services nor on geography, the directors and management of the enterprise should choose either business segments or geographical segments as the enterprise's primary segment reporting format based on their assessment of which reflects the primary source of the enterprise's risks and returns, with the other its secondary reporting format. In that case, the directors and management of the enterprise must determine its business segments and geographical segments for external reporting purposes based on the factors in the definitions in the Standard, rather than on the basis of its system of internal financial reporting to the board of directors and chief executive officer, consistent with the following:

(a)   if one or more of the segments reported internally to the directors and management is a business segment or a geographical segment based on the factors in the definitions in the Standard but others are not, subparagraph (b) below should be applied only to those internal segments that do not meet those definitions (that is, an internally reported segment that meets the definition should not be further segmented);

(b)   for those segments reported internally to the directors and management that do not satisfy the definitions in the Standard, management of the enterprise should look to the next lower level of internal segmentation that reports information along product and service lines or geographical lines, as appropriate; and

(c)   if such an internally reported lower-level segment meets the definition of business segment or geographical segment based on the factors in the Standard, the criteria in paragraphs discussed below for identifying reportable segments should be applied to that segment. *(14.32)*

Reportable Segments

Two or more internally reported business segments or geographical segments that are substantially similar may be combined as a single business segment or geographical segment. Two or more business segments or geographical segments are substantially similar only if:

(a)   they exhibit similar long-term financial performance; and

(b)   they are similar in all of the factors in the appropriate principal definition. *(14.34)*

A business segment or geographical segment should be identified as a reportable segment if a majority of its revenue is earned from sales to external customers and:

(a)   its revenue from sales to external customers and from transactions with other segments is 10 per cent or more of the total revenue, external and internal, of all segments; or

(b)   its segment result, whether profit or loss, is 10 per cent or more of the combined result of all segments in profit or the combined result of all segments in loss, whichever is the greater in absolute amount; or

(c)   its assets are 10 per cent or more of the total assets of all segments. *(14.35)*

If an internally reported segment is below all of these thresholds of significance:

(a)   that segment may be designated as a reportable segment despite its size;

(b)   if not designated as a reportable segment despite its size, that segment may be combined into a separately reportable segment with one or more other similar internally reported segment(s) that are also below all of the thresholds of significance (two or more business segments or geographical segments are similar if they share a majority of the factors in the appropriate principal definition); and

(c)   if that segment is not separately reported or combined, it should be included as an unallocated reconciling item. *(14.36)*

If total external revenue attributable to reportable segments constitutes less than 75 per cent of the total consolidated or enterprise revenue, additional segments should be identified as reportable segments, even if they do not meet the 10 per cent thresholds described above, until at least 75 per cent of total consolidated or enterprise revenue is included in reportable segments. *(14.37)*

If an enterprise's internal reporting system treats vertically integrated activities as separate segments and the enterprise does not choose to report them externally as business segments, the selling segment should be combined into the buying segment(s) in identifying externally reportable business segments unless there is no reasonable basis for doing so, in which case the selling segment would be included as an unallocated reconciling item. *(14.41)*

A segment identified as a reportable segment in the immediately preceding period because it satisfied the relevant 10 per cent thresholds should continue to be a reportable segment for the current period notwithstanding that its revenue, result, and assets all no longer exceed the 10 per cent thresholds, if the management of the enterprise judges the segment to be of continuing significance. *(14.42)*

If a segment is identified as a reportable segment in the current period because it satisfies the relevant 10 per cent thresholds, prior period segment data that is presented for comparative purposes should be restated to reflect the newly reportable segment as a separate segment, even if that segment did not satisfy the 10 per cent thresholds in the prior period, unless it is impractical to do so. *(14.43)*

Segment Accounting Policies

Segment information should be prepared in conformity with the accounting policies adopted for preparing and presenting the financial statements of the consolidated group or enterprise. *(14.44)*

Assets that are jointly used by two or more segments should be allocated to segments if, and only if, their related revenues and expenses also are allocated to those segments. *(14.47)*

The way in which asset, liability, revenue, and expense items are allocated to segments depends on such factors as the nature of those items, the activities conducted by the segment, and the relative autonomy of that segment. It is not possible or appropriate to specify a single basis of allocation that should be adopted by all enterprises. Nor is it appropriate to force allocation of enterprise asset, liability, revenue, and expense items that relate jointly to two or more segments, if the only basis for making those allocations is arbitrary or difficult to understand. At the same time, the definitions of segment revenue, segment expense, segment assets, and segment liabilities are interrelated, and the resulting allocations should be consistent. Therefore, jointly-used assets are allocated to segments if, and only if, their related revenues and expenses also are allocated to those segments. For example, an asset is included in segment assets if, and only if, the related depreciation or amortisation is deducted in measuring segment result. *(14.48)*

Disclosure

Primary Reporting Format

The following disclosure requirements are applicable to each reportable segment based on an enterprise's primary reporting format. *(14.50)*

An enterprise should disclose, for each reportable segment:

(a)   segment revenue from sales to external customers and segment revenue from transactions with other segments should be reported separately; *(14.51)*

(b)   segment result; *(14.52)*

(c)   the total carrying amount of segment assets; *(14.55)*

(d)   segment liabilities; *(14.56)*

(e)   the total cost incurred during the period to acquire segment assets that are expected to be used during more than one period (property, plant, equipment, and intangible assets). While this sometimes is referred to as capital additions or capital expenditure, the measurement required by this principle should be on an accrual basis, not a cash basis; *(14.57)*

(f)   the total amount of expense included in segment result for depreciation and amortisation of segment assets for the period; *(14.58)*

(g)   the total amount of significant non-cash expenses, other than depreciation and amortisation for which separate disclosure is required, that were included in segment expense and, therefore, deducted in measuring segment result. *(14.61)*. An enterprise that provides the segment cash flow disclosures that are encouraged by IAS 7 (see section 2.2.4, p. 111) need not also disclose depreciation and amortisation expense or non-cash expenses; *(14.63)* and

(h)   the aggregate of the enterprise's share of the net profit or loss of associates, joint ventures, or other investments accounted for under the equity method if substantially all of those associates' operations are within that single segment. *(14.64)*

If an enterprise's aggregate share of the net profit or loss of associates, joint ventures, or other investments accounted for under the equity method is disclosed by reportable segment, the aggregate investments in those associates and joint ventures should also be disclosed by reportable segment. *(14.66)*

An enterprise is encouraged, but not required to disclose the nature and amount of any items of segment revenue and segment expense that are of such size, nature, or incidence that their disclosure is relevant to explain the performance of each reportable segment for the period. *(14.59)*

An enterprise should present a reconciliation between the information disclosed for reportable segments and the aggregated information in the consolidated or enterprise financial statements. In presenting the reconciliation, segment revenue should be reconciled to enterprise revenue from external customers (including disclosure of the amount of enterprise revenue from external customers not included in any segment's revenue); segment result should be reconciled to a comparable measure of enterprise operating profit or loss as well as to enterprise net profit or loss; segment assets should be reconciled to enterprise assets; and segment liabilities should be reconciled to enterprise liabilities. *(14.67)*

Secondary Segment Information

If an enterprise's primary format for reporting segment information is business segments, it should also report the following information:

(a)   segment revenue from external customers by geographical area based on the geographical location of its customers, for each geographical segment whose revenue from sales to external customers is 10 per cent or more of total enterprise revenue from sales to all external customers;

(b)   the total carrying amount of segment assets by geographical location of assets, for each geographical segment whose segment assets are 10 per cent or more of the total assets of all geographical segments; and

(c)   the total cost incurred during the period to acquire segment assets that are expected to be used during more than one period (property, plant, equipment, and intangible assets) by geographical location of assets, for each geographical segment whose segment assets are 10 per cent or more of the total assets of all geographical segments. *(14.69)*

If an enterprise's primary format for reporting segment information is geographical segments (whether based on location of assets or location of customers), it should also report the following segment information for each business segment whose revenue from sales to external customers is 10 per cent or more of total enterprise revenue from sales to all external customers or whose segment assets are 10 per cent or more of the total assets of all business segments:

(a)   segment revenue from external customers;

(b)   the total carrying amount of segment assets; and

(c)   the total cost incurred during the period to acquire segment assets that are expected to be used during more than one period (property, plant, equipment, and intangible assets). *(14.70)*

If an enterprise's primary format for reporting segment information is geographical segments that are based on location of assets, and if the location of its customers is different from the location of its assets, then the enterprise should also report revenue from sales to external customers for each customer-based geographical segment whose revenue from sales to external customers is 10 per cent or more of total enterprise revenue from sales to all external customers. *(14.71)*

If an enterprise's primary format for reporting segment information is geographical segments that are based on location of customers, and if the enterprise's assets are located in different geographical areas from its customers, then the enterprise should also report the following segment information for each asset-based geographical segment whose revenue from sales to external customers or segment assets are 10 per cent or more of related consolidated or total enterprise amounts:

(a)   the total carrying amount of segment assets by geographical location of the assets; and

(b)   the total cost incurred during the period to acquire segment assets that are expected to be used during more than one period (property, plant, equipment, and intangible assets) by location of the assets. *(14.72)*

Other Disclosure Matters

If a business segment or geographical segment for which information is reported to the board of directors and chief executive officer is not a reportable segment because it earns a majority of its revenue from sales to other segments, but nonetheless its revenue from sales to external customers is 10 per cent or more of total enterprise revenue from sales to all external customers, the enterprise should disclose that fact and the amounts of revenue from (a) sales to external customers and (b) internal sales to other segments. *(14.74)*

Summary of Required Disclosure (1/3)

PRIMARY FORMAT IS BUSINESS SEGMENTS	PRIMARY FORMAT IS GEOGRAPHICAL SEGMENTS BY LOCATION OF ASSETS	PRIMARY FORMAT IS GEOGRAPHICAL SEGMENTS BY LOCATION OF CUSTOMERS
Required Primary Disclosures:	*Required Primary Disclosures:*	*Required Primary Disclosures:*
Revenue from external customers by business segment	Revenue from external customers by location of assets	Revenue from external customers by location of customers
Revenue from transactions with other segments by business segment	Revenue from transactions with other segments by location of assets	Revenue from transactions with other segments by location of customers
Segment result by business segment	Segment result by location of assets	Segment result by location of customers
Carrying amount of segment assets by business segment	Carrying amount of segment assets by location of assets	Carrying amount of segment assets by location of customers
Segment liabilities by business segment	Segment liabilities by location of assets	Segment liabilities by location of customers
Cost to acquire property, plant, equipment, and intangibles by business segment	Cost to acquire property, plant, equipment, and intangibles by location of assets	Cost to acquire property, plant, equipment, and intangibles by location of customers
Depreciation and amortisation expense by business segment	Depreciation and amortisation expense by location of assets	Depreciation and amortisation expense by location of customers
Non-cash expenses other than depreciation and amortisation by business segment	Non-cash expenses other than depreciation and amortisation by location of assets	Non-cash expenses other than depreciation and amortisation by location of customers
Share of net profit or loss of and investment in equity method associates or joint ventures by business segment (if substantially all within a single business segment)	Share of net profit or loss of and investment in equity method associates or joint ventures by location of assets (if substantially all within a single segment)	Share of net profit or loss of and investment in equity method associates or joint ventures by location of customers (if substantially all within a single segment)

Figure 5   **Summary of Required Disclosure (Table 1 of 3)**

Summary of Required Disclosure (2/3)

PRIMARY FORMAT IS BUSINESS SEGMENTS	PRIMARY FORMAT IS GEOGRAPHICAL SEGMENTS BY LOCATION OF ASSETS	PRIMARY FORMAT IS GEOGRAPHICAL SEGMENTS BY LOCATION OF CUSTOMERS
Required Secondary Disclosures:	*Required Secondary Disclosures:*	*Required Secondary Disclosures:*
Revenue from external customers by location of customers	Revenue from external customers by business segment	Revenue from external customers by business segment
Carrying amount of segment assets by location of assets	Carrying amount of segment assets by business segment	Carrying amount of segment assets by business segment
Cost to acquire property, plant, equipment, and intangibles by location of assets	Cost to acquire property, plant, equipment, and intangibles by business segment	Cost to acquire property, plant, equipment, and intangibles by business segment
	Revenue from external customers by geographical customers if different from location of assets	
		Carrying amount of segment assets by location of assets if different from location of customers
		Cost to acquire property, plant, equipment, and intangibles by location of assets if different from location of customers
Revenue for any business or geographical segment whose external revenue is more than 10 per cent of enterprise revenue but that is not a reportable segment because a majority of its revenue is from internal transfers	Revenue for any business or geographical segment whose external revenue is more than 10 per cent of enterprise revenue but that is not a reportable segment because a majority of its revenue is from internal transfers	Revenue for any business or geographical segment whose external revenue is more than 10 per cent of enterprise revenue but that is not a reportable segment because a majority of its revenue is from internal transfers

Figure 6 **Summary of Required Disclosure (Table 2 of 3)**

Summary of Required Disclosure (3/3)

PRIMARY FORMAT IS BUSINESS SEGMENTS	PRIMARY FORMAT IS GEOGRAPHICAL SEGMENTS BY LOCATION OF ASSETS	PRIMARY FORMAT IS GEOGRAPHICAL SEGMENTS BY LOCATION OF CUSTOMERS
Other Required Disclosures:	*Other Required Disclosures:*	*Other Required Disclosures:*
Revenue for any business or geographical segment whose external revenue is more than 10 per cent of enterprise revenue but that is not a reportable segment because a majority of its revenue is from internal transfers	Revenue for any business or geographical segment whose external revenue is more than 10 per cent of enterprise revenue but that is not a reportable segment because a majority of its revenue is from internal transfers	Revenue for any business or geographical segment whose external revenue is more than 10 per cent of enterprise revenue but that is not a reportable segment because a majority of its revenue is from internal transfers
Basis of pricing inter-segment transfers and any change therein	Basis of pricing inter-segment transfers and any change therein	Basis of pricing inter-segment transfers and any change therein
Changes in segment accounting policies	Changes in segment accounting policies	Changes in segment accounting policies
Types of products and services in each business segment	Types of products and services in each business segment	Types of products and services in each business segment
Composition of each geographical segment	Composition of each geographical segment	Composition of each geographical segment [14.81]

Figure 7   **Summary of Required Disclosure (Table 3 of 3)**

In measuring and reporting segment revenue from transactions with other segments, inter-segment transfers should be measured on the basis that the enterprise actually used to price those transfers. The basis of pricing inter-segment transfers and any change therein should be disclosed in the financial statements. *(14.75)*

Changes in accounting policies adopted for segment reporting that have a material effect on segment information should be disclosed, and prior period segment information presented for comparative purposes should be restated unless it is impractical to do so. Such disclosure should include a description of the nature of the change, the reasons for the change, the fact that comparative information has been restated or that it is impractical to do so, and the financial effect of the change, if it is reasonably determinable. If an enterprise changes the identification of its segments and it does not restate prior period segment information on the new basis because it is impractical to do so, then for the purpose of comparison the enterprise should report segment data for both the old and the new bases of segmentation in the year in which it changes the identification of its segments. *(14.76)*

An enterprise should indicate the types of products and services included in each reported business segment and indicate the composition of each reported geographical segment, both primary and secondary, if not otherwise disclosed in the financial statements or elsewhere in the financial report. *(14.81)*

2.4	**Earnings Per Share**

Enterprises Whose Shares are Publicly Traded

IAS 33 should be applied by enterprises whose ordinary shares or potential ordinary shares are publicly traded and by enterprises that are in the process of issuing ordinary shares or potential ordinary shares in public securities markets. *(33.1)*

When both parent and consolidated financial statements are presented, the information called for by IAS 33 need be presented only on the basis of consolidated information. *(33.2)*

Enterprises Whose Shares are Not Publicly Traded

An enterprise which has neither ordinary shares nor potential ordinary shares which are publicly traded, but which discloses earnings per share, should calculate and disclose earnings per share in accordance with IAS 33. *(33.4)*

IAS 33 uses the following terms:

- An *ordinary share* is an equity instrument that is subordinate to all other classes of equity instruments.

- A *potential ordinary share* is a financial instrument or other contract that may entitle its holder to ordinary shares.

- *Warrants* or *options* are financial instruments that give the holder the right to purchase ordinary shares. *(33.6)*

Ordinary shares participate in the net profit for the period only after other types of shares such as preference shares. An enterprise may have more than one class of ordinary shares. Ordinary shares of the same class will have the same rights to receive dividends. *(33.7)*

Examples of potential ordinary shares are:

(a)   debt or equity instruments, including preference shares, that are convertible into ordinary shares;

(b)   share warrants and options;

(c)   employee plans that allow employees to receive ordinary shares as part of their remuneration and other share purchase plans; and

(d)   shares which would be issued upon the satisfaction of certain conditions resulting from contractual arrangements, such as the purchase of a business or other assets. *(33.8)*

The following terms are used with the meanings specified in IAS 32, *Financial Instruments: Disclosure and Presentation* (see section 6.2, p. 370):

- A *financial instrument* is any contract that gives rise to both a financial asset of one enterprise and a financial liability or equity instrument of another enterprise.

- An *equity instrument* is any contract that evidences a residual interest in the assets of an enterprise after deducting all of its liabilities.

- *Fair value* is the amount for which an asset could be exchanged, or a liability settled, between knowledgeable, willing parties in an arm's length transaction. *(33.9)*

Measurement

Basic Earnings Per Share

Basic earnings per share should be calculated by dividing the net profit or loss for the period attributable to ordinary shareholders by the weighted average number of ordinary shares outstanding during the period. *(33.10)*

Earnings – Basic

For the purpose of calculating basic earnings per share, the net profit or loss for the period attributable to ordinary shareholders should be the net profit or loss for the period after deducting preference dividends. *(33.11)*

The amount of preference dividends that is deducted from the net profit for the period is:

(a)   the amount of any preference dividends on non-cumulative preference shares declared in respect of the period; and

(b)   the full amount of the required preference dividends for cumulative preference shares for the period, whether or not the dividends have been declared. The amount of preference dividends for the period does not include the amount of any preference dividends for cumulative preference shares paid or declared during the current period in respect of previous periods. *(33.13)*

Per Share – Basic

For the purpose of calculating basic earnings per share, the number of ordinary shares should be the weighted average number of ordinary shares outstanding during the period. *(33.14)*

The weighted average number of ordinary shares outstanding during the period reflects the fact that the amount of shareholders' capital may have varied during the period as a result of a larger or lesser number of shares being outstanding at any time. It is the number of ordinary shares outstanding at the beginning of the period, adjusted by the number of ordinary shares bought back or issued during the period multiplied by a time-weighting factor. The time-weighting factor is the number of days that the specific shares are outstanding as a proportion of the total number of days in the period; a reasonable approximation of the weighted average is adequate in many circumstances. *(33.15)*

The weighted average number of ordinary shares outstanding during the period and for all periods presented should be adjusted for events, other than the conversion of potential ordinary shares, that have changed the number of ordinary shares outstanding, without a corresponding change in resources. *(33.20)*

Diluted Earnings Per Share

For the purpose of calculating diluted earnings per share, the net profit attributable to ordinary shareholders and the weighted average number of shares outstanding should be adjusted for the effects of all dilutive potential ordinary shares. *(33.24)*

The calculation of diluted earnings per share is consistent with the calculation of basic earnings per share while giving effect to all dilutive potential ordinary shares that were outstanding during the period, that is:

(a)   the net profit for the period attributable to ordinary shares is increased by the after-tax amount of dividends and interest recognised in the period in respect of the dilutive potential ordinary shares and adjusted for any other changes in income or expense that would result from the conversion of the dilutive potential ordinary shares;

(b)   the weighted average number of ordinary shares outstanding is increased by the weighted average number of additional ordinary shares which would have been outstanding assuming the conversion of all dilutive potential ordinary shares. *(33.25)*

Earnings – Diluted

For the purpose of calculating diluted earnings per share, the amount of net profit or loss for the period attributable to ordinary shareholders, as calculated for the purposes of basic earnings per share, should be adjusted by the after-tax effect:

(a)   any dividends on dilutive potential ordinary shares which have been deducted in arriving at the net profit attributable to ordinary shareholders;

(b)   interest recognised in the period for the dilutive potential ordinary shares; and

(c)   any other changes in income or expense that would result from the conversion of the dilutive potential ordinary shares. *(33.26)*

Per Share – Diluted

For the purpose of calculating diluted earnings per share, the number of ordinary shares should be the weighted average number of ordinary shares calculated for the purposes of basic earnings per share, plus the weighted average number of ordinary shares which would be issued on the conversion of all the dilutive potential ordinary shares into ordinary shares. Dilutive potential ordinary shares should be deemed to have been converted into ordinary shares at the beginning of the period or, if later, the date of the issue of the potential ordinary shares. *(33.29)*

For the purpose of calculating diluted earnings per share, an enterprise should assume the exercise of dilutive options and other dilutive potential ordinary shares of the enterprise. The assumed proceeds from these issues should be considered to have been received from the issue of shares at fair value. The difference between the number of shares issued and the number of shares that would have been issued at fair value should be treated as an issue of ordinary shares for no consideration. *(33.33)*

Fair value for this purpose is calculated on the basis of the average price of the ordinary shares during the period. *(33.34)*

Dilutive Potential Ordinary Shares

Potential ordinary shares should be treated as dilutive when, and only when, their conversion to ordinary shares would decrease net profit per share from continuing ordinary operations. *(33.38)*

Restatement

If the number of ordinary or potential ordinary shares outstanding increases as a result of a capitalisation or bonus issue or share split or decreases as a result of a reverse share split, the calculation of basic and diluted earnings per share for all periods presented should be adjusted retrospectively. If these changes occur after the balance sheet date but before issue of the financial statements, the per share calculations for those and any prior period financial statements presented should be based on the new number of shares. When per share calculations reflect such changes in the number of shares, that fact should be disclosed. In addition, basic and diluted earnings per share of all periods presented should be adjusted for:

(a)   the effects of fundamental errors, and adjustments resulting from changes in accounting policies, dealt with in accordance with the benchmark treatment in IAS 8 (see section 2.5.4, p. 145); and

(b)   the effects of a business combination which is a uniting of interests. *(33.43)*

Presentation

An enterprise should present basic and diluted earnings per share on the face of the income statement for each class of ordinary shares that has a different right to share in the net profit for the period. An enterprise should present basic and diluted earnings per share with equal prominence for all periods presented. *(33.47)*

IAS 33 requires an enterprise to present basic and diluted earnings per share, even if the amounts disclosed are negative (a loss per share). *(33.48)*

Disclosure

An enterprise should disclose the following:

(a)   the amounts used as the numerators in calculating basic and diluted earnings per share, and a reconciliation of those amounts to the net profit or loss for the period; and

(b)   the weighted average number of ordinary shares used as the denominator in calculating basic and diluted earnings per share, and a reconciliation of these denominators to each other. *(33.49)*

If an enterprise discloses, in addition to basic and diluted earnings per share, per share amounts using a reported component of net profit other than net profit or loss for the period attributable to ordinary shareholders, such amounts should be calculated using the weighted average number of ordinary shares determined in accordance with this Standard. If a component of net profit is used which is not reported as a line item in the income statement, a reconciliation should be provided between the component used and a line item which is reported in the income statement. Basic and diluted per share amounts should be disclosed with equal prominence. *(33.51)*

2.5   Other Disclosure Issues

2.5.1   Effects of Changes in Foreign Exchange Rates

Generally, enterprises carry on foreign activities in two ways. They may have transactions in foreign currencies and/or they may have foreign operations. In order to include foreign currency transactions and foreign operations in the financial statements of an enterprise, transactions must be expressed in the enterprise's reporting currency and the financial statements of foreign operations must be translated into the enterprise's reporting currency.

IAS 21 should be applied:

(a)   in accounting for transactions in foreign currencies; and

(b)   in translating the financial statements of foreign operations that are included in the financial statements of the enterprise by consolidation, proportionate consolidation or by the equity method. *(21.1)*

Exclusions

IAS 21 does not address hedge accounting for foreign currency items other than the classification of exchange differences arising on a foreign currency liability accounted for as a hedge of a net investment in a foreign entity. Other aspects of hedge accounting, including the criteria to use hedge accounting, are dealt with in IAS 39, *Financial Instruments: Recognition and Measurement* (see section 6.1, p. 349). *(21.2)*

IAS 21 does not deal with the restatement of an enterprise's financial statements from its reporting currency into another currency for the convenience of users accustomed to that currency or for similar purposes. *(21.5)*

IAS 21 does not deal with the presentation in a cash flow statement of cash flows arising from transactions in a foreign currency and the translation of cash flows of a foreign operation (see IAS 7, *Cash Flow Statements*, under section 2.2.4, p. 111). *(21.6)*

Definitions

IAS 21 uses the following terms:

- *Foreign operation* is a subsidiary, associate, joint venture or branch of the reporting enterprise, the activities of which are based or conducted in a country other than the country of the reporting enterprise.

- *Foreign entity* is a foreign operation, the activities of which are not an integral part of those of the reporting enterprise.

- *Reporting currency* is the currency used in presenting the financial statements.

- *Foreign currency* is a currency other than the reporting currency of an enterprise.

- *Exchange rate* is the ratio for exchange of two currencies.

- *Exchange difference* is the difference resulting from reporting the same number of units of a foreign currency in the reporting currency at different exchange rates.

- *Closing rate* is the spot exchange rate at the balance sheet date.

- *Net investment* in a foreign entity is the reporting enterprise's share in the net assets of that entity.

- *Monetary items* are money held and assets and liabilities to be received or paid in fixed or determinable amounts of money.

- *Fair value* is the amount for which an asset could be exchanged, or a liability settled, between knowledgeable, willing parties in an arm's length transaction. *(21.7)*

Foreign Currency Transactions

Initial Recognition

A foreign currency transaction should be recorded, on initial recognition in the reporting currency, by applying to the foreign currency amount the exchange rate between the reporting currency and the foreign currency at the date of the transaction. *(21.9)*

Reporting at Subsequent Balance Sheet Dates

At each balance sheet date:

(a)   foreign currency monetary items should be reported using the closing rate;

(b)   non-monetary items which are carried in terms of historical cost denominated in a foreign currency should be reported using the exchange rate at the date of the transaction; and

(c)   non-monetary items which are carried at fair value denominated in a foreign currency should be reported using the exchange rates that existed when the values were determined. *(21.11)*

Recognition of Exchange Differences

Exchange differences arising on the settlement of monetary items or on reporting an enterprise's monetary items at rates different from those at which they were initially recorded during the period, or reported in previous financial statements, should be recognised as income or as expenses in the period in which they arise, with the exception of exchange differences arising in relation to the net investment in a foreign entity. *(21.15)*

Net Investment in a Foreign Entity

Exchange differences arising on a monetary item that, in substance, forms part of an enterprise's net investment in a foreign entity should be classified as equity in the enterprise's financial statements until the disposal of the net investment, at which time they should be recognised as income or as expenses. *(21.17)*

Exchange differences arising on a foreign currency liability accounted for as a hedge of an enterprise's net investment in a foreign entity should be classified as equity in the enterprise's financial statements until the disposal of the net investment, at which time they should be recognised as income or as expenses. *(21.19)*

Allowed Alternative Treatment

Exchange differences may result from a severe devaluation or depreciation of a currency against which there is no practical means of hedging and that affects liabilities which cannot be settled and which arise directly on the recent acquisition of an asset invoiced in a foreign currency. Such exchange differences should be included in the carrying amount of the related asset, provided that the adjusted carrying amount does not exceed the lower of the replacement cost and the amount recoverable from the sale or use of the asset. *(21.21)*

Financial Statements of Foreign Operations

Classification of Foreign Operations

A foreign operation that is integral to the operations of the reporting enterprise carries on its business as if it were an extension of the reporting enterprise's operations. *(21.24)*

In contrast, a foreign entity accumulates cash and other monetary items, incurs expenses, generates income and perhaps arranges borrowings, all substantially in its local currency. It may also enter into transactions in foreign currencies, including transactions in the reporting currency. *(21.25)*

Foreign Operations that are Integral to the Operations of the Reporting Enterprise

The financial statements of a foreign operation that is integral to the operations of the reporting enterprise should be translated using the standards and procedures specified above for foreign currency transactions as if the transactions of the foreign operation had been those of the reporting enterprise itself. *(21.27)*

Foreign Entities

In translating the financial statements of a foreign entity for incorporation in its financial statements, the reporting enterprise should use the following procedures:

(a)   the assets and liabilities, both monetary and non-monetary, of the foreign entity should be translated at the closing rate;

(b)   income and expense items of the foreign entity should be translated at exchange rates at the dates of the transactions, except when the foreign entity reports in the currency of a hyperinflationary economy, in which case income and expense items should be translated at the closing rate; and

(c)   all resulting exchange differences should be classified as equity until the disposal of the net investment. *(21.30)*

The financial statements of a foreign entity that reports in the currency of a hyperinflationary economy should be restated in accordance with IAS 29, *Financial Reporting in Hyperinflationary Economies* (see section 2.5.6, p. 158), before they are translated into the reporting currency of the reporting enterprise. When the economy ceases to be hyperinflationary and the foreign entity discontinues the preparation and presentation of financial statements prepared in accordance with IAS 29, *Financial Reporting in Hyperinflationary Economies*, it should use the amounts expressed in the measuring unit current at the date of discontinuation as the historical costs for translation into the reporting currency of the reporting enterprise. *(21.36)*

Disposal of a Foreign Entity

On the disposal of a foreign entity, the cumulative amount of the exchange differences which have been deferred and which relate to that foreign entity should be recognised as income or as expenses in the same period in which the gain or loss on disposal is recognised. *(21.37)*

Change in the Classification of a Foreign Operation

When there is a change in the classification of a foreign operation, the translation procedures applicable to the revised classification should be applied from the date of the change in the classification. *(21.39)*

All Changes in Foreign Exchange Rates

Tax Effects of Exchange Differences

Gains and losses on foreign currency transactions and exchange differences arising on the translation of the financial statements of foreign operations may have associated tax effects which are accounted for in accordance with IAS 12, *Income Taxes* (see section 4.1, p. 247). *(21.41)*

Disclosure

An enterprise should disclose:

(a)   the amount of exchange differences included in the net profit or loss for the period;

(b)   net exchange differences classified as equity as a separate component of equity, and a reconciliation of the amount of such exchange differences at the beginning and end of the period; and

(c)   the amount of exchange differences arising during the period which is included in the carrying amount of an asset in accordance with the allowed alternative treatment in paragraph 21.21. *(21.42)*

When the reporting currency is different from the currency of the country in which the enterprise is domiciled, the reason for using a different currency should be disclosed. The reason for any change in the reporting currency should also be disclosed. *(21.43)*

When there is a change in the classification of a significant foreign operation, an enterprise should disclose:

(a)   the nature of the change in classification;

(b)   the reason for the change;

(c)   the impact of the change in classification on shareholders' equity; and

(d)   the impact on net profit or loss for each prior period presented had the change in classification occurred at the beginning of the earliest period presented. *(21.44)*

An enterprise should disclose the method selected to translate goodwill and fair value adjustments arising on the acquisition of a foreign entity. *(21.45)*

2.5.2	**Related Party Disclosures**

IAS 24 should be applied in dealing with related parties and transactions between a reporting enterprise and its related parties. The requirements of this Standard apply to the financial statements of each reporting enterprise. *(24.1)*

IAS 24 applies only to those related party relationships described below and deals only with those related party relationships described in (a) to (e) below:

(a) enterprises that directly, or indirectly through one or more intermediaries, control, or are controlled by, or are under common control with, the reporting enterprise. (This includes holding companies, subsidiaries and fellow subsidiaries.);

(b) associates (*see IAS 28, Accounting for Investments in Associates,* section 7.3, p. 407);

(c) individuals owning, directly or indirectly, an interest in the voting power of the reporting enterprise that gives them significant influence over the enterprise, and close members of the family[1] of any such individual;

(d) key management personnel, that is, those persons having authority and responsibility for planning, directing and controlling the activities of the reporting enterprise, including directors and officers of companies and close members of the families of such individuals; and

(e) enterprises in which a substantial interest in the voting power is owned, directly or indirectly, by any person described in (c) or (d) or over which such a person is able to exercise significant influence. This includes enterprises owned by directors or major shareholders of the reporting enterprise and enterprises that have a member of key management in common with the reporting enterprise.

In considering each possible related party relationship, attention is directed to the substance of the relationship, and not merely the legal form. *(24.3)*

No disclosure of transactions is required:

(a) in consolidated financial statements in respect of intragroup transactions;

(b) in parent financial statements when they are made available or published with the consolidated financial statements;

---

[1] *Close members of the family of an individual are those that may be expected to influence, or be influenced by, that person in their dealings with the enterprise.*

(c)   in financial statements of a wholly-owned subsidiary if its parent is incorporated in the same country and provides consolidated financial statements in that country; and

(d)   in financial statements of state-controlled enterprises of transactions with other state-controlled enterprises. *(24.4)*

IAS 24 uses the following terms:

• *Related party* – parties are considered to be related if one party has the ability to control the other party or exercise significant influence over the other party in making financial and operating decisions.

• *Related party transaction* – a transfer of resources or obligations between related parties, regardless of whether a price is charged.

• *Control* – ownership, directly, or indirectly through subsidiaries, of more than one half of the voting power of an enterprise, or a substantial interest in voting power and the power to direct, by statute or agreement, the financial and operating policies of the management of the enterprise.

• *Significant influence* (for the purpose of IAS 24) – participation in the financial and operating policy decisions of an enterprise, but not control of those policies. Significant influence may be exercised in several ways, usually by representation on the board of directors but also by, for example, participation in the policy-making process, material inter-company transactions, interchange of managerial personnel or dependence on technical information. Significant influence may be gained by share ownership, statute or agreement. With share ownership, significant influence is presumed in accordance with the definition contained in IAS 28, *Accounting for Investments in Associates* (see section 6.3, p. 407). *(24.5)*

The Related Party Issue

Related party relationships are a normal feature of commerce and business. For example, enterprises frequently carry on separate parts of their activities through subsidiary or associated enterprises and acquire interests in other enterprises – for investment purposes or for trading reasons – that are of sufficient proportions that the investing company can control or exercise significant influence on the financial and operating decisions of its investee. *(24.7)*

A related party relationship could have an effect on the financial position and operating results of the reporting enterprise. Related parties may enter into transactions which unrelated parties would not enter into. Also, transactions between related parties may not be effected at the same amounts as between unrelated parties. *(24.8)*

The operating results and financial position of an enterprise may be affected by a related party relationship even if related party transactions do not occur. The mere existence of the relationship may be sufficient to affect the transactions of the reporting enterprise with other parties. For example, a subsidiary may terminate relations with a trading partner on acquisition by the parent of a fellow subsidiary engaged in the same trade as the former partner. Alternatively, one party may refrain from acting because of the significant influence of another – for example, a subsidiary may be instructed by its parent not to engage in research and development. *(24.9)*

Accounting recognition of a transfer of resources is normally based on the price agreed between the parties. Between unrelated parties the price is an arm's length price. Related parties may have a degree of flexibility in the price-setting process that is not present in transactions between unrelated parties. *(24.11)*

A variety of methods is used to price transactions between related parties. *(24.12)*

Disclosure

In many countries the laws require financial statements to give disclosures about certain categories of related parties. In particular, attention is focused on transactions with the directors of an enterprise, especially their remuneration and borrowings, because of the fiduciary nature of their relationship with the enterprise, as well as disclosures of significant intercompany transactions and investments in and balances with group and associated companies and with directors. IAS 28, *Accounting for Investments in Associates* (see section 7.3. p 407) requires disclosure of a list of significant subsidiaries and associates. IAS 8, *Net Profit or Loss for the Period* (see section 2.2.2, p. 106), *Fundamental Errors and Changes in Accounting Policies* (see section 2.5.4, p. 145), requires disclosure of extraordinary items and items of income and expense within profit or loss from ordinary activities that are of such size, nature or incidence that their disclosure is relevant to explain the performance of the enterprise for the period. *(24.18)*

Related party relationships where control exists should be disclosed irrespective of whether there have been transactions between the related parties. *(24.20)*

If there have been transactions between related parties, the reporting enterprise should disclose the nature of the related party relationships as well as the types of transactions and the elements of the transactions necessary for an understanding of the financial statements. *(24.22)*

Items of a similar nature may be disclosed in aggregate except when separate disclosure is necessary for an understanding of the effects of related party transactions on the financial statements of the reporting enterprise. *(24.24)*

2.5.3   Events After the Balance Sheet Date

IAS 10 should be applied in the accounting for, and disclosure of, events after the balance sheet date. *(10.1)*

IAS 10 uses the following terms:

Events after the balance sheet date are those events, both favourable and unfavourable, that occur between the balance sheet date and the date when the financial statements are authorised for issue. Two types of events can be identified:

(a)   those that provide evidence of conditions that existed at the balance sheet date *(adjusting events after the balance sheet date)*; and

(b)   those that are indicative of conditions that arose after the balance sheet date *(non-adjusting events after the balance sheet date). (10.2)*

The process involved in authorising the financial statements for issue will vary depending upon the management structure, statutory requirements and procedures followed in preparing and finalising the financial statements. In some cases, an enterprise is required to submit its financial statements to its shareholders for approval after the financial statements have already been issued. In such cases, the financial statements are authorised for issue on the date of original issuance, not on the date when shareholders approve the financial statements. *(10.3, 10.4)*

➤ Example

The management of an enterprise completes draft financial statements for the year to 31 December 20X1 on 28 February 20X2. On 18 March 20X2, the board of directors reviews the financial statements and authorises them for issue. The enterprise announces its profit and selected other financial information on 19 March 20X2. The financial statements are made available to shareholders and others on 1 April 20X2. The annual meeting of shareholders approves the financial statements on 15 May 20X2 and the approved financial statements are then filed with a regulatory body on 17 May 20X2.

The financial statements are authorised for issue on 18 March 20X2 (date of Board authorisation for issue).

Figure 8

In some cases, the management of an enterprise is required to issue its financial statements to a supervisory board (made up solely of non-executives) for approval. In such cases, the financial statements are authorised for issue when the management authorises them for issue to the supervisory board. *(10.5)*

➤ Example

On 18 March 20X2, the management of an enterprise authorises financial statements for issue to its supervisory board. The supervisory board is made up solely of non-executives and may include representatives of employees and other outside interests. The supervisory board approves the financial statements on 26 March 20X2. The financial statements are made available to shareholders and others on 1 April 20X2. The annual meeting of shareholders receives the financial statements on 15 May 20X2 and the financial statements are then filed with a regulatory body on 17 May 20X2.

The financial statements are authorised for issue on 18 March 20X2 (date of management authorisation for issue to the supervisory board).

Figure 9

Recognition and Measurement

An enterprise should adjust the amounts recognised in its financial statements to reflect adjusting events after the balance sheet date and should not adjust the amounts recognised in its financial statements to reflect non-adjusting events after the balance sheet date. *(10.7, 10.9)*

Dividends

If dividends to holders of equity instruments (as defined in IAS 32, *Financial Instruments: Disclosure and Presentation*, see section 6.2, p. 370) are proposed or declared after the balance sheet date, an enterprise should not recognise those dividends as a liability at the balance sheet date. *(10.11)*

IAS 1, *Presentation of Financial Statements* (see section 2.1, p. 98), requires an enterprise to disclose the amount of dividends that were proposed or declared after the balance sheet date but before the financial statements were authorised for issue. IAS 1 permits an enterprise to make this disclosure either:

(a)   on the face of the balance sheet as a separate component of equity; or

(b)   in the notes to the financial statements. *(10.12)*

Going Concern

An enterprise should not prepare its financial statements on a going concern basis if management determines after the balance sheet date either that it intends to liquidate the enterprise or to cease trading, or that it has no realistic alternative but to do so. *(10.13)*

Deterioration in operating results and financial position after the balance sheet date may indicate a need to consider whether the going concern assumption is still appropriate. If the going concern assumption is no longer appropriate, the effect is so pervasive that this Standard requires a fundamental change in the basis of accounting, rather than an adjustment to the amounts recognised within the original basis of accounting. *(10.14)*

IAS 1, *Presentation of Financial Statements*, requires certain disclosures if:

(a)   the financial statements are not prepared on a going concern basis; or

(b)   management is aware of material uncertainties related to events or conditions that may cast significant doubt upon the enterprise's ability to continue as a going concern. The events or conditions requiring disclosure may arise after the balance sheet date. *(10.15)*

Disclosure

Date of Authorisation for Issue

An enterprise should disclose the date when the financial statements were authorised for issue and who gave that authorisation. If the enterprise's owners or others have the power to amend the financial statements after issuance, the enterprise should disclose that fact. *(10.16)*

Updating Disclosure about Conditions at the Balance Sheet Date

If an enterprise receives information after the balance sheet date about conditions that existed at the balance sheet date, the enterprise should update disclosures that relate to these conditions, in the light of the new information. *(10.18)*

Non-Adjusting Events After the Balance Sheet Date

Where non-adjusting events after the balance sheet date are of such importance that non-disclosure would affect the ability of the users of the financial statements to make proper evaluations and decisions, an enterprise should disclose the following information for each significant category of non-adjusting event after the balance sheet date:

(a)   the nature of the event; and

(b)   an estimate of its financial effect, or a statement that such an estimate cannot be made. *(10.20)*

2.5.4	# Fundamental Errors and Changes in Accounting Policies

Besides the presentation of profit or loss from ordinary activities and extraordinary items in the income statement and the accounting for changes in accounting estimates, IAS 8 should be applied in presenting fundamental errors and changes in accounting policies. *(8.1)*

IAS 8 uses the following terms:

• *Fundamental errors* are errors discovered in the current period that are of such significance that the financial statements of one or more prior periods can no longer be considered to have been reliable at the date of their issue.

• *Accounting policies* are the specific principles, bases, conventions, rules and practices adopted by an enterprise in preparing and presenting financial statements. *(8.6)*

Fundamental Errors

On rare occasions, an error has such a significant effect on the financial statements of one or more prior periods that those financial statements can no longer be considered to have been reliable at the date of their issue. These errors are referred to as fundamental errors. *(8.32)*

The correction of fundamental errors can be distinguished from changes in accounting estimates. Accounting estimates by their nature are approximations that may need revision as additional information becomes known. *(8.33)*

Benchmark Treatment

The amount of the correction of a fundamental error that relates to prior periods should be reported by adjusting the opening balance of retained earnings. Comparative information should be restated, unless it is impractical to do so. *(8.34)*

The restatement of comparative information does not necessarily give rise to the amendment of financial statements which have been approved by shareholders or registered or filed with regulatory authorities. However, national laws may require the amendment of such financial statements. *(8.36)*

An enterprise should disclose the following:

(a)   the nature of the fundamental error;

(b)   the amount of the correction for the current period and for each prior period presented;

(c)   the amount of the correction relating to periods prior to those included in the comparative information; and

(d)   the fact that comparative information has been restated or that it is impractical to do so. *(8.37)*

Allowed Alternative Treatment

The amount of the correction of a fundamental error should be included in the determination of net profit or loss for the current period. Comparative information should be presented as reported in the financial statements of the prior period. Additional pro forma information, prepared in accordance with paragraph 8.34, should be presented unless it is impractical to do so. *(8.38)*
An enterprise should disclose the following:

(a)   the nature of the fundamental error;

(b)   the amount of the correction recognised in net profit or loss for the current period; and

(c)   the amount of the correction included in each period for which pro forma information is presented and the amount of the correction relating to periods prior to those included in the pro forma information. If it is impractical to present pro forma information, this fact should be disclosed. *(8.40)*

➤ Examples: Fundamental Errors

During 20X2, Beta Co discovered that certain products that had been sold during 20X1 were incorrectly included in inventory at 31 December 20X1 at 6,500.

Beta's accounting records for 20X2 show sales of 104,000, cost of goods sold of 86,500 (including 6,500 for error in opening inventory), and income taxes of 5,250.

In 20X1, Beta reported:

Sales	73,500
Cost of goods sold	(53,500)
Profit from ordinary activities before income taxes	20,000
Income taxes	(6,000)
Net Profit	14,000

20X1 opening retained earnings was 20,000 and closing retained earnings was 34,000.
Beta's income tax rate was 30% for 20X2 and 20X1.

Beta Co: *Extract from the Income Statement under the Benchmark Treatment*

	20X2	20X1 (restated)
Sales	104,000	73,500
Cost of goods sold	(80,000)	(60,000)
Profit from ordinary activities before income taxes	24,000	13,500
Income taxes	(7,200)	(4,050)
Net Profit	16,800	9,450

Beta Co: *Statement of Retained Earnings under the Benchmark Treatment*

	20X2	20X1 (restated)
Opening retained earnings as previously reported	34,000	20,000
Correction of fundamental error (Net of income taxes of 1,950) (Note 1)	(4,550)	-
Opening retained earnings as restated	29,450	20,000
Net Profit	16,800	9,450
Closing Retained Earnings	46,250	29,450

Extracts from Notes to the Financial Statements

1. Certain products that had been sold in 20X1 were incorrectly included in inventory at 31 December 20X1 at 6,500. The financial statements of 20X1 have been restated to correct this error.

Cont.

➤ **Examples: Fundamental Errors** *(cont.)*

Beta Co: *Extract from the Income Statement under the Allowed Alternative Treatment*

	20X2	20X1	Pro forma 20X2 (restated)	Pro forma 20X1 (restated)
Sales	104,000	73,500	104,000	73,500
Cost of goods sold (Note 1)	(86,500)	(53,500)	(80,000)	(60,000)
Profit from ordinary activities before income taxes	17,500	20,000	24,000	13,500
Income taxes (includes the effects of the correction of a fundamental error)	(5,250)	(6,000)	(7,200)	(4,050)
Net Profit	12,250	14,000	16,800	9,450

Beta Co: *Statement of Retained Earnings under the Allowed Alternative Treatment*

	20X2	20X1	Pro forma 20X2 (restated)	Pro forma 20X1 (restated)
Opening retained earnings as previously reported	34,000	20,000	34,000	20,000
Correction of fundamental error (Net of income taxes of 1,950)	-	-	(4,550)	-
Opening retained earnings as restated	34,000	20,000	29,450	20,000
Net Profit	12,250	14,000	16,800	9,450
Closing Retained Earnings	46,250	34,000	46,250	29,450

Extracts from Notes to the Financial Statements

1. Cost of goods sold for 20X2 includes 6,500 for certain products that had been sold in 20X1 but were incorrectly included in inventory at 31 December 20X1. Restated pro forma information for 20X2 and 20X1 is presented as if the error had been corrected in 20X1.

Figure 10

Changes in Accounting Policies

A change in accounting policy should be made only if required by statute, or by an accounting standard setting body, or if the change will result in a more appropriate presentation of events or transactions in the financial statements of the enterprise. *(8.42)*

The following are not changes in accounting policies:

(a)   the adoption of an accounting policy for events or transactions that differ in substance from previously occurring events or transactions; and

(b)   the adoption of a new accounting policy for events or transactions which did not occur previously or that were immaterial.

The initial adoption of a policy to carry assets at revalued amounts is a change in accounting policy but it is dealt with as a revaluation in accordance with IAS 16, *Property, Plant and Equipment* (see under section 3.2, p. 190), or IAS 40, *Investment Property* (see section 3.3, p. 196) as appropriate, rather than in accordance with IAS 8. *(8.44)*

A change in accounting policy is applied retrospectively or prospectively in accordance with the requirements of IAS 8. Retrospective application results in the new accounting policy being applied to events and transactions as if the new accounting policy had always been in use. Therefore, the accounting policy is applied to events and transactions from the date of origin of such items. Prospective application means that the new accounting policy is applied to the events and transactions occurring after the date of the change. No adjustments relating to prior periods are made either to the opening balance of retained earnings or in reporting the net profit or loss for the current period because existing balances are not recalculated. However, the new accounting policy is applied to existing balances as from the date of the change. *(8.45)*

Adoption of an International Accounting Standard

A change in accounting policy which is made on the adoption of a Standard should be accounted for in accordance with the specific transitional provisions, if any, in that Standard. In the absence of any transitional provisions, the change in accounting policy should be applied in accordance with the requirement of benchmark treatment or the allowed alternative treatment in the Standard. *(8.46)*

Other Changes in Accounting Policies – Benchmark Treatment

A change in accounting policy should be applied retrospectively unless the amount of any resulting adjustment that relates to prior periods is not reasonably determinable. Any resulting adjustment should be reported as an adjustment to the opening balance of retained earnings. Comparative information should be restated unless it is impractical to do so. *(8.49)*

The change in accounting policy should be applied prospectively when the amount of the adjustment to the opening balance of retained earnings cannot be reasonably determined. *(8.52)*

When a change in accounting policy has a material effect on the current period or any prior period presented, or may have a material effect in subsequent periods, an enterprise should disclose the following:

(a)   the reasons for the change;

(b)   the amount of the adjustment for the current period and for each period presented;

(c)   the amount of the adjustment relating to periods prior to those included in the comparative information; and

(d)   the fact that comparative information has been restated or that it is impractical to do so. *(8.53)*

Other Changes in Accounting Policies – Allowed Alternative Treatment

A change in accounting policy should be applied retrospectively unless the amount of any resulting adjustment that relates to prior periods is not reasonably determinable. Any resulting adjustment should be included in the determination of the net profit or loss for the current period. Comparative information should be presented as reported in the financial statements of the prior period. Additional pro forma comparative information, should be presented unless it is impractical to do so. *(8.54)*

The change in accounting policy should be applied prospectively when the amount to be included in net profit or loss for the current period cannot be reasonably determined. *(8.56)*

When a change in accounting policy has a material effect on the current period or any prior period presented, or may have a material effect in subsequent periods, an enterprise should disclose the following:

(a)   the reasons for the change;

(b)   the amount of the adjustment recognised in net profit or loss in the current period; and

(c)   the amount of the adjustment included in each period for which pro forma information is presented and the amount of the adjustment relating to periods prior to those included in the financial statements. If it is impractical to present pro forma information, this fact should be disclosed. *(8.57)*

➤ Examples: Accounting Policy

During 20X2, Gamma Co changed its accounting policy with respect to the treatment of borrowing costs that are directly attributable to the acquisition of a hydro-electric power station which is in course of construction for use by Gamma. In previous periods, Gamma had capitalised such costs, net of income taxes, in accordance with the allowed alternative treatment in IAS 23, *Borrowing Costs* (see section 5.4, p. 343). Gamma has now decided to expense, rather than capitalise, these costs in order to conform with the benchmark treatment in IAS 23.

Gamma capitalised borrowing costs incurred of 2,600 during 20X1 and 5,200 in periods prior to 20X1. All borrowing costs incurred in previous years in respect to the acquisition of the power station were capitalised.

Gamma's accounting records for 20X2 show profit from ordinary activities before interest and income taxes of 30,000; interest expense of 3,000 (which relates only to 20X2); and income taxes of 8,100.

Gamma has not yet recognised any depreciation on the power station because it is not yet in use.

In 20X1, Gamma reported:

Sales	18,000
Cost of goods sold	-
Profit from ordinary activities before income taxes	18,000
Income taxes	(5,400)
Net Profit	12,600

20X1 opening retained earnings was 20,000 and closing retained earnings was 32,600.

Gamma's tax rate was 30% for 20X2 and 20X1.

Gamma Co: *Extract from the Income Statement under the Benchmark Treatment*

	20X2	20X1 (restated)
Profit from ordinary activities before interest and income taxes	30,000	18,000
Interest expense	(3,000)	(2,600)
Profit from ordinary activities before income taxes	27,000	15,400
Income taxes	(8,100)	(4,620)
Net Profit	18,900	10,780

Gamma Co: *Statement of Retained Earnings under the Benchmark Treatment*

	20X2	20X1 (restated)
Opening retained earnings as previously reported	32,600	20,000
Change in accounting policy with respect to the capitalisation of interest (Net of income taxes of 2,340 for 20X2 and 1,560 for 20X1) (Note 1)	(5,460)	(3,640)
Opening retained earnings as restated	27,140	16,360
Net profit	18,900	10,780

Cont.

➤ Examples: Accounting Policy *(cont.)*

Extracts from notes to the Financial Statements

During 19X2, Gamma changed its accounting policy with respect to the treatment of borrowing costs related to a hydro-electric power station which is in course of construction for use by Gamma. In order to conform with the benchmark treatment in IAS 23, *Borrowing Costs*, the enterprise now expenses rather than capitalises such costs. This change in accounting policy has been accounted for retrospectively. The comparative statements for 19X1 have been restated to conform to the changed policy. The effect of the change is an increase in interest expense of 3,000 (19X2) and 2,600 (19X1). Opening retained earnings for 19X1 have been reduced by 5,200 which is the amount of the adjustment relating to periods prior to 19X1.

Gamma Co: *Extract from the Income Statement under the Allowed Alternative Treatment*

	20X2	20X1	Pro forma 20X2 (restated)	Pro forma 20X1 (restated)
Profit from ordinary activities before interest and income taxes	30,000	18,000	30,000	18,000
Interest expense	(3,000)	-	(3,000)	(2,600)
Cumulative effect of change in accounting policy	(7,800)	-	-	-
Profit from ordinary activities before income taxes	19,200	18,000	27,000	15,400
Income taxes (includes the effect of a change in accounting policy)	(5,760)	(5,400)	(8,100)	(4,620)
Net Profit	13,440	12,600	18,900	10,780

Extracts from notes to the Financial Statements

1. An adjustment of 7,800 has been made in the income statement for 20X2 representing the effect of a change in accounting policy with respect to the treatment of borrowing costs related to a hydro-electric power station which is in course of construction for use by Gamma. In order to conform with the benchmark treatment in IAS 23, *Borrowing Costs*, the enterprise now expenses rather than capitalises such costs. This change in accounting policy has been accounted for retrospectively. Restated pro forma information, which assumes that the new policy had always been in use, is presented. Opening retained earnings in the pro forma information for 20X1 have been reduced by 5,200 which is the amount of the adjustment relating to periods prior to 20X1.

Gamma Co: *Statement of Retained Earnings under the Allowed Alternative Treatment*

	20X2	20X1	Pro forma 20X2 (restated)	Pro forma 20X1 (restated)
Opening retained earnings as previously reported	32,600	20,000	32,600	20,000
Change in accounting policy with respect to the capitalisation of interest (Net of income taxes of 2,340 for 20X2 and 1,560 for 20X1) (Note 1)	-	-	(5,460)	(3,640)
Opening retained earnings as restated	32,600	20,000	27,140	16,360
Net Profit	13,440	12,600	18,900	10,780
Closing Retained Earnings	46,040	32,600	46,040	27,140

Figure 12

| 2.5.5 | **Discontinuing Operations** |

IAS 35 applies to all discontinuing operations of all enterprises, and establishes principles for reporting information about discontinuing operations, thereby enhancing the ability of users of financial statements to make projections of an enterprise's cash flows, earnings-generating capacity, and financial position by segregating information about discontinuing operations from information about continuing operations. *(35.1)*

IAS 35 uses the following terms:

* A *discontinuing operation* is a component of an enterprise:

(a)   that the enterprise, pursuant to a single plan, is:

    (i)   disposing of substantially in its entirety, such as by selling the component in a single transaction, by demerger or spin-off of ownership of the component to the enterprise's shareholders;

    (ii)   disposing of piecemeal, such as by selling off the component's assets and settling its liabilities individually; or

    (iii)   terminating through abandonment;

(b)   that represents a separate major line of business or geographical area of operations; and

(c)   that can be distinguished operationally and for financial reporting purposes. *(35.2)*

* The *initial disclosure event* is the occurrence of one of the following, whichever occurs earlier:

(a)   the enterprise has entered into a binding sale agreement for substantially all of the assets attributable to the discontinuing operation; or

(b)   the enterprise's board of directors or similar governing body has both (i) approved a detailed, formal plan for the discontinuance and (ii) made an announcement of the plan. *(35.16)*

Recognition and Measurement

An enterprise should apply the principles of recognition and measurement that are set out in other Standards for the purpose of deciding when and how to recognise and measure the changes in assets and liabilities and the income, expenses, and cash flows relating to a discontinuing operation. *(35.17)*

Provisions

A discontinuing operation is a restructuring as that term is defined in IAS 37, *Provisions, Contingent Liabilities and Contingent Assets*. IAS 37 provides guidance for certain of the requirements of IAS 35, including:

(a)   what constitutes a "detailed, formal plan for the discontinuance" as that term is used in IAS 35; and

(b)   what constitutes an "announcement of the plan" as that term is used in IAS 35. *(35.20)*

Presentation and Disclosure

Initial Disclosure

An enterprise should include the following information relating to a discontinuing operation in its financial statements beginning with the financial statements for the period in which the "initial disclosure event" occurs:

(a)   a description of the discontinuing operation;

(b)   the business or geographical segment(s) in which it is reported in accordance with IAS 14;

(c)   the date and nature of the initial disclosure event;

(d)   the date or period in which the discontinuance is expected to be completed if known or determinable;

(e)   the carrying amounts, as of the balance sheet date, of the total assets and the total liabilities to be disposed of;

(f)   the amounts of revenue, expenses, and pre-tax profit or loss from ordinary activities attributable to the discontinuing operation during the current financial reporting period, and the income tax expense relating thereto as required by IAS 12, paragraph 81(h) (see section 4.1, p. 247); and

(g)   the amounts of net cash flows attributable to the operating, investing, and financing activities of the discontinuing operation during the current financial reporting period. *(35.27)*

If an initial disclosure event occurs after the end of an enterprise's financial reporting period but before the financial statements for that period are authorised for issue, specific disclosures are required. *(35.29)*

Other Disclosures

When an enterprise disposes of assets or settles liabilities attributable to a discontinuing operation or enters into binding agreements for the sale of such assets or the settlement of such liabilities, it should include in its financial statements the following information when the events occur:

(a)   for any gain or loss that is recognised on the disposal of assets or settlement of liabilities attributable to the discontinuing operation, (i) the amount of the pre-tax gain or loss and (ii) income tax expense relating to the gain or loss, as required by IAS 12; and

(b)   the net selling price or range of prices (which is after deducting the expected disposal costs) of those net assets for which the enterprise has entered into one or more binding sale agreements, the expected timing of receipt of those cash flows, and the carrying amount of those net assets. *(35.31)*

Updating the Disclosures

In addition to these disclosures, an enterprise should include in its financial statements for periods subsequent to the one in which the initial disclosure event occurs a description of any significant changes in the amount or timing of cash flows relating to the assets and liabilities to be disposed of or settled and the events causing those changes. *(35.33)*

The preceding disclosures should continue in financial statements for periods up to and including the period in which the discontinuance is completed. A discontinuance is completed when the plan is substantially completed or abandoned, though payments from the buyer(s) to the seller may not yet be completed. *(35.35)*

If an enterprise abandons or withdraws from a plan that was previously reported as a discontinuing operation, that fact and its effect should be disclosed. *(35.36)*

Separate Disclosure for Each Discontinuing Operation

Any disclosures required by IAS 35 should be presented separately for each discontinuing operation. *(35.38)*

Presentation of the Required Disclosures

Face of Financial Statements or Notes

The preceding disclosures may be presented either in the notes to the financial statements or on the face of the financial statements except that the disclosure of the amount of the pre-tax gain or loss recognised on the disposal of assets or settlement of liabilities attributable to the discontinuing operation should be shown on the face of the income statement. *(35.39)*

Not an Extraordinary Item

A discontinuing operation should not be presented as an extraordinary item. *(35.41)*

Restricted Use of the Term 'Discontinuing Operation'

A restructuring, transaction, or event that does not meet the definition of a discontinuing operation in this Standard should not be called a discontinuing operation. *(35.43)*

Restatement of Prior Periods

Comparative information for prior periods that is presented in financial statements prepared after the initial disclosure event should be restated to segregate continuing and discontinuing assets, liabilities, income, expenses, and cash flows in a manner similar to that required for the current period. *(35.45)*

Disclosure in Interim Financial Reports

The notes to an interim financial report should describe any significant activities or events since the end of the most recent annual reporting period relating to a discontinuing operation and any significant changes in the amount or timing of cash flows relating to the assets and liabilities to be disposed of or settled. *(35.47)*

➤ **Example: Classification of Prior Period Operations**

Facts

1. IAS 35 requires that comparative information for prior periods that is presented in financial statements prepared after the initial disclosure event be restated to segregate continuing and discontinuing assets, liabilities, income, expenses, and cash flows in a manner similar to that required for the current period.

2. Consider the following set of changes to an enterprise:

    (a)   operations *A, B, C,* and *D* were all continuing in Years 1 and 2;

    (b)   in Year 3, operation *D* is discontinued (approved for disposal and actually disposed of);

    (c)   in Year 4, operation *B* is discontinued (approved for disposal and actually disposed of) and operation *E* is acquired; and

    (d)   in Year 5 operation *F* is acquired.

3. The following table illustrates the classification of continuing and discontinuing operations in the foregoing circumstances:

FINANCIAL STATEMENTS FOR YEAR 3 (Approved and Published Early in Year 4)			
Year 2 Comparatives		Year 3	
Continuing	*Discontinuing*	*Continuing*	*Discontinuing*
A		A	
B		B	
C		C	
	D		D

FINANCIAL STATEMENTS FOR YEAR 4 (Approved and Published Early in Year 5)			
Year 3 Comparatives		Year 4	
Continuing	*Discontinuing*	*Continuing*	*Discontinuing*
A		A	
	B		B
C		C	
	D		
		E	

Cont.

➤ Example: Classification of Prior Period Operations *(cont.)*

FINANCIAL STATEMENTS FOR YEAR 5 (Approved and Published Early in Year 6)			
Year 4 Comparatives		Year 5	
Continuing	*Discontinuing*	*Continuing*	*Discontinuing*
A		A	
	B		
C		C	
E		E	
		F	

4. If the approval and announcement of the discontinuance of operation *B* had occurred early in year 4, before the financial statements for year 3 had been approved by the enterprise's board of directors, operation *B* would have been classified as a discontinuing operation in the financial statements for year 3 and the year 2 comparatives, as follows:

FINANCIAL STATEMENTS FOR YEAR 3 (Approved in Year 4 After the Discontinuance of Operation B was Approved and Announced)			
Year 2 Comparatives		Year 3	
Continuing	*Discontinuing*	*Continuing*	*Discontinuing*
A		A	
	B		B
C		C	
	D		D

5. If, for whatever reason, five-year comparative financial statements were prepared in year 5, the classification of continuing and discontinuing operations would be as follows:

FINANCIAL STATEMENTS FOR YEAR 5									
Year 1 Comparatives		Year 2 Comparatives		Year 3 Comparatives		Year 4 Comparatives		Year 5	
Cont.	*Disc.*	*Cont.*	*Disc.*	*Cont.*	*Disc.*	*Cont.*	*Disc.*	*Cont.*	*Disc.*
A		A		A		A		A	
	B		B		B		B		
C		C		C		C		C	
	D		D		D				
						E		E	
								F	

Figure 13

| 2.5.6 | **Hyperinflation** |

Financial Reporting in Hyperinflationary Economies

IAS 29 should be applied to the primary financial statements, including the consolidated financial statements, of any enterprise that complies with IAS and reports in the currency of a hyperinflationary economy. *(29.1)*

The Restatement of Financial Statements

The financial statements of an enterprise that reports in the currency of a hyperinflationary economy, whether they are based on a historical cost approach or a current cost approach, should be stated in terms of the measuring unit current at the balance sheet date. The corresponding figures for the previous period required by IAS 1, *Presentation of Financial Statements*, and any information in respect of earlier periods should also be stated in terms of the measuring unit current at the balance sheet date. *(29.8)*

The gain or loss on the net monetary position should be included in net income and separately disclosed. *(29.9)*

Historical Cost Financial Statements

Balance Sheet
Balance sheet amounts not already expressed in terms of the measuring unit current at the balance sheet date are restated by applying a general price index. *(29.11)*

Monetary items are not restated because they are already expressed in terms of the monetary unit current at the balance sheet date. Monetary items are money held and items to be received or paid in money. *(29.12)*

Assets and liabilities linked by agreement to changes in prices, such as index-linked bonds and loans, are adjusted in accordance with the agreement in order to ascertain the amount outstanding at the balance sheet date. These items are carried at this adjusted amount in the restated balance sheet. *(29.13)*

All other assets and liabilities are non-monetary. Some non-monetary items are carried at amounts current at the balance sheet date, such as net realisable value and market value, so they are not restated. All other non-monetary assets and liabilities are restated. *(29.14)*

Many non-monetary items are carried at cost or cost less depreciation; hence they are expressed at amounts current at their date of acquisition. The restated cost, or cost less depreciation, of each item is determined by applying to its historical cost and accumulated depreciation the change in a general price index from the date of acquisition to the balance sheet date. Hence, property, plant and equipment, investments, inventories of raw materials and merchandise, goodwill, patents, trademarks and similar assets are restated from the dates of their purchase. Inventories of partly-finished and finished goods are restated from the dates on which the costs of purchase and of conversion were incurred. (29.15)

At the beginning of the first period of application of IAS 29, the components of owners' equity, except retained earnings and any revaluation surplus, are restated by applying a general price index from the dates the components were contributed or otherwise arose. Any revaluation surplus that arose in previous periods is eliminated. Restated retained earnings are derived from all the other amounts in the restated balance sheet. (29.24)

At the end of the first period and in subsequent periods, all components of owners' equity are restated by applying a general price index from the beginning of the period or the date of contribution, if later. The movements for the period in owners' equity are disclosed in accordance with IAS 1, *Presentation of Financial Statements*. (29.25)

Income Statement

IAS 29 requires all items in the income statement to be expressed in terms of the measuring unit current at the balance sheet date. Therefore all amounts need to be restated by applying the change in the general price index from the dates when the items of income and expenses were initially recorded in the financial statements. (29.26)

Gain or Loss on Net Monetary Position

In a period of inflation, an enterprise holding an excess of monetary assets over monetary liabilities loses purchasing power and an enterprise with an excess of monetary liabilities over monetary assets gains purchasing power to the extent the assets and liabilities are not linked to a price level. This gain or loss on the net monetary position may be derived as the difference resulting from the restatement of non-monetary assets, owners' equity and income statement items and the adjustment of index-linked assets and liabilities. The gain or loss may be estimated by applying the change in a general price index to the weighted average for the period of the difference between monetary assets and monetary liabilities. (29.27)

The gain or loss on the net monetary position is included in net income. The adjustment to those assets and liabilities linked by agreement to changes in prices made in accordance with paragraph 29.13 is offset against the gain or loss on net monetary position. Other income statement items, such as interest income and expense, and foreign exchange differences related to invested or borrowed funds, are also associated with the net monetary position. Although such items are separately disclosed, it may be helpful if they are presented together with the gain or loss on net monetary position in the income statement. (29.28)

Current Cost Financial Statements

Balance Sheet

Items stated at current cost are not restated because they are already expressed in terms of the measuring unit current at the balance sheet date. Other items in the balance sheet are restated in a manner similar to that for historical cost financial statements. *(29.29)*

Income Statement

The current cost income statement, before restatement, generally reports costs current at the time at which the underlying transactions or events occurred. Cost of sales and depreciation are recorded at current costs at the time of consumption; sales and other expenses are recorded at their money amounts when they occurred. Therefore all amounts need to be restated into the measuring unit current at the balance sheet date by applying a general price index. *(29.30)*

Gain or Loss on Net Monetary Position

The gain or loss on the net monetary position is accounted for in the same manner as that for historical cost financial statements. The current cost income statement may, however, already include an adjustment reflecting the effects of changing prices on monetary items in accordance with IAS 15 (see"Information Reflecting the Effects of Changing Prices", p. 161). Such an adjustment is part of the gain or loss on net monetary position. *(29.31)*

Taxes

The restatement of financial statements in accordance with IAS 29 may give rise to differences between taxable income and accounting income. These differences are accounted for in accordance with IAS 12, *Income Taxes* (see section 4.1, p. 247). *(29.32)*

Cash Flow Statement

IAS 29 requires that all items in the cash flow statement are expressed in terms of the measuring unit current at the balance sheet date. *(29.33)*

Corresponding Figures

Corresponding figures for the previous reporting period, whether they were based on a historical cost approach or a current cost approach, are restated by applying a general price index so that the comparative financial statements are presented in terms of the measuring unit current at the end of the current reporting period. Information that is disclosed in respect of the earlier periods is also expressed in terms of the measuring unit current at the end of the reporting period. *(29.34)*

Consolidated Financial Statements

A parent that reports in the currency of a hyperinflationary economy may have subsidiaries that also report in the currencies of hyperinflationary economies. The financial statements of any such subsidiary need to be restated by applying a general price index of the country in whose currency it reports before they are included in the consolidated financial statements issued by its parent. Where such a subsidiary is a foreign subsidiary, its restated financial statements are translated at closing rates. The financial statements of subsidiaries that do not report in the currencies of hyperinflationary economies are dealt with in accordance with IAS 21, *Accounting for the Effects of Changes in Foreign Exchange Rates* (see section 2.5.1, p. 135). *(29.35)*

Selection and Use of the General Price Index

The restatement of financial statements in accordance with IAS 29 requires the use of a general price index that reflects changes in general purchasing power. It is preferable that all enterprises that report in the currency of the same economy use the same index. *(29.37)*

Economies Ceasing to be Hyperinflationary

When an economy ceases to be hyperinflationary and an enterprise discontinues the preparation and presentation of financial statements prepared in accordance with IAS 29, it should treat the amounts expressed in the measuring unit current at the end of the previous reporting period as the basis for the carrying amounts in its subsequent financial statements. *(29.38)*

Disclosures

The following disclosures should be made:

(a)   the fact that the financial statements and the corresponding figures for previous periods have been restated for the changes in the general purchasing power of the reporting currency and, as a result, are stated in terms of the measuring unit current at the balance sheet date;

(b)   whether the financial statements are based on a historical cost approach or a current cost approach; and

(c)   the identity and level of the price index at the balance sheet date and the movement in the index during the current and the previous reporting period. *(29.39)*

Information Reflecting the Effects of Changing Prices

IAS 15 is currently a non-mandatory Standard – that is, it need not be applied in order for financial statements to 'comply with IAS', as that term is used in IAS 1. The IASC Board encourages enterprises to present the information required by IAS 15.

IAS 15 should be applied in reflecting the effects of changing prices on the measurements used in the determination of an enterprise's results of operation and financial position. *(15.1)*

IAS 15 applies to enterprises whose levels of revenues, profit, assets or employment are significant in the economic environment in which they operate. When both parent company and consolidated financial statements are presented, the information called for by this Standard need only be presented on the basis of consolidated information. (15.3)

The information called for by IAS 15 is not required for a subsidiary operating in the country of domicile of its parent if consolidated information on this basis is presented by the parent. For subsidiaries operating in a country other than the country of domicile of the parent, the information called for by IAS 15 is only required when it is accepted practice for similar information to be presented by enterprises of economic significance in that country. (15.4)

Presentation of information reflecting the effects of changing prices is encouraged for other entities in the interest of promoting more informative financial reporting. (15.5)

Explanation

Prices change over time as the result of various specific or general economic and social forces. In most countries financial statements are prepared on the historical cost basis of accounting without regard either to changes in the general level of prices or to changes in specific prices of assets held, except to the extent that property, plant and equipment may have been revalued or inventories or other current assets reduced to net realisable value. The information required by IAS 15 is designed to make users of an enterprise's financial statements aware of the effects of changing prices on the results of its operations. Financial statements, however, whether prepared under the historical cost method or under a method that reflects the effects of changing prices, are not intended to indicate directly the value of the enterprise as a whole. (15.6, 15.7)

Responding to Changing Prices

Enterprises to which IAS 15 applies should present information disclosing the items set out in paragraphs 15.21 to 15.23 using an accounting method reflecting the effects of changing prices. (15.8)

Financial information intended as a response to the effects of changing prices is prepared in a number of ways. One way shows financial information in terms of general purchasing power. Another way shows current cost in place of historical cost, recognising changes in specific prices of assets. A third way combines features of both these methods. (15.9)

Underlying these responses are two basic approaches to the determination of income. One recognises income after the general purchasing power of the shareholders' equity in the enterprise has been maintained. The other recognises income after the operating capacity of the enterprise has been maintained, and may or may not include a general price level adjustment. (15.10)

General Purchasing Power Approach

The general purchasing power approach involves the restatement of some or all of the items in the financial statements for changes in the general price level. Proposals on this subject emphasise that general purchasing power restatements change the unit of account but do not change the underlying measurement bases. Under this approach, income normally reflects the effects, using an appropriate index, of general price level changes on depreciation, cost of sales and net monetary items and is reported after the general purchasing power of the shareholders' equity in the enterprise has been maintained. *(15.11)*

Current Cost Approach

The current cost approach is found in a number of different methods. In general, these use replacement cost as the primary measurement basis. If, however, replacement cost is higher than both net realisable value and present value, the higher of net realisable value and present value is usually used as the measurement basis. *(15.12)*

The replacement cost of a specific asset is normally derived from the current acquisition cost of a similar asset, new or used, or of an equivalent productive capacity or service potential. Net realisable value usually represents the net current selling price of the asset. Present value represents a current estimate of future net receipts attributable to the asset, appropriately discounted. *(15.13)*

Specific price indices are often used as a means to determine current costs for items, particularly if no recent transaction involving those items has occurred, no price lists are available or the use of price lists is not practical. *(15.14)*

Minimum Disclosures

The items to be presented are:

(a)   the amount of the adjustment to or the adjusted amount of depreciation of property, plant and equipment;

(b)   the amount of the adjustment to or the adjusted amount of cost of sales;

(c)   the adjustments relating to monetary items, the effect of borrowing, or equity interests when such adjustments have been taken into account in determining income under the accounting method adopted; and

(d)   the overall effect on results of the adjustments described in (a) and (b) and, where appropriate, (c), as well as any other items reflecting the effects of changing prices that are reported under the accounting method adopted. *(15.21)*

When a current cost method is adopted the current cost of property, plant and equipment, and of inventories, should be disclosed. *(15.22)*

Enterprises should describe the methods adopted to compute this information, including the nature of any indices used. The information should be provided on a supplementary basis unless such information is presented in the primary financial statements. *(15.23, 15.24)*

IAS 15 does not apply to the accounting and reporting policies required to be used by an enterprise in the preparation of its primary financial statements, unless those financial statements are presented on a basis that reflects the effects of changing prices. *(15.25)*

Other Disclosures

Enterprises are encouraged to provide additional disclosures, and in particular a discussion of the significance of the information in the circumstances of the enterprise. Disclosure of any adjustments to tax provisions or tax balances is usually helpful. *(15.26)*

| 2.6 | Interim Financial Reporting |

Timely and reliable interim financial reporting improves the ability of investors, creditors, and others to understand an enterprise's capacity to generate earnings and cash flows and its financial condition and liquidity.

IAS 34 does not mandate which enterprises should be required to publish interim financial reports, how frequently, or how soon after the end of an interim period. However, governments, securities regulators, stock exchanges, and accountancy bodies often require enterprises whose debt or equity securities are publicly traded to publish interim financial reports. IAS 34 applies if an enterprise is required or elects to publish an interim financial report in accordance with International Accounting Standards. The International Accounting Standards Committee encourages publicly traded enterprises to provide interim financial reports that conform to the recognition, measurement, and disclosure principles set out in IAS 34. Specifically, publicly traded enterprises are encouraged:

(a)   to provide interim financial reports at least as of the end of the first half of their financial year; and

(b)   to make their interim financial reports available not later than 60 days after the end of the interim period. *(34.1)*

Each financial report, annual or interim, is evaluated on its own for conformity to IAS. The fact that an enterprise may not have provided interim financial reports during a particular financial year or may have provided interim financial reports that do not comply with IAS 34 does not prevent the enterprise's annual financial statements from conforming to IAS if they otherwise do so. *(34.2)*

If an enterprise's interim financial report is described as complying with IAS, it must comply with all of the requirements of IAS 34. Paragraph 34.19 requires certain disclosures in that regard. *(34.3)*

IAS 34 uses the following terms:

- *Interim period* is a financial reporting period shorter than a full financial year.
- *Interim financial report* means a financial report containing either a complete set of financial statements (as described in IAS 1, *Presentation of Financial Statements,* see 2.1, p. 98), or a set of condensed financial statements (as described in IAS 34) for an interim period. *(34.4)*

Content of an Interim Financial Report

Minimum Components of an Interim Financial Report

An interim financial report should include, at a minimum, the following components:

(a) condensed balance sheet;

(b) condensed income statement;

(c) condensed statement showing either (i) all changes in equity or (ii) changes in equity other than those arising from capital transactions with owners and distributions to owners;

(d) condensed cash flow statement; and

(e) selected explanatory notes. *(34.8)*

Form and Content of Interim Financial Statements

If an enterprise publishes a complete set of financial statements in its interim financial report, the form and content of those statements should conform to the requirements of IAS 1 (see sections 2.1 - 2.3) for a complete set of financial statements. *(34.9)*

If an enterprise publishes a set of condensed financial statements in its interim financial report, those condensed statements should include, at a minimum, each of the headings and subtotals that were included in its most recent annual financial statements and the selected explanatory notes as required by IAS 34. Additional line items or notes should be included if their omission would make the condensed interim financial statements misleading. *(34.10)*

Basic and diluted earnings per share calculated in accordance with IAS 33, *Earnings Per Share*, should be presented on the face of an income statement, complete or condensed, for an interim period. *(34.11)*

Selected Explanatory Notes

An enterprise should include the following information, as a minimum, in the notes to its interim financial statements, if material and if not disclosed elsewhere in the interim financial report. The information should normally be reported on a financial year-to-date basis. However, the enterprise should also disclose any events or transactions that are material to an understanding of the current interim period:

(a)   a statement that the same accounting policies and methods of computation are followed in the interim financial statements as compared with the most recent annual financial statements or, if those policies or methods have been changed, a description of the nature and effect of the change;

(b)   explanatory comments about the seasonality or cyclicality of interim operations;

(c)   the nature and amount of items affecting assets, liabilities, equity, net income, or cash flows that are unusual because of their nature, size, or incidence;

(d)   the nature and amount of changes in estimates of amounts reported in prior interim periods of the current financial year or changes in estimates of amounts reported in prior financial years, if those changes have a material effect in the current interim period;

(e)   issuances, repurchases, and repayments of debt and equity securities;

(f)   dividends paid (aggregate or per share) separately for ordinary shares and other shares;

(g)   segment revenue and segment result for business segments or geographical segments, whichever is the enterprise's primary basis of segment reporting (disclosure of segment data is required in an enterprise's interim financial report only if IAS 14, *Segment Reporting* (see section 2.3, p. 119), requires that enterprise to disclose segment data in its annual financial statements);

(h)   material events subsequent to the end of the interim period that have not been reflected in the financial statements for the interim period;

(i)   the effect of changes in the composition of the enterprise during the interim period, including business combinations, acquisition or disposal of subsidiaries and long-term investments, restructurings, and discontinuing operations; and

(j)   changes in contingent liabilities or contingent assets since the last annual balance sheet date. *(34.16)*

Disclosure of Compliance with IAS

If an enterprise's interim financial report is in compliance with IAS 34 that fact should be disclosed. An interim financial report should not be described as complying with IAS unless it complies with all of the requirements of each applicable Standard and each applicable Interpretation of the SIC. *(34.19)*

Periods for which Interim Financial Statements are Required to be Presented

Interim reports should include interim financial statements (condensed or complete) for periods as follows:

(a)   balance sheet as of the end of the current interim period and a comparative balance sheet as of the end of the immediately preceding financial year;

(b)   income statements for the current interim period and cumulatively for the current financial year to date, with comparative income statements for the comparable interim periods (current and year to date) of the immediately preceding financial year;

(c)   statement showing changes in equity cumulatively for the current financial year to date, with a comparative statement for the comparable year-to-date period of the immediately preceding financial year; and

(d)   cash flow statement cumulatively for the current financial year to date, with a comparative statement for the comparable year-to-date period of the immediately preceding financial year. *(34.20)*

Materiality

In deciding how to recognise, measure, classify, or disclose an item for interim financial reporting purposes, materiality should be assessed in relation to the interim period financial data. In making assessments of materiality, it should be recognised that interim measurements may rely on estimates to a greater extent than measurements of annual financial data. *(34.23)*

Disclosure in Annual Financial Statements

If an estimate of an amount reported in an interim period is changed significantly during the final interim period of the financial year but a separate financial report is not published for that final interim period, the nature and amount of that change in estimate should be disclosed in a note to the annual financial statements for that financial year. *(34.26)*

Recognition and Measurement

Accounting Policies

An enterprise should apply the same accounting policies in its interim financial statements as are applied in its annual financial statements, except for accounting policy changes made after the date of the most recent annual financial statements that are to be reflected in the next annual financial statements. However, the frequency of an enterprise's reporting (annual, half-yearly, or quarterly) should not affect the measurement of its annual results. To achieve that objective, measurements for interim reporting purposes should be made on a year-to-date basis. *(34.28)*

Revenues Received Seasonally, Cyclically, or Occasionally

Revenues that are received seasonally, cyclically, or occasionally within a financial year should not be anticipated or deferred as of an interim date if anticipation or deferral would not be appropriate at the end of the enterprise's financial year. *(34.37)*

Costs Incurred Unevenly During the Financial Year

Costs that are incurred unevenly during an enterprise's financial year should be anticipated or deferred for interim reporting purposes if, and only if, it is also appropriate to anticipate or defer that type of cost at the end of the financial year. *(34.39)*

Use of Estimates

The measurement procedures to be followed in an interim financial report should be designed to ensure that the resulting information is reliable and that all material financial information that is relevant to an understanding of the financial position or performance of the enterprise is appropriately disclosed. While measurements in both annual and interim financial reports are often based on reasonable estimates, the preparation of interim financial reports generally will require a greater use of estimation methods than annual financial reports. *(34.41)*

Restatement of Previously Reported Interim Periods

A change in accounting policy, other than one for which the transition is specified by a new International Accounting Standard, should be reflected by:

(a)   restating the financial statements of prior interim periods of the current financial year and the comparable interim periods of prior financial years, if the enterprise follows the benchmark treatment under IAS 8 (see section 2.5.4. p.145); or

(b)   restating the financial statements of prior interim periods of the current financial year, if the enterprise follows the allowed alternative treatment under IAS 8. In this case, comparable interim periods of prior financial years are not restated. *(34.43)*

2.6.1	**Illustration of Periods Required to be Presented**

Enterprise Publishes Interim Financial Reports Quarterly

The enterprise's financial year ends 31 December (calendar year). The enterprise will present the following financial statements (condensed or complete) in its quarterly interim financial report as of 30 June 2001:

Balance Sheet:		
At	30 June 2001	31 December 2000
Income Statement:		
6 months ending	30 June 2001	30 June 2000
3 months ending	30 June 2001	30 June 2000
Cash Flow Statement:		
6 months ending	30 June 2001	30 June 2000
Statement of Changes in Equity:		
6 months ending	30 June 2001	30 June 2000

Figure 14

2.6.2 Examples of Applying the Recognition and Measurement Principles in IAS 34

Employer Payroll Taxes and Insurance Contributions

1. If employer payroll taxes or contributions to government-sponsored insurance funds are assessed on an annual basis, the employer's related expense is recognised in interim periods using an estimated average annual effective payroll tax or contribution rate, even though a large portion of the payments may be made early in the financial year. A common example is an employer payroll tax or insurance contribution that is imposed up to a certain maximum level of earnings per employee. For higher income employees, the maximum income is reached before the end of the financial year, and the employer makes no further payments through the end of the year.

Major Planned Periodic Maintenance or Overhaul

2. The cost of a planned major periodic maintenance or overhaul or other seasonal expenditure that is expected to occur late in the year is not anticipated for interim reporting purposes unless an event has caused the enterprise to have a legal or constructive obligation. The mere intention or necessity to incur expenditure related to the future is not sufficient to give rise to an obligation.

Provisions

3. A provision is recognised when an enterprise has no realistic alternative but to make a transfer of economic benefits as a result of an event that has created a legal or constructive obligation. The amount of the obligation is adjusted upward or downward, with a corresponding loss or gain recognised in the income statement, if the enterprise's best estimate of the amount of the obligation changes.

4. IAS 34 requires that an enterprise apply the same criteria for recognising and measuring a provision at an interim date as it would at the end of its financial year. The existence or non-existence of an obligation to transfer benefits is not a function of the length of the reporting period. It is a question of fact.

Year-End Bonuses

5. The nature of year-end bonuses varies widely. Some are earned simply by continued employment during a time period. Some bonuses are earned based on a monthly, quarterly, or annual measure of operating result. They may be purely discretionary, contractual, or based on years of historical precedent.

6. A bonus is anticipated for interim reporting purposes if, and only if, (a) the bonus is a legal obligation or past practice would make the bonus a constructive obligation for which the enterprise has no realistic alternative but to make the payments, and (b) a reliable estimate of the obligation can be made. IAS 19, *Employee Benefits* (see section 4.2, p. 277), provides guidance.

Contingent Lease Payments

7.   Contingent lease payments can be an example of a legal or constructive obligation that is recognised as a liability. If a lease provides for contingent payments based on the lessee achieving a certain level of annual sales, an obligation can arise in the interim periods of the financial year before the required annual level of sales has been achieved, if that required level of sales is expected to be achieved and the enterprise, therefore, has no realistic alternative but to make the future lease payment.

Intangible Assets

8.   An enterprise will apply the definition and recognition criteria for an intangible asset in the same way in an interim period as in an annual period. Costs incurred before the recognition criteria for an intangible asset are met are recognised as an expense. Costs incurred after the specific point in time at which the criteria are met are recognised as part of the cost of an intangible asset. "Deferring" costs as assets in an interim balance sheet in the hope that the recognition criteria will be met later in the financial year is not justified.

Pensions

9.   Pension cost for an interim period is calculated on a year-to-date basis by using the actuarially determined pension cost rate at the end of the prior financial year, adjusted for significant market fluctuations since that time and for significant curtailments, settlements, or other significant one-time events.

Vacations, Holidays, and Other Short-term Compensated Absences

10.   Accumulating compensated absences are those that are carried forward and can be used in future periods if the current period's entitlement is not used in full. IAS 19, *Employee Benefits*, requires that an enterprise measure the expected cost of and obligation for accumulating compensated absences at the amount the enterprise expects to pay as a result of the unused entitlement that has accumulated at the balance sheet date. That principle is also applied at interim financial reporting dates. Conversely, an enterprise recognises no expense or liability for non-accumulating compensated absences at an interim reporting date, just as it recognises none at an annual reporting date.

Other Planned but Irregularly Occurring Costs

11.   An enterprise's budget may include certain costs expected to be incurred irregularly during the financial year, such as charitable contributions and employee training costs. Those costs generally are discretionary even though they are planned and tend to recur from year to year. Recognising an obligation at an interim financial reporting date for such costs that have not yet been incurred generally is not consistent with the definition of a liability.

Measuring Interim Income Tax Expense

12.   Interim period income tax expense is accrued using the tax rate that would be applicable to expected total annual earnings, that is, the estimated average annual effective income tax rate applied to the pre-tax income of the interim period.

13.   This is consistent with the basic concept set out in IAS 34 that the same accounting recognition and measurement principles should be applied in an interim financial report as are applied in annual financial statements. Income taxes are assessed on an annual basis. Interim period income tax expense is calculated by applying to an interim period's pre-tax income the tax rate that would be applicable to expected total annual earnings, that is, the estimated average annual effective income tax rate. That estimated average annual rate would reflect a blend of the progressive tax rate structure expected to be applicable to the full year's earnings including enacted or substantively enacted changes in the income tax rates scheduled to take effect later in the financial year. IAS 12, *Income Taxes*, provides guidance on substantively enacted changes in tax rates. The estimated average annual income tax rate would be re-estimated on a year-to-date basis. IAS 34 requires disclosure of a significant change in estimate.

14.   To the extent practicable, a separate estimated average annual effective income tax rate is determined for each taxing jurisdiction and applied individually to the interim period pre-tax income of each jurisdiction. Similarly, if different income tax rates apply to different categories of income (such as capital gains or income earned in particular industries), to the extent practicable a separate rate is applied to each individual category of interim period pre-tax income. While that degree of precision is desirable, it may not be achievable in all cases, and a weighted average of rates across jurisdictions or across categories of income is used if it is a reasonable approximation of the effect of using more specific rates.

15.   To illustrate the application of the foregoing principle, an enterprise reporting quarterly expects to earn 10,000 pre-tax each quarter and operates in a jurisdiction with a tax rate of 20 per cent on the first 20,000 of annual earnings and 30 per cent on all additional earnings. Actual earnings match expectations. The following table shows the amount of income tax expense that is reported in each quarter:

	1st Quarter	2nd Quarter	3rd Quarter	4th Quarter	Annual
Tax expense	2,500	2,500	2,500	2,500	10,000

Figure 15

10,000 of tax is expected to be payable for the full year on 40,000 of pre-tax income.

16.   As another illustration, an enterprise reports quarterly, earns 15,000 pre-tax profit in the first quarter but expects to incur losses of 5,000 in each of the three remaining quarters (thus having zero income for the year), and operates in a jurisdiction in which its estimated average annual income tax rate is expected to

be 20 per cent. The following table shows the amount of income tax expense that is reported in each quarter:

	1st Quarter	2nd Quarter	3rd Quarter	4th Quarter	Annual
Tax expense	3,000	(1,000)	(1,000)	(1,000)	0

Figure 16

Difference in Financial Reporting Year and Tax Year

17.   If the financial reporting year and the income tax year differ, income tax expense for the interim periods of that financial reporting year is measured using separate weighted average estimated effective tax rates for each of the income tax years applied to the portion of pre-tax income earned in each of those income tax years.

18.   To illustrate, an enterprise's financial reporting year ends 30 June and it reports quarterly. Its taxable year ends 31 December. For the financial year that begins 1 July, Year 1 and ends 30 June, Year 2, the enterprise earns 10,000 pre-tax each quarter. The estimated average annual income tax rate is 30 per cent in Year 1 and 40 per cent in Year 2.

	Qtr Ending 30 Sept. Year 1	Qtr Ending 31 Dec. Year 1	Qtr Ending 31 Mar. Year 2	Qtr Ending 30 June Year 2	Year Ending 30 June Year 2
Tax expense	3,000	3,000	4,000	4,000	14,000

Figure 17

Tax Credits

19.   Some tax jurisdictions give taxpayers credits against the tax payable based on amounts of capital expenditures, exports, research and development expenditures, or other bases. Anticipated tax benefits of this type for the full year are generally reflected in computing the estimated annual effective income tax rate, because those credits are granted and calculated on an annual basis under most tax laws and regulations. On the other hand, tax benefits that relate to a one-time event are recognised in computing income tax expense in that interim period, in the same way that special tax rates applicable to particular categories of income are not blended into a single effective annual tax rate. Moreover, in some jurisdictions tax benefits or credits, including those related to capital expenditures and levels of exports, while reported on the income tax return, are more similar to a government grant and are recognised in the interim period in which they arise.

Tax Loss and Tax Credit Carrybacks and Carryforwards

20.   The benefits of a tax loss carryback are reflected in the interim period in which the related tax loss occurs. IAS 12 (see section 4.1, p. 247) provides that *"the*

benefit relating to a tax loss that can be carried back to recover current tax of a previous period should be recognised as an asset". A corresponding reduction of tax expense or increase of tax income is also recognised.

21.   IAS 12 provides that *"a deferred tax asset should be recognised for the carryforward of unused tax losses and unused tax credits to the extent that it is probable that future taxable profit will be available against which the unused tax losses and unused tax credits can be utilised".* IAS 12 provides criteria for assessing the probability of taxable profit against which the unused tax losses and credits can be utilised. Those criteria are applied at the end of each interim period and, if they are met, the effect of the tax loss carryforward is reflected in the computation of the estimated average annual effective income tax rate.

22.   To illustrate, an enterprise that reports quarterly has an operating loss carryforward of 10,000 for income tax purposes at the start of the current financial year for which a deferred tax asset has not been recognised. The enterprise earns 10,000 in the first quarter of the current year and expects to earn 10,000 in each of the three remaining quarters. Excluding the carryforward, the estimated average annual income tax rate is expected to be 40 per cent. Tax expense is as follows:

	1st Quarter	2nd Quarter	3rd Quarter	4th Quarter	Annual
Tax expense	3,000	3,000	3,000	3,000	12,000

Figure 18

Contractual or Anticipated Purchase Price Changes

23.   Volume rebates or discounts and other contractual changes in the prices of raw materials, labour, or other purchased goods and services are anticipated in interim periods, by both the payer and the recipient, if it is probable that they have been earned or will take effect. Thus, contractual rebates and discounts are anticipated but discretionary rebates and discounts are not anticipated because the resulting asset or liability would not satisfy the conditions in the Framework that an asset must be a resource controlled by the enterprise as a result of a past event and that a liability must be a present obligation whose settlement is expected to result in an outflow of resources.

Depreciation and Amortisation

24.   Depreciation and amortisation for an interim period is based only on assets owned during that interim period. It does not take into account asset acquisitions or dispositions planned for later in the financial year.

Inventories

25.   Inventories are measured for interim financial reporting by the same principles as at financial year end. IAS 2, *Inventories* (see section 3.1, p. 185), establishes standards for recognising and measuring inventories. Inventories pose particular problems at any financial reporting date because of the need to

determine inventory quantities, costs, and net realisable values. Nonetheless, the same measurement principles are applied for interim inventories. To save cost and time, enterprises often use estimates to measure inventories at interim dates to a greater extent than at annual reporting dates. Following are examples of how to apply the net realisable value test at an interim date, how interim LIFO inventories should be determined, and how to treat manufacturing variances at interim dates.

Net Realisable Value of Inventories

26. The net realisable value of inventories is determined by reference to selling prices and related costs to complete and dispose at interim dates. An enterprise will reverse a writedown to net realisable value in a subsequent interim period only if it would be appropriate to do so at the end of the financial year.

Estimating LIFO Inventories at Interim Dates

27. A reduction in the quantity of LIFO inventories is not reflected in an inventory valuation at an interim date if that reduction is expected to be restored by year end. Such a temporary reduction may result, for example, from normal seasonal fluctuations in inventory quantities or from a one-time event beyond the control of the management of the enterprise such as a shipping strike. Excluding the effects of temporary reductions in LIFO inventories is consistent with (and not an exception to) the provision of paragraph 34.28 that the frequency of an enterprise's reporting (annual, half-yearly, or quarterly) should not affect the measurement of its annual results. This principle is justified because investors and creditors can otherwise be misled by the potentially significant effect on reported earnings that would result from a temporary reduction of low-cost LIFO inventory that is expected to be replenished at much higher current costs. Also, for many companies, the use of LIFO to measure inventory costs in financial statements is income tax driven. Since income taxes are assessed on an annual basis in most jurisdictions, LIFO inventory measurements are also made on an annual basis, an approach consistent with the use of the estimated average annual income tax rate as discussed in paragraph 12, above.

Interim Period Manufacturing Cost Variances

28. Price, efficiency, spending, and volume variances of a manufacturing enterprise are recognised in income at interim reporting dates to the same extent that those variances are recognised in income at financial year end. Deferral of variances that are expected to be absorbed by year end is not appropriate because it could result in reporting inventory at the interim date at more or less than its portion of the actual cost of manufacture.

Foreign Currency Translation Gains and Losses

29. Foreign currency translation gains and losses are measured for interim financial reporting by the same principles as at financial year end.

30.   IAS 21, *The Effects of Changes in Foreign Exchange Rates* (see section 2.5.1, p. 135), specifies how to translate the financial statements for foreign operations into the reporting currency, including guidelines for using historical, average, or closing foreign exchange rates and guidelines for including the resulting adjustments in income or in equity. Consistent with IAS 21, the actual average and closing rates for the interim period are used. Enterprises do not anticipate some future changes in foreign exchange rates in the remainder of the current financial year in translating foreign operations at an interim date.

31.   If IAS 21 requires that translation adjustments be recognised as income or as expenses in the period in which they arise, that principle is applied during each interim period. Enterprises do not defer some foreign currency translation adjustments at an interim date if the adjustment is expected to reverse before the end of the financial year.

Interim Financial Reporting in Hyperinflationary Economies

32.   Interim financial reports in hyperinflationary economies are prepared by the same principles as at financial year end.

33.   IAS 29, *Financial Reporting in Hyperinflationary Economies* (see section 2.5.6, p. 158), requires that the financial statements of an enterprise that reports in the currency of a hyperinflationary economy be stated in terms of the measuring unit current at balance sheet date, and the gain or loss on the net monetary position is included in net income. Also, comparative financial data reported for prior periods is restated to the current measuring unit.

34.   Enterprises follow those same principles at interim dates, thereby presenting all interim data in the measuring unit as of the end of the interim period, with the resulting gain or loss on the net monetary position included in the interim period's net income. Enterprises do not annualise the recognition of the gain or loss. Nor do they use an estimated annual inflation rate in preparing an interim financial report in a hyperinflationary economy.

Impairment of Assets

35.   IAS 36, *Impairment of Assets* (see section 3.5, p. 214), requires that an impairment loss be recognised if the recoverable amount has declined below carrying amount.

36.   IAS 34 requires that an enterprise apply the same impairment testing, recognition, and reversal criteria at an interim date as it would at the end of its financial year. That does not mean, however, that an enterprise must necessarily make a detailed impairment calculation at the end of each interim period. Rather, an enterprise will review for indications of significant impairment since the end of the most recent financial year to determine whether such a calculation is needed.

2.6.3 Examples of the Use of Estimates in IAS 34

1. **Inventories**: Full stock-taking and valuation procedures may not be required for inventories at interim dates, although it may be done at financial year end. It may be sufficient to make estimates at interim dates based on sales margins. Similarly, at interim dates LIFO inventories can be estimated by using representative samples for each LIFO layer or pool and inflation indices.

2. **Classifications of current and non-current assets and liabilities**: Enterprises may do a more thorough investigation for classifying assets and liabilities as current or non-current at annual reporting dates than at interim dates.

3. **Provisions**: Determination of the appropriate amount of a provision (such as a provision for warranties, environmental costs, and site restoration costs) may be complex and often costly and time-consuming. Enterprises sometimes engage outside experts to assist in the annual calculations. Making similar estimates at interim dates often entails updating of the prior annual provision rather than the engaging of outside experts to do a new calculation.

4. **Pensions**: IAS 19, *Employee Benefits* (see section 4.2, p. 277), requires that an enterprise determine the present value of defined benefit obligations and the market value of plan assets at each balance sheet date and encourages an enterprise to involve a professionally qualified actuary in measurement of the obligations. For interim reporting purposes, reliable measurement is often obtainable by extrapolation of the latest actuarial valuation.

5. **Income taxes:** Enterprises may calculate income tax expense and deferred income tax liability at annual dates by applying the tax rate for each individual jurisdiction to measures of income for each jurisdiction. IAS 34, Appendix 2, paragraph 14 (see section 2.6.2, p. 171) acknowledges that while that degree of precision is desirable at interim reporting dates as well, it may not be achievable in all cases, and a weighted average of rates across jurisdictions or across categories of income is used if it is a reasonable approximation of the effect of using more specific rates.

6. **Contingencies**: The measurement of contingencies may involve the opinions of legal experts or other advisers. Formal reports from independent experts are sometimes obtained with respect to contingencies. Such opinions about litigation, claims, assessments, and other contingencies and uncertainties may or may not also be needed at interim dates.

7. **Revaluations**: IAS 16, *Property, Plant and Equipment* (see section 3.2, p. 190), allows as an alternative treatment the revaluation of property, plant, and equipment to fair value. For those revaluations, an enterprise may rely on professionally qualified valuers at annual reporting dates though not at interim reporting dates.

8. **Intercompany reconciliations**: Some intercompany balances that are reconciled on a detailed level in preparing consolidated financial statements at financial year end might be reconciled at a less detailed level in preparing consolidated financial statements at an interim date.

9.   **Specialised industries**: Because of complexity, costliness, and time, interim period measurements in specialised industries might be less precise than at financial year end. An example would be calculation of insurance reserves by insurance companies.

| 2.7 | **Disclosures in the Financial Statements of Banks and Similar Financial Institutions** |

IAS 30 should be applied in the financial statements of banks and similar financial institutions (subsequently referred to as banks). *(30.1)*

For the purposes of IAS 30, the term "bank" includes all financial institutions, one of whose principal activities is to take deposits and borrow with the objective of lending and investing and which are within the scope of banking or similar legislation. The Standard is relevant to such enterprises whether or not they have the word "bank" in their name. *(30.2)*

Accounting Policies

Banks use differing methods for the recognition and measurement of items in their financial statements. In order to comply with IAS 1, *Presentation of Financial Statements* (see section 2.1, p. 98), and thereby enable users to understand the basis on which the financial statements of a bank are prepared, accounting policies dealing with the following items may need to be disclosed:

(a)   the recognition of the principal types of income;

(b)   the valuation of investment and dealing securities;

(c)   the distinction between those transactions and other events that result in the recognition of assets and liabilities on the balance sheet and those transactions and other events that only give rise to contingencies and commitments;

(d)   the basis for the determination of losses on loans and advances and for writing off uncollectable loans and advances; and

(e)   the basis for the determination of charges for general banking risks and the accounting treatment of such charges.

Some of these topics are the subject of existing IAS while others may be dealt with at a later date. *(30.8)*

Income Statement

A bank should present an income statement which groups income and expenses by nature and discloses the amounts of the principal types of income and expenses. *(30.9)*

In addition to the requirements of other International Accounting Standards, the disclosures in the income statement or the notes to the financial statements should include, but are not limited to, the following items of income and expenses:

- Interest and similar income;
- Interest expense and similar charges;
- Dividend income;
- Fee and commission income;
- Fee and commission expense;
- Gains less losses arising from dealing securities;
- Gains less losses arising from investment securities;
- Gains less losses arising from dealing in foreign currencies;
- Other operating income;
- Losses on loans and advances;
- General administrative expenses; and
- Other operating expenses. *(30.10)*

Income and expense items should not be offset except for those relating to hedges and to assets and liabilities which have been offset in accordance with paragraph 30.23. *(30.13)*

Gains and losses arising from each of the following are normally reported on a net basis:

(a)   disposals and changes in the carrying amount of dealing securities;

(b)   disposals of investment securities; and

(c)   dealings in foreign currencies. *(30.15)*

Balance Sheet

A bank should present a balance sheet that groups assets and liabilities by nature and lists them in an order that reflects their relative liquidity. *(30.18)*

In addition to the requirements of other International Accounting Standards, the disclosures in the balance sheet or the notes to the financial statements should include, but are not limited to, the following assets and liabilities:

Assets

- Cash and balances with the central bank;
- Treasury bills and other bills eligible for rediscounting with the central bank;
- Government and other securities held for dealing purposes;
- Placements with, and loans and advances to, other banks;
- Other money market placements;
- Loans and advances to customers; and
- Investment securities.

Liabilities

- Deposits from other banks;
- Other money market deposits;
- Amounts owed to other depositors;
- Certificates of deposits;
- Promissory notes and other liabilities evidenced by paper; and
- Other borrowed funds. *(30.19)*

The distinction between balances with other banks and those with other parts of the money market and from other depositors is relevant information because it gives an understanding of a bank's relations with, and dependence on, other banks and the money market. Hence, a bank discloses separately:

(a)   balances with the central bank;

(b)   placements with other banks;

(c)   other money market placements;

(d)   deposits from other banks;

(e)   other money market deposits; and

(f)   other deposits. *(30.21)*

A bank generally does not know the holders of its certificates of deposit because they are usually traded on an open market. Hence, a bank discloses separately deposits that have been obtained through the issue of its own certificates of deposit or other negotiable paper. *(30.22)*

The amount at which any asset or liability is stated in the balance sheet should not be offset by the deduction of another liability or asset unless a legal right of set-off exists and the offsetting represents the expectation as to the realisation or settlement of the asset or liability. *(30.23)*

A bank should disclose the fair values of each class of its financial assets and liabilities as required by IAS 32, *Financial Instruments: Disclosure and Presentation* (see section 6.2, p. 370), and IAS 39, *Financial Instruments: Recognition and Measurement* (see section 6.1, p. 349). *(30.24)*

Contingent Liabilities and Commitments Including Off Balance Sheet Items

A bank should disclose the following contingent liabilities and commitments:

(a)   the nature and amount of commitments to extend credit that are irrevocable because they cannot be withdrawn at the discretion of the bank without the risk of incurring significant penalty or expense; and

(b)   the nature and amount of contingent liabilities and commitments arising from off balance sheet items including those relating to:

(i)   direct credit substitutes including general guarantees of indebtedness, bank acceptance guarantees and standby letters of credit serving as financial guarantees for loans and securities;

(ii)   certain transaction-related contingent liabilities including performance bonds, bid bonds, warranties and standby letters of credit related to particular transactions;

(iii) short-term self-liquidating trade-related contingent liabilities arising from the movement of goods, such as documentary credits where the underlying shipment is used as security;

(iv)   those sale and repurchase agreements not recognised in the balance sheet;

(v)   interest and foreign exchange rate related items including swaps, options and futures; and

(vi)   other commitments, note issuance facilities and revolving underwriting facilities. *(30.26)*

Maturities of Assets and Liabilities

A bank should disclose an analysis of assets and liabilities into relevant maturity groupings based on the remaining period at the balance sheet date to the contractual maturity date. *(30.30)*

The maturity groupings applied to individual assets and liabilities differ between banks and in their appropriateness to particular assets and liabilities. Examples of periods used include the following:

(a)   up to 1 month;

(b)   from 1 month to 3 months;

(c)   from 3 months to 1 year;

(d)   from 1 year to 5 years; and

(e)   from 5 years and over.

Frequently the periods are combined, for example, in the case of loans and advances, by grouping those under one year and those over one year. When repayment is spread over a period of time, each instalment is allocated to the period in which it is contractually agreed or expected to be paid or received. *(30.33)*

Maturities could be expressed in terms of:

(a)   the remaining period to the repayment date;

(b)   the original period to the repayment date; or

(c)   the remaining period to the next date at which interest rates may be changed. *(30.35)*

Concentrations of Assets, Liabilities and Off Balance Sheet Items

A bank should disclose any significant concentrations of its assets, liabilities and off balance sheet items. Such disclosures should be made in terms of geographical areas, customer or industry groups or other concentrations of risk. A bank should also disclose the amount of significant net foreign currency exposures. *(30.40)*

Losses on Loans and Advances

A bank should disclose the following:

(a) the accounting policy which describes the basis on which uncollectable loans and advances are recognised as an expense and written off;

(b) details of the movements in the provision for losses on loans and advances during the period. It should disclose separately the amount recognised as an expense in the period for losses on uncollectable loans and advances, the amount charged in the period for loans and advances written off and the amount credited in the period for loans and advances previously written off that have been recovered;

(c) the aggregate amount of the provision for losses on loans and advances at the balance sheet date; and

(d) the aggregate amount included in the balance sheet for loans and advances on which interest is not being accrued and the basis used to determine the carrying amount of such loans and advances. *(30.43)*

Any amounts set aside in respect of losses on loans and advances in addition to those losses that have been specifically identified or potential losses which experience indicates are present in the portfolio of loans and advances should be accounted for as appropriations of retained earnings. Any credits resulting from the reduction of such amounts result in an increase in retained earnings and are not included in the determination of net profit or loss for the period. *(30.44)*

General Banking Risks

Any amounts set aside in respect of general banking risks, including future losses and other unforeseeable risks or contingencies in addition to those for which accrual must be made in accordance with IAS 10, *Contingencies and Events Occurring After the Balance Sheet Date*, should be disclosed separately as appropriations of retained earnings. Any credits resulting from the reduction of such amounts result in an increase in retained earnings and are not included in the determination of net profit or loss for the period. *(30.50)*

Assets Pledged as Security

A bank should disclose the aggregate amount of secured liabilities and the nature and carrying amount of the assets pledged as security. *(30.53)*

2.8 Accounting and Reporting by Retirement Benefit Plans

IAS 26 should be applied in the financial statements of retirement benefit plans where such Statements are prepared. *(26.1)*

The Standard deals with accounting and reporting by the plan to all participants as a group. It does not deal with reports to individual participants about their retirement benefit rights. *(26.3)*

IAS 19, *Employee Benefits* (see section 4.2, p. 277), is concerned with the determination of the cost of retirement benefits in the financial statements of employers having plans. Hence IAS 26 complements IAS 19. *(26.4)*

Retirement benefit plans may be defined contribution plans or defined benefit plans. Many require the creation of separate funds, which may or may not have separate legal identity and may or may not have trustees, to which contributions are made and from which retirement benefits are paid. IAS 26 applies regardless of whether such a fund is created and regardless of whether there are trustees. *(26.5)*

IAS 26 uses the following terms:
- *Retirement benefit plans* are arrangements whereby an enterprise provides benefits for its employees on or after termination of service (either in the form of an annual income or as a lump sum) when such benefits, or the employer's contributions towards them, can be determined or estimated in advance of retirement from the provisions of a document or from the enterprise's practices.
- *Defined contribution plans* are retirement benefit plans under which amounts to be paid as retirement benefits are determined by contributions to a fund together with investment earnings thereon.
- *Defined benefit plans* are retirement benefit plans under which amounts to be paid as retirement benefits are determined by reference to a formula usually based on employees' earnings and/or years of service.
- *Funding* is the transfer of assets to an entity (the *fund*) separate from the employer's enterprise to meet future obligations for the payment of retirement benefits.

For the purposes of IAS 26 the following terms are also used:
- *Participants* are the members of a retirement benefit plan and others who are entitled to benefits under the plan.
- *Net assets available for benefits* are the assets of a plan less liabilities other than the actuarial present value of promised retirement benefits.
- *Actuarial present value of promised retirement benefits* is the present value of the expected payments by a retirement benefit plan to existing and past employees, attributable to the service already rendered.
- *Vested benefits* are benefits, the rights to which, under the conditions of a retirement benefit plan, are not conditional on continued employment. *(26.8)*

Defined Contribution Plans

The report of a defined contribution plan should contain a statement of net assets available for benefits and a description of the funding policy. *(26.13)*

Defined Benefit Plans

The report of a defined benefit plan should contain either:

(a)   a statement that shows:

   (i)   the net assets available for benefits;

   (ii)   the actuarial present value of promised retirement benefits, distinguishing between vested benefits and non-vested benefits; and

   (iii) the resulting excess or deficit; or

(b)   a statement of net assets available for benefits including either:

   (i)   a note disclosing the actuarial present value of promised retirement benefits, distinguishing between vested benefits and non-vested benefits; or

   (ii)   a reference to this information in an accompanying actuarial report.

If an actuarial valuation has not been prepared at the date of the report, the most recent valuation should be used as a base and the date of the valuation disclosed. *(26.17)*

The actuarial present value of promised retirement benefits should be based on the benefits promised under the terms of the plan on service rendered to date using either current salary levels or projected salary levels with disclosure of the basis used. The effect of any changes in actuarial assumptions that have had a significant effect on the actuarial present value of promised retirement benefits should also be disclosed. *(26.18)*

The report should explain the relationship between the actuarial present value of promised retirement benefits and the net assets available for benefits, and the policy for the funding of promised benefits. *(26.19)*

Actuarial Present Value of Promised Retirement Benefits

The present value of the expected payments by a retirement benefit plan may be calculated and reported using current salary levels or projected salary levels up to the time of retirement of participants. *(26.23)*

Frequency of Actuarial Valuations

In many countries, actuarial valuations are not obtained more frequently than every three years. If an actuarial valuation has not been prepared at the date of the report, the most recent valuation is used as a base and the date of the valuation disclosed. *(26.27)*

Report Content

For defined benefit plans, information is presented in one of the following formats which reflect different practices in the disclosure and presentation of actuarial information:

(a)   a statement is included in the report that shows the net assets available for benefits, the actuarial present value of promised retirement benefits, and the resulting excess or deficit. The report of the plan also contains statements of changes in net assets available for benefits and changes in the actuarial present value of promised retirement benefits. The report may include a separate actuary's report supporting the actuarial present value of promised retirement benefits;

(b)   a report that includes a statement of net assets available for benefits and a statement of changes in net assets available for benefits. The actuarial present value of promised retirement benefits is disclosed in a note to the statements. The report may also include a report from an actuary supporting the actuarial present value of promised retirement benefits; and

(c)   a report that includes a statement of net assets available for benefits and a statement of changes in net assets available for benefits with the actuarial present value of promised retirement benefits contained in a separate actuarial report.

In each format a trustees' report in the nature of a management or directors' report and an investment report may also accompany the statements. *(26.28)*

The formats described in (a) and (b) above are considered acceptable under this Standard, as is the format described in (c) so long as the financial information contains a reference to, and is accompanied by, an actuarial report that includes the actuarial present value of promised retirement benefits. *(26.31)*

All Plans

Valuation of Plan Assets

Retirement benefit plan investments should be carried at fair value. In the case of marketable securities fair value is market value. Where plan investments are held for which an estimate of fair value is not possible disclosure should be made of the reason why fair value is not used. *(26.32)*

Disclosure

The report of a retirement benefit plan, whether defined benefit or defined contribution, should also contain the following information:

(a)   a statement of changes in net assets available for benefits;

(b)   a summary of significant accounting policies; and

(c)   a description of the plan and the effect of any changes in the plan during the period. *(26.34)*

Chapter 3

Accounting for Assets

The accounting for tangible assets is covered by the following IAS:

- **IAS 2** deals with the accounting treatment for inventories under the historical cost system.

- **IAS 16** prescribes the accounting treatment for property, plant and equipment.

- **IAS 40** prescribes the permitted alternative treatments for accounting for investment property.

- **IAS 38** prescribes the accounting treatment for intangible assets that are not dealt with specifically in another International Accounting Standard comprise.

- **IAS 36** requires the enterprise to recognise an impairment loss whenever an asset is impaired. IAS 36 also specifies when an enterprise should reverse an impairment loss and it prescribes certain disclosures for impaired assets.

3.1	Inventories

IAS 2 prescribes the accounting treatment for inventories under the historical cost system. A primary issue in accounting for inventories is the amount of cost to be recognised as an asset and carried forward until the inventory is sold and the related revenues are recognised. IAS 2 provides practical guidance on the determination of cost and its subsequent recognition as an expense, including any write-down to net realisable value. It also provides guidance on the cost formulas that are used to assign costs to inventories.

IAS 2 should be applied in financial statements prepared in the context of the historical cost system in accounting for inventories other than:

(a) work in progress arising under construction contracts, including directly related service contracts (see IAS 11, *Construction Contracts*, section 5.2, p. 331);

(b) financial instruments (see chapter 6); and

(c) producers' inventories of livestock, agricultural and forest products, and mineral ores to the extent that they are measured at net realisable value in accordance with well established practices in certain industries. *(2.1)*

The inventories referred to in paragraph (c) are measured at net realisable value at certain stages of production. This occurs, for example, when agricultural crops have been harvested or mineral ores have been extracted and sale is assured under a forward contract or a government guarantee, or when a homogenous market exists and there is a negligible risk of failure to sell. These inventories are excluded from the scope of IAS 2. *(2.3)*

IAS 2 uses the following terms:

- *Inventories* are assets:

    (a)   held for sale in the ordinary course of business;

    (b)   in the process of production for such sale; or

    (c)   in the form of materials or supplies to be consumed in the production process or in the rendering of services.

- *Net realisable value* is the estimated selling price in the ordinary course of business less the estimated costs of completion and the estimated costs necessary to make the sale. *(2.4)*

Inventories encompass goods purchased and held for resale including, for example, merchandise purchased by a retailer and held for resale, or land and other property held for resale. Inventories also encompass finished goods produced, or work in progress being produced, by the enterprise and include materials and supplies awaiting use in the production process. In the case of a service provider, inventories include the costs of the service, as described in paragraph 2.16, for which the enterprise has not yet recognised the related revenue (see IAS 18, *Revenue*, section 5.1, p. 321). *(2.5)*

Measurement of Inventories

Inventories should be measured at the lower of cost and net realisable value. *(2.6)*

Cost of Inventories

The cost of inventories should comprise all costs of purchase, costs of conversion and other costs incurred in bringing the inventories to their present location and condition. *(2.7)*

Costs of Purchase

The costs of purchase of inventories comprise the purchase price, import duties and other taxes (other than those subsequently recoverable by the enterprise from the taxing authorities), and transport, handling and other costs directly attributable to the acquisition of finished goods, materials and services. Trade discounts, rebates and other similar items are deducted in determining the costs of purchase. *(2.8)*

The costs of purchase may include foreign exchange differences which arise directly on the recent acquisition of inventories invoiced in a foreign currency in the rare circumstances permitted in the allowed alternative treatment in IAS 21, *The Effects of Changes in Foreign Exchange Rates* (see section 2.5.1, p. 135). These exchange differences are limited to those resulting from a severe devaluation or depreciation of a currency against which there is no practical means of hedging and that affects liabilities which cannot be settled and which arise on the recent acquisition of the inventories. *(2.9)*

Costs of Conversion

The costs of conversion of inventories include costs directly related to the units of production, such as direct labour. They also include a systematic allocation of fixed and variable production overheads that are incurred in converting materials into finished goods. Fixed production overheads are those indirect costs of production that remain relatively constant regardless of the volume of production, such as depreciation and maintenance of factory buildings and equipment, and the cost of factory management and administration. Variable production overheads are those indirect costs of production that vary directly, or nearly directly, with the volume of production, such as indirect materials and indirect labour. *(2.10)*

Other Costs

Other costs are included in the cost of inventories only to the extent that they are incurred in bringing the inventories to their present location and condition. For example, it may be appropriate to include non-production overheads or the costs of designing products for specific customers in the cost of inventories. *(2.13)*

Examples of costs excluded from the cost of inventories and recognised as expenses in the period in which they are incurred are:

(a)   abnormal amounts of wasted materials, labour, or other production costs;

(b)   storage costs, unless those costs are necessary in the production process prior to a further production stage;

(c)   administrative overheads that do not contribute to bringing inventories to their present location and condition; and

(d)   selling costs. *(2.14)*

In limited circumstances, borrowing costs are included in the cost of inventories. These circumstances are identified in the allowed alternative treatment in IAS 23, *Borrowing Costs* (see section 5.4, p. 345). *(2.15)*

Cost of Inventories of a Service Provider

The cost of inventories of a service provider consists primarily of the labour and other costs of personnel directly engaged in providing the service, including supervisory personnel, and attributable overheads. Labour and other costs relating to sales and general administrative personnel are not included but are recognised as expenses in the period in which they are incurred. *(2.16)*

Techniques for the Measurement of Cost

Techniques for the measurement of the cost of inventories, such as the standard cost method or the retail method, may be used for convenience if the results approximate cost. Standard costs take into account normal levels of materials and supplies, labour, efficiency and capacity utilisation. They are regularly reviewed and, if necessary, revised in the light of current conditions. *(2.17)*

Cost Formulas

The cost of inventories of items that are not ordinarily interchangeable and goods or services produced and segregated for specific projects should be assigned by using specific identification of their individual costs. *(2.19)*

Benchmark Treatment

The cost of inventories, other than those dealt with in paragraph 2.19, should be assigned by using the first-in, first-out (FIFO), or weighted average cost formulas. *(2.21)*

Allowed Alternative Treatment

The cost of inventories, other than those dealt with in paragraph 2.19, should be assigned by using the last-in, first-out (LIFO) formula. *(2.23)*

Consistency of Cost Formulas

An enterprise should use the same cost formula for all inventories having similar nature and use to the enterprise. For inventories with different nature or use (for example, certain commodities used in one business segment and the same type of commodities used in another business segment), different cost formulas may be justified. A difference in geographical location of inventories (and in the respective tax rules), by itself, is not sufficient to justify the use of different cost formulas. *(SIC-1)*

Net Realisable Value

The cost of inventories may not be recoverable if those inventories are damaged, if they have become wholly or partially obsolete, or if their selling prices have declined. The cost of inventories may also not be recoverable if the estimated costs of completion or the estimated costs to be incurred to make the sale have increased. The practice of writing inventories down below cost to net realisable value is consistent with the view that assets should not be carried in excess of amounts expected to be realised from their sale or use. *(2.25)*

Inventories are usually written down to net realisable value on an item by item basis. In some circumstances, however, it may be appropriate to group similar or related items. *(2.26)*

Estimates of net realisable value are based on the most reliable evidence available at the time the estimates are made as to the amount the inventories are expected to realise. These estimates take into consideration fluctuations of price or cost directly relating to events occurring after the end of the period to the extent that such events confirm conditions existing at the end of the period. *(2.27)*

Estimates of net realisable value also take into consideration the purpose for which the inventory is held. For example, the net realisable value of the quantity of inventory held to satisfy firm sales or service contracts is based on the contract price.

If the sales contracts are for less than the inventory quantities held, the net realisable value of the excess is based on general selling prices. *(2.28)*

Materials and other supplies held for use in the production of inventories are not written down below cost if the finished products in which they will be incorporated are expected to be sold at or above cost. However, when a decline in the price of materials indicates that the cost of the finished products will exceed net realisable value, the materials are written down to net realisable value. In such circumstances, the replacement cost of the materials may be the best available measure of their net realisable value. *(2.29)*

A new assessment is made of net realisable value in each subsequent period. When the circumstances which previously caused inventories to be written down below cost no longer exist, the amount of the write-down is reversed so that the new carrying amount is the lower of the cost and the revised net realisable value. *(2.30)*

Recognition as an Expense

When inventories are sold, the carrying amount of those inventories should be recognised as an expense in the period in which the related revenue is recognised. The amount of any write-down of inventories to net realisable value and all losses of inventories should be recognised as an expense in the period the write-down or loss occurs. The amount of any reversal of any write-down of inventories, arising from an increase in net realisable value, should be recognised as a reduction in the amount of inventories recognised as an expense in the period in which the reversal occurs. *(2.31)*

Disclosure

The financial statements should disclose:

(a)   the accounting policies adopted in measuring inventories, including the cost formula used;

(b)   the total carrying amount of inventories and the carrying amount in classifications appropriate to the enterprise;

(c)   the carrying amount of inventories carried at net realisable value;

(d)   the amount of any reversal of any write-down that is recognised as income in the period of reversal;

(e)   the circumstances or events that led to the reversal of a write-down of inventories; and

(f)   the carrying amount of inventories pledged as security for liabilities. *(2.34)*

When the cost of inventories is determined using the LIFO formula in accordance with the allowed alternative treatment, the financial statements should disclose the difference between the amount of inventories as shown in the balance sheet and either:

(a)   the lower of the amount arrived at using the FIFO formula under the Benchmark treatment and net realisable value; or

(b)   the lower of current cost at the balance sheet date and net realisable value. *(2.36)*

The financial statements should disclose either:

(a)   the cost of inventories recognised as an expense during the period; or

(b)   the operating costs, applicable to revenues, recognised as an expense during the period, classified by their nature. *(2.37)*

3.2   Tangible Assets

Property, Plant and Equipment

The principal issues in accounting for property, plant and equipment are the timing of recognition of the assets, the determination of their carrying amounts and the depreciation charges to be recognised in relation to them.

IAS 16 requires an item of property, plant and equipment to be recognised as an asset when it satisfies the definition and recognition criteria for an asset in the Framework for the Preparation and Presentation of Financial Statements.

IAS 16 Standard does not apply to:

(a)   forests and similar regenerative natural resources; and

(b)   mineral rights, the exploration for and extraction of minerals, oil, natural gas and similar non-regenerative resources.

However, IAS 16 does apply to property, plant and equipment used to develop or maintain the activities or assets covered in (a) or (b) but separable from those activities or assets. *(16.2)*

IAS 16 uses the following terms:

• *Property, plant and equipment* are tangible assets that:

(a)   are held by an enterprise for use in the production or supply of goods or services, for rental to others, or for administrative purposes; and

(b)   are expected to be used during more than one period.

• *Depreciation* is the systematic allocation of the depreciable amount of an asset over its useful life.

• *Depreciable amount* is the cost of an asset, or other amount substituted for cost in the financial statements, less its residual value.

- *Useful life* is either:

  (a) the period of time over which an asset is expected to be used by the enterprise; or

  (b) the number of production or similar units expected to be obtained from the asset by the enterprise.

- *Cost* is the amount of cash or cash equivalents paid or the fair value of the other consideration given to acquire an asset at the time of its acquisition or construction.

- *Residual value* is the net amount which the enterprise expects to obtain for an asset at the end of its useful life after deducting the expected costs of disposal.

- *Fair value* is the amount for which an asset could be exchanged between knowledgeable, willing parties in an arm's length transaction.

- An *impairment loss* is the amount by which the carrying amount of an asset exceeds its recoverable amount.

- *Carrying amount* is the amount at which an asset is recognised in the balance sheet after deducting any accumulated depreciation and accumulated impairment losses thereon. *(16.6)*

Recognition of Property, Plant and Equipment

An item of property, plant and equipment should be recognised as an asset when:

(a) it is probable that future economic benefits associated with the asset will flow to the enterprise; and

(b) the cost of the asset to the enterprise can be measured reliably. *(16.7)*

In determining whether an item satisfies the first criterion for recognition, an enterprise needs to assess the degree of certainty attaching to the flow of future economic benefits on the basis of the available evidence at the time of initial recognition. Existence of sufficient certainty that the future economic benefits will flow to the enterprise necessitates an assurance that the enterprise will receive the rewards attaching to the asset and will undertake the associated risks. This assurance is usually only available when the risks and rewards have passed to the enterprise. *(16.9)*

The second criterion for recognition is usually readily satisfied because the exchange transaction evidencing the purchase of the asset identifies its cost. In the case of a self-constructed asset, a reliable measurement of the cost can be made from the transactions with parties external to the enterprise for the acquisition of the materials, labour and other inputs used during the construction process. *(16.10)*

Initial Measurement of Property, Plant and Equipment

An item of property, plant and equipment which qualifies for recognition as an asset should initially be measured at its cost. *(16.14)*

Components of Cost

The cost of an item of property, plant and equipment comprises its purchase price, including import duties and non-refundable purchase taxes, and any directly attributable costs of bringing the asset to working condition for its intended use; any trade discounts and rebates are deducted in arriving at the purchase price. *(16.15)*

Subsequent Expenditure

Subsequent expenditure relating to an item of property, plant and equipment that has already been recognised should be added to the carrying amount of the asset when it is probable that future economic benefits, in excess of the originally assessed standard of performance of the existing asset, will flow to the enterprise. All other subsequent expenditure should be recognised as an expense in the period in which it is incurred. *(16.23)*

Measurement Subsequent to Initial Recognition

Benchmark Treatment

Subsequent to initial recognition as an asset, an item of property, plant and equipment should be carried at its cost less any accumulated depreciation and any accumulated impairment losses. *(16.28)*

Allowed Alternative Treatment

Subsequent to initial recognition as an asset, an item of property, plant and equipment should be carried at a revalued amount, being its fair value at the date of the revaluation less any subsequent accumulated depreciation and subsequent accumulated impairment losses. Revaluations should be made with sufficient regularity such that the carrying amount does not differ materially from that which would be determined using fair value at the balance sheet date. *(16.29)*

Revaluations

The fair value of land and buildings is usually its market value. This value is determined by appraisal normally undertaken by professionally qualified valuers. *(16.30)*

The fair value of items of plant and equipment is usually their market value determined by appraisal. When there is no evidence of market value because of the specialised nature of the plant and equipment and because these items are rarely sold, except as part of a continuing business, they are valued at their depreciated replacement cost. *(16.31)*

The frequency of revaluations depends upon the movements in the fair values of the items of property, plant and equipment being revalued. *(16.32)*

When an item of property, plant and equipment is revalued, any accumulated depreciation at the date of the revaluation is either:

(a)   restated proportionately with the change in the gross carrying amount of the asset so that the carrying amount of the asset after revaluation equals its revalued amount. This method is often used when an asset is revalued by means of an index to its depreciated replacement cost; or

(b)   eliminated against the gross carrying amount of the asset and the net amount restated to the revalued amount of the asset. For example, this method is used for buildings which are revalued to their market value.

The amount of the adjustment arising on the restatement or elimination of accumulated depreciation forms part of the increase or decrease in carrying amount. *(16.33)*

When an item of property, plant and equipment is revalued, the entire class of property, plant and equipment to which that asset belongs should be revalued. A class of property, plant and equipment is a grouping of assets of a similar nature and use in an enterprise's operations. (16.34, 16.35)

When an asset's carrying amount is increased as a result of a revaluation, the increase should be credited directly to equity under the heading of revaluation surplus. However, a revaluation increase should be recognised as income to the extent that it reverses a revaluation decrease of the same asset previously recognised as an expense. *(16.37)*

When an asset's carrying amount is decreased as a result of a revaluation, the decrease should be recognised as an expense. However, a revaluation decrease should be charged directly against any related revaluation surplus to the extent that the decrease does not exceed the amount held in the revaluation surplus in respect of that same asset. *(16.38)*

The revaluation surplus included in equity may be transferred directly to retained earnings when the surplus is realised. The whole surplus may be realised on the retirement or disposal of the asset. However, some of the surplus may be realised as the asset is used by the enterprise; in such a case, the amount of the surplus realised is the difference between depreciation based on the revalued carrying amount of the asset and depreciation based on the asset's original cost. The transfer from revaluation surplus to retained earnings is not made through the income statement. *(16.39)*

Depreciation

The depreciable amount of an item of property, plant and equipment should be allocated on a systematic basis over its useful life. The depreciation method used should reflect the pattern in which the asset's economic benefits are consumed by the enterprise. The depreciation charge for each period should be recognised as an expense unless it is included in the carrying amount of another asset. *(16.41)*

The depreciable amount of an asset is determined after deducting the residual value of the asset. In practice, the residual value of an asset is often insignificant and therefore is immaterial in the calculation of the depreciable amount. When the benchmark treatment is adopted and the residual value is likely to be significant, the residual value is estimated at the date of acquisition and is not subsequently increased for changes in prices. However, when the allowed alternative treatment is adopted, a new estimate is made at the date of any subsequent revaluation of the asset. The estimate is based on the residual value prevailing at the date of the estimate for similar assets which have reached the end of their useful lives and which have operated under conditions similar to those in which the asset will be used. *(16.46)*

A variety of depreciation methods can be used to allocate the depreciable amount of an asset on a systematic basis over its useful life. These methods include the straight-line method, the diminishing balance method and the sum-of-the-units method. Straight-line depreciation results in a constant charge over the useful life of the asset. The diminishing balance method results in a decreasing charge over the useful life of the asset. The sum-of-the-units method results in a charge based on the expected use or output of the asset. The method used for an asset is selected based on the expected pattern of economic benefits and is consistently applied from period to period unless there is a change in the expected pattern of economic benefits from that asset. *(16.47)*

The depreciation charge for a period is usually recognised as an expense. However, in some circumstances, the economic benefits embodied in an asset are absorbed by the enterprise in producing other assets rather than giving rise to an expense. In this case, the depreciation charge comprises part of the cost of the other asset and is included in its carrying amount. *(16.48)*

Review of Useful Life

The useful life of an item of property, plant and equipment should be reviewed periodically and, if expectations are significantly different from previous estimates, the depreciation charge for the current and future periods should be adjusted. *(16.49)*

Review of Depreciation Method

The depreciation method applied to property, plant and equipment should be reviewed periodically and, if there has been a significant change in the expected pattern of economic benefits from those assets, the method should be changed to reflect the changed pattern. When such a change in depreciation method is necessary the change should be accounted for as a change in accounting estimate and the depreciation charge for the current and future periods should be adjusted. *(16.52)*

Recoverability of the Carrying Amount - Impairment Losses

To determine whether an item of property, plant and equipment is impaired, an enterprise applies IAS 36, *Impairment of Assets* (see section 3.5, p. 314). That Standard explains how an enterprise reviews the carrying amount of its assets, how it determines the recoverable amount of an asset and when it recognises or reverses an impairment loss. *(16.53)*

IAS 22, *Business Combinations* (see section 7.1, p. 389), explains how to deal with an impairment loss recognised before the end of the first annual accounting period commencing after a business combination that is an acquisition. *(16.54)*

Retirements and Disposals

An item of property, plant and equipment should be eliminated from the balance sheet on disposal or when the asset is permanently withdrawn from use and no future economic benefits are expected from its disposal. *(16.55)*

Gains or losses arising from the retirement or disposal of an item of property, plant and equipment should be determined as the difference between the estimated net disposal proceeds and the carrying amount of the asset and should be recognised as income or expense in the income statement. *(16.56)*

Disclosure

The financial statements should disclose, for each class of property, plant and equipment:

(a)   the measurement bases used for determining the gross carrying amount. When more than one basis has been used, the gross carrying amount for that basis in each category should be disclosed;

(b)   the depreciation methods used;

(c)   the useful lives or the depreciation rates used;

(d)   the gross carrying amount and the accumulated depreciation (aggregated with accumulated impairment losses) at the beginning and end of the period;

(e)   a reconciliation of the carrying amount at the beginning and end of the period showing:

  (i)   additions;

  (ii)   disposals;

  (iii) acquisitions through business combinations;

  (iv)   increases or decreases during the period resulting from revaluations under this Standard and from impairment losses recognised or reversed directly in equity under IAS 36, *Impairment of Assets* (if any);

  (v)   impairment losses recognised in the income statement during the period under IAS 36 (if any);

  (vi)   impairment losses reversed in the income statement during the period under IAS 36 (if any);

  (vii) depreciation;

  (viii) the net exchange differences arising on the translation of the financial statements of a foreign entity; and

  (ix)   other movements.

Comparative information is not required for the reconciliation in (e) above. *(16.60)*

The financial statements should also disclose:

(a)   the existence and amounts of restrictions on title, and property, plant and equipment pledged as security for liabilities;

(b)   the accounting policy for the estimated costs of restoring the site of items of property, plant or equipment;

(c)   the amount of expenditures on account of property, plant and equipment in the course of construction; and

(d)   the amount of commitments for the acquisition of property, plant and equipment. *(16.61)*

When items of property, plant and equipment are stated at revalued amounts the following should be disclosed:

(a)   the basis used to revalue the assets;

(b)   the effective date of the revaluation;

(c)   whether an independent valuer was involved;

(d)   the nature of any indices used to determine replacement cost;

(e)   the carrying amount of each class of property, plant and equipment that would have been included in the financial statements had the assets been carried under the benchmark treatment in this Standard; and

(f)   the revaluation surplus, indicating the movement for the period and any restrictions on the distribution of the balance to shareholders. *(16.64)*

3.3   Investment Property

IAS 40 should be applied in the recognition, measurement and disclosure of investment property *(40.1)*.

Definitions

IAS 40 uses the following terms:

- *Investment property* is property (land or a building - or part of a building - or both) held (by the owner or by the lessee under a finance lease) to earn rentals or for capital appreciation or both, rather than for:

  (a)   use in the production or supply of goods or services or for administrative purposes; or

  (b)   sale in the ordinary course of business.

- *Owner-occupied property* is property held (by the owner or by the lessee under a finance lease) for use in the production or supply of goods or services or for administrative purposes.
- *Fair value* is the amount for which an asset could be exchanged between knowledgeable, willing parties in an arm's length transaction.
- *Cost* is the amount of cash or cash equivalents paid or the fair value of other consideration given to acquire an asset at the time of its acquisition or construction.
- *Carrying amount* is the amount at which an asset is recognised in the balance sheet. *(40.4)*

Investment property is held to earn rentals or for capital appreciation or both. Therefore, an investment property generates cash flows largely independently of the other assets held by an enterprise. This distinguishes investment property from owner-occupied property. The production or supply of goods or services (or the use of property for administrative purposes) generates cash flows that are attributable not merely to property, but also to other assets used in the production or supply process. IAS 16, *Property, Plant and Equipment*, applies to owner-occupied property. *(40.5)*

The following are examples of investment property:

(a)   land held for long-term capital appreciation rather than for short-term sale in the ordinary course of business;

(b)   land held for a currently undetermined future use. (If an enterprise has not determined that it will use the land either as owner-occupied property or for short-term sale in the ordinary course of business, the land is considered to be held for capital appreciation);

(c)   a building owned by the reporting enterprise (or held by the reporting enterprise under a finance lease) and leased out under one or more operating leases; and

(d)   a building that is vacant but is held to be leased out under one or more operating leases. *(40.6)*

The following are examples of items that are not investment property and therefore fall outside the scope of this Standard:

(a)   property held for sale in the ordinary course of business or in the process of construction or development for such sale (see IAS 2, *Inventories*, section 3.1, p. 185), for example, property acquired exclusively with a view to subsequent disposal in the near future or for development and resale;

(b)   property being constructed or developed on behalf of third parties (see IAS 11, *Construction Contracts*, section 5.2, p. 331);

(c)   owner-occupied property (see IAS 16, p. 190), including (among other things) property held for future use as owner-occupied property, property held for future development and subsequent use as owner-occupied property, property occupied by employees (whether or not the employees pay rent at market rates) and owner-occupied property awaiting disposal; and

(d)   property that is being constructed or developed for future use as investment property. IAS 16 applies to such property until construction or development is complete, at which time the property becomes investment property and this Standard applies. However, this Standard does apply to existing investment property that is being redeveloped for continued future use as investment property. *(40.7)*

Certain properties include a portion that is held to earn rentals or for capital appreciation and another portion that is held for use in the production or supply of goods or services or for administrative purposes. If these portions could be sold separately (or leased out separately under a finance lease), an enterprise accounts for the portions separately. If the portions could not be sold separately, the property is investment property only if an insignificant portion is held for use in the production or supply of goods or services or for administrative purposes. *(40.8)*

Recognition

Investment property should be recognised as an asset when, and only when:

(a)   it is probable that the future economic benefits that are associated with the investment property will flow to the enterprise; and

(b)   the cost of the investment property can be measured reliably. *(40.15)*

Initial Measurement

An investment property should be measured initially at its cost. Transaction costs should be included in the initial measurement *(40.17)*.

The cost of a purchased investment property comprises its purchase price, and any directly attributable expenditure. Directly attributable expenditure includes, for example, professional fees for legal services, property transfer taxes and other transaction costs. *(40.18)*

The cost of a self-constructed investment property is its cost at the date when the construction or development is complete. Until that date, an enterprise applies IAS 16. At that date, the property becomes investment property and this Standard applies. *(40.19)*

Subsequent Expenditure

Subsequent expenditure relating to an investment property that has already been recognised should be added to the carrying amount of the investment property when it is probable that future economic benefits, in excess of the originally assessed standard of performance of the existing investment property, will flow to the enterprise. All other subsequent expenditure should be recognised as an expense in the period in which it is incurred. *(40.22)*

Measurement Subsequent to Initial Recognition

An enterprise should choose either the 'fair value model' or the 'cost model' as its accounting policy and should apply that policy to all of its investment property. *(40.24)*

Fair Value Model

After initial recognition, an enterprise that chooses the fair value model should measure all of its investment property at its fair value, except in the exceptional cases described later in this section. *(40.27)*

A gain or loss arising from a change in the fair value of investment property should be included in net profit or loss for the period in which it arises. *(40.28)*

The fair value of investment property is usually its market value. Fair value is measured as the most probable price reasonably obtainable in the market at the balance sheet date in keeping with the fair value definition. It is the best price reasonably obtainable by the seller and the most advantageous price reasonably obtainable by the buyer. This estimate specifically excludes an estimated price inflated or deflated by special terms or circumstances such as atypical financing, sale and leaseback arrangements, special considerations or concessions granted by anyone associated with the sale. *(40.29)*

An enterprise determines fair value without any deduction for transaction costs that the enterprise may incur on sale or other disposal. *(40.30)*

The fair value of investment property should reflect the actual market state and circumstances as of the balance sheet date, not as of either a past or future date. *(40.31)*

In the absence of current prices on an active market, an enterprise considers information from a variety of sources, including:

(a)   current prices on an active market for properties of different nature, condition or location (or subject to different lease or other contracts), adjusted to reflect those differences;

(b)   recent prices on less active markets, with adjustments to reflect any changes in economic conditions since the date of the transactions that occurred at those prices; and

(c)   discounted cash flow projections based on reliable estimates of future cash flows, supported by the terms of any existing lease and other contracts and (where possible) by external evidence such as current market rents for similar properties in the same location and condition, and using discount rates that reflect current market assessments of the uncertainty in the amount and timing of the cash flows. *(40.40)*

Inability to Measure Fair Value Reliably

There is a rebuttable presumption that an enterprise will be able to determine the fair value of an investment property reliably on a continuing basis. However, in exceptional cases, there is clear evidence when an enterprise first acquires an investment property (or when an existing property first becomes investment property following the completion of construction or development, or after a change in use) that the enterprise will not be able to determine the fair value of the investment property reliably on a continuing basis. This arises when, and only when, comparable market transactions are infrequent and alternative estimates of fair value (for example, based on discounted cash flow projections) are not available. In such cases, an enterprise should measure that investment property using the benchmark treatment in IAS 16. The residual value of the investment property should be assumed to be zero. The enterprise should continue to apply IAS 16 until the disposal of the investment property. *(40.47)*

If an enterprise has previously measured an investment property at fair value, the enterprise should continue to measure the property at fair value until disposal (or until the property becomes owner-occupied property or the enterprise begins to develop the property for subsequent sale in the ordinary course of business) even if comparable market transactions become less frequent or market prices become less readily available. *(40.49)*

Cost Model

After initial recognition, an enterprise that chooses the cost model should measure all of its investment property using the benchmark treatment in IAS 16, that is, at cost less any accumulated depreciation and any accumulated impairment losses. *(40.50)*

Transfers

Transfers to, or from, investment property should be made when, and only when, there is a change in use, evidenced by:

(a)   commencement of owner-occupation, for a transfer from investment property to owner-occupied property;

(b)   commencement of development with a view to sale, for a transfer from investment property to inventories;

(c)   end of owner-occupation, for a transfer from owner-occupied property to investment property;

(d)   commencement of an operating lease to another party, for a transfer from inventories to investment property; or

(e)   end of construction or development, for a transfer from property in the course of construction or development (covered by IAS 16) to investment property. *(40.51)*

For a transfer from investment property carried at fair value to owner-occupied property or inventories, the property's cost for subsequent accounting under IAS 16 or IAS 2 should be its fair value at the date of change in use. *(40.54)*

If an owner-occupied property becomes an investment property that will be carried at fair value, an enterprise should apply IAS 16 up to the date of change in use. The enterprise should treat any difference at that date between the carrying amount of the property under IAS 16 and its fair value in the same way as a revaluation under IAS 16. *(40.55)*

For a transfer from inventories to investment property that will be carried at fair value, any difference between the fair value of the property at that date and its previous carrying amount should be recognised in net profit or loss for the period. *(40.57)*

When an enterprise completes the construction or development of a self-constructed investment property that will be carried at fair value, any difference between the fair value of the property at that date and its previous carrying amount should be recognised in net profit or loss for the period. *(40.59)*

Disposals

An investment property should be derecognised (eliminated from the balance sheet) on disposal or when the investment property is permanently withdrawn from use and no future economic benefits are expected from its disposal. *(40.60)*

Gains or losses arising from the retirement or disposal of investment property should be determined as the difference between the net disposal proceeds and the carrying amount of the asset and should be recognised as income or expense in the income statement (unless IAS 17, *Leases*, requires otherwise on a sale and leaseback). *(40.62)*

Disclosure

Fair Value Model and Cost Model

An enterprise should disclose:

(a)   when classification is difficult, the criteria developed by the enterprise to distinguish investment property from owner-occupied property and from property held for sale in the ordinary course of business;

(b)   the methods and significant assumptions applied in determining the fair value of investment property, including a statement whether the determination of fair value was supported by market evidence or was more heavily based on other factors (which the enterprise should disclose) because of the nature of the property and lack of comparable market data;

(c)   the extent to which the fair value of investment property (as measured or disclosed in the financial statements) is based on a valuation by an independent valuer who holds a recognised and relevant professional qualification and who has recent experience in the location and category of the investment property being valued. If there has been no such valuation, that fact should be disclosed;

(d)   the amounts included in the income statement for:

(i)   rental income from investment property;

(ii)   direct operating expenses (including repairs and maintenance) arising from investment property that generated rental income during the period; and

(iii) direct operating expenses (including repairs and maintenance) arising from investment property that did not generate rental income during the period;

(e)   the existence and amounts of restrictions on the realisability of investment property or the remittance of income and proceeds of disposal; and

(f)   material contractual obligations to purchase, construct or develop investment property or for repairs, maintenance or enhancements. *(40.66)*.

Fair Value Model

In addition to the disclosure required by the preceding paragraph, an enterprise that applies the fair value model should also disclose a reconciliation of the carrying amount of investment property at the beginning and end of the period showing the following (comparative information is not required):

(a)   additions, disclosing separately those additions resulting from acquisitions and those resulting from capitalised subsequent expenditure;

(b)   additions resulting from acquisitions through business combinations;

(c)   disposals;

(d)   net gains or losses from fair value adjustments;

(e)   the net exchange differences arising on the translation of the financial statements of a foreign entity;

(f)   transfers to and from inventories and owner-occupied property; and

(g)   other movements. *(40.67)*

In the exceptional cases when an enterprise measures investment property using the benchmark treatment in IAS 16, (because of the lack of a reliable fair value), the reconciliation required by the previous paragraph should disclose amounts relating to that investment property separately from amounts relating to other investment property. In addition, an enterprise should disclose:

(a)   a description of the investment property;

(b)   an explanation of why fair value cannot be reliably measured;

(c)   if possible, the range of estimates within which fair value is highly likely to lie; and

(d)   on disposal of investment property not carried at fair value:

(i)   the fact that the enterprise has disposed of investment property not carried at fair value;

(ii)   the carrying amount of that investment property at the time of sale; and

(iii)   the amount of gain or loss recognised. *(40.68)*

Cost Model

In addition to the general disclosures required, an enterprise that applies the cost model in paragraph 40.50 should also disclose:

(a)   the depreciation methods used;

(b)   the useful lives or the depreciation rates used;

(c)   the gross carrying amount and the accumulated depreciation (aggregated with accumulated impairment losses) at the beginning and end of the period;

(d)   a reconciliation of the carrying amount of investment property at the beginning and end of the period showing the following (comparative information is not required):

(i)   additions, disclosing separately those additions resulting from acquisitions and those resulting from capitalised subsequent expenditure;

(ii)   additions resulting from acquisitions through business combinations;

(iii)   disposals;

(iv)   depreciation;

(v)   the amount of impairment losses recognised, and the amount of impairment losses reversed, during the period under IAS 36, *Impairment of Assets*;

(vi)   the net exchange differences arising on the translation of the financial statements of a foreign entity;

(vii)   transfers to and from inventories and owner-occupied property; and

(viii) other movements; and

(e)   the fair value of investment property. In exceptional cases when an enterprise cannot determine the fair value of the investment property reliably, the enterprise should disclose:

(i)   a description of the investment property;

(ii)   an explanation of why fair value cannot be determined reliably; and

(iii)   if possible, the range of estimates within which fair value is highly likely to lie. *(40.69)*

| 3.4 | **Intangible Assets** |

IAS 38 requires an enterprise to recognise an intangible asset if, and only if, certain criteria are met. The Standard also specifies how to measure the carrying amount of intangible assets and requires certain disclosures about intangible assets.

IAS 38 should be applied by all enterprises in accounting for intangible assets, except:

(a)   intangible assets that are covered by another International Accounting Standard;

(b)   financial assets, as defined in IAS 32, *Financial Instruments: Disclosure and Presentation* (see section 6.2, p. 370);

(c)   mineral rights and expenditure on the exploration for, or development and extraction of, minerals, oil, natural gas and similar non-regenerative resources; and

(d)   intangible assets arising in insurance enterprises from contracts with policyholders. *(38.1)*

IAS 38 uses the following terms:

- An *intangible asset* is an identifiable non-monetary asset without physical substance held for use in the production or supply of goods or services, for rental to others, or for administrative purposes.

- An *asset* is a resource:

    (a)   controlled by an enterprise as a result of past events; and

    (b)   from which future economic benefits are expected to flow to the enterprise.

- *Monetary assets* are money held and assets to be received in fixed or determinable amounts of money.

- *Research* is original and planned investigation undertaken with the prospect of gaining new scientific or technical knowledge and understanding.

- *Development* is the application of research findings or other knowledge to a plan or design for the production of new or substantially improved materials, devices, products, processes, systems or services prior to the commencement of commercial production or use.

- *Amortisation* is the systematic allocation of the depreciable amount of an intangible asset over its useful life.

- *Depreciable amount* is the cost of an asset, or other amount substituted for cost in the financial statements, less its residual value.

- *Useful life* is either:

    (a)   the period of time over which an asset is expected to be used by the enterprise; or

(b)   the number of production or similar units expected to be obtained from the asset by the enterprise.

- *Cost* is the amount of cash or cash equivalents paid or the fair value of the other consideration given to acquire an asset at the time of its acquisition or production.

- *Residual value* is the net amount which an enterprise expects to obtain for an asset at the end of its useful life after deducting the expected costs of disposal.

- *Fair value of an asset* is the amount for which that asset could be exchanged between knowledgeable, willing parties in an arm's length transaction.

- An *active market* is a market where all the following conditions exist:

   (a)   the items traded within the market are homogeneous;

   (b)   willing buyers and sellers can normally be found at any time; and

   (c)   prices are available to the public.

- An *impairment loss* is the amount by which the carrying amount of an asset exceeds its recoverable amount.

- *Carrying amount* is the amount at which an asset is recognised in the balance sheet after deducting any accumulated amortisation and accumulated impairment losses thereon. *(38.7)*

Intangible Assets

Enterprises frequently expend resources, or incur liabilities, on the acquisition, development, maintenance or enhancement of intangible resources such as scientific or technical knowledge, design and implementation of new processes or systems, licences, intellectual property, market knowledge and trademarks (including brand names and publishing titles). Common examples of items encompassed by these broad headings are computer software, patents, copyrights, motion picture films, customer lists, mortgage servicing rights, fishing licences, import quotas, franchises, customer or supplier relationships, customer loyalty, market share and marketing rights. *(38.8)*

Identifiability

The definition of an intangible asset requires that an intangible asset be identifiable to distinguish it clearly from goodwill. Goodwill arising on a business combination that is an acquisition represents a payment made by the acquirer in anticipation of future economic benefits. The future economic benefits may result from synergy between the identifiable assets acquired or from assets which, individually, do not qualify for recognition in the financial statements but for which the acquirer is prepared to make a payment in the acquisition. *(38.10)*

Control

An enterprise controls an asset if the enterprise has the power to obtain the future economic benefits flowing from the underlying resource and also can restrict the access of others to those benefits. The capacity of an enterprise to control the future economic benefits from an intangible asset would normally stem from legal rights that are enforceable in a court of law. In the absence of legal rights, it is more difficult to demonstrate control. However, legal enforceability of a right is not a necessary condition for control since an enterprise may be able to control the future economic benefits in some other way. *(38.13)*

Future Economic Benefits

The future economic benefits flowing from an intangible asset may include revenue from the sale of products or services, cost savings, or other benefits resulting from the use of the asset by the enterprise. For example, the use of intellectual property in a production process may reduce future production costs rather than increase future revenues. *(38.17)*

Recognition and Initial Measurement of an Intangible Asset

An intangible asset should be recognised if, and only if:

(a)   it is probable that the future economic benefits that are attributable to the asset will flow to the enterprise; and

(b)   the cost of the asset can be measured reliably. *(38.19)*

An enterprise should assess the probability of future economic benefits using reasonable and supportable assumptions that represent management's best estimate of the set of economic conditions that will exist over the useful life of the asset. *(38.20)*

An intangible asset should be measured initially at cost. *(38.22)*

Separate Acquisition

If an intangible asset is acquired separately, the cost of the intangible asset can usually be measured reliably. This is particularly so when the purchase consideration is in the form of cash or other monetary assets. *(38.23)*

Acquisition as Part of a Business Combination

Under IAS 22 (revised 1998), *Business Combinations* (see section 7.1, p. 389), if an intangible asset is acquired in a business combination that is an acquisition, the cost of that intangible asset is based on its fair value at the date of acquisition. *(38.27)*

Acquisition by Way of a Government Grant

In some cases, an intangible asset may be acquired free of charge, or for nominal consideration, by way of a government grant. This may occur when a government transfers or allocates to an enterprise intangible assets such as airport landing rights, licences to operate radio or television stations, import licences or quotas or rights to access other restricted resources. Under IAS 20, *Accounting for Government Grants and Disclosure of Government Assistance* (see section 5.3, p. 342), an enterprise may choose to recognise both the intangible asset and the grant at fair value initially. If an enterprise chooses not to recognise the asset initially at fair value, the enterprise recognises the asset initially at a nominal amount (under the other treatment permitted by IAS 20) plus any expenditure that is directly attributable to preparing the asset for its intended use. *(38.33)*

Exchanges of Assets

An intangible asset may be acquired in exchange or part exchange for a dissimilar intangible asset or other asset. The cost of such an item is measured at the fair value of the asset received, which is equivalent to the fair value of the asset given up, adjusted by the amount of any cash or cash equivalents transferred. *(38.34)*

An intangible asset may be acquired in exchange for a similar asset that has a similar use in the same line of business and that has a similar fair value. An intangible asset may also be sold in exchange for an equity interest in a similar asset. In both cases, since the earnings process is incomplete, no gain or loss is recognised on the transaction. Instead, the cost of the new asset is the carrying amount of the asset given up. However, the fair value of the asset received may provide evidence of an impairment loss in the asset given up. Under these circumstances an impairment loss is recognised for the asset given up and the carrying amount after impairment is assigned to the new asset. *(38.35)*

Internally Generated Goodwill

Internally generated goodwill should not be recognised as an asset. *(38.36)*

Internally Generated Intangible Assets

To assess whether an internally generated intangible asset meets the criteria for recognition, an enterprise classifies the generation of the asset into:

(a)   a research phase; and

(b)   a development phase.

Although the terms 'research' and 'development' are defined, the terms 'research phase' and 'development phase' have a broader meaning for the purpose of IAS 38. *(38.40)*

Research Phase

No intangible asset arising from research (or from the research phase of an internal project) should be recognised. Expenditure on research (or on the research phase of an internal project) should be recognised as an expense when it is incurred. *(38.42)*

Development Phase

An intangible asset arising from development (or from the development phase of an internal project) should be recognised if, and only if, an enterprise can demonstrate all of the following:

(a)   the technical feasibility of completing the intangible asset so that it will be available for use or sale;

(b)   its intention to complete the intangible asset and use or sell it;

(c)   its ability to use or sell the intangible asset;

(d)   how the intangible asset will generate probable future economic benefits. Among other things, the enterprise should demonstrate the existence of a market for the output of the intangible asset or the intangible asset itself or, if it is to be used internally, the usefulness of the intangible asset;

(e)   the availability of adequate technical, financial and other resources to complete the development and to use or sell the intangible asset; and

(f)   its ability to measure reliably the expenditure attributable to the intangible asset during its development. *(38.45)*

Internally generated brands, mastheads, publishing titles, customer lists and items similar in substance should not be recognised as intangible assets. *(38.51)*

Cost of an Internally Generated Intangible Asset

The cost of an internally generated intangible asset for the purpose of IAS 38 is the sum of expenditure incurred from the date when the intangible asset first meets the recognition criteria in the Standard. The Standard prohibits reinstatement of expenditure recognised as an expense in previous annual financial statements or interim financial reports. *(38.53)*

The cost of an internally generated intangible asset comprises all expenditure that can be directly attributed, or allocated on a reasonable and consistent basis, to creating, producing and preparing the asset for its intended use. *(38.54)*.

► Example – Cost of an Internally Generated Intangible Asset

An enterprise is developing a new production process. During 20X5, expenditure incurred was 1,000, of which 900 was incurred before 1 December 20X5 and 100 was incurred between 1 December 20X5 and 31 December 20X5. The enterprise is able to demonstrate that, at 1 December 20X5, the production process met the criteria for recognition as an intangible asset. The recoverable amount of the know-how embodied in the process (including future cash outflows to complete the process before it is available for use) is estimated to be 500.

At the end of 20X5, the production process is recognised as an intangible asset at a cost of 100 (expenditure incurred since the date when the recognition criteria were met, that is, 1 December 20X5). The 900 expenditure incurred before 1 December 20X5 is recognised as an expense because the recognition criteria were not met until 1 December 20X5. This expenditure will never form part of the cost of the production process recognised in the balance sheet.

During 20X6, expenditure incurred is 2,000. At the end of 20X6, the recoverable amount of the know-how embodied in the process (including future cash outflows to complete the process before it is available for use) is estimated to be 1,900.

At the end of 20X6, the cost of the production process is 2,100 (100 expenditure recognised at the end of 20X5 plus 2,000 expenditure recognised in 20X6). The enterprise recognises an impairment loss of 200 to adjust the carrying amount of the process before impairment loss (2,100) to its recoverable amount (1,900). This impairment loss will be reversed in a subsequent period if the requirements for the reversal of an impairment loss in IAS 36, *Impairment of Assets* are met.

Figure 19

Recognition of an Expense

Expenditure on an intangible item should be recognised as an expense when it is incurred unless:

(a)   it forms part of the cost of an intangible asset that meets the recognition criteria; or

(b)   the item is acquired in a business combination that is an acquisition and cannot be recognised as an intangible asset. If this is the case, this expenditure (included in the cost of acquisition) should form part of the amount attributed to goodwill (negative goodwill) at the date of acquisition (see IAS 22 (revised 1998), *Business Combinations*, under section 7.1, p. 331). *(38.56)*

Past Expenses not to be Recognised as an Asset

Expenditure on an intangible item that was initially recognised as an expense by a reporting enterprise in previous annual financial statements or interim financial reports should not be recognised as part of the cost of an intangible asset at a later date. *(38.59)*

Subsequent Expenditure

Subsequent expenditure on an intangible asset after its purchase or its completion should be recognised as an expense when it is incurred unless:

(a)   it is probable that this expenditure will enable the asset to generate future economic benefits in excess of its originally assessed standard of performance; and

(b)   this expenditure can be measured and attributed to the asset reliably.

If these conditions are met, the subsequent expenditure should be added to the cost of the intangible asset. *(38.60)*

Measurement Subsequent to Initial Recognition

Benchmark Treatment

After initial recognition, an intangible asset should be carried at its cost less any accumulated amortisation and any accumulated impairment losses. *(38.63)*

Allowed Alternative Treatment

After initial recognition, an intangible asset should be carried at a revalued amount, being its fair value at the date of the revaluation less any subsequent accumulated amortisation and any subsequent accumulated impairment losses. For the purpose of revaluations under IAS 38, fair value should be determined by reference to an active market. Revaluations should be made with sufficient regularity such that the carrying amount does not differ materially from that which would be determined using fair value at the balance sheet date. *(38.64)*

If an intangible asset is revalued, all the other assets in its class should also be revalued, unless there is no active market for those assets. *(38.70)*

If an intangible asset in a class of revalued intangible assets cannot be revalued because there is no active market for this asset, the asset should be carried at its cost less any accumulated amortisation and impairment losses. *(38.72)*

If the fair value of a revalued intangible asset can no longer be determined by reference to an active market, the carrying amount of the asset should be its revalued amount at the date of the last revaluation by reference to the active market less any subsequent accumulated amortisation and any subsequent accumulated impairment losses. *(38.73)*

If an intangible asset's carrying amount is increased as a result of a revaluation, the increase should be credited directly to equity under the heading of revaluation surplus. However, a revaluation increase should be recognised as income to the extent that it reverses a revaluation decrease of the same asset and that revaluation decrease was previously recognised as an expense. *(38.76)*

If an asset's carrying amount is decreased as a result of a revaluation, the decrease should be recognised as an expense. However, a revaluation decrease should be charged directly against any related revaluation surplus to the extent that the decrease does not exceed the amount held in the revaluation surplus in respect of that same asset. *(38.77)*

Amortisation

Amortisation Period

The depreciable amount of an intangible asset should be allocated on a systematic basis over the best estimate of its useful life. There is a rebuttable presumption that the useful life of an intangible asset will not exceed twenty years from the date when the asset is available for use. Amortisation should commence when the asset is available for use. *(38.79)*

Estimates of the useful life of an intangible asset generally become less reliable as the length of the useful life increases. IAS 38 adopts a presumption that the useful life of intangible assets is unlikely to exceed twenty years. *(38.82)*

The useful life of an intangible asset may be very long but it is always finite. Uncertainty justifies estimating the useful life of an intangible asset on a prudent basis, but it does not justify choosing a life that is unrealistically short. *(38.84)*

If control over the future economic benefits from an intangible asset is achieved through legal rights that have been granted for a finite period, the useful life of the intangible asset should not exceed the period of the legal rights unless:

(a)   the legal rights are renewable; and

(b)   renewal is virtually certain. *(38.85)*

Amortisation Method

The amortisation method used should reflect the pattern in which the asset's economic benefits are consumed by the enterprise. If that pattern cannot be determined reliably, the straight-line method should be used. The amortisation charge for each period should be recognised as an expense unless another International Accounting Standard permits or requires it to be included in the carrying amount of another asset. *(38.88)*

Residual Value

The residual value of an intangible asset should be assumed to be zero unless:

(a)   there is a commitment by a third party to purchase the asset at the end of its useful life; or

(b)   there is an active market for the asset and:

    (i)   residual value can be determined by reference to that market; and

    (ii)   it is probable that such a market will exist at the end of the asset's useful life. *(38.91)*

The depreciable amount of an asset is determined after deducting its residual value. A residual value other than zero implies that an enterprise expects to dispose of the intangible asset before the end of its economic life. *(38.92)*

Review of Amortisation Period and Amortisation Method

The amortisation period and the amortisation method should be reviewed at least at each financial year end. If the expected useful life of the asset is significantly different from previous estimates, the amortisation period should be changed accordingly. If there has been a significant change in the expected pattern of economic benefits from the asset, the amortisation method should be changed to reflect the changed pattern. Such changes should be accounted for as changes in accounting estimates under IAS 8, *Net Profit or Loss for the Period* (see section 2.2.2, p. 106), *Fundamental Errors and Changes in Accounting Policies* (see section 2.5.4, p. 145), by adjusting the amortisation charge for the current and future periods. *(38.94)*

Recoverability of the Carrying Amount - Impairment Losses

In addition to the following requirements included in IAS 36, *Impairment of Assets* (see section 3.5, p. 214), an enterprise should estimate the recoverable amount of the following intangible assets at least at each financial year end, even if there is no indication that the asset is impaired:

(a)   an intangible asset that is not yet available for use; and

(b)   an intangible asset that is amortised over a period exceeding twenty years from the date when the asset is available for use.

The recoverable amount should be determined under IAS 36 and impairment losses recognised accordingly. *(38.99)*

Retirements and Disposals

An intangible asset should be derecognised (eliminated from the balance sheet) on disposal or when no future economic benefits are expected from its use and subsequent disposal. *(38.103)*

Gains or losses arising from the retirement or disposal of an intangible asset should be determined as the difference between the net disposal proceeds and the carrying amount of the asset and should be recognised as income or expense in the income statement. *(38.104)*

Disclosure

General

The financial statements should disclose the following for each class of intangible assets, distinguishing between internally generated intangible assets and other intangible assets:

(a)   the useful lives or the amortisation rates used;

(b)   the amortisation methods used;

(c)   the gross carrying amount and the accumulated amortisation (aggregated with accumulated impairment losses) at the beginning and end of the period;

(d)   the line item(s) of the income statement in which the amortisation of intangible assets is included;

(e)   a reconciliation of the carrying amount at the beginning and end of the period showing:

   (i)   additions, indicating separately those from internal development and through business combinations;

   (ii)   retirements and disposals;

   (iii)   increases or decreases during the period resulting from revaluations under this Standard and from impairment losses recognised or reversed directly in equity under IAS 36, *Impairment of Assets* (see section 3.5, p. 214) (if any);

   (iv)   impairment losses recognised in the income statement during the period under IAS 36 (if any);

   (v)   impairment losses reversed in the income statement during the period under IAS 36 (if any);

   (vi)   amortisation recognised during the period;

   (vii)   net exchange differences arising on the translation of the financial statements of a foreign entity; and

   (viii) other changes in the carrying amount during the period.

Comparative information is not required. *(38.107)*

The financial statements should also disclose:

(a)   if an intangible asset is amortised over more than twenty years, the reasons why the presumption that the useful life of an intangible asset will not exceed twenty years from the date when the asset is available for use is rebutted. In giving these reasons, the enterprise should describe the factor(s) that played a significant role in determining the useful life of the asset;

(b)   a description, the carrying amount and remaining amortisation period of any individual intangible asset that is material to the financial statements of the enterprise as a whole;

(c)   for intangible assets acquired by way of a government grant and initially recognised at fair value:

(i)   the fair value initially recognised for these assets;

(ii)   their carrying amount; and

(iii)   whether they are carried under the benchmark or the allowed alternative treatment for subsequent measurement;

(d)   the existence and carrying amounts of intangible assets whose title is restricted and the carrying amounts of intangible assets pledged as security for liabilities; and

(e)   the amount of commitments for the acquisition of intangible assets. *(38.111)*

Intangible Assets Carried Under the Allowed Alternative Treatment

If intangible assets are carried at revalued amounts, the following should be disclosed:

(a)   by class of intangible assets:

(i)   the effective date of the revaluation;

(ii)   the carrying amount of revalued intangible assets; and

(iii)   the carrying amount that would have been included in the financial statements had the revalued intangible assets been carried under the benchmark treatment in this Standard.

(b)   the amount of the revaluation surplus that relates to intangible assets at the beginning and end of the period, indicating the changes during the period and any restrictions on the distribution of the balance to shareholders. (38.113)

Research and Development Expenditure

The financial statements should disclose the aggregate amount of research and development expenditure recognised as an expense during the period. *(38.115)*

Other Information

An enterprise is encouraged, but not required, to give the following information:

(a)   a description of any fully amortised intangible asset that is still in use; and

(b)   a brief description of significant intangible assets controlled by the enterprise but not recognised as assets because they did not meet the recognition criteria in this Standard or because they were acquired or generated before IAS 38 was effective. *(38.117)*

3.5 | Impairment of Assets

The objective of IAS 36 is to prescribe the procedures that an enterprise applies to ensure that its assets are carried at no more than their recoverable amount. An asset is carried at more than its recoverable amount if its carrying amount exceeds the amount to be recovered through use or sale of the asset.

IAS 36 should be applied in accounting for the impairment of all assets, other than:

(a)   inventories;

(b)   assets arising from construction contracts;

(c)   deferred tax assets;

(d)   assets arising from employee benefits; and

(e)   financial assets that are included in the scope of IAS 32, *Financial Instruments: Disclosure and Presentation* (see section 6.2, p. 370). *(36.1)*

IAS 36 uses the following terms:

• *Recoverable amount* is the higher of an asset's net selling price and its value in use.

• *Value in use* is the present value of estimated future cash flows expected to arise from the continuing use of an asset and from its disposal at the end of its useful life.

• *Net selling price* is the amount obtainable from the sale of an asset in an arm's length transaction between knowledgeable, willing parties, less the costs of disposal.

• *Costs of disposal* are incremental costs directly attributable to the disposal of an asset, excluding finance costs and income tax expense.

• An *impairment loss* is the amount by which the carrying amount of an asset exceeds its recoverable amount.

• *Carrying amount* is the amount at which an asset is recognised in the balance sheet after deducting any accumulated depreciation (amortisation) and accumulated impairment losses thereon.

• *Depreciation (Amortisation)* is the systematic allocation of the depreciable amount of an asset over its useful life.[1]

• *Depreciable amount* is the cost of an asset, or other amount substituted for cost in the financial statements, less its residual value.

• *Useful life* is either:

    (a)   the period of time over which an asset is expected to be used by the enterprise; or

    (b)   the number of production or similar units expected to be obtained from the asset by the enterprise.

---

[1] *In the case of an intangible asset or goodwill, the term 'amortisation' is generally used instead of 'depreciation'. Both terms have the same meaning.*

- A *cash-generating unit* is the smallest identifiable group of assets that generates cash inflows from continuing use that are largely independent of the cash inflows from other assets or groups of assets.

- *Corporate assets* are assets other than goodwill that contribute to the future cash flows of both the cash-generating unit under review and other cash-generating units.

- An *active market* is a market where all the following conditions exist:

    (a)   the items traded within the market are homogeneous;

    (b)   willing buyers and sellers can normally be found at any time; and

    (c)   prices are available to the public. *(36.5)*

Identifying an Asset that may be Impaired

An enterprise should assess at each balance sheet date whether there is any indication that an asset may be impaired. If any such indication exists, the enterprise should estimate the recoverable amount of the asset. *(36.8)*

In assessing whether there is any indication that an asset may be impaired, an enterprise should consider, as a minimum, the following indications:

External sources of information

(a)   during the period, an asset's market value has declined significantly more than would be expected as a result of the passage of time or normal use;

(b)   significant changes with an adverse effect on the enterprise have taken place during the period, or will take place in the near future, in the technological, market, economic or legal environment in which the enterprise operates or in the market to which an asset is dedicated;

(c)   market interest rates or other market rates of return on investments have increased during the period, and those increases are likely to affect the discount rate used in calculating an asset's value in use and decrease the asset's recoverable amount materially;

(d)   the carrying amount of the net assets of the reporting enterprise is more than its market capitalisation;

Internal sources of information

(e)   evidence is available of obsolescence or physical damage of an asset;

(f)   significant changes with an adverse effect on the enterprise have taken place during the period, or are expected to take place in the near future, in the extent to which, or manner in which, an asset is used or is expected to be used. These changes include plans to discontinue or restructure the operation to which an asset belongs or to dispose of an asset before the previously expected date; and

(g)   evidence is available from internal reporting that indicates that the economic performance of an asset is, or will be, worse than expected. *(36.9)*

Measurement of Recoverable Amount

IAS 36 defines recoverable amount as the higher of an asset's net selling price and value in use. The following paragraphs set out the requirements for measuring recoverable amount. These requirements use the term 'an asset' but apply equally to an individual asset or a cash-generating unit. *(36.15)*

It is not always necessary to determine both an asset's net selling price and its value in use. For example, if either of these amounts exceeds the asset's carrying amount, the asset is not impaired and it is not necessary to estimate the other amount. *(36.16)*

If there is no reason to believe that an asset's value in use materially exceeds its net selling price, the asset's recoverable amount may be taken to be its net selling price. This will often be the case for an asset that is held for disposal. This is because the value in use of an asset held for disposal will consist mainly of the net disposal proceeds, since the future cash flows from continuing use of the asset until its disposal are likely to be negligible. *(36.18)*

Recoverable amount is determined for an individual asset, unless the asset does not generate cash inflows from continuing use that are largely independent of those from other assets or groups of assets. If this is the case, recoverable amount is determined for the cash-generating unit to which the asset belongs, unless either:

(a)   the asset's net selling price is higher than its carrying amount; or

(b)   the asset's value in use can be estimated to be close to its net selling price and net selling price can be determined. *(36.19)*

Net Selling Price

The best evidence of an asset's net selling price is a price in a binding sale agreement in an arm's length transaction, adjusted for incremental costs that would be directly attributable to the disposal of the asset. *(36.21)*

Costs of disposal, other than those that have already been recognised as liabilities, are deducted in determining net selling price. Examples of such costs are legal costs, stamp duty and similar transaction taxes, costs of removing the asset, and direct incremental costs to bring an asset into condition for its sale. However, termination benefits (as defined in IAS 19, *Employee Benefits*, see section 4.2, p. 277) and costs associated with reducing or reorganising a business following the disposal of an asset are not direct incremental costs to dispose of the asset. *(36.24)*

Value in Use

Basis for Estimates of Future Cash Flows

In measuring value in use:

(a)   cash flow projections should be based on reasonable and supportable assumptions that represent management's best estimate of the set of economic conditions that will exist over the remaining useful life of the asset. Greater weight should be given to external evidence;

(b)   cash flow projections should be based on the most recent financial budgets/that have been approved by management. Projections based on these budgets/forecasts should cover a maximum period of five years, unless a longer period can be justified; and

(c)   cash flow projections beyond the period covered by the most recent budgets/should be estimated by extrapolating the projections based on the budgets/using a steady or declining growth rate for subsequent years, unless an increasing rate can be justified. This growth rate should not exceed the long-term average growth rate for the products, industries, or country or countries in which the enterprise operates, or for the market in which the asset is used, unless a higher rate can be justified. *(36.27)*

Detailed, explicit and reliable financial budgets/forecasts of future cash flows for periods longer than five years are generally not available. For this reason, management's estimates of future cash flows are based on the most recent budgets/forecasts for a maximum of five years. Management may use cash flow projections based on financial budgets/forecasts over a period longer than five years if management is confident that these projections are reliable and it can demonstrate its ability, based on past experience, to forecast cash flows accurately over that longer period. *(36.28)*

Composition of Estimates of Future Cash Flows

Estimates of future cash flows should include:

(a)   projections of cash inflows from the continuing use of the asset;

(b)   projections of cash outflows that are necessarily incurred to generate the cash inflows from continuing use of the asset (including cash outflows to prepare the asset for use) and that can be directly attributed, or allocated on a reasonable and consistent basis, to the asset; and

(c)   net cash flows, if any, to be received (or paid) for the disposal of the asset at the end of its useful life. *(36.32)*

Future cash flows should be estimated for the asset in its current condition. Estimates of future cash flows should not include estimated future cash inflows or outflows that are expected to arise from:

(a)   a future restructuring to which an enterprise is not yet committed; or

(b)   future capital expenditure that will improve or enhance the asset in excess of its originally assessed standard of performance. *(36.37)*

Estimates of future cash flows should not include:

(a)   cash inflows or outflows from financing activities; or

(b)   income tax receipts or payments. *(36.43)*

The estimate of net cash flows to be received (or paid) for the disposal of an asset at the end of its useful life should be the amount that an enterprise expects to obtain from the disposal of the asset in an arm's length transaction between knowledgeable, willing parties, after deducting the estimated costs of disposal. *(36.45)*

Foreign Currency Future Cash Flows

Future cash flows are estimated in the currency in which they will be generated and then discounted using a discount rate appropriate for that currency. An enterprise translates the present value obtained using the spot exchange rate at the balance sheet date (described in IAS 21, *The Effects of Changes in Foreign Exchange Rates* (see section 2.5.1, p. 135), as the closing rate). *(36.47)*

Discount Rate

The discount rate (or rates) should be a pre-tax rate (or rates) that reflect(s) current market assessments of the time value of money and the risks specific to the asset. The discount rate(s) should not reflect risks for which future cash flow estimates have been adjusted. *(36.48)*

Recognition and Measurement of an Impairment Loss

If, and only if, the recoverable amount of an asset is less than its carrying amount, the carrying amount of the asset should be reduced to its recoverable amount. That reduction is an impairment loss. *(36.58)*

An impairment loss should be recognised as an expense in the income statement immediately, unless the asset is carried at revalued amount under another International Accounting Standard (for example, under the allowed alternative treatment in IAS 16, *Property, Plant and Equipment*, see section 3.2, p. 190). Any impairment loss of a revalued asset should be treated as a revaluation decrease under that other International Accounting Standard. *(36.59)*

When the amount estimated for an impairment loss is greater than the carrying amount of the asset to which it relates, an enterprise should recognise a liability if, and only if, that is required by another International Accounting Standard. *(36.61)*

After the recognition of an impairment loss, the depreciation (amortisation) charge for the asset should be adjusted in future periods to allocate the asset's revised carrying amount, less its residual value (if any), on a systematic basis over its remaining useful life. *(36.62)*

Cash-Generating Units

The following paragraphs set out the requirements for identifying the cash-generating unit to which an asset belongs and determining the carrying amount of, and recognising impairment losses for, cash-generating units. *(36.64)*

Identification of the Cash-Generating Unit to Which an Asset Belongs

If there is any indication that an asset may be impaired, recoverable amount should be estimated for the individual asset. If it is not possible to estimate the recoverable amount of the individual asset, an enterprise should determine the recoverable amount of the cash-generating unit to which the asset belongs (the asset's cash-generating unit). *(36.65)*

If an active market exists for the output produced by an asset or a group of assets, this asset or group of assets should be identified as a cash-generating unit, even if some or all of the output is used internally. If this is the case, management's best estimate of future market prices for the output should be used:

(a)   in determining the value in use of this cash-generating unit, when estimating the future cash inflows that relate to the internal use of the output; and

(b)   in determining the value in use of other cash-generating units of the reporting enterprise, when estimating the future cash outflows that relate to the internal use of the output. *(36.69)*

Cash-generating units should be identified consistently from period to period for the same asset or types of assets, unless a change is justified. *(36.71)*

Recoverable Amount and Carrying Amount of a Cash-Generating Unit

The carrying amount of a cash-generating unit should be determined consistently with the way the recoverable amount of the cash-generating unit is determined. *(36.74)*

Goodwill

In testing a cash-generating unit for impairment, an enterprise should identify whether goodwill that relates to this cash-generating unit is recognised in the financial statements. If this is the case, an enterprise should:

(a)   perform a 'bottom-up' test, that is, the enterprise should:

   (i)   identify whether the carrying amount of goodwill can be allocated on a reasonable and consistent basis to the cash-generating unit under review; and

   (ii)   then, compare the recoverable amount of the cash-generating unit under review to its carrying amount (including the carrying amount of allocated goodwill, if any) and recognise any impairment loss in accordance with paragraph 36.88.

The enterprise should perform the second step of the 'bottom-up' test even if none of the carrying amount of goodwill can be allocated on a reasonable and consistent basis to the cash-generating unit under review; and

(b)   if, in performing the 'bottom-up' test, the enterprise could not allocate the carrying amount of goodwill on a reasonable and consistent basis to the cash-generating unit under review, the enterprise should also perform a 'top-down' test, that is, the enterprise should:

   (i)   identify the smallest cash-generating unit that includes the cash-generating unit under review and to which the carrying amount of goodwill can be allocated on a reasonable and consistent basis (the 'larger' cash-generating unit); and

(ii)   then, compare the recoverable amount of the larger cash-generating unit to its carrying amount (including the carrying amount of allocated goodwill) and recognise any impairment loss in accordance with requirements for impairment losses on cash generating units. *(36.80)*

Corporate Assets

In testing a cash-generating unit for impairment, an enterprise should identify all the corporate assets that relate to the cash-generating unit under review. For each identified corporate asset, an enterprise should then:

(a)   if the carrying amount of the corporate asset can be allocated on a reasonable and consistent basis to the cash-generating unit under review, an enterprise should apply the 'bottom-up' test only; and

(b)   if the carrying amount of the corporate asset cannot be allocated on a reasonable and consistent basis to the cash-generating unit under review, an enterprise should apply both the 'bottom-up' and 'top-down' tests. *(36.86)*

Impairment Loss for a Cash-Generating Unit

An impairment loss should be recognised for a cash-generating unit if, and only if, its recoverable amount is less than its carrying amount. The impairment loss should be allocated to reduce the carrying amount of the assets of the unit in the following order:

(a)   first, to goodwill allocated to the cash-generating unit (if any); and

(b)   then, to the other assets of the unit on a pro-rata basis based on the carrying amount of each asset in the unit.

These reductions in carrying amounts should be treated as impairment losses on individual assets and recognised in accordance with the general requirements for the recognition of impairment losses. *(36.88)*

In allocating an impairment loss of a cash generating unit, the carrying amount of an asset should not be reduced below the highest of:

(a)   its net selling price (if determinable);

(b)   its value in use (if determinable); and

(c)   zero.

The amount of the impairment loss that would otherwise have been allocated to the asset should be allocated to the other assets of the unit on a pro-rata basis. *(36.89)*

After these requirements have been applied, a liability should be recognised for any remaining amount of an impairment loss for a cash-generating unit if, and only if, that is required by other International Accounting Standards. *(36.93)*

Reversal of an Impairment Loss

An enterprise should assess at each balance sheet date whether there is any indication that an impairment loss recognised for an asset in prior years may no longer exist or may have decreased. If any such indication exists, the enterprise should estimate the recoverable amount of that asset. *(36.95)*

In assessing whether there is any indication that an impairment loss recognised for an asset in prior years may no longer exist or may have decreased, an enterprise should consider, as a minimum, the following indications:

External sources of information

(a)   the asset's market value has increased significantly during the period;

(b)   significant changes with a favourable effect on the enterprise have taken place during the period, or will take place in the near future, in the technological, market, economic or legal environment in which the enterprise operates or in the market to which the asset is dedicated;

(c)   market interest rates or other market rates of return on investments have decreased during the period, and those decreases are likely to affect the discount rate used in calculating the asset's value in use and increase the asset's recoverable amount materially;

Internal sources of information

(d)   significant changes with a favourable effect on the enterprise have taken place during the period, or are expected to take place in the near future, in the extent to which, or manner in which, the asset is used or is expected to be used. These changes include capital expenditure that has been incurred during the period to improve or enhance an asset in excess of its originally assessed standard of performance or a commitment to discontinue or restructure the operation to which the asset belongs; and

(e)   evidence is available from internal reporting that indicates that the economic performance of the asset is, or will be, better than expected. *(36.96)*

An impairment loss recognised for an asset in prior years should be reversed if, and only if, there has been a change in the estimates used to determine the asset's recoverable amount since the last impairment loss was recognised. If this is the case, the carrying amount of the asset should be increased to its recoverable amount. That increase is a reversal of an impairment loss. *(36.99)*

Reversal of an Impairment Loss for an Individual Asset

The increased carrying amount of an asset due to a reversal of an impairment loss should not exceed the carrying amount that would have been determined (net of amortisation or depreciation) had no impairment loss been recognised for the asset in prior years. *(36.102)*
A reversal of an impairment loss for an asset should be recognised as income immediately in the income statement, unless the asset is carried at revalued amount

under another International Accounting Standard (for example, under the allowed alternative treatment in IAS 16, *Property, Plant and Equipment*, see section 3.2, p. 190). Any reversal of an impairment loss on a revalued asset should be treated as a revaluation increase under that other International Accounting Standard. *(36.104)*

After a reversal of an impairment loss is recognised, the depreciation (amortisation) charge for the asset should be adjusted in future periods to allocate the asset's revised carrying amount, less its residual value (if any), on a systematic basis over its remaining useful life. *(36.106)*

Reversal of an Impairment Loss for a Cash-Generating Unit

A reversal of an impairment loss for a cash-generating unit should be allocated to increase the carrying amount of the assets of the unit in the following order:

(a)   first, assets other than goodwill on a pro-rata basis based on the carrying amount of each asset in the unit; and

(b)   then, to goodwill allocated to the cash-generating unit (if any), if the requirements in paragraph 36.109 are met.

These increases in carrying amounts should be treated as reversals of impairment losses for individual assets and recognised in accordance with paragraph 36.104. *(36.107)*

In allocating a reversal of an impairment loss for a cash-generating unit under paragraph 36.107, the carrying amount of an asset should not be increased above the lower of:

(a)   its recoverable amount (if determinable); and

(b)   the carrying amount that would have been determined (net of amortisation or depreciation) had no impairment loss been recognised for the asset in prior years.

The amount of the reversal of the impairment loss that would otherwise have been allocated to the asset should be allocated to the other assets of the unit on a pro-rata basis. *(36.108)*

Reversal of an Impairment Loss for Goodwill

As an exception to the general requirement in IAS 36, an impairment loss recognised for goodwill should not be reversed in a subsequent period unless:

(a)   the impairment loss was caused by a specific external event of an exceptional nature that is not expected to recur; and

(b)   subsequent external events have occurred that reverse the effect of that event. *(36.109)*

Disclosure

For each class of assets, the financial statements should disclose:

(a) the amount of impairment losses recognised in the income statement during the period and the line item(s) of the income statement in which those impairment losses are included;

(b) the amount of reversals of impairment losses recognised in the income statement during the period and the line item(s) of the income statement in which those impairment losses are reversed;

(c) the amount of impairment losses recognised directly in equity during the period; and

(d) the amount of reversals of impairment losses recognised directly in equity during the period. *(36.113)*

An enterprise that applies IAS 14, *Segment Reporting* (see section 2.3, p. 119), should disclose the following for each reportable segment based on an enterprise's primary format (as defined in IAS 14):

(a) the amount of impairment losses recognised in the income statement and directly in equity during the period; and

(b) the amount of reversals of impairment losses recognised in the income statement and directly in equity during the period. *(36.116)*

If an impairment loss for an individual asset or a cash-generating unit is recognised or reversed during the period and is material to the financial statements of the reporting enterprise as a whole, an enterprise should disclose:

(a) the events and circumstances that led to the recognition or reversal of the impairment loss;

(b) the amount of the impairment loss recognised or reversed;

(c) for an individual asset:

   (i) the nature of the asset; and

   (ii) the reportable segment to which the asset belongs, based on the enterprise's primary format (as defined in IAS 14, *Segment Reporting*, if the enterprise applies IAS 14);

(d) for a cash-generating unit:

   (i) a description of the cash-generating unit (such as whether it is a product line, a plant, a business operation, a geographical area, a reportable segment as defined in IAS 14 or other);

   (ii) the amount of the impairment loss recognised or reversed by class of assets and by reportable segment based on the enterprise's primary format (as defined in IAS 14, if the enterprise applies IAS 14); and

(iii) if the aggregation of assets for identifying the cash-generating unit has changed since the previous estimate of the cash-generating unit's recoverable amount (if any), the enterprise should describe the current and former way of aggregating assets and the reasons for changing the way the cash-generating unit is identified;

(e)   whether the recoverable amount of the asset (cash-generating unit) is its net selling price or its value in use;

(f)   if recoverable amount is net selling price, the basis used to determine net selling price (such as whether selling price was determined by reference to an active market or in some other way); and

(g)   if recoverable amount is value in use, the discount rate(s) used in the current estimate and previous estimate (if any) of value in use. *(36.117)*

If impairment losses recognised (reversed) during the period are material in aggregate to the financial statements of the reporting enterprise as a whole, an enterprise should disclose a brief description of the following:

(a)   the main classes of assets affected by impairment losses (reversals of impairment losses) for which no information is disclosed under the preceding paragraph; and

(b)   the main events and circumstances that led to the recognition (reversal) of these impairment losses for which no information is disclosed under paragraph 36.117. *(36.118)*

Appendix A:

Accounting for Assets: Illustrative Examples

Contents

Example 7

Application of the 'Bottom-Up' and 'Top- Down' Tests to Goodwill   A62 - A71

A - Goodwill Can Be Allocated on a Reasonable and Consistent Basis   A64 - A66

B - Goodwill Cannot Be Allocated on a Reasonable and Consistent Basis   A67 - A71

Example 8

Allocation of Corporate Assets   A72 - A83

Example 1 — Identification of Cash-Generating Units

The purpose of this example is:

(a)   to give an indication of how cash-generating units are identified in various situations; and

(b)   to highlight certain factors that an enterprise may consider in identifying the cash-generating unit to which an asset belongs.

A - Retail Store Chain

Background

A1.   Store *X* belongs to a retail store chain *M*. *X* makes all its retail purchases through *M*'s purchasing centre. Pricing, marketing, advertising and human resources policies (except for hiring *X*'s cashiers and salesmen) are decided by *M*. *M* also owns five other stores in the same city as *X* (although in different neighbourhoods) and 20 other stores in other cities. All stores are managed in the same way as *X*. *X* and four other stores were purchased five years ago and goodwill was recognised.

What is X's cash-generating unit?

Analysis

A2.   In identifying *X*'s cash-generating unit, an enterprise considers whether, for example:

(a)   internal management reporting is organised to measure performance on a store-by-store basis; and

(b)   the business is run on a store-by-store profit basis or on a region/city basis.

A3.   All *M*'s stores are in different neighbourhoods and probably have different customer bases. So, although *X* is managed at a corporate level, *X* generates cash inflows that are largely independent from those of M's other stores. Therefore, it is likely that X is a cash-generating unit.

A4.   If the carrying amount of the goodwill can be allocated on a reasonable and consistent basis to X's cash-generating unit, M applies the 'bottom-up' test described in paragraph 36.80. If the carrying amount of the goodwill cannot be allocated on a reasonable and consistent basis to X's cash-generating unit, M applies the 'bottom-up' and 'top-down' tests.

B - Plant for an Intermediate Step in a Production Process

Background

A5.   A significant raw material used for plant Y's final production is an intermediate product bought from plant X of the same enterprise. X's products are sold to Y at a transfer price that passes all margins to X. 80% of Y's final production is sold to customers outside of the reporting enterprise. 60% of X's final production is sold to Y and the remaining 40% is sold to customers outside of the reporting enterprise.

For each of the following cases, what are the cash-generating units for X and Y?

Case 1: X could sell the products it sells to Y in an active market. Internal transfer prices are higher than market prices.

Case 2:   There is no active market for the products X sells to Y.

Analysis

❏   Case 1

A6. X could sell its products on an active market and, so, generate cash inflows from continuing use that would be largely independent of the cash inflows from Y. Therefore, it is likely that X is a separate cash-generating unit, although part of its production is used by Y (see paragraph 36.69, p. 219).

A7.   It is likely that Y is also a separate cash-generating unit. Y sells 80% of its products to customers outside of the reporting enterprise. Therefore, its cash inflows from continuing use can be considered to be largely independent.

A8.   Internal transfer prices do not reflect market prices for X's output. Therefore, in determining value in use of both X and Y, the enterprise adjusts financial budgets/forecasts to reflect management's best estimate of future market prices for those of X's products that are used internally (see paragraph 36.69, p. 219).

❏   Case 2

A9.   It is likely that the recoverable amount of each plant cannot be assessed independently from the recoverable amount of the other plant because:

(a)   the majority of X's production is used internally and could not be sold in an active market. So, cash inflows of X depend on demand for Y's products. Therefore, X cannot be considered to generate cash inflows that are largely independent from those of Y; and

(b)   the two plants are managed together.

A10. As a consequence, it is likely that X and Y together are the smallest group of assets that generates cash inflows from continuing use that are largely independent.

C - Single Product Enterprise

Background

A11. Enterprise M produces a single product and owns plants A, B and C. Each plant is located in a different continent. A produces a component that is assembled in either B or C. The combined capacity of B and C is not fully utilised. M's products are sold world-wide from either B or C. For example, B's production can be sold in C's continent if the products can be delivered faster from B than from C. Utilisation levels of B and C depend on the allocation of sales between the two sites.

For each of the following cases, what are the cash-generating units for A, B and C?

Case 1:   There is an active market for A's products.

Case 2:   There is no active market for A's products.

Analysis

❏   Case 1

A12. It is likely that A is a separate cash-generating unit because there is an active market for its products (*see Example B - Plant for an Intermediate Step in a Production Process, Case 1*).

A13. Although there is an active market for the products assembled by B and C, cash inflows for B and C depend on the allocation of production across the two sites. It is unlikely that the future cash inflows for B and C can be determined individually. Therefore, it is likely that B and C together is the smallest identifiable group of assets that generates cash inflows from continuing use that are largely independent.

A14. In determining the value in use of A and B plus C, M adjusts financial budgets/ forecasts to reflect its best estimate of future market prices for A's products (see paragraph 36.69, p. 219).

❏   Case 2

A15. It is likely that the recoverable amount of each plant cannot be assessed independently because:

(a) there is no active market for A's products. Therefore, A's cash inflows depend on sales of the final product by B and C; and

(b) although there is an active market for the products assembled by B and C, cash inflows for B and C depend on the allocation of production across the two sites. It is unlikely that the future cash inflows for B and C can be determined individually.

A16. As a consequence, it is likely that A, B and C together (i.e. M as a whole) are the smallest identifiable group of assets that generates cash inflows from continuing use that are largely independent.

D - Magazine Titles

Background

A17. A publisher owns 150 magazine titles of which 70 were purchased and 80 were self-created. The price paid for a purchased magazine title is recognised as an intangible asset. The costs of creating magazine titles and maintaining the existing titles are recognised as an expense when incurred. Cash inflows from direct sales and advertising are identifiable for each magazine title. Titles are managed by customer segments. The level of advertising income for a magazine title depends on the range of titles in the customer segment to which the magazine title relates. Management has a policy to abandon old titles before the end of their economic lives and replace them immediately with new titles for the same customer segment.

What is the cash-generating unit for an individual magazine title?

Analysis

A18. It is likely that the recoverable amount of an individual magazine title can be assessed. Even though the level of advertising income for a title is influenced, to a certain extent, by the other titles in the customer segment, cash inflows from direct sales and advertising are identifiable for each title. In addition, although titles are managed by customer segments, decisions to abandon titles are made on an individual title basis.

A19. Therefore, it is likely that individual magazine titles generate cash inflows that are largely independent one from another and that each magazine title is a separate cash-generating unit.

E - Building Half-Rented to Others and Half-Occupied for Own Use

Background

A20. M is a manufacturing company. It owns a headquarter building that used to be fully occupied for internal use. After down-sizing, half of the building is now used internally and half-rented to third parties. The lease agreement with the tenant is for five years.

What is the cash-generating unit of the building?

Analysis

A21. The primary purpose of the building is to serve as a corporate asset, supporting M's manufacturing activities. Therefore, the building as a whole cannot be considered to generate cash inflows that are largely independent of the cash inflows from the enterprise as a whole. So, it is likely that the cash-generating unit for the building is M as a whole.

A22. The building is not held as an investment. Therefore, it would not be appropriate to determine the value in use of the building based on projections of future market related rents.

Example 2	**Calculation of Value in Use and Recognition of an Impairment Loss**

In this example, tax effects are ignored.

Background and Calculation of Value in Use

A23. At the end of 20X0, enterprise T acquires enterprise M for 10,000. M has manufacturing plants in three countries. The anticipated useful life of the resulting merged activities is 15 years.

End of 20X0	Allocation of purchase price	Fair value of identifiable assets	Goodwill[1]
Activities in Country A	3,000	2,000	1,000
Activities in Country B	2,000	1,500	500
Activities in Country C	5,000	3,500	1,500
Total	10,000	7,000	3,000

[1] *Activities in each country are the smallest cash-generating units to which goodwill can be allocated on a reasonable and consistent basis (allocation based on the purchase price of the activities in each country, as specified in the purchase agreement).*

Figure 20 **Schedule 1: Data at the end of 20X0**

A24. T uses straight-line depreciation and amortisation over a 15-year life for the Country A assets and no residual value is anticipated.

A25. In 20X4, a new government is elected in Country *A*. It passes legislation significantly restricting exports of *T*'s main product. As a result, and for the foreseeable future, *T*'s production will be cut by 40%.

A26. The significant export restriction and the resulting production decrease require *T* to estimate the recoverable amount of the goodwill and net assets of the Country *A* operations. The cash-generating unit for the goodwill and the identifiable assets of the Country *A* operations is the Country *A* operations, since no independent cash inflows can be identified for individual assets.

A27. The net selling price of the Country *A* cash-generating unit is not determinable, as it is unlikely that a ready buyer exists for all the assets of that unit.

A28. To determine the value in use for the Country *A* cash-generating unit (see Schedule 2, Figure 21), *T*:

(a)   prepares cash flow forecasts derived from the most recent financial budgets/forecasts for the next five years (years 20X5-20X9) approved by management;

(b)   estimates subsequent cash flows (years 20X10-20X15) based on declining growth rates. The growth rate for 20X10 is estimated to be 3%. This rate is lower than the average long-term growth rate for the market in Country *A*; and

(c)   selects a 15% discount rate, which represents a pre-tax rate that reflects current market assessments of the time value of money and the risks specific to the Country *A* cash-generating unit.

Recognition and Measurement of Impairment Loss

A29. The recoverable amount of the Country *A* cash-generating unit is 1,360: the higher of the net selling price of the Country *A* cash-generating unit (not determinable) and its value in use (1,360).

A30. *T* compares the recoverable amount of the Country *A* cash-generating unit to its carrying amount (see Schedule 3, Figure 22).

A31. *T* recognises an impairment loss of 840 immediately in the income statement. The carrying amount of the goodwill that relates to the Country *A* operations is eliminated before reducing the carrying amount of other identifiable assets within the Country *A* cash-generating unit.

A32. Tax effects are accounted for separately in accordance with IAS 12, *Income Taxes* (see Example 3A, overleaf).

Year	Long-term growth rates	Future cash flows	Present value factor at 15% discount rate[3]	Discounted future cash flows
20X5 (n=1)		230[1]	0.86957	200
20X6		253[1]	0.75614	191
20X7		273[1]	0.65752	180
20X8		290[1]	0.57175	166
20X9		304[1]	0.49718	151
20X10	3%	313[2]	0.43233	135
20X11	-2%	307[2]	0.37594	115
20X12	-6%	289[2]	0.32690	94
20X13	-15%	245[2]	0.28426	70
20X14	-25%	184[2]	0.24719	45
20X15	-67%	61[2]	0.21494	13
Value in use				1,360

[1] *Based on management's best estimate of net cash flow projections (after the 40% cut).*
[2] *Based on an extrapolation from preceding year cash flow using declining growth rates.*
[3] *The present value factor is calculated as $k = 1/(1+a)^n$, where a = discount rate and n = period of discount.*

Figure 21 **Schedule 2: Calculation of the value in use of the Country *A* cash-generating unit at the end of 20X4**

End of 20X4	Goodwill	Identifiable assets	Total
Historical cost	1,000	2,000	3,000
Accumulated depreciation/ amortisation (20X1- 20X4)	(267)	(533)	(800)
Carrying amount	733	1,467	2,200
Impairment loss	(733)	(107)	(840)
Carrying amount after impairment loss	0	1,360	1,360

Figure 22 **Schedule 3: Calculation and allocation of the impairment loss for the Country *A* cash-generating unit at the end of 20X4**

Example 3   **Deferred Tax Effects**

A - Deferred Tax Effects of the Recognition of an Impairment Loss

Use the data for enterprise T as presented in Example 2, with supplementary information as provided in this example.

A33. At the end of 20X4, the tax base of the identifiable assets of the Country *A* cash-generating unit is 1,100. Impairment losses are not deductible for tax purposes. The tax rate is 40%.

A34. The recognition of an impairment loss on the assets of the Country *A* cash-generating unit reduces the taxable temporary difference related to those assets. The deferred tax liability is reduced accordingly.

End of 20X4	Identifiable assets before impairment loss	Impairment loss	Identifiable assets after impairment loss
Carrying amount (Example 2)	1,467	(107)	1,360
Tax base	1,100	-	1,100
Taxable temporary difference	367	(107)	260
Deferred tax liability at 40%	146	(42)	104

Figure 23

A35. In accordance with IAS 12, *Income Taxes* (see section 4.1, p. 247), no deferred tax relating to the goodwill was recognised initially. Therefore, the impairment loss relating to the goodwill does not give rise to a deferred tax adjustment.

B - Recognition of an Impairment Loss Creates a Deferred Tax Asset

A36. An enterprise has an asset with a carrying amount of 1,000. Its recoverable amount is 650. The tax rate is 30% and the tax base of the asset is 800. Impairment losses are not deductible for tax purposes. The effect of the impairment loss is as as follows:

	Before impairment	Effect of impairment	After impairment
Carrying amount	1,000	(350)	650
Tax base	800	-	800
Taxable (deductible) temporary difference	200	(350)	(150)
Deferred tax liability (asset) at 30%	60	(105)	(45)

Figure 24

A37. In accordance with IAS 12, *Income Taxes*, the enterprise recognises the deferred tax asset to the extent that it is probable that taxable profit will be available against which the deductible temporary difference can be utilised.

Example 4	Reversal of an Impairment Loss

Use the data for enterprise T as presented in Example 2, with supplementary information as provided in this example. In this example, tax effects are ignored.

Background

A38. In 20X6, the government is still in office in Country *A*, but the business situation is improving. The effects of the export laws on *T*'s production are proving to be less drastic than initially expected by management. As a result, management estimates that production will increase by 30%. This favourable change requires *T* to re-estimate the recoverable amount of the net assets of the Country *A* operations (see paragraphs 36.95 and 36.96, p. 221). The cash-generating unit for the net assets of the Country *A* operations is still the Country *A* operations.

A39. Calculations similar to those in Example 2 show that the recoverable amount of the Country *A* cash-generating unit is now 1,710.

Reversal of Impairment Loss

End of 20X4 (Example 2)	Goodwill	Identifiable assets	Total
Historical cost	1,000	2,000	3,000
Accumulated depreciation/amortisation (4 years)	(267)	(533)	(800)
Impairment loss	(733)	(107)	(840)
Carrying amount after impairment loss	0	1,360	1,360

Figure 25 **Schedule 1: Calculation of the carrying amount of the Country *A* cash-generating unit at the end of 20X6**

A40. *T* compares the recoverable amount and the net carrying amount of the Country *A* cash-generating unit.

End of 20X6	Goodwill	Identifiable assets	Total
Additional depreciation (2 years) [1]	-	(247)	(247)
Carrying amount	0	1,113	1,113
Recoverable amount			1,710
Excess of recoverable amount over carrying amount			597

Figure 26 **Schedule 2: Calculation of the carrying amount of the Country *A* cash-generating unit at the end of 20X6 (continued)**

[1] *After recognition of the impairment loss at the end of 20X4, T revised the depreciation charge for the Country A identifiable assets (from 133.3 per year to 123.7 per year), based on the revised carrying amount and remaining useful life (11 years).*

A41. There has been a favourable change in the estimates used to determine the recoverable amount of the Country *A* net assets since the last impairment loss was recognised. Therefore, in accordance with paragraph 36.99 (p. 221), *T* recognises a reversal of the impairment loss recognised in 20X4.

A42. In accordance with paragraphs 36.107 and 36.108, *T* increases the carrying amount of the Country *A* identifiable assets by 87 (see Schedule 3, Figure 28), i.e. up to the lower of recoverable amount (1,710) and the identifiable assets' depreciated historical cost (1,200) (see Schedule 2, Figure 27). This increase is recognised in the income statement immediately.

A43. In accordance with paragraph 36.109 (p. 222), the impairment loss on goodwill is not reversed because the external event that led to the recognition of the impairment loss on goodwill has not reversed. The legislation that significantly restricts exports of *T*'s product is still in place, even though its effect is not as severe as expected.

End of 20X6	Identifiable assets
Historical cost	2,000
Accumulated depreciation (133.3 * 6 years)	(800)
Depreciated historical cost	1,200
Carrying amount (Schedule 1)	1,113
Difference	87

Figure 27 **Schedule 2: Determination of the depreciated historical cost of the Country *A* identifiable assets at the end of 20X6**

End of 20X6	Goodwill	Identifiable assets	Total
Gross carrying amount	1,000	2,000	3,000
Accumulated amortisation	(267)	(780)	(1,047)
Accumulated impairment loss	(733)	(107)	(840)
Carrying amount	0	1,113	1,113
Reversal of impairment loss	0	87	87
Carrying amount after reversal of impairment loss	0	1,200	1,200

Figure 28 **Schedule 3: Carrying amount of the Country *A* assets at the end of 20X6**

Example 5	Treatment of a Future Restructuring

In this example, tax effects are ignored.

Background

A44. At the end of 20X0, enterprise K tests a plant for impairment. The plant is a cash-generating unit. The plant's assets are carried at depreciated historical cost. The plant has a carrying amount of 3,000 and a remaining useful life of 10 years.

A45. The plant is so specialised that it is not possible to determine its net selling price. Therefore, the plant's recoverable amount is its value in use. Value in use is calculated using a pre-tax discount rate of 14%.

A46. Management approved budgets reflect that:

(a)   at the end of 20X3, the plant will be restructured at an estimated cost of 100. Since K is not yet committed to the restructuring, a provision has not been recognised for the future restructuring costs; and

(b)   there will be future benefits from this restructuring in the form of reduced future cash outflows.

A47. At the end of 20X2, K becomes committed to the restructuring. The costs are still estimated to be 100 and a provision is recognised accordingly. The plant's estimated future cash flows reflected in the most recent management approved budgets are given in paragraph A51 and a current discount rate is the same as at the end of 20X0.

A48. At the end of 20X3, actual restructuring costs of 100 are incurred and paid. Again, the plant's estimated future cash flows reflected in the most recent management approved budgets and a current discount rate are the same as those estimated at the end of 20X2.

At the End of 20X0

Year	Future cash flows	Discounted at 14%
20X1	300	263
20X2	280	215
20X3	420[1]	283
20X4	520[2]	308
20X5	350[2]	182
20X6	420[2]	191
20X7	480[2]	192
20X8	480[2]	168
20X9	460[2]	141
20X10	400[2]	108
Value in use		2,051

Figure 29 **Schedule 1: Calculation of the plant's value in use at the end of 20X0**

[1] *Excludes estimated restructuring costs reflected in management budgets.*
[2] *Excludes estimated benefits expected from the restructuring reflected in management budgets.*

A49. The plant's recoverable amount (value in use) is less than its carrying amount. Therefore, *K* recognises an impairment loss for the plant.

	Plant
Carrying amount before impairment loss	3,000
Recoverable amount (Schedule 1)	2,051
Impairment loss	(949)
Carrying amount after impairment loss	2,051

Figure 30 **Schedule 2: Calculation of the impairment loss at the end of 20X0**

At the End of 20X1

A50. No event occurs that requires the plant's recoverable amount to be re-estimated. Therefore, no calculation of the recoverable amount is required to be performed.

At the End of 20X2

A51. The enterprise is now committed to the restructuring. Therefore, in determining the plant's value in use, the benefits expected from the restructuring are considered in forecasting cash flows. This results in an increase in the estimated future cash flows used to determine value in use at the end of 20X0. In accordance with paragraphs 36.95 and 36.96, the recoverable amount of the plant is re-determined at the end of 20X2.

Year	Future cash flows	Discounted at 14%
20X3	420[1]	368
20X4	570[2]	439
20X5	380[2]	256
20X6	450[2]	266
20X7	510[2]	265
20X8	510[2]	232
20X9	480[2]	192
20X10	410[2]	144
Value in use		2,162

Figure 31 **Schedule 3: Calculation of the plant's value in use at the end of 20X2**

[1] *Excludes estimated restructuring costs because a liability has already been recognised.*
[2] *Includes estimated benefits expected from the restructuring reflected in management budgets.*

A52. The plant's recoverable amount (value in use) is higher than its carrying amount (see Schedule 4. Figure 32). Therefore, *K* reverses the impairment loss recognised for the plant at the end of 20X0.

	Plant
Carrying amount at the end of 20X0 (Schedule 2)	2,051
End of 20X2	
Depreciation charge (for 20X1 and 20X2 – Schedule 5)	(410)
Carrying amount before reversal	1,641
Recoverable amount (Schedule 3)	2,162
Reversal of the impairment loss	521
Carrying amount after reversal	2,162
Carrying amount: depreciated historical cost (Schedule 5)	2,400[1]

Figure 32 **Schedule 4: Calculation of the reversal of the impairment loss at the end of 20X2**

[1] *The reversal does not result in the carrying amount of the plant exceeding what its carrying amount would have been at depreciated historical cost. Therefore, the full reversal of the impairment loss is recognised.*

At the End of 20X3

A53. There is a cash outflow of 100 when the restructuring costs are paid. Even though a cash outflow has taken place, there is no change in the estimated future cash flows used to determine value in use at the end of 20X2. Therefore, the plant's recoverable amount is not calculated at the end of 20X3.

End of year	Depreciated historical cost	Recoverable amount	Adjusted depreciation charge	Impairment loss	Carrying amount after impairment
20X0	3,000	2,051	0	(949)	2,051
20X1	2,700	n.c.	(205)	0	1,846
20X2	2,400	2,162	(205)	521	2,162
20X3	2,100	n.c.	(270)	0	1,892

Figure 33 **Schedule 5: Summary of the carrying amount of the plant**

n.c. = *not calculated as there is no indication that the impairment loss may have increased/decreased.*

Example 6 **Treatment of Future Capital Expenditure**

In this example, tax effects are ignored.

Background

A54. At the end of 20X0, enterprise *F* tests a plane for impairment. The plane is a cash-generating unit. It is carried at depreciated historical cost and its carrying amount is 150,000. It has an estimated remaining useful life of 10 years.

A55. For the purpose of this example, it is assumed that the plane's net selling price is not determinable. Therefore, the plane's recoverable amount is its value in use. Value in use is calculated using a pre-tax discount rate of 14%.

A56. Management approved budgets reflect that:

(a) in 20X4, capital expenditure of 25,000 will be incurred to renew the engine of the plane; and

(b) this capital expenditure will improve the performance of the plane by decreasing fuel consumption.

A57. At the end of 20X4, renewal costs are incurred. The plane's estimated future cash flows reflected in the most recent management approved budgets are given in paragraph A60 and a current discount rate is the same as at the end of 20X0.

At the End of 20X0

Year	Future cash flows	Discounted at 14%
20X1	22,165	19,443
20X2	21,450	16,505
20X3	20,550	13,871
20X4	24,725[1]	14,639
20X5	25,325[2]	13,153
20X6	24,825[2]	11,310
20X7	24,123[2]	9,640
20X8	25,533[2]	8,951
20X9	24,234[2]	7,452
20X10	22,850[2]	6,164
Value in use		121,128

Figure 34 **Schedule 1: Calculation of the plane's value in use at the end of 20X0**

[1] *Excludes estimated renewal costs reflected in management budgets.*
[2] *Excludes estimated benefits expected from the renewal of the engine reflected in management budgets.*

A58. The plane's carrying amount is less than its recoverable amount (value in use). Therefore, F recognises an impairment loss for the plane.

	Plane
Carrying amount before impairment loss	150,000
Recoverable amount (Schedule 1)	121,128
Impairment loss	(28,872)
Carrying amount after impairment loss	121,128

Figure 35 **Schedule 2: Calculation of the impairment loss at the end of 20X0**

Years 20X1 - 20X3

A59. No event occurs that requires the plane's recoverable amount to be re-estimated. Therefore, no calculation of recoverable amount is required to be performed.

At the End of 20X4

A60. The capital expenditure is incurred. Therefore, in determining the plane's value in use, the future benefits expected from the renewal of the engine are considered in forecasting cash flows. This results in an increase in the estimated future cash flows used to determine value in use at the end of 20X0. As a consequence, in accordance with paragraphs 95-96 of IAS 36, the recoverable amount of the plane is recalculated at the end of 20X4.

Year	Future cash flows[1]	Discounted at 14%
20X5	30,321	26,597
20X6	32,750	25,200
20X7	31,721	21,411
20X8	31,950	18,917
20X9	33,100	17,191
20X10	27,999	12,756
Value in use		122,072

Figure 36 **Schedule 3: Calculation of the plane's value in use at the end of 20X4**

[1] *Includes estimated benefits expected from the renewal of the engine reflected in management budgets.*

A61. The plane's recoverable amount (value in use) is higher than the plane's carrying amount and depreciated historical cost (see Schedule 4 below). Therefore, F reverses the impairment loss recognised for the plane at the end of 20X0 so that the plane is carried at depreciated historical cost.

	Plane
Carrying amount at the end of 20X0 (Schedule 2)	121,128
End of 20X4	
Depreciation charge (20X1 to 20X4 – Schedule 5)	(48,452)
Renewal expenditure	25,000
Carrying amount before reversal	97,676
Recoverable amount (Schedule 3)	122,072
Reversal of the impairment loss	17,324
Carrying amount after reversal	115,000
Carrying amount: depreciated historical cost (Schedule 5)	115,000[1]

Figure 37 **Schedule 4: Calculation of the reversal of the impairment loss at the end of 20X4**

[1] *The value in use of the plane exceeds what its carrying amount would have been at depreciated historical cost. Therefore, the reversal is limited to an amount that does not result in the carrying amount of the plane exceeding depreciated historical cost.*

Year	Depreciated historical cost	Recoverable amount	Adjusted depreciation charge	Impairment loss	Carrying amount after impairment
20X0	150,000	121,128	0	(28,872)	121,128
20X1	135,000	n.c.	(12,113)	0	109,015
20X2	120,000	n.c.	(12,113)	0	96,902
20X3	105,000	n.c.	(12,113)	0	84,789
20X4	90,000		(12,113)		
renewal	25,000		-		
	115,000	122,072	(12,113)	17,324	115,000
20X5	95,833	n.c.	(19,167)	0	95,833

Figure 38 **Schedule 5: Summary of the carrying amount of the plane**

n.c. = not calculated as there is no indication that the impairment loss may have increased/decreased.

Example 7

Application of the 'Bottom-Up' and 'Top-Down' Tests to Goodwill

---

In this example, tax effects are ignored.

A62. At the end of 20X0, enterprise M acquired 100% of enterprise Z for 3,000. Z has 3 cash-generating units A, B and C with net fair values of 1,200, 800 and 400 respectively. M recognises goodwill of 600 (3,000 less 2,400) that relates to Z.

A63. At the end of 20X5, A makes significant losses. Its recoverable amount is estimated to be 1,400. Carrying amounts are detailed below.

End of 20X5	A	B	C	Goodwill	Total
Net carrying amount	1,300	1,200	800	450	3,750

Figure 39 **Schedule 1: Carrying amounts at the end of 20X5**

A - Goodwill Can be Allocated on a Reasonable and Consistent Basis

A64. At the date of acquisition of Z, the net fair values of A, B and C are considered a reasonable basis for a pro-rata allocation of the goodwill to A, B and C.

End of 20X0	A	B	C	Total
Net fair values	1,200	800	400	2,400
Pro rata	50%	33%	17%	100%
End of 20X5				
Net carrying amount	1,300	1,200	800	3,300
Allocation of goodwill (using the pro rata above)	225	150	75	450
Net carrying amount (after allocation of goodwill)	1,525	1,350	875	3,750

Figure 40 **Schedule 2: Allocation of goodwill at the end of 20X5**

A65. In accordance with the 'bottom-up' test in paragraph 36.80(a) of IAS 36 (p. 219), *M* compares *A*'s recoverable amount to its carrying amount after the allocation of the carrying amount of goodwill.

End of 20X5	A
Carrying amount after allocation of goodwill (Schedule 2)	1,525
Recoverable amount	1,400
Impairment loss	125

Figure 41 **Schedule 3: Application of 'bottom-up' test**

A66. *M* recognises an impairment loss of 125 for *A*. The impairment loss is fully allocated to the goodwill in accordance with paragraph 36.88 (p. 220).

B - Goodwill Cannot be Allocated on a Reasonable and Consistent Basis

A67. There is no reasonable way to allocate the goodwill that arose on the acquisition of *Z* to *A*, *B* and *C*. At the end of 20X5, *Z*'s recoverable amount is estimated to be 3,500.

A68. At the end of 20X5, *M* first applies the 'bottom-up' test in accordance with paragraph 36.80(a). It compares *A*'s recoverable amount to its carrying amount excluding the goodwill.

End of 20X5	A
Carrying amount	1,300
Recoverable amount	1,400
Impairment loss	0

Figure 42 **Schedule 4: Application of 'bottom-up' test**

A69. Therefore, no impairment loss is recognised for A as a result of the 'bottom-up' test.

A70. Since the goodwill could not be allocated on a reasonable and consistent basis to A, M also performs a 'top-down' test in accordance with paragraph 36.80(b). It compares the carrying amount of Z as a whole to its recoverable amount (Z as a whole is the smallest cash-generating unit that includes A and to which goodwill can be allocated on a reasonable and consistent basis).

End of 20X5	A	B	C	Goodwill	Z
Carrying amount	1,300	1,200	800	450	3,750
Impairment loss arising from the 'bottom-up' test	0	-	-	-	0
Carrying amount after the 'bottom-up' test	1,300	1,200	800	450	3,750
Recoverable amount					3,500
Impairment loss arising from 'top-down' test					(250)

Figure 43 **Schedule 5: Application of the 'top-down' test**

A71. Therefore, M recognises an impairment loss of 250 that it allocates fully to goodwill in accordance with paragraph 36.88.

Example 8	**Allocation of Corporate Assets**

In this example, tax effects are ignored.

Background

A72. Enterprise M has three cash-generating units: A, B and C. There are adverse changes in the technological environment in which M operates. Therefore, M

conducts impairment tests of each of its cash-generating units. At the end of 20X0, the carrying amounts of *A*, *B* and *C* are 100, 150 and 200 respectively.

A73. The operations are conducted from a headquarter. The carrying amount of the headquarter assets is 200: a headquarter building of 150 and a research centre of 50. The relative carrying amounts of the cash-generating units are a reasonable indication of the proportion of the headquarter building devoted to each cash-generating unit. The carrying amount of the research centre cannot be allocated on a reasonable basis to the individual cash-generating units.

A74. The remaining estimated useful life of cash-generating unit *A* is 10 years. The remaining useful lives of *B*, *C* and the headquarter assets are 20 years. The headquarter assets are depreciated on a straight-line basis.

A75. There is no basis on which to calculate a net selling price for each cash-generating unit. Therefore, the recoverable amount of each cash-generating unit is based on its value in use. Value in use is calculated using a pre-tax discount rate of 15%.

Identification of Corporate Assets

A76. In accordance with paragraph 36.86, *M* first identifies all the corporate assets that relate to the individual cash-generating units under review. The corporate assets are the headquarter building and the research centre.

A77. *M* then decides how to deal with each of the corporate assets:

(a)   the carrying amount of the headquarter building can be allocated on a reasonable and consistent basis to the cash-generating units under review. Therefore, only a 'bottom-up' test is necessary; and

(b)   the carrying amount of the research centre cannot be allocated on a reasonable and consistent basis to the individual cash-generating units under review. Therefore, a 'top-down' test will be applied in addition to the 'bottom-up' test.

Allocation of Corporate Assets

A78. The carrying amount of the headquarter building is allocated to the carrying amount of each individual cash-generating unit. A weighted allocation basis is used because the estimated remaining useful life of *A*'s cash-generating unit is 10 years, whereas the estimated remaining useful lives of *B* and *C*'s cash-generating units are 20 years.

End of 20X0	A	B	C	Total
Carrying amount	100	150	200	450
Useful life	10 years	20 years	20 years	
Weighting based on useful life	1	2	2	
Carrying amount after weighting	100	300	400	800
Pro-rata allocation of the building	12% (100/800)	38% (300/800)	50% (400/800)	100%
Allocation of the carrying amount of the building (based on pro-rata above)	19	56	75	(150)
Carrying amount (after allocation of the building)	119	206	275	600

Figure 44 **Schedule 1: Calculation of a weighted allocation of the carrying amount of the headquarter building**

Determination of Recoverable Amount

A79. The 'bottom-up' test requires calculation of the recoverable amount of each individual cash-generating unit. The 'top-down' test requires calculation of the recoverable amount of M as a whole (the smallest cash-generating unit that includes the research centre).

	A		B		C		M	
Year	Future cash flows	Discount at 15%	Future cash flows	Discount at 15%	Future cash flows	Discount at 15%	Future cash flows	Discount at 15%
1	18	16	9	8	10	9	39	34
2	31	23	16	12	20	15	72	54
3	37	24	24	16	34	22	105	69
4	42	24	29	17	44	25	128	73
5	47	24	32	16	51	25	143	71
6	52	22	33	14	56	24	155	67
7	55	21	34	13	60	22	162	61
8	55	18	35	11	63	21	166	54
9	53	15	35	10	65	18	167	48
10	48	12	35	9	66	16	169	42
11			36	8	66	14	132	28
12			35	7	66	12	131	25
13			35	6	66	11	131	21
14			33	5	65	9	128	18
15			30	4	62	8	122	15
16			26	3	60	6	115	12
17			22	2	57	5	108	10
18			18	1	51	4	97	8
19			14	1	43	3	85	6
20		—	10	1	35	2	71	4
Value in use		199		164		271		720[1]

Figure 45 **Schedule 2: Calculation of A, B, C and M's value in use at the end of 20X0**

[1] *It is assumed that the research centre generates additional future cash flows for the enterprise as a whole. Therefore, the sum of the value in use of each individual cash-generating unit is less than the value in use of the business as a whole. The additional cash flows are not attributable to the headquarter building.*

Calculation of Impairment Losses

A80. In accordance with the 'bottom-up' test, M compares the carrying amount of each cash-generating unit (after allocation of the carrying amount of the building) to its recoverable amount.

End of 20X0	A	B	C
Carrying amount (after allocation of the building) (Schedule 1)	119	206	
			275
Recoverable amount (Schedule 2)	199	164	271
Impairment loss	0	(42)	(4)

Figure 46 **Schedule 3: Application of 'bottom-up' test**

A81. The next step is to allocate the impairment losses between the assets of the cash-generating units and the headquarter building.

Cash-generating unit	B	C
To headquarter building	(12) *(42 × 56/206)*	(1) *(4 × 75/275)*
To assets in cash-generating unit	(30) *(42 × 150/206)*	(3) *(4 × 200/275)*
	(42)	(4)

Figure 47 **Schedule 4: Allocation of the impairment losses for cash-generating units B and C**

A82. In accordance with the 'top-down' test, since the research centre could not be allocated on a reasonable and consistent basis to A, B and C's cash-generating units, M compares the carrying amount of the smallest cash-generating unit to which the carrying amount of the research centre can be allocated (i.e. M as a whole) to its recoverable amount.

End of 20X0	A	B	C	Building	Research centre	M
Carrying amount	100	150	200	150	50	650
Impairment loss arising from the 'bottom-up' test	-	(30)	(3)	(13)	-	(46)
Carrying amount after the 'bottom-up' test	100	120	197	137	50	604
Recoverable amount (Schedule 2)						720
Impairment loss arising from 'top-down' test						0

Figure 48 **Schedule 5: Application of the 'top-down' test**

A83. Therefore, no additional impairment loss results from the application of the 'top-down' test. Only an impairment loss of 46 is recognised as a result of the application of the 'bottom-up' test.

Chapter 4

Accounting for Liabilities

IAS 12 prescribes the accounting treatment of income taxes. IAS 12 also addresses the recognition of deferred tax assets arising from unused tax losses or unused tax credits, the presentation of income taxes in the financial statements and the disclosure of information relating to income taxes.

IAS 19 prescribes the accounting and disclosure by employers for employee benefits.

IAS 17 prescribes the appropriate policies and disclosure applicable to finance and operating leases, from the perspective of both lessees and lessors.

IAS 37 ensures that appropriate recognition criteria and measurement bases are applied to provisions, contingent liabilities and contingent assets and that sufficient information is disclosed in the notes to the financial statements to enable users to understand their nature, timing and amount.

4.1	**Income Taxes**

The principal issue in accounting for income taxes is how to account for the current and future tax consequences of:

(a)   the future recovery (settlement) of the carrying amount of assets (liabilities) that are recognised in an enterprise's balance sheet; and

(b)   transactions and other events of the current period that are recognised in an enterprise's financial statements.

It is inherent in the recognition of an asset or liability that the reporting enterprise expects to recover or settle the carrying amount of that asset or liability. If it is probable that recovery or settlement of that carrying amount will make future tax payments larger (smaller) than they would be if such recovery or settlement were to have no tax consequences, IAS 12 requires an enterprise to recognise a deferred tax liability (deferred tax asset), with certain limited exceptions.

IAS 12 should be applied in accounting for income taxes. *(12.1)*

For the purposes of this Standard, income taxes include all domestic and foreign taxes which are based on taxable profits. Income taxes also include taxes, such as withholding taxes, which are payable by a subsidiary, associate or joint venture on distributions to the reporting enterprise. *(12.2)*

In some jurisdictions, income taxes are payable at a higher or lower rate if part or all of the net profit or retained earnings is paid out as a dividend. In some other jurisdictions, income taxes may be refundable if part or all of the net profit or retained earnings is paid out as a dividend. IAS 12 does not specify when, or how, an enterprise should account for the tax consequences of dividends and other distributions by the reporting enterprise. *(12.3)*

IAS 12 does not deal with the methods of accounting for government grants (see IAS 20, *Accounting for Government Grants and Disclosure of Government Assistance,* under section 5.3, p. 342) or investment tax credits. However, this Standard does deal with the accounting for temporary differences that may arise from such grants or investment tax credits. (12.4)

IAS 12 uses the following terms:

- *Accounting profit* is net profit or loss for a period before deducting tax expense.
- *Taxable profit (tax loss)* is the profit (loss) for a period, determined in accordance with the rules established by the taxation authorities, upon which income taxes are payable (recoverable).
- *Tax expense (tax income)* is the aggregate amount included in the determination of net profit or loss for the period in respect of current tax and deferred tax.
- *Current tax* is the amount of income taxes payable (recoverable) in respect of the taxable profit (tax loss) for a period.
- *Deferred tax liabilities* are the amounts of income taxes payable in future periods in respect of taxable temporary differences.
- *Deferred tax assets* are the amounts of income taxes recoverable in future periods in respect of:

    (a)   deductible temporary differences;

    (b)   the carryforward of unused tax losses; and

    (c)   the carryforward of unused tax credits.

- *Temporary differences* are differences between the carrying amount of an asset or liability in the balance sheet and its tax base. Temporary differences may be either:

    (a)   **taxable temporary differences,** which are temporary differences that will result in taxable amounts in determining taxable profit (tax loss) of future periods when the carrying amount of the asset or liability is recovered or settled; or

    (b)   **deductible temporary differences,** which are temporary differences that will result in amounts that are deductible in determining taxable profit (tax loss) of future periods when the carrying amount of the asset or liability is recovered or settled.

- The *tax base* of an asset or liability is the amount attributed to that asset or liability for tax purposes. *(12.5)*

Tax Base

The tax base of an asset is the amount that will be deductible for tax purposes against any taxable economic benefits that will flow to an enterprise when it recovers the carrying amount of the asset. If those economic benefits will not be taxable, the tax base of the asset is equal to its carrying amount. *(12.7)*

The tax base of a liability is its carrying amount, less any amount that will be deductible for tax purposes in respect of that liability in future periods. In the case of revenue which is received in advance, the tax base of the resulting liability is its carrying amount, less any amount of the revenue that will not be taxable in future periods. *(12.8)*

Some items have a tax base but are not recognised as assets and liabilities in the balance sheet. For example, research costs are recognised as an expense in determining accounting profit in the period in which they are incurred but may not be permitted as a deduction in determining taxable profit (tax loss) until a later period. The difference between the tax base of the research costs, being the amount the taxation authorities will permit as a deduction in future periods, and the carrying amount of nil is a deductible temporary difference that results in a deferred tax asset. *(12.9)*

In consolidated financial statements, temporary differences are determined by comparing the carrying amounts of assets and liabilities in the consolidated financial statements with the appropriate tax base. The tax base is determined by reference to a consolidated tax return in those jurisdictions in which such a return is filed. In other jurisdictions, the tax base is determined by reference to the tax returns of each enterprise in the group. *(12.11)*

Recognition of Current Tax Liabilities and Current Tax Assets

Current tax for current and prior periods should, to the extent unpaid, be recognised as a liability. If the amount already paid in respect of current and prior periods exceeds the amount due for those periods, the excess should be recognised as an asset. *(12.12)*

The benefit relating to a tax loss that can be carried back to recover current tax of a previous period should be recognised as an asset. *(12.13)*

Recognition of Deferred Tax Liabilities and Deferred Tax Assets

Taxable Temporary Differences

A deferred tax liability should be recognised for all taxable temporary differences, unless the deferred tax liability arises from:

(a)   goodwill for which amortisation is not deductible for tax purposes; or

(b)   the initial recognition of an asset or liability in a transaction which:

   (i)   is not a business combination; and

   (ii)   at the time of the transaction, affects neither accounting profit nor taxable profit (tax loss).

However, for taxable temporary differences associated with investments in subsidiaries, branches and associates, and interests in joint ventures, a deferred tax liability should be recognised in accordance with the requirements discussed in "Investments in Subsidiaries, Branches and Associates and Interests in Joint Ventures" on page 253. *(12.15)*

Business Combinations

In a business combination that is an acquisition, the cost of the acquisition is allocated to the identifiable assets and liabilities acquired by reference to their fair values at the date of the exchange transaction. Temporary differences arise when the tax bases of the identifiable assets and liabilities acquired are not affected by the business combination or are affected differently. For example, when the carrying amount of an asset is increased to fair value but the tax base of the asset remains at cost to the previous owner, a taxable temporary difference arises which results in a deferred tax liability. The resulting deferred tax liability affects goodwill. *(12.19)*

Assets Carried at Fair Value

International Accounting Standards permit certain assets to be carried at fair value or to be revalued (see, for example, IAS 16, *Property, Plant and Equipment*, and IAS 40, *Investment Property*). In some jurisdictions, the revaluation or other restatement of an asset to fair value affects taxable profit (tax loss) for the current period. As a result, the tax base of the asset is adjusted and no temporary difference arises. In other jurisdictions, the revaluation or restatement of an asset does not affect taxable profit in the period of the revaluation or restatement and, consequently, the tax base of the asset is not adjusted. Nevertheless, the future recovery of the carrying amount will result in a taxable flow of economic benefits to the enterprise and the amount that will be deductible for tax purposes will differ from the amount of those economic benefits. The difference between the carrying amount of a revalued asset and its tax base is a temporary difference and gives rise to a deferred tax liability or asset. This is true even if:

(a)   the enterprise does not intend to dispose of the asset. In such cases, the revalued carrying amount of the asset will be recovered through use and this will generate taxable income which exceeds the depreciation that will be allowable for tax purposes in future periods; or

(b)   tax on capital gains is deferred if the proceeds of the disposal of the asset are invested in similar assets. In such cases, the tax will ultimately become payable on sale or use of the similar assets. *(12.20)*

Goodwill

Goodwill is the excess of the cost of an acquisition over the acquirer's interest in the fair value of the identifiable assets and liabilities acquired. Many taxation authorities do not allow the amortisation of goodwill as a deductible expense in determining taxable profit. Moreover, in such jurisdictions, the cost of goodwill is often not deductible when a subsidiary disposes of its underlying business. In such jurisdictions, goodwill has a tax base of nil. Any difference between the carrying amount of goodwill and its tax base of nil is a taxable temporary difference. However, this Standard does not permit the recognition of the resulting deferred tax liability because goodwill is a residual and the recognition of the deferred tax liability would increase the carrying amount of goodwill. *(12.21)*

Initial Recognition of an Asset or Liability

A temporary difference may arise on initial recognition of an asset or liability, for example, if part or all of the cost of an asset will not be deductible for tax purposes. The method of accounting for such a temporary difference depends on the nature of the transaction which led to the initial recognition of the asset:

(a)   in a business combination, an enterprise recognises any deferred tax liability or asset and this affects the amount of goodwill or negative goodwill;

(b)   if the transaction affects either accounting profit or taxable profit, an enterprise recognises any deferred tax liability or asset and recognises the resulting deferred tax expense or income in the income statement; and

(c)   if the transaction is not a business combination, and affects neither accounting profit nor taxable profit, an enterprise would, in the absence of an exemption, recognise the resulting deferred tax liability or asset and adjust the carrying amount of the asset or liability by the same amount. Such adjustments would make the financial statements less transparent. Therefore, IAS 12 does not permit an enterprise to recognise the resulting deferred tax liability or asset, either on initial recognition or subsequently. Furthermore, an enterprise does not recognise subsequent changes in the unrecognised deferred tax liability or asset as the asset is depreciated. *(12.22)*

In accordance with IAS 32, *Financial Instruments: Disclosure and Presentation*, the issuer of a compound financial instrument (for example, a convertible bond) classifies the instrument's liability component as a liability and the equity component as equity. In some jurisdictions, the tax base of the liability component on initial recognition is equal to the initial carrying amount of the sum of the liability and equity components. The resulting taxable temporary difference arises from the initial recognition of the equity component separately from the liability component. An enterprise recognises the resulting deferred tax liability. In accordance with the Standard, the deferred tax is charged directly to the carrying amount of the equity component, and subsequent changes in the deferred tax liability are recognised in the income statement as deferred tax expense (income). *(12.23)*

Deductible Temporary Differences

A deferred tax asset should be recognised for all deductible temporary differences to the extent that it is probable that taxable profit will be available against which the deductible temporary difference can be utilised, unless the deferred tax asset arises from:

(a)   negative goodwill which is treated as deferred income in accordance with IAS 22, *Business Combinations* (see section 7.1, p. 389); or

(b)   the initial recognition of an asset or liability in a transaction which:

   (i)   is not a business combination; and

   (ii)   at the time of the transaction, affects neither accounting profit nor taxable profit (tax loss).

However, for deductible temporary differences associated with investments in subsidiaries, branches and associates, and interests in joint ventures, a deferred tax asset should be recognised as required by the Standard. *(12.24)*

It is inherent in the recognition of a liability that the carrying amount will be settled in future periods through an outflow from the enterprise of resources embodying economic benefits. When resources flow from the enterprise, part or all of their amounts may be deductible in determining taxable profit of a period later than the period in which the liability is recognised. In such cases, a temporary difference exists between the carrying amount of the liability and its tax base. Accordingly, a deferred tax asset arises in respect of the income taxes that will be recoverable in the future periods when that part of the liability is allowed as a deduction in determining taxable profit. Similarly, if the carrying amount of an asset is less than its tax base, the difference gives rise to a deferred tax asset in respect of the income taxes that will be recoverable in future periods. *(12.25)*

Negative Goodwill

IAS 12 does not permit the recognition of a deferred tax asset arising from deductible temporary differences associated with negative goodwill which is treated as deferred income in accordance with IAS 22, because negative goodwill is a residual and the recognition of the deferred tax asset would increase the carrying amount of negative goodwill. *(12.32)*

Initial Recognition of an Asset or Liability

One case when a deferred tax asset arises on initial recognition of an asset is when a non-taxable government grant related to an asset is deducted in arriving at the carrying amount of the asset but, for tax purposes, is not deducted from the asset's depreciable amount (in other words its tax base); the carrying amount of the asset is less than its tax base and this gives rise to a deductible temporary difference. Government grants may also be set up as deferred income in which case the difference between the deferred income and its tax base of nil is a deductible temporary difference. Whichever method of presentation an enterprise adopts, the enterprise does not recognise the resulting deferred tax asset. *(12.33)*

Unused Tax Losses and Unused Tax Credits

A deferred tax asset should be recognised for the carryforward of unused tax losses and unused tax credits to the extent that it is probable that future taxable profit will be available against which the unused tax losses and unused tax credits can be utilised. *(12.34)*

Re-assessment of Unrecognised Deferred Tax Assets

At each balance sheet date, an enterprise re-assesses unrecognised deferred tax assets. The enterprise recognises a previously unrecognised deferred tax asset to the extent that it has become probable that future taxable profit will allow the deferred tax asset to be recovered. For example, an improvement in trading conditions may make it more probable that the enterprise will be able to generate sufficient taxable profit in the future for the deferred tax asset to meet the recognition criteria set out in the Standard. *(12.37)*

Investments in Subsidiaries, Branches and Associates and Interests in Joint Ventures

An enterprise should recognise a deferred tax liability for all taxable temporary differences associated with investments in subsidiaries, branches and associates, and interests in joint ventures, except to the extent that both of the following conditions are satisfied:

(a)   the parent, investor or venturer is able to control the timing of the reversal of the temporary difference; and

(b)   it is probable that the temporary difference will not reverse in the foreseeable future. *(12.39)*

An enterprise should recognise a deferred tax asset for all deductible temporary differences arising from investments in subsidiaries, branches and associates, and interests in joint ventures, to the extent that, and only to the extent that, it is probable that:

(a)   the temporary difference will reverse in the foreseeable future; and

(b)   taxable profit will be available against which the temporary difference can be utilised. *(12.44)*

Measurement

Current tax liabilities (assets) for the current and prior periods should be measured at the amount expected to be paid to (recovered from) the taxation authorities, using the tax rates (and tax laws) that have been enacted or substantively enacted by the balance sheet date. *(12.46)*

Deferred tax assets and liabilities should be measured at the tax rates that are expected to apply to the period when the asset is realised or the liability is settled, based on tax rates (and tax laws) that have been enacted or substantively enacted by the balance sheet date. *(12.47)*

The measurement of deferred tax liabilities and deferred tax assets should reflect the tax consequences that would follow from the manner in which the enterprise expects, at the balance sheet date, to recover or settle the carrying amount of its assets and liabilities. *(12.51)*

Deferred tax assets and liabilities should not be discounted. *(12.53)*

The carrying amount of a deferred tax asset should be reviewed at each balance sheet date. An enterprise should reduce the carrying amount of a deferred tax asset to the extent that it is no longer probable that sufficient taxable profit will be available to allow the benefit of part or all of that deferred tax asset to be utilised. Any such reduction should be reversed to the extent that it becomes probable that sufficient taxable profit will be available. *(12.56)*

Recognition of Current and Deferred Tax

Accounting for the current and deferred tax effects of a transaction or other event is consistent with the accounting for the transaction or event itself. The following paragraphs implement this principle. *(12.57)*

Income Statement

Current and deferred tax should be recognised as income or an expense and included in the net profit or loss for the period, except to the extent that the tax arises from:

(a)   a transaction or event which is recognised, in the same or a different period, directly in equity; or

(b)   a business combination that is an acquisition. *(12.58)*

Items Credited or Charged Directly to Equity

Current tax and deferred tax should be charged or credited directly to equity if the tax relates to items that are credited or charged, in the same or a different period, directly to equity. *(12.61)*

Deferred Tax Arising from a Business Combination

Temporary differences may arise in a business combination that is an acquisition. In accordance with IAS 22, an enterprise recognises any resulting deferred tax assets (to the extent that they meet the recognition criteria), or deferred tax liabilities as identifiable assets and liabilities at the date of the acquisition. Consequently, those deferred tax assets and liabilities affect goodwill or negative goodwill. However, an enterprise does not recognise deferred tax liabilities arising from goodwill itself (if amortisation of the goodwill is not deductible for tax purposes) and deferred tax assets arising from non-taxable negative goodwill which is treated as deferred income. *(12.66)*

As a result of a business combination, an acquirer may consider it probable that it will recover its own deferred tax asset that was not recognised prior to the business combination. For example, the acquirer may be able to utilise the benefit of its unused tax losses against the future taxable profit of the acquiree. In such cases, the acquirer recognises a deferred tax asset and takes this into account in determining the goodwill or negative goodwill arising on the acquisition. *(12.67)*

When an acquirer did not recognise a deferred tax asset of the acquiree as an identifiable asset at the date of a business combination and that deferred tax asset is subsequently recognised in the acquirer's consolidated financial statements, the resulting deferred tax income is recognised in the income statement. In addition, the acquirer:

(a)   adjusts the gross carrying amount of the goodwill and the related accumulated amortisation to the amounts that would have been recorded if the deferred tax asset had been recognised as an identifiable asset at the date of the business combination; and

(b)   recognises the reduction in the net carrying amount of the goodwill as an expense.

However, the acquirer does not recognise negative goodwill, nor does it increase the carrying amount of negative goodwill. *(12.68)*

Presentation

Tax Assets and Tax Liabilities

Tax assets and tax liabilities should be presented separately from other assets and liabilities in the balance sheet. Deferred tax assets and liabilities should be distinguished from current tax assets and liabilities. *(12.69)*

When an enterprise makes a distinction between current and non-current assets and liabilities in its financial statements, it should not classify deferred tax assets (liabilities) as current assets (liabilities). *(12.70)*

Offset

An enterprise should offset current tax assets and current tax liabilities if, and only if, the enterprise:

(a)   has a legally enforceable right to set off the recognised amounts; and

(b)   intends either to settle on a net basis, or to realise the asset and settle the liability simultaneously. *(12.71)*

An enterprise should offset deferred tax assets and deferred tax liabilities if, and only if:

(a)   the enterprise has a legally enforceable right to set off current tax assets against current tax liabilities; and

(b)   the deferred tax assets and the deferred tax liabilities relate to income taxes levied by the same taxation authority on either:

(i)   the same taxable entity; or

(ii)   different taxable entities which intend either to settle current tax liabilities and assets on a net basis, or to realise the assets and settle the liabilities simultaneously, in each future period in which significant amounts of deferred tax liabilities or assets are expected to be settled or recovered. *(12.74)*

Tax Expense

Tax Expense (Income) Related to Profit or Loss from Ordinary Activities

The tax expense (income) related to profit or loss from ordinary activities should be presented on the face of the income statement. *(12.77)*

Exchange Differences on Deferred Foreign Tax Liabilities or Assets

IAS 21, *The Effects of Changes in Foreign Exchange Rates* (see section 2.5.1, p. 135), requires certain exchange differences to be recognised as income or expense but does not specify where such differences should be presented in the income statement. Accordingly, where exchange differences on deferred foreign tax liabilities or assets are recognised in the income statement, such differences may be classified as deferred tax expense (income) if that presentation is considered to be the most useful to financial statement users. *(12.78)*

Disclosure

The major components of tax expense (income) should be disclosed separately. *(12.79)*

The following should also be disclosed separately:

(a)   the aggregate current and deferred tax relating to items that are charged or credited to equity;

(b)   tax expense (income) relating to extraordinary items recognised during the period;

(c)   an explanation of the relationship between tax expense (income) and accounting profit;

(d)   an explanation of changes in the applicable tax rate(s) compared to the previous accounting period;

(e)   the amount (and expiry date, if any) of deductible temporary differences, unused tax losses, and unused tax credits for which no deferred tax asset is recognised in the balance sheet;

(f)   the aggregate amount of temporary differences associated with investments in subsidiaries, branches and associates and interests in joint ventures, for which deferred tax liabilities have not been recognised;

(g)   in respect of each type of temporary difference, and in respect of each type of unused tax losses and unused tax credits:

    (i)   the amount of the deferred tax assets and liabilities recognised in the balance sheet for each period presented;

> (ii) the amount of the deferred tax income or expense recognised in the income statement, if this is not apparent from the changes in the amounts recognised in the balance sheet; and

(h) in respect of discontinued operations, the tax expense relating to:

> (i) the gain or loss on discontinuance; and

> (ii) the profit or loss from the ordinary activities of the discontinued operation for the period, together with the corresponding amounts for each prior period presented. *(12.81)*

An enterprise should disclose the amount of a deferred tax asset and the nature of the evidence supporting its recognition, when:

(a) the utilisation of the deferred tax asset is dependent on future taxable profits in excess of the profits arising from the reversal of existing taxable temporary differences; and

(b) the enterprise has suffered a loss in either the current or preceding period in the tax jurisdiction to which the deferred tax asset relates. *(12.82)*

Appendix B:

Examples of Temporary Differences

A - Examples of Circumstances that Give Rise to Taxable Temporary Differences

All taxable temporary differences give rise to a deferred tax liability.

Transactions that Affect the Income Statement

1. Interest revenue is received in arrears and is included in accounting profit on a time apportionment basis but is included in taxable profit on a cash basis.

2. Revenue from the sale of goods is included in accounting profit when goods are delivered but is included in taxable profit when cash is collected.

    ▲ *Note: as explained in B3 below, there is also a deductible temporary difference associated with any related inventory.*

3. Depreciation of an asset is accelerated for tax purposes.

4. Development costs have been capitalised and will be amortised to the income statement but were deducted in determining taxable profit in the period in which they were incurred.

5. Prepaid expenses have already been deducted on a cash basis in determining the taxable profit of the current or previous periods.

Transactions that Affect the Balance Sheet

6. Depreciation of an asset is not deductible for tax purposes and no deduction will be available for tax purposes when the asset is sold or scrapped.

    ▲ *Note: the Standard prohibits recognition of the resulting deferred tax liability unless the asset was acquired in a business combination.*

7. A borrower records a loan at the proceeds received (which equals the amount due at maturity), less transaction costs. Subsequently, the carrying amount of the loan is increased by amortisation of the transaction costs to accounting profit. The transaction costs were deducted for tax purposes in the period when the loan was first recognised.

    ▲ *Notes: (1) the taxable temporary difference is the amount of transaction costs already deducted in determining the taxable profit of current or prior periods, less the cumulative amount amortised to accounting profit; and (2) as the initial recognition of the loan affects taxable profit, the exception in the Standard does not apply. Therefore, the borrower recognises the deferred tax liability.*

8. A loan payable was measured on initial recognition at the amount of the net proceeds, net of transaction costs. The transaction costs are amortised to accounting profit over the life of the loan. Those transaction costs are not deductible in determining the taxable profit of future, current, or prior periods.

   ▲ *Notes: (1) the taxable temporary difference is the amount of unamortised transaction costs; and (2) the Standard prohibits recognition of the resulting deferred tax liability.*

9. The liability component of a compound financial instrument (for example, a convertible bond) is measured at a discount to the amount repayable on maturity, after assigning a portion of the cash proceeds to the equity component (see IAS 32, *Financial Instruments: Disclosure and Presentation*, section 6.2, p. 370). The discount is not deductible in determining taxable profit (tax loss).

   ▲ *Notes: (1) the taxable temporary difference is the amount of unamortised discount, (see Example 4 in Appendix C, p. 263); and (2) an enterprise recognises the resulting deferred tax liability and charges the deferred tax directly to the carrying amount of the equity component. In accordance with the Standard, subsequent changes in the deferred tax liability are recognised in the income statement as deferred tax expense (income).*

Fair Value Adjustments and Revaluations

10. Current investments or financial instruments are carried at fair value which exceeds cost but no equivalent adjustment is made for tax purposes.

11. An enterprise revalues property, plant and equipment (under the allowed alternative treatment in IAS 16), but no equivalent adjustment is made for tax purposes.

    ▲ *Note: the Standard requires the related deferred tax to be charged directly to equity.*

Business Combinations and Consolidation

12. The carrying amount of an asset is increased to fair value in a business combination that is an acquisition and no equivalent adjustment is made for tax purposes.

    ▲ *Note: on initial recognition, the resulting deferred tax liability increases goodwill or decreases negative goodwill.*

13. Amortisation of goodwill is not deductible in determining taxable profit and the cost of the goodwill would not be deductible on disposal of the business.

    ▲ *Note: the Standard prohibits recognition of the resulting deferred tax liability.*

14. Unrealised losses resulting from intragroup transactions are eliminated by inclusion in the carrying amount of inventory or property, plant and equipment.

15.   Retained earnings of subsidiaries, branches, associates and joint ventures are included in consolidated retained earnings, but income taxes will be payable if the profits are distributed to the reporting parent.

▲ *Note: the Standard prohibits recognition of the resulting deferred tax liability if the parent, investor or venturer is able to control the timing of the reversal of the temporary difference and it is probable that the temporary difference will not reverse in the foreseeable future.*

16.   Investments in foreign subsidiaries, branches or associates or interests in foreign joint ventures are affected by changes in foreign exchange rates.

▲ *Notes: (1) there may be either a taxable temporary difference or a deductible temporary difference; and (2) prohibits recognition of the resulting deferred tax liability if the parent, investor or venturer is able to control the timing of the reversal of the temporary difference and it is probable that the temporary difference will not reverse in the foreseeable future.*

17.   An enterprise accounts in its own currency for the cost of the non-monetary assets of a foreign operation that is integral to the reporting enterprise's operations but the taxable profit or tax loss of the foreign operation is determined in the foreign currency.

▲ *Notes: (1) there may be either a taxable temporary difference or a deductible temporary difference; (2) where there is a taxable temporary difference, the resulting deferred tax liability is recognised, because it relates to the foreign operation's own assets and liabilities, rather than to the reporting enterprise's investment in that foreign operation; and (3) the deferred tax is charged in the income statement.*

Hyperinflation

18.   Non-monetary assets are restated in terms of the measuring unit current at the balance sheet date (see IAS 29, *Financial Reporting in Hyperinflationary Economies,* section 2.5.6, p. 158) and no equivalent adjustment is made for tax purposes.

▲ *Notes: (1) the deferred tax is charged in the income statement; and (2) if, in addition to the restatement, the non-monetary assets are also revalued, the deferred tax relating to the revaluation is charged to equity and the deferred tax relating to the restatement is charged in the income statement.*

B - Examples of Circumstances that Give Rise to Deductible Temporary Differences

All deductible temporary differences give rise to a deferred tax asset. However, some deferred tax assets may not satisfy the recognition criteria.

Transactions that affect the income statement

1.   Retirement benefit costs are deducted in determining accounting profit as service is provided by the employee, but are not deducted in determining

taxable profit until the enterprise pays either retirement benefits or contributions to a fund.

▲ *Note: similar deductible temporary differences arise where other expenses, such as product warranty costs or interest, are deductible on a cash basis in determining taxable profit.*

2. Accumulated depreciation of an asset in the financial statements is greater than the cumulative depreciation allowed up to the balance sheet date for tax purposes.

3. The cost of inventories sold before the balance sheet date is deducted in determining accounting profit when goods or services are delivered but is deducted in determining taxable profit when cash is collected.

▲ *Note: as explained in A2 above, there is also a taxable temporary difference associated with the related trade receivable.*

4. The net realisable value of an item of inventory, or the recoverable amount of an item of property, plant or equipment, is less than the previous carrying amount and an enterprise therefore reduces the carrying amount of the asset, but that reduction is ignored for tax purposes until the asset is sold.

5. Research costs (or organisation or other start up costs) are recognised as an expense in determining accounting profit but are not permitted as a deduction in determining taxable profit until a later period.

6. Income is deferred in the balance sheet but has already been included in taxable profit in current or prior periods.

7. A government grant which is included in the balance sheet as deferred income will not be taxable in future periods.

▲ *Note: the Standard prohibits the recognition of the resulting deferred tax asset.*

Fair Value Adjustments and Revaluations

8. Current investments or financial instruments are carried at fair value which is less than cost, but no equivalent adjustment is made for tax purposes.

Business Combinations and Consolidation

9. A liability is recognised at its fair value in a business combination that is an acquisition, but none of the related expense is deducted in determining taxable profit until a later period.

▲ *Note: the resulting deferred tax asset decreases goodwill or increases negative goodwill.*

10. Negative goodwill is included in the balance sheet as deferred income and the income will not be included in the determination of taxable profit.

▲ *Note: the Standard prohibits recognition of the resulting deferred tax asset.*

11.   Unrealised profits resulting from intragroup transactions are eliminated from the carrying amount of assets, such as inventory or property, plant or equipment, but no equivalent adjustment is made for tax purposes.

12.   Investments in foreign subsidiaries, branches or associates or interests in foreign joint ventures are affected by changes in foreign exchange rates.

▲ *Notes: (1) there may be a taxable temporary difference or a deductible temporary difference; and (2) the Standard requires recognition of the resulting deferred tax asset to the extent, and only to the extent, that it is probable that: (a) the temporary difference will reverse in the foreseeable future; and (b) taxable profit will be available against which the temporary difference can be utilised.*

13.   An enterprise accounts in its own currency for the cost of the non-monetary assets of a foreign operation that is integral to the reporting enterprise's operations but the taxable profit or tax loss of the foreign operation is determined in the foreign currency.

▲ *Notes: (1) there may be either a taxable temporary difference or a deductible temporary difference; (2) where there is a deductible temporary difference, the resulting deferred tax asset is recognised to the extent that it is probable that sufficient taxable profit will be available, because the deferred tax asset relates to the foreign operation's own assets and liabilities, rather than to the reporting enterprise's investment in that foreign operation; and (3) the deferred tax is charged in the income statement.*

C - Examples of Circumstances where the Carrying Amount of an Asset or Liability is Equal to its Tax Base

1.   Accrued expenses have already been deducted in determining an enterprise's current tax liability for the current or earlier periods.

2.   A loan payable is measured at the amount originally received and this amount is the same as the amount repayable on final maturity of the loan.

3.   Accrued expenses will never be deductible for tax purposes.

4.   Accrued income will never be taxable.

Appendix C:

Illustrative Computations and Presentation

All the examples in this Appendix assume that the enterprises concerned have no transaction other than those described.

| Example 1 | **Depreciable Assets** |

An enterprise buys equipment for 10,000 and depreciates it on a straight line basis over its expected useful life of five years. For tax purposes, the equipment is depreciated at 25% per annum on a straight line basis. Tax losses may be carried back against taxable profit of the previous five years. In year 0, the enterprise's taxable profit was 5,000. The tax rate is 40 %.

The enterprise will recover the carrying amount of the equipment by using it to manufacture goods for resale. Therefore, the enterprise's current tax computation is as follows:

| | Year | | | | |
	1	2	3	4	5
Taxable income	2,000	2,000	2,000	2,000	2,000
Depreciation for tax purposes	2,500	2,500	2,500	2,500	0
Taxable profit (tax loss)	(500)	(500)	(500)	(500)	2,000
Current tax expense (income) at 40%	(200)	(200)	(200)	(200)	800

Figure 49

The enterprise recognises a current tax asset at the end of years 1 to 4 because it recovers the benefit of the tax loss against the taxable profit of year 0.

The temporary differences associated with the equipment and the resulting deferred tax asset and liability and deferred tax expense and income are as follows:

	Year				
	1	2	3	4	5
Carrying amount	8,000	6,000	4,000	2,000	0
Tax base	7,500	5,000	2,500	0	0
Taxable temporary difference	500	1,000	1,500	2,000	0
Opening deferred tax liability	0	200	400	600	800
Deferred tax expense (income)	200	200	200	200	(800)
Closing deferred tax liability	200	400	600	800	0

Figure 50

The enterprise recognises the deferred tax liability in years 1 to 4 because the reversal of the taxable temporary difference will create taxable income in subsequent years. The enterprise's income statement is as follows:

	Year				
	1	2	3	4	5
Income	2,000	2,000	2,000	2,000	2,000
Depreciation	2,000	2,000	2,000	2,000	2,000
Profit before tax	0	0	0	0	0
Current tax expense (income)	(200)	(200)	(200)	(200)	800
Deferred tax expense (income)	200	200	200	200	(800)
Total tax expense (income)	0	0	0	0	0

Figure 51

Example 2

Deferred Tax Assets and Liabilities

The example deals with an enterprise over the two year period, X5 and X6. In X5 the enacted income tax rate was 40% of taxable profit. In X6 the enacted income tax rate was 35% of taxable profit.

Charitable donations are recognised as an expense when they are paid and are not deductible for tax purposes.

In X5, the enterprise was notified by the relevant authorities that they intend to pursue an action against the enterprise with respect to sulphur emissions. Although as at December X6 the action had not yet come to court the enterprise recognised a liability of 700 in X5 being its best estimate of the fine arising from the action. Fines are not deductible for tax purposes.

In X2, the enterprise incurred 1,250 of costs in relation to the development of a new product. These costs were deducted for tax purposes in X2. For accounting purposes, the enterprise capitalised this expenditure and amortised it on the straight line basis over five years. At 31/12/X4, the unamortised balance of these product development costs was 500.

In X5, the enterprise entered into an agreement with its existing employees to provide health care benefits to retirees. The enterprise recognises as an expense the cost of this plan as employees provide service. No payments to retirees were made for such benefits in X5 or X6. Health care costs are deductible for tax purposes when payments are made to retirees. The enterprise has determined that it is probable that taxable profit will be available against which any resulting deferred tax asset can be utilised.

Buildings are depreciated for accounting purposes at 5% a year on a straight line basis and at 10% a year on a straight line basis for tax purposes. Motor vehicles are depreciated for accounting purposes at 20% a year on a straight line basis and at 25% a year on a straight line basis for tax purposes. A full year's depreciation is charged for accounting purposes in the year that an asset is acquired.

At 1/1/X6, the building was revalued to 65,000 and the enterprise estimated that the remaining useful life of the building was 20 years from the date of the revaluation. The revaluation did not affect taxable profit in X6 and the taxation authorities did not adjust the tax base of the building to reflect the revaluation. In X6, the enterprise transferred 1,033 from revaluation reserve to retained earnings. This represents the difference of 1,590 between the actual depreciation on the building (3,250) and equivalent depreciation based on the cost of the building (1,660, which is the book value at 1/1/X6 of 33,200 divided by the remaining useful life of 20 years), less the related deferred tax of 557 (see IAS 12, paragraph 64).

Current Tax Expense

	X5	X6
Accounting profit	8,775	8,740
Add		
Depreciation for accounting purposes	4,800	8,250
Charitable donations	500	350
Fine for environmental pollution	700	-
Product development costs	250	250
Health care benefits	2,000	1,000
	17,025	18,590
Deduct		
Depreciation for tax purposes	(8,100)	(11,850)
Taxable Profit	8,925	6,740
Current tax expense at 40%	3,570	
Current tax expense at 35%		2,359

Figure 52

Carrying Amounts of Property, Plant and Equipment

Cost	Building	Motor Vehicles	Total
Balance at 31/12/X4	50,000	10,000	60,000
Additions X5	6,000	-	6,000
Balance at 31/12/X5	56,000	10,000	66,000
Elimination of accumulated depreciation on revaluation at 1/1/X6			
	(22,800)	-	(22,800)
Revaluation at 1/1/X6	31,800	-	31,800
Balance at 1/1/X6	65,000	10,000	75,000
Additions X6	-	15,000	15,000
	65,000	25,000	90,000
Accumulated Depreciation	5%	20%	
Balance at 31/12/X4	20,000	4,000	24,000
Depreciation X5	2,800	2,000	4,800
Balance at 31/12/X5	22,800	6,000	28,800
Revaluation at 1/1/X6	(22,800)	-	(22,800)
Balance at 1/1/X6	-	6,000	6,000
Depreciation X6	3,250	5,000	8,250
Balance at 31/12/X6	3,250	11,000	14,250
Carrying Amount			
31/12/X4	30,000	6,000	36,000
31/12/X5	33,200	4,000	37,200
31/12/X6	61,750	14,000	75,750

Figure 53

Tax Base of Property, Plant and Equipment

Cost	Building	Motor Vehicles	Total
Balance at 31/12/X4	50,000	10,000	60,000
Additions X5	6,000	-	6,000
Balance at 31/12/X5	56,000	10,000	66,000
Additions X6	-	15,000	15,000
Balance at 31/12/X6	56,000	25,000	81,000
Accumulated Depreciation	10%	25%	
Balance at 31/12/X4	40,000	5,000	45,000
Depreciation X5	5,600	2,500	8,100
Balance at 31/12/X5	45,600	7,500	53,100
Depreciation X6	5,600	6,250	11,850
Balance 31/12/X6	51,200	13,750	64,950
Tax Base			
31/12/X4	10,000	5,000	15,000
31/12/X5	10,400	2,500	12,900
31/12/X6	4,800	11,250	16,050

Figure 54

Deferred Tax Assets, Liabilities and Expense at 31/12/X4

	Carrying Amount	Tax Base	Temporary Differences
Accounts receivable	500	500	-
Inventory	2,000	2,000	-
Product development costs	500	-	500
Investments	33,000	33,000	-
Property, plant & equipment	36,000	15,000	21,000
TOTAL ASSETS	72,000	50,500	21,500
Current income taxes payable	3,000	3,000	-
Accounts payable	500	500	-
Fines payable	-	-	-
Liability for health care benefits	-	-	-
Long term debt	20,000	20,000	-
Deferred income taxes	8,600	8,600	-
TOTAL LIABILITIES	32,100	32,100	
Share capital	5,000	5,000	-
Revaluation surplus	-	-	-
Retained earnings	34,900	13,400	-
TOTAL LIABILITIES/EQUITY	72,000	50,500	
TEMPORARY DIFFERENCES			21,500
Deferred tax liability	21,500 at 40%		8,600
Deferred tax asset	-	-	-
Net deferred tax liability			8,600

Figure 55

Deferred Tax Assets, Liabilities and Expense at 31/12/X5

	Carrying Amount	Tax Base	Temporary Differences
Accounts receivable	500	500	-
Inventory	2,000	2,000	-
Product development costs	250	-	250
Investments	33,000	33,000	-
Property, plant & equipment	37,200	12,900	24,300
TOTAL ASSETS	72,950	48,400	24,550
Current income taxes payable	3,570	3,570	-
Accounts payable	500	500	-
Fines payable	700	700	-
Liability for health care benefits	2,000	-	(2,000)
Long term debt	12,475	12,475	-
Deferred income taxes	9,020	9,020	-
TOTAL LIABILITIES	28,265	26,265	(2,000)
Share capital	5,000	5,000	-
Revaluation surplus	-	-	-
Retained earnings	39,685	17,135	
TOTAL LIABILITIES/EQUITY	72,950	48,400	
TEMPORARY DIFFERENCES			22,550
Deferred tax liability	24,550 at 40%		9,820
Deferred tax asset	(2,000) at 40%		(800)
Net deferred tax liability			9,020
Less: Opening deferred tax liability			(8,600)
Deferred tax expense (income) related to the origination and reversal of temporary differences			420

Figure 56

Deferred Tax Assets, Liabilities and Expense at 31/12/X6

	Carrying Amount	Tax Base	Temporary Differences
Accounts receivable	500	500	-
Inventory	2,000	2,000	-
Product development costs	-	-	-
Investments	33,000	33,000	-
Property, plant & equipment	75,750	16,050	59,700
TOTAL ASSETS	111,250	51,550	59,700
Current income taxes payable	2,359	2,359	-
Accounts payable	500	500	-
Fines payable	700	700	
Liability for health care benefits	3,000	-	(3,000)
Long term debt	12,805	12,805	-
Deferred income taxes	19,845	19,845	-
TOTAL LIABILITIES	39,209	36,209	(3,000)
Share capital	5,000	5,000	-
Revaluation surplus	19,637	-	-
Retained earnings	47,404	10,341	
TOTAL LIABILITIES/EQUITY	111,250	51,550	
TEMPORARY DIFFERENCES			56,700
Deferred tax liability	59,700 at 35%		20,895
Deferred tax asset	(3,000 at 35%)		(1,050)
Net deferred tax liability			19,845
Less: Opening deferred tax liability			
			(9,020)
Adjustment to opening deferred tax liability resulting from reduction in tax rate	22,550 at 5 %		1,127
Deferred tax attributable to revaluation surplus	31,800 at 35%		(11,130)
Deferred tax expense (income) related to the origination and reversal of temporary differences			822

Figure 57

Illustrative Disclosure

The amounts to be disclosed in accordance with IAS 12 are as follows:

Major components of tax expense (income)

	X5	X6
Current tax expense	3,570	2,359
Deferred tax expense relating to the origination and reversal of temporary differences	420	822
Deferred tax expense (income) resulting from reduction in tax rate	-	(1,127)
Tax expense	3,990	2,054

Figure 58

Aggregate current and deferred tax relating to items charged or credited to equity

Deferred tax relating to revaluation of building	-	(11,130)

Figure 59

In addition, deferred tax of 557 was transferred in X6 from retained earnings to revaluation reserve. This relates to the difference between the actual depreciation on the building and equivalent depreciation based on the cost of the building.

Explanation of the relationship between tax expense and accounting profit

IAS 12 permits two alternative methods of explaining the relationship between tax expense (income) and accounting profit. Both of these formats are illustrated on the next page.

(i)   *a numerical reconciliation between tax expense (income) and the product of accounting profit multiplied by the applicable tax rate(s), disclosing also the basis on which the applicable tax rate(s) is (are) computed*

	X5	X6
Accounting profit	8,775	8,740
Tax at the applicable tax rate of 35% (X5: 40%)	3,510	3,059
Tax effect of expenses that are not deductible in determining taxable profit:		
Charitable donations	200	122
Fines for environmental pollution	280	-
Reduction in opening deferred taxes resulting from reduction in tax rate	-	(1,127)
Tax expense	3,990	2,054

Figure 60

The applicable tax rate is the aggregate of the national income tax rate of 30% (X5: 35%) and the local income tax rate of 5%.

(ii)   *a numerical reconciliation between the average effective tax rate and the applicable tax rate, disclosing also the basis on which the applicable tax rate is computed*

	X5 %	X6 %
Applicable tax rate	40.0	35.0
Tax effect of expenses that are not deductible for tax purposes:		
Charitable donations	2.3	1.4
Fines for environmental pollution	3.2	-
Effect on opening deferred taxes of reduction in tax rate	-	(12.9)
Average effective tax rate (tax expense divided by profit before tax)	45.5	23.5

Figure 61

The applicable tax rate is the aggregate of the national income tax rate of 30% (X5: 35%) and the local income tax rate of 5%.

An explanation of changes in the applicable tax rate(s) compared to the previous accounting period

In X6, the government enacted a change in the national income tax rate from 35% to 30%.

In respect of each type of temporary difference, and in respect of each type of unused tax losses and unused tax credits:

(i)   the amount of the deferred tax assets and liabilities recognised in the balance sheet for each period presented;

(ii) the amount of the deferred tax income or expense recognised in the income statement for each period presented, if this is not apparent from the changes in the amounts recognised in the balance sheet.

	X5	X6
Accelerated depreciation for tax purposes	9,720	10,322
Liabilities for health care benefits that are deducted for tax purposes only when paid	(800)	(1,050)
Product development costs deducted from taxable profit in earlier years	100	-
Revaluation, net of related depreciation		10,573
Deferred tax liability	9,020	19,845

Figure 62

▲ *Note: the amount of the deferred tax income or expense recognised in the income statement for the current year is apparent from the changes in the amounts recognised in the balance sheet.*

Example 3 — Business Combinations

On 1 January X5, enterprise *A* acquired 100% of the shares of enterprise *B* at a cost of 600. *A* amortises goodwill over 5 years. Goodwill amortisation is not deductible for tax purposes. The tax rate in *A*'s tax jurisdiction is 30% and the tax rate in *B*'s tax jurisdiction is 40%.

The fair value of the identifiable assets and liabilities (excluding deferred tax assets and liabilities) acquired by *A* is set out in the following table, together with their tax base in *B*'s tax jurisdiction and the resulting temporary differences.

	Cost of Acquisition	Tax Base	Temporary Differences
Property, plant and equipment	270	155	115
Accounts receivable	210	210	-
Inventory	174	124	50
Retirement benefit obligations	(30)	-	(30)
Accounts payable	(120)	(120)	-
Fair value of the identifiable assets and liabilities acquired, excluding deferred tax	504	369	135

Figure 63

The deferred tax asset arising from the retirement benefit obligations is offset against the deferred tax liabilities arising from the property, plant and equipment and inventory.

No deduction is available in *B*'s tax jurisdiction for the cost of the goodwill. Therefore, the tax base of the goodwill (in *B*'s jurisdiction) is nil. However, in accordance with the Standard, *A* recognises no deferred tax liability for the taxable temporary difference associated, in *B*'s tax jurisdiction, with the goodwill.

The carrying amount, in *A*'s consolidated financial statements, of its investment in *B* is made up as follows:

Fair value of identifiable assets and liabilities acquired, excluding deferred tax	504
Deferred tax liability (135 at 40%)	(54)
Fair value of identifiable assets and liabilities acquired	450
Goodwill (net of amortisation of nil)	150
Carrying amount	600

Figure 64

At the date of acquisition, the tax base, in *A*'s tax jurisdiction, of *A*'s investment in *B* is 600. Therefore, no temporary difference is associated, in *A*'s jurisdiction, with the investment.

During X5, *B*'s equity (incorporating the fair value adjustments made on acquisition) changed as follows:

At 1 January X5	450
Retained profit for X5 (net profit of 150, less dividend payable of 80)	70
At 31 December X5	520

Figure 65

A recognises a liability for any withholding tax or other taxes that it will suffer on the accrued dividend receivable of 80.

At 31 December X5, the carrying amount of A's underlying investment in B, excluding the accrued dividend receivable, is as follows:

Net assets of B	520
Goodwill (net of amortisation of 30)	120
Carrying amount	640

Figure 66

The temporary difference associated with A's underlying investment is 40 as follows:

Cumulative retained profit since acquisition	70
Cumulative amortisation of goodwill	(30)
	40

Figure 67

If A has determined that it will not sell the investment in the foreseeable future and that B will not distribute its retained profits in the foreseeable future, no deferred tax liability is recognised in relation to A's investment in B. Note that this exception would apply for an investment in an associate only if there is an agreement requiring that the profits of the associate will not be distributed in the foreseeable future. A discloses the amount (40) of the temporary difference for which no deferred tax is recognised.

If A expects to sell the investment in B, or that B will distribute its retained profits in the foreseeable future, A recognises a deferred tax liability to the extent that the temporary difference is expected to reverse. The tax rate reflects the manner in which A expects to recover the carrying amount of its investment. A credits or charges the deferred tax to equity to the extent that the deferred tax results from foreign exchange translation differences which have been charged or credited directly to equity. A discloses separately:

(a)   the amount of deferred tax which has been charged or credited directly to equity; and

(b)   the amount of any remaining temporary difference which is not expected to reverse in the foreseeable future and for which, therefore, no deferred tax is recognised.

Example 4

Compound Financial Instruments

An enterprise receives a non-interest-bearing convertible loan of 1,000 on 31 December X4 repayable at par on 1 January X8. In accordance with IAS 32, *Financial Instruments: Disclosure and Presentation*, the enterprise classifies the instrument's liability component as a liability and the equity component as equity. The enterprise assigns an initial carrying amount of 751 to the liability component of the convertible loan and 249 to the equity component. Subsequently, the enterprise recognises imputed discount as interest expense at an annual rate of 10% on the carrying amount of the liability component at the beginning of the year. The tax authorities do not allow the enterprise to claim any deduction for the imputed discount on the liability component of the convertible loan. The tax rate is 40%.

The temporary differences associated with the liability component and the resulting deferred tax liability and deferred tax expense and income are as follows:

		Year		
	X4	X5	X6	X7
Carrying amount of liability component	751	826	909	1,000
Tax base	1,000	1,000	1,000	1,000
Taxable temporary difference	249	174	91	-
Opening deferred tax liability at 40%	0	100	70	37
Deferred tax charged to equity	100	-	-	-
Deferred tax expense (income)	-	(30)	(33)	(37)

Figure 68

At 31 December X4, the enterprise recognises the resulting deferred tax liability by adjusting the initial carrying amount of the equity component of the convertible liability. Therefore, the amounts recognised at that date are as follows:

Liability component	751
Deferred tax liability	100
Equity component (249 less 100)	149
	1,000

Figure 69

Subsequent changes in the deferred tax liability are recognised in the income statement as tax income. Therefore, the enterprise's income statement is as follows:

		Year		
	X4	X5	X6	X7
Interest expense (imputed discount)	-	75	83	91
Deferred tax (income)	-	(30)	(33)	(37)
	-	45	50	54

Figure 70

| 4.2 | **Employee Benefits** |

IAS 19 should be applied by an employer in accounting for employee benefits. *(19.1)*

IAS 19 requires an enterprise to recognise:

(a)   a liability when an employee has provided service in exchange for employee benefits to be paid in the future; and

(b)   an expense when the enterprise consumes the economic benefit arising from service provided by an employee in exchange for employee benefits.

IAS 19 does not deal with reporting by employee benefit plans (see IAS 26, *Accounting and Reporting by Retirement Benefit Plans,* section 2.8, p. 182). *(19.2)*

IAS 19 applies to all employee benefits, including those provided:

(a)   under formal plans or other formal agreements between an enterprise and individual employees, groups of employees or their representatives;

(b)   under legislative requirements, or through industry arrangements, whereby enterprises are required to contribute to national, state, industry or other multi-employer plans; or

(c)   by those informal practices that give rise to a constructive obligation. Informal practices give rise to a constructive obligation where the enterprise has no realistic alternative but to pay employee benefits. An example of a constructive obligation is where a change in the enterprise's informal practices would cause unacceptable damage to its relationship with employees. *(19.3)*

Employee benefits include:

(a)   short-term employee benefits, such as wages, salaries and social security contributions, paid annual leave and paid sick leave, profit-sharing and bonuses (if payable within twelve months of the end of the period) and non-monetary benefits (such as medical care, housing, cars and free or subsidised goods or services) for current employees;

(b)   post-employment benefits such as pensions, other retirement benefits, post-employment life insurance and post-employment medical care;

(c)   other long-term employee benefits, including long-service leave or sabbatical leave, jubilee or other long-service benefits, long-term disability benefits and, if they are not payable wholly within twelve months after the end of the period, profit-sharing, bonuses and deferred compensation;

(d)   termination benefits; and

(e)   equity compensation benefits.

Because each category identified in (a) to (e) above has different characteristics, IAS 19 establishes separate requirements for each category. *(19.4)*

Employee benefits include benefits provided to either employees or their dependants and may be settled by payments (or the provision of goods or services) made either directly to the employees, to their spouses, children or other dependants or to others, such as insurance companies. *(19.5)*

An employee may provide services to an enterprise on a full-time, part-time, permanent, casual or temporary basis. For the purpose of IAS 19, employees include directors and other management personnel. *(19.6)*

IAS 19 uses the following terms:

- *Employee benefits* are all forms of consideration given by an enterprise in exchange for service rendered by employees.
- *Short-term employee benefits* are employee benefits (other than termination benefits and equity compensation benefits) which fall due wholly within twelve months after the end of the period in which the employees render the related service.
- *Post-employment benefits* are employee benefits (other than termination benefits and equity compensation benefits) which are payable after the completion of employment.
- *Post-employment benefit* **plans** are formal or informal arrangements under which an enterprise provides post-employment benefits for one or more employees.
- *Defined contribution plans* are post-employment benefit plans under which an enterprise pays fixed contributions into a separate entity (a fund) and will have no legal or constructive obligation to pay further contributions if the fund does not hold sufficient assets to pay all employee benefits relating to employee service in the current and prior periods.
- *Defined benefit plans* are post-employment benefit plans other than defined contribution plans.
- *Multi-employer plans* are defined contribution plans (other than state plans), or defined benefit plans (other than state plans) that:

    (a)   pool the assets contributed by various enterprises that are not under common control; and

    (b)   use those assets to provide benefits to employees of more than one enterprise, on the basis that contribution and benefit levels are determined without regard to the identity of the enterprise that employs the employees concerned.

- *Other long-term employee benefits* are employee benefits (other than post-employment benefits, termination benefits and equity compensation benefits) which do not fall due wholly within twelve months after the end of the period in which the employees render the related service.

- *Termination benefits* are employee benefits payable as a result of either:
  - (a)   an enterprise's decision to terminate an employee's employment before the normal retirement date; or
  - (b)   an employee's decision to accept voluntary redundancy in exchange for those benefits.
- *Equity compensation benefits* are employee benefits under which either:
  - (a)   employees are entitled to receive equity financial instruments issued by the enterprise (or its parent); or
  - (b)   the amount of the enterprise's obligation to employees depends on the future price of equity financial instruments issued by the enterprise.
- *Equity compensation plans* are formal or informal arrangements under which an enterprise provides equity compensation benefits for one or more employees.
- *Vested* employee benefits are employee benefits that are not conditional on future employment.
- The *present value of a defined benefit obligation* is the present value, without deducting any plan assets, of expected future payments required to settle the obligation resulting from employee service in the current and prior periods.
- *Current service cost* is the increase in the present value of the defined benefit obligation resulting from employee service in the current period.
- *Interest cost* is the increase during a period in the present value of a defined benefit obligation which arises because the benefits are one period closer to settlement.
- *Plan assets* are assets (other than non-transferable financial instruments issued by the reporting enterprise) held by an entity (a fund) that satisfies all of the following conditions:
  - (a)   the entity is legally separate from the reporting enterprise;
  - (b)   the assets of the fund are to be used only to settle the employee benefit obligations, are not available to the enterprise's own creditors and cannot be returned to the enterprise (or can be returned to the enterprise only if the remaining assets of the fund are sufficient to meet the plan's obligations); and
  - (c)   to the extent that sufficient assets are in the fund, the enterprise will have no legal or constructive obligation to pay the related employee benefits directly.
- *Fair value* is the amount for which an asset could be exchanged or a liability settled between knowledgeable, willing parties in an arm's length transaction.
- The *return on plan assets* is interest, dividends and other revenue derived from the plan assets, together with realised and unrealised gains or losses on the plan assets, less any costs of administering the plan and less any tax payable by the plan itself.
- *Actuarial gains and losses* comprise:
  - (a)   experience adjustments (the effects of differences between the previous actuarial assumptions and what has actually occurred); and
  - (b)   the effects of changes in actuarial assumptions.

- *Past service cost* is the increase in the present value of the defined benefit obligation for employee service in prior periods, resulting in the current period from the introduction of, or changes to, post-employment benefits or other long-term employee benefits. Past service cost may be either positive (where benefits are introduced or improved), or negative (where existing benefits are reduced). *(19.7)*

Short-term Employee Benefits

Recognition and Measurement

All Short-term Employee Benefits

When an employee has rendered service to an enterprise during an accounting period, the enterprise should recognise the undiscounted amount of short-term employee benefits expected to be paid in exchange for that service:

(a)   as a liability (accrued expense), after deducting any amount already paid. If the amount already paid exceeds the undiscounted amount of the benefits, an enterprise should recognise that excess as an asset (prepaid expense) to the extent that the prepayment will lead to, for example, a reduction in future payments or a cash refund; and

(b)   as an expense, unless another International Accounting Standard requires or permits the inclusion of the benefits in the cost of an asset (see, for example, IAS 2, *Inventories*, and IAS 16, *Property, Plant and Equipment*).

IAS 19 explains how an enterprise should apply this requirement to short-term employee benefits in the form of compensated absences and profit-sharing and bonus plans. *(19.10)*

Short-term Compensated Absences

An enterprise should recognise the expected cost of short-term employee benefits in the form of compensated absences as follows:

(a)   in the case of accumulating compensated absences, when the employees render service that increases their entitlement to future compensated absences; and

(b)   in the case of non-accumulating compensated absences, when the absences occur. *(19.11)*

An enterprise should measure the expected cost of accumulating compensated absences as the additional amount that the enterprise expects to pay as a result of the unused entitlement that has accumulated at the balance sheet date. *(19.14)*

The method specified in the previous paragraph measures the obligation at the amount of the additional payments that are expected to arise solely from the fact that the benefit accumulates. In many cases, an enterprise may not need to make detailed computations to estimate that there is no material obligation for unused compensated absences. For example, a sick leave obligation is likely to be material only if there is a formal or informal understanding that unused paid sick leave may be taken as paid vacation. *(19.15)*

➤ Example

An enterprise has 100 employees, who are each entitled to five working days of paid sick leave for each year. Unused sick leave may be carried forward for one calendar year. Sick leave is taken first out of the current year's entitlement and then out of any balance brought forward from the previous year (a LIFO basis). At 31 December 20X1, the average unused entitlement is two days per employee. The enterprise expects, based on past experience which is expected to continue, that 92 employees will take no more than five days of paid sick leave in 20X2 and that the remaining 8 employees will take an average of six and a half days each.

The enterprise expects that it will pay an additional 12 days of sick pay as a result of the unused entitlement that has accumulated at 31 December 20X1 (one and a half days each, for 8 employees). Therefore, the enterprise recognises a liability equal to 12 days of sick pay.

Figure 71

Profit-Sharing and Bonus Plans

An enterprise should recognise the expected cost of profit-sharing and bonus payments under paragraph 19.10 when, and only when:

(a)   the enterprise has a present legal or constructive obligation to make such payments as a result of past events; and

(b)   a reliable estimate of the obligation can be made.

A present obligation exists when, and only when, the enterprise has no realistic alternative but to make the payments. *(19.17)*

Post-employment Benefits: Distinction between Defined Contribution Plans and Defined Benefit Plans

Post-employment benefit plans are classified as either defined contribution plans or defined benefit plans, depending on the economic substance of the plan as derived from its principal terms and conditions. Under defined contribution plans:

(a)   the enterprise's legal or constructive obligation is limited to the amount that it agrees to contribute to the fund. Thus, the amount of the post-employment benefits received by the employee is determined by the amount of contributions paid by an enterprise (and perhaps also the employee) to a post-employment benefit plan or to an insurance company, together with investment returns arising from the contributions; and

(b)   in consequence, actuarial risk (that benefits will be less than expected) and investment risk (that assets invested will be insufficient to meet expected benefits) fall on the employee. *(19.25)*

Under defined benefit plans:

(a)   the enterprise's obligation is to provide the agreed benefits to current and former employees; and

(b)   actuarial risk (that benefits will cost more than expected) and investment risk fall, in substance, on the enterprise. If actuarial or investment experience are worse than expected, the enterprise's obligation may be increased. *(19.27)*

Multi-employer Plans

An enterprise should classify a multi-employer plan as a defined contribution plan or a defined benefit plan under the terms of the plan (including any constructive obligation that goes beyond the formal terms). Where a multi-employer plan is a defined benefit plan, an enterprise should:

(a)   account for its proportionate share of the defined benefit obligation, plan assets and cost associated with the plan in the same way as for any other defined benefit plan; and

(b)   disclose the information required by the Standard for defined contribution plans. *(19.29)*

When sufficient information is not available to use defined benefit accounting for a multi-employer plan that is a defined benefit plan, an enterprise should:

(a)   account for the plan as if it were a defined contribution plan;

(b)   disclose the fact that the plan is a defined benefit plan and the reason why sufficient information is not available to enable the enterprise to account for the plan as a defined benefit plan; and

(c)   to the extent that a surplus or deficit in the plan may affect the amount of future contributions, disclose in addition any available information about that surplus or deficit, the basis used to determine that surplus or deficit, and the implications, if any, for the enterprise. *(19.30)*

State Plans

An enterprise should account for a state plan in the same way as for a multi-employer plan. *(19.36)*

Insured Benefits

An enterprise may pay insurance premiums to fund a post-employment benefit plan. The enterprise should treat such a plan as a defined contribution plan unless the enterprise will have (either directly, or indirectly through the plan) a legal or constructive obligation to either:

(a)   pay the employee benefits directly when they fall due; or

(b)   pay further contributions if the insurer does not pay all future employee benefits relating to employee service in the current and prior periods.

If the enterprise retains such a legal or constructive obligation, the enterprise should treat the plan as a defined benefit plan. *(19.39)*

Post-employment Benefits: Defined Contribution Plans

Recognition and Measurement

When an employee has rendered service to an enterprise during a period, the enterprise should recognise the contribution payable to a defined contribution plan in exchange for that service:

(a)   as a liability (accrued expense), after deducting any contribution already paid. If the contribution already paid exceeds the contribution due for service before the balance sheet date, an enterprise should recognise that excess as an asset (prepaid expense) to the extent that the prepayment will lead to, for example, a reduction in future payments or a cash refund; and

(b)   as an expense, unless another International Accounting Standard requires or permits the inclusion of the contribution in the cost of an asset (*see*, for example, IAS 2, and IAS 16). *(19.44)*

Where contributions to a defined contribution plan do not fall due wholly within twelve months after the end of the period in which the employees render the related service, they should be discounted using the discount rate specified for defined benefit obligations. *(19.45)*

Disclosure

An enterprise should disclose the amount recognised as an expense for defined contribution plans. *(19.46)*

Post-employment Benefits: Defined Benefit Plans

Recognition and Measurement

Defined benefit plans may be unfunded, or they may be wholly or partly funded by contributions by an enterprise, and sometimes its employees, into an entity, or fund, that is legally separate from the reporting enterprise and from which the employee benefits are paid. The payment of funded benefits when they fall due depends not only on the financial position and the investment performance of the fund but also on an enterprise's ability (and willingness) to make good any shortfall in the fund's assets. Therefore, the enterprise is, in substance, underwriting the actuarial and investment risks associated with the plan. Consequently, the expense recognised for a defined benefit plan is not necessarily the amount of the contribution due for the period. *(19.49)*

Accounting by an enterprise for defined benefit plans involves the following steps:

(a)   using actuarial techniques to make a reliable estimate of the amount of benefit that employees have earned in return for their service in the current and prior periods. This requires an enterprise to determine how much benefit is attributable to the current and prior periods and to make estimates (actuarial assumptions) about demographic variables (such as employee turnover and mortality) and financial variables (such as future increases in salaries and medical costs) that will influence the cost of the benefit;

(b)   discounting that benefit using the Projected Unit Credit Method in order to determine the present value of the defined benefit obligation and the current service cost;

(c)   determining the fair value of any plan assets;

(d)   determining the total amount of actuarial gains and losses and the amount of those actuarial gains and losses that should be recognised;

(e)   where a plan has been introduced or changed, determining the resulting past service cost; and

(f)   where a plan has been curtailed or settled, determining the resulting gain or loss.

Where an enterprise has more than one defined benefit plan, the enterprise applies these procedures for each material plan separately. *(19.50)*

Accounting for the Constructive Obligation

An enterprise should account not only for its legal obligation under the formal terms of a defined benefit plan, but also for any constructive obligation that arises from the enterprise's informal practices. Informal practices give rise to a constructive obligation where the enterprise has no realistic alternative but to pay employee benefits. An example of a constructive obligation is where a change in the enterprise's informal practices would cause unacceptable damage to its relationship with employees. *(19.52)*

Balance Sheet

The amount recognised as a defined benefit liability should be the net total of the following amounts:

(a)   the present value of the defined benefit obligation at the balance sheet date;

(b)   plus any actuarial gains (less any actuarial losses) not recognised because of the 'corridor' treatment of recognising actuarial gains and losses;

(c)   minus any past service cost not yet recognised;

(d)   minus the fair value at the balance sheet date of plan assets (if any) out of which the obligations are to be settled directly. *(19.54)*

An enterprise should determine the present value of defined benefit obligations and the fair value of any plan assets with sufficient regularity that the amounts recognised in the financial statements do not differ materially from the amounts that would be determined at the balance sheet date. *(19.56)*

The amount recognised as a defined benefit liability may be negative (an asset). An enterprise should measure the resulting asset at the lower of:

(a)   the amount determined; and

(b)   the net total of:

    (i)   any unrecognised actuarial losses and past service cost; and

    (ii)   the present value of any economic benefits available in the form of refunds from the plan or reductions in future contributions to the plan. The present value of these economic benefits should be determined using the discount rate specified for determining the defined benefit obligation. *(19.58)*

Income Statement

An enterprise should recognise the net total of the following amounts as expense or (subject to the limit in paragraph 19.58(b)) income, except to the extent that another International Accounting Standard requires or permits their inclusion in the cost of an asset:

(a)   current service cost;

(b)   interest cost;

(c)   the expected return on any plan assets;

(d)   actuarial gains and losses, to the extent that they are recognised under the 'corridor' approach;

(e)   past service cost, to the extent that an enterprise is required to recognise it; and

(f)   the effect of any curtailments or settlements. *(19.61)*

Recognition and Measurement: Present Value of Defined Benefit Obligations and Current Service Cost

In order to measure the present value of the post-employment benefit obligations and the related current service cost, it is necessary to:

(a)   apply an actuarial valuation method;

(b)   attribute benefit to periods of service; and

(c)   make actuarial assumptions. *(19.63)*

Actuarial Valuation Method

An enterprise should use the Projected Unit Credit Method to determine the present value of its defined benefit obligations and the related current service cost and, where applicable, past service cost. *(19.64)*

The Projected Unit Credit Method (sometimes known as the accrued benefit method pro rated on service or as the benefit/years of service method) sees each period of service as giving rise to an additional unit of benefit entitlement and measures each unit separately to build up the final obligation. *(19.65)*

➤ Example

A lump sum benefit is payable on termination of service and equal to 1% of final salary for each year of service. The salary in year 1 is 10,000 and is assumed to increase at 7% (compound) each year. The discount rate used is 10% per annum. The following table shows how the obligation builds up for an employee who is expected to leave at the end of year 5, assuming that there are no changes in actuarial assumptions. For simplicity, this example ignores the additional adjustment needed to reflect the probability that the employee may leave the enterprise at an earlier or later date.

Year	1	2	3	4	5
Benefit attributed to:					
- prior years	0	131	262	393	524
- current year (1% of final salary)	131	131	131	131	131
- current and prior years	131	262	393	524	655
Opening Obligation	-	89	196	324	476
Interest at 10%	-	9	20	33	48
Current Service Cost	89	98	108	119	131
Closing Obligation	89	196	324	476	655

Figure 72

Note:
1. The Opening Obligation is the present value of benefit attributed to prior years.
2. The Current Service Cost is the present value of benefit attributed to the current year.
3. The Closing Obligation is the present value of benefit attributed to current and prior years.

Attributing Benefit to Periods of Service

In determining the present value of its defined benefit obligations and the related current service cost and, where applicable, past service cost, an enterprise should attribute benefit to periods of service under the plan's benefit formula. However, if an employee's service in later years will lead to a materially higher level of benefit than in earlier years, an enterprise should attribute benefit on a straight-line basis from:

(a) the date when service by the employee first leads to benefits under the plan (whether or not the benefits are conditional on further service); until

(b) the date when further service by the employee will lead to no material amount of further benefits under the plan, other than from further salary increases. *(19.67)*

Actuarial Assumptions

Actuarial assumptions should be unbiased and mutually compatible. *(19.72)*

Financial assumptions should be based on market expectations, at the balance sheet date, for the period over which the obligations are to be settled. *(19.77)*

Actuarial Assumptions: Discount Rate

The rate used to discount post-employment benefit obligations (both funded and unfunded) should be determined by reference to market yields at the balance sheet date on high quality corporate bonds. In countries where there is no deep market in such bonds, the market yields (at the balance sheet date) on government bonds should be used. The currency and term of the corporate bonds or government bonds should be consistent with the currency and estimated term of the post-employment benefit obligations. *(19.78)*

Actuarial Assumptions: Salaries, Benefits and Medical Costs

Post-employment benefit obligations should be measured on a basis that reflects:

(a)   estimated future salary increases;

(b)   the benefits set out in the terms of the plan (or resulting from any constructive obligation that goes beyond those terms) at the balance sheet date; and

(c)   estimated future changes in the level of any state benefits that affect the benefits payable under a defined benefit plan, if, and only if, either:

    (i)   those changes were enacted before the balance sheet date; or

    (ii)   past history, or other reliable evidence, indicates that those state benefits will change in some predictable manner, for example, in line with future changes in general price levels or general salary levels. *(19.83)*

Assumptions about medical costs should take account of estimated future changes in the cost of medical services, resulting from both inflation and specific changes in medical costs. *(19.88)*

Actuarial Gains and Losses – The 'Corridor'

In measuring its defined benefit liability, an enterprise should recognise a portion of its actuarial gains and losses as income or expense if the net cumulative unrecognised actuarial gains and losses at the end of the previous reporting period exceeded the greater of:

(a)   10% of the present value of the defined benefit obligation at that date (before deducting plan assets); and

(b)   10% of the fair value of any plan assets at that date.

These limits should be calculated and applied separately for each defined benefit plan. *(19.92)*

The portion of actuarial gains and losses to be recognised for each defined benefit plan is the excess determined under the preceding paragraph, divided by the expected average remaining working lives of the employees participating in that plan. However, an enterprise may adopt any systematic method that results in faster recognition of actuarial gains and losses, provided that the same basis is applied to both gains and losses and the basis is applied consistently from period to period. An enterprise may apply such systematic methods to actuarial gains and losses even if they fall within the limits specified in the preceding paragraph. *(19.93)*

Past Service Cost

In measuring its defined benefit liability, an enterprise should recognise past service cost as an expense on a straight-line basis over the average period until the benefits become vested. To the extent that the benefits are already vested immediately following the introduction of, or changes to, a defined benefit plan, an enterprise should recognise past service cost immediately. *(19.96)*

Recognition and Measurement: Plan Assets

Fair Value of Plan Assets

The fair value of any plan assets is deducted in determining the amount of the defined benefit liability recognised in the balance sheet. When no market price is available, the fair value of plan assets is estimated; for example, by discounting expected future cash flows using a discount rate that reflects both the risk associated with the plan assets and the maturity or expected disposal date of those assets (or, if they have no maturity, the expected period until the settlement of the related obligation). *(19.102)*

Plan assets exclude unpaid contributions due from the reporting enterprise to the fund, as well as any non-transferable financial instruments issued by the enterprise and held by the fund. *(19.103)*

Where plan assets include insurance policies that exactly match the amount and timing of some or all of the benefits payable under the plan, the plan's rights under those insurance policies are measured at the same amount as the related obligations. *(19.104)*

Return on Plan Assets

The expected return on plan assets is one component of the expense recognised in the income statement. The difference between the expected return on plan assets and the actual return on plan assets is an actuarial gain or loss; it is included with the actuarial gains and losses on the defined benefit obligation in determining the net amount that is compared with the limits of the 10% 'corridor'. *(19.105)*

The expected return on plan assets is based on market expectations, at the beginning of the period, for returns over the entire life of the related obligation. The expected return on plan assets reflects changes in the fair value of plan assets held during the period as a result of actual contributions paid into the fund and actual benefits paid out of the fund. *(19.106)*

Curtailments and Settlements

An enterprise should recognise gains or losses on the curtailment or settlement of a defined benefit plan when the curtailment or settlement occurs. The gain or loss on a curtailment or settlement comprises the change in the present value of the defined benefit obligation together with the change in the fair value of the plan assets and any related actuarial gains and losses and past service cost that had not previously been recognised. *(19.109)*

Before determining the effect of a curtailment or settlement, an enterprise should remeasure the obligation (and the related plan assets, if any) using current actuarial assumptions (including current market interest rates and other current market prices). *(19.110)*

Presentation

Offset

An enterprise should offset an asset relating to one plan against a liability relating to another plan when, and only when, the enterprise:

(a)   has a legally enforceable right to use a surplus in one plan to settle obligations under the other plan; and

(b)   intends either to settle the obligations on a net basis, or to realise the surplus in one plan and settle its obligations under the other plan simultaneously. *(19.116)*

Current/Non-current Distinction

Some enterprises distinguish current assets and liabilities from non-current assets and liabilities. IAS 19 does not specify whether an enterprise should distinguish current and non-current portions of assets and liabilities arising from post-employment benefits. *(19.118)*

Financial Components of Post-employment Benefit Costs

IAS 19 does not specify whether an enterprise should present current service cost, interest cost and the expected return on plan assets as components of a single item of income or expense on the face of the income statement. *(19.119)*

Disclosure

An enterprise should disclose the following information about defined benefit plans:

(a)   the enterprise's accounting policy for recognising actuarial gains and losses;

(b)   a general description of the type of plan;

(c)   a reconciliation of the assets and liabilities recognised in the balance sheet;

(d)   the amounts included in the fair value of plan assets for:

    (i)   each category of the reporting enterprise's own financial instruments; and

    (ii)   any property occupied by, or other assets used by, the reporting enterprise;

(e)   a reconciliation showing the movements during the period in the net liability (or asset) recognised in the balance sheet;

(f)   the total expense recognised in the income statement for each of the following, and the line item(s) of the income statement in which they are included:

    (i)   current service cost;

    (ii)   interest cost;

(iii)   expected return on plan assets;

(iv)   actuarial gains and losses;

(v)   past service cost; and

(vi)   the effect of any curtailment or settlement;

(g)   the actual return on plan assets; and

(h)   the principal actuarial assumptions used as at the balance sheet date, including, where applicable:

(i)   the discount rates;

(ii)   the expected rates of return on any plan assets for the periods presented in the financial statements;

(iii)   the expected rates of salary increases (and of charges in an index or other variable specified in the formal or constructive terms of a plan as the basis for future benefit increases);

(iv)   medical cost trend rates; and

(v)   any other material actuarial assumptions used.

An enterprise should disclose each actuarial assumption in absolute terms (for example, as an absolute percentage) and not just as a margin between different percentages or other variables. *(19.120)*

Other Long-term Employee Benefits

IAS 19 requires a simplified method of accounting for other long-term employee benefits. This method differs from the accounting required for post-employment benefits as follows:

(a)   actuarial gains and losses are recognised immediately and no 'corridor' is applied; and

(b)   all past service cost is recognised immediately. *(19.127)*

Recognition and Measurement

The amount recognised as a liability for other long-term employee benefits should be the net total of the following amounts:

(a)   the present value of the defined benefit obligation at the balance sheet date;

(b)   minus the fair value at the balance sheet date of plan assets (if any) out of which the obligations are to be settled directly.

In measuring the liability, an enterprise should apply the general principles for defined benefit plans, with the exception of the determination of the balance sheet and income statement amounts. *(19.128)*

For other long-term employee benefits, an enterprise should recognise the net total of the following amounts as expense or income, except to the extent that another International Accounting Standard requires or permits their inclusion in the cost of an asset:

(a)   current service cost;

(b)   interest cost;

(c)   the expected return on any plan assets;

(d)   actuarial gains and losses, which should all be recognised immediately;

(e)   past service cost, which should all be recognised immediately; and

(f)   the effect of any curtailments or settlements. *(19.129)*

Termination Benefits

Recognition

An enterprise should recognise termination benefits as a liability and an expense when, and only when, the enterprise is demonstrably committed to either:

(a)   terminate the employment of an employee or group of employees before the normal retirement date; or

(b)   provide termination benefits as a result of an offer made in order to encourage voluntary redundancy. *(19.133)*

An enterprise is demonstrably committed to a termination when, and only when, the enterprise has a detailed formal plan for the termination and is without realistic possibility of withdrawal. The detailed plan should include, as a minimum:

(a)   the location, function, and approximate number of employees whose services are to be terminated;

(b)   the termination benefits for each job classification or function; and

(c)   the time at which the plan will be implemented. Implementation should begin as soon as possible and the period of time to complete implementation should be such that material changes to the plan are not likely. *(19.134)*

Measurement

Where termination benefits fall due more than 12 months after the balance sheet date, they should be discounted using the discount rate specified for the defined benefit obligation. (19.139)

In the case of an offer made to encourage voluntary redundancy, the measurement of termination benefits should be based on the number of employees expected to accept the offer. *(19.140)*

Equity Compensation Benefits

Recognition and Measurement

IAS 19 does not specify recognition and measurement requirements for equity compensation benefits. *(19.145)*

Disclosure

An enterprise should disclose:

(a)   the nature and terms (including any vesting provisions) of equity compensation plans;

(b)   the accounting policy for equity compensation plans;

(c)   the amounts recognised in the financial statements for equity compensation plans;

(d)   the number and terms (including, where applicable, dividend and voting rights, conversion rights, exercise dates, exercise prices and expiry dates) of the enterprise's own equity financial instruments which are held by equity compensation plans (and, in the case of share options, by employees) at the beginning and end of the period. The extent to which employees' entitlements to those instruments are vested at the beginning and end of the period should be specified;

(e)   the number and terms (including, where applicable, dividend and voting rights, conversion rights, exercise dates, exercise prices and expiry dates) of equity financial instruments issued by the enterprise to equity compensation plans or to employees (or of the enterprise's own equity financial instruments distributed by equity compensation plans to employees) during the period and the fair value of any consideration received from the equity compensation plans or the employees;

(f)   the number, exercise dates and exercise prices of share options exercised under equity compensation plans during the period;

(g)   the number of share options held by equity compensation plans, or held by employees under such plans, that lapsed during the period; and

(h)   the amount, and principal terms, of any loans or guarantees granted by the reporting enterprise to, or on behalf of, equity compensation plans. *(19.147)*

An enterprise should also disclose:

(a)   the fair value, at the beginning and end of the period, of the enterprise's own equity financial instruments (other than share options) held by equity compensation plans; and

(b)   the fair value, at the date of issue, of the enterprise's own equity financial instruments (other than share options) issued by the enterprise to equity compensation plans or to employees, or by equity compensation plans to employees, during the period.

If it is not practical to determine the fair value of the equity financial instruments (other than share options), that fact should be disclosed. *(19.148)*

Example 1	Applying IAS 19

Background Information

The following information is given about a funded defined benefit plan. To keep interest computations simple, all transactions are assumed to occur at the year end. The present value of the obligation and the fair value of the plan assets were both 1,000 at 1 January 20X1. Net cumulative unrecognised actuarial gains at that date were 140.

	20X1	*20X2*	*20X3*
Discount rate at start of year	10.0%	9.0%	8.0%
Expected rate of return on plan assets at start of year	12.0%	11.1%	10.3%
Current service cost	130	140	150
Benefits paid	150	180	190
Contributions paid	90	100	110
Present value of obligation at 31 December	1,141	1,197	1,295
Fair value of plan assets at 31 December	1,092	1,109	1,093
Expected average remaining working lives of employees (years)	10	10	10

Figure 73

In 20X2, the plan was amended to provide additional benefits with effect from 1 January 20X2. The present value as at 1 January 20X2 of additional benefits for employee service before 1 January 20X2 was 50 for vested benefits and 30 for non-vested benefits. As at 1 January 20X2, the enterprise estimated that the average period until the non-vested benefits would become vested was three years; the past service cost arising from additional non-vested benefits is therefore recognised on a straight-line basis over three years. The past service cost arising from additional vested benefits is recognised immediately. The enterprise has adopted a policy of recognising actuarial gains and losses under the minimum requirements of IAS 19.

Changes in the Present Value of the Obligation and in the Fair Value of the Plan Assets

The first step is to summarise the changes in the present value of the obligation and in the fair value of the plan assets and use this to determine the amount of the actuarial gains or losses for the period. These are as follows:

	20X1	20X2	20X3
Present value of obligation, 1 January	1,000	1,141	1,197
Interest cost	100	103	96
Current service cost	130	140	150
Past service cost – non-vested benefits	-	30	-
Past service cost – vested benefits	-	50	-
Benefits paid	(150)	(180)	(190)
Actuarial (gain) loss on obligation (balancing figure)	61	(87)	42
Present value of obligation, 31 December	1,141	1,197	1,295
Fair value of plan assets, 1 January	1,000	1,092	1,109
Expected return on plan assets	120	121	114
Contributions	90	100	110
Benefits paid	(150)	(180)	(190)
Actuarial gain (loss) on plan assets (balancing figure)	32	(24)	(50)

Figure 74

Limits of the 'Corridor'

The next step is to determine the limits of the corridor and then compare these with the cumulative unrecognised actuarial gains and losses in order to determine the net actuarial gain or loss to be recognised in the following period. The limits of the 'corridor' are set at the greater of:

(a)   10% of the present value of the obligation before deducting plan assets; and

(b)   10% of the fair value of any plan assets.

These limits, and the recognised and unrecognised actuarial gains and losses, are as shown in Figure 75 overleaf:

	20X1	20X2	20X3
Net cumulative unrecognised actuarial gains (losses) at 1 January	140	107	170
Limits of 'corridor' at 1 January	100	114	120
Excess [A]	40	-	50
Average expected remaining working lives (years) [B]	10	10	10
Actuarial gain (loss) to be recognised [A/B]	4	-	5
Unrecognised actuarial gains (losses) at 1 January	140	107	170
Actuarial gain (loss) for year - obligation	(61)	87	(42)
Actuarial gain (loss) for year - plan assets	32	(24)	(50)
Subtotal	111	170	78
Actuarial (gain) loss recognised	(4)	-	(5)
Unrecognised actuarial gains (losses) at 31 December	107	170	73

Figure 75

Amounts Recognised in the Balance Sheet and Income Statement, and Related Analyses

The final step is to determine the amounts to be recognised in the balance sheet and income statement, and the related analyses to be disclosed. These are as follows:

	20X1	20X2	20X3
Present value of the obligation	1,141	1,197	1,295
Fair value of plan assets	(1,092)	(1,109)	(1,093)
	49	88	202
Unrecognised actuarial gains (losses)	107	170	73
Unrecognised past service cost – non-vested benefits	-	(20)	(10)
Liability recognised in balance sheet	**156**	**238**	**265**
Current service cost	130	140	150
Interest cost	100	103	96
Expected return on plan assets	(120)	(121)	(114)
Net actuarial (gain) loss recognised in year	(4)	-	(5)
Past service cost – non-vested benefits	-	10	10
Past service cost – vested benefits	-	50	-
Expense recognised in the income statement	**106**	**182**	**137**

Figure 76

Movements in the net liability recognised in the balance sheet:

Opening net liability	140	156	238
Expense as above	106	182	137
Contributions paid	(90)	(100)	(110)
Closing net liability	156	238	265

Figure 77

Actual return on plan assets:

Expected return on plan assets	120	121	114
Actuarial gain (loss) on plan assets	32	(24)	(50)
Actual return on plan assets	152	97	64

Figure 78

Example 2

Employee Benefit Obligations

The amounts recognised in the balance sheet are as follows:

	Defined benefit pension plans		Post-employment medical benefits	
	20X2	*20X1*	*20X2*	*20X1*
Present value of funded obligations	12,310	11,772	2,819	2,721
Fair value of plan assets	(11,982)	(11,188)	(2,480)	(2,415)
	328	584	339	306
Present value of unfunded obligations	6,459	6,123	5,160	5,094
Unrecognised actuarial gains (losses)	(97)	(17)	31	72
Unrecognised past service cost	(450)	(650)	-	-
Net liability in balance sheet	6,240	6,040	5,530	5,472

Cont.

(cont.)

	Defined benefit pension plans		Post-employment medical benefits	
	20X2	*20X1*	*20X2*	*20X1*
Amounts in the balance sheet:				
Liabilities	6,451	6,278	5,530	5,472
Assets	(211)	(238)	-	-
Net liability in balance sheet	6,240	6,040	5,530	5,472

Figure 79

The pension plan assets include ordinary shares issued by [name of reporting enterprise] with a fair value of 317 (20X1: 281). Plan assets also include property occupied by [name of reporting enterprise] with a fair value of 200 (20X1: 185).

The amounts recognised in the income statement are as follows:

	Defined benefit pension plans		Post-employment medical benefits	
	20X2	*20X1*	*20X2*	*20X1*
Current service cost	1,679	1,554	471	411
Interest on obligation	1,890	1,650	819	705
Expected return on plan assets	(1,392)	(1,188)	(291)	(266)
Net actuarial losses (gains) recognised in year	90	(187)	-	-
Past service cost	200	200	-	-
Losses (gains) on curtailments and settlements	221	(47)	-	-
Total, included in 'staff costs'	2,688	1,982	999	850
Actual return on plan assets	1,232	1,205	275	254

Figure 80

Movements in the net liability recognised in the balance sheet are as follows:

	Defined benefit pension plans		Post-employment medical benefits	
	20X2	20X1	20X2	20X1
Net liability at start of year	6,040	5,505	5,472	5,439
Net expense recognised in the income statement	2,688	1,982	999	850
Contributions	(2,261)	(1,988)	(941)	(817)
Exchange differences on foreign plan	(227)	221	-	-
Liabilities acquired in business combinations	-	320	-	-
Net liability at end of year	6,240	6,040	5,530	5,472

Figure 81

Principal actuarial assumptions at the balance sheet date (expressed as weighted averages):

	20X2	20X1
Discount rate at 31 December	10.0%	9.1%
Expected return on plan assets at 31 December	12.0%	10.9%
Future salary increases	5%	4%
Future pension increases	3%	2%
Proportion of employees opting for early retirement	30%	30%
Annual increase in health care costs	8%	8%
Future changes in maximum state health care benefits	3%	2%

Figure 82

The group also participates in an industry-wide defined benefit plan which provides pensions linked to final salaries and is funded on a pay-as-you-go basis. It is not practical to determine the present value of the group's obligation or the related current service cost as the plan computes its obligations on a basis that differs materially from the basis used in [name of reporting enterprise]'s financial statements. [describe basis] On that basis, the plan's financial statements to 30 June 20X0 show an unfunded liability of 27,525. The unfunded liability will result in future payments by participating employers. The plan has approximately 75,000 members, of whom approximately 5,000 are current or former employees of [name of reporting enterprise], or their dependants. The expense recognised in the income statement, which is equal to contributions due for the year, and is not included in the above amounts, was 230 (20X1: 215). The group's future contributions may be increased substantially if other enterprises withdraw from the plan.

Equity Compensation Benefits

Share Option Plan

The group offers vested share options, without payment, to directors and other senior employees with more than three years' service. Movements in the number of share options held by employees are as follows:

	20X2	20X1
Outstanding at 1 January	10,634	10,149
Issued	2,001	1,819
Exercised	(957)	(891)
Lapsed	(481)	(443)
Outstanding at 31 December	11,197	10,634

Figure 83

Details of share options granted during the period:

	1/1/X7	1/1/X6
Expiry date		
Exercise price per share	12.17 -12.27	10.05 - 10.22
Aggregate proceeds if shares are issued ('000)	24	20
Amounts recognised in the balance sheet and income statement (and accounting policy)	*Not shown in this example, as the Standard prescribes no particular accounting treatment.*	

Figure 84

Details of share options exercised during the period:

	1/1/X2	1/1/X1
Expiry date		
Exercise price per share	7.45-7.49	7.37-7.48
Aggregate issue proceeds ('000)	7	7

Figure 85

Terms of the options outstanding at 31 December:

		20X2	20X1
Expiry date	Exercise price	Number	Number
1 January 20X2	7.43 - 7.51	-	1,438
1 January 20X3	7.57 - 7.65	1,952	1,952
1 January 20X4	7.89 - 8.01	2,118	2,118
1 January 20X5	9.09 - 9.12	3,307	3,307
1 January 20X6	10.05 - 10.22	1,819	1,819
1 January 20X7	12.17 - 12.27	2,001	-

Figure 86

Employee Share Ownership Plan

The Enterprise operates an Employee Share Ownership Plan for senior employees with more than three years' service. The Enterprise grants unsecured, interest-free loans with no fixed repayment terms to the Plan which enable the Plan to acquire Ordinary Shares in the Enterprise. The shares carry full dividend and voting rights. The Plan subsequently allocates shares to employees who meet certain performance criteria. Employees are not required to contribute to the cost of the shares. Movements in shares held by the Plan were as follows:

Outstanding at 1 January	125	100
Issued to the Plan for consideration of 60 (20X1: 52)	42	37
Allocated to employees	(18)	(12)
Outstanding at 31 December	149	125
Fair value of shares held at 31 December	781	607
Loans outstanding at 31 December	590	530
Fair value, on issuance, of shares issued in the year	166	137
Fair value of shares allocated to employees in the year	57	41
Amounts recognised in the balance sheet and income statement (and accounting policy)	*Not shown in this example, as the Standard prescribes no particular accounting treatment.*	

Figure 87

4.3   Leases

IAS 17 should be applied in accounting for all leases other than:

(a)   lease agreements to explore for or use natural resources, such as oil, gas, timber, metals and other mineral rights; and

(b)   licensing agreements for such items as motion picture films, video recordings, plays, manuscripts, patents and copyrights. *(17.1)*

IAS 17 applies to agreements that transfer the right to use assets even though substantial services by the lessor may be called for in connection with the operation or maintenance of such assets. On the other hand, this Standard does not apply to agreements that are contracts for services that do not transfer the right to use assets from one contracting party to the other. *(17.2)*

IAS 17 uses following terms:

• A *lease* is an agreement whereby the lessor conveys to the lessee in return for a payment or series of payments the right to use an asset for an agreed period of time.

• A *finance lease* is a lease that transfers substantially all the risks and rewards incident to ownership of an asset. Title may or may not eventually be transferred.

- An *operating lease* is a lease other than a finance lease.
- A *non-cancellable lease* is a lease that is cancellable only:

    (a)   upon the occurrence of some remote contingency;

    (b)   with the permission of the lessor;

    (c)   if the lessee enters into a new lease for the same or an equivalent asset with the same lessor; or

    (d)   upon payment by the lessee of an additional amount such that, at inception, continuation of the lease is reasonably certain.

- The *inception of the lease* is the earlier of the date of the lease agreement or of a commitment by the parties to the principal provisions of the lease.
- The *lease term* is the non-cancellable period for which the lessee has contracted to lease the asset together with any further terms for which the lessee has the option to continue to lease the asset, with or without further payment, which option at the inception of the lease it is reasonably certain that the lessee will exercise.
- *Minimum lease payments* are the payments over the lease term that the lessee is, or can be required, to make excluding contingent rent, costs for services and taxes to be paid by and reimbursed to the lessor, together with:

    (a)   in the case of the lessee, any amounts guaranteed by the lessee or by a party related to the lessee; or

    (b)   in the case of the lessor, any residual value guaranteed to the lessor by either:

        (i)   the lessee;

        (ii)   a party related to the lessee; or

        (iii)   an independent third party financially capable of meeting this guarantee.

    However, if the lessee has an option to purchase the asset at a price which is expected to be sufficiently lower than the fair value at the date the option becomes exercisable that, at the inception of the lease, is reasonably certain to be exercised, the minimum lease payments comprise the minimum payments payable over the lease term and the payment required to exercise this purchase option.

- *Fair value* is the amount for which an asset could be exchanged or a liability settled, between knowledgeable, willing parties in an arm's length transaction.
- *Economic life* is either:

    (a)   the period over which an asset is expected to be economically usable by one or more users; or

    (b)   the number of production or similar units expected to be obtained from the asset by one or more users.

- *Useful life* is the estimated remaining period, from the beginning of the lease term, without limitation by the lease term, over which the economic benefits embodied in the asset are expected to be consumed by the enterprise.

- *Guaranteed residual value* is:

    (a)   in the case of the lessee, that part of the residual value which is guaranteed by the lessee or by a party related to the lessee (the amount of the guarantee being the maximum amount that could, in any event, become payable); and

    (b)   in the case of the lessor, that part of the residual value which is guaranteed by the lessee or by a third party unrelated to the lessor who is financially capable of discharging the obligations under the guarantee.

- *Unguaranteed residual value* is that portion of the residual value of the leased asset, the realisation of which by the lessor is not assured or is guaranteed solely by a party related to the lessor.

- *Gross investment in the lease* is the aggregate of the minimum lease payments under a finance lease from the standpoint of the lessor and any unguaranteed residual value accruing to the lessor.

- *Unearned finance income* is the difference between:

    (a)   the aggregate of the minimum lease payments under a finance lease from the standpoint of the lessor and any unguaranteed residual value accruing to the lessor; and

    (b)   the present value of (a) above, at the interest rate implicit in the lease.

- *Net investment in the lease* is the gross investment in the lease less unearned finance income.

- The *interest rate implicit in the lease* is the discount rate that, at the inception of the lease, causes the aggregate present value of:

    (a)   the minimum lease payments; and

    (b)   the unguaranteed residual value to be equal to the fair value of the leased asset.

- The *lessee's incremental borrowing rate of interest* is the rate of interest the lessee would have to pay on a similar lease or, if that is not determinable, the rate that, at the inception of the lease, the lessee would incur to borrow over a similar term, and with a similar security, the funds necessary to purchase the asset.

- *Contingent rent* is that portion of the lease payments that is not fixed in amount but is based on a factor other than just the passage of time (e.g. percentage of sales, amount of usage, price indices, market rates of interest). *(17.3)*

The definition of a lease includes contracts for the hire of an asset which contain a provision giving the hirer an option to acquire title to the asset upon the fulfilment of agreed conditions. These contracts are sometimes known as hire purchase contracts. *(17.4)*

The classification of leases adopted in IAS 17 is based on the extent to which risks and rewards incident to ownership of a leased asset lie with the lessor or the lessee. Risks include the possibilities of losses from idle capacity or technological obsolescence and of variations in return due to changing economic conditions. Rewards may be represented by the expectation of profitable operation over the asset's economic life and of gain from appreciation in value or realisation of a residual value. *(17.5)*

A lease is classified as a finance lease if it transfers substantially all the risks and rewards incident to ownership. A lease is classified as an operating lease if it does not transfer substantially all the risks and rewards incident to ownership. *(17.6)*

Since the transaction between a lessor and a lessee is based on a lease agreement common to both parties, it is appropriate to use consistent definitions. The application of these definitions to the differing circumstances of the two parties may sometimes result in the same lease being classified differently by lessor and lessee. *(17.7)*

Whether a lease is a finance lease or an operating lease depends on the substance of the transaction rather than the form of the contract. Examples of situations which would normally lead to a lease being classified as a finance lease are:

(a)   the lease transfers ownership of the asset to the lessee by the end of the lease term;

(b)   the lessee has the option to purchase the asset at a price which is expected to be sufficiently lower than the fair value at the date the option becomes exercisable such that, at the inception of the lease, it is reasonably certain that the option will be exercised;

(c)   the lease term is for the major part of the economic life of the asset even if title is not transferred;

(d)   at the inception of the lease the present value of the minimum lease payments amounts to at least substantially all of the fair value of the leased asset; and

(e)   the leased assets are of a specialised nature such that only the lessee can use them without major modifications being made. *(17.8)*

Indicators of situations which individually or in combination could also lead to a lease being classified as a finance lease are:

(a)   if the lessee can cancel the lease, the lessor's losses associated with the cancellation are borne by the lessee;

(b)   gains or losses from the fluctuation in the fair value of the residual fall to the lessee (for example, in the form of a rent rebate equalling most of the sales proceeds at the end of the lease); and

(c)   the lessee has the ability to continue the lease for a secondary period at a rent which is substantially lower than market rent. *(17.9)*

Leases in the Financial Statements of Lessees

Finance Leases

Lessees should recognise finance leases as assets and liabilities in their balance sheets at amounts equal at the inception of the lease to the fair value of the leased property or, if lower, at the present value of the minimum lease payments. In calculating the present value of the minimum lease payments the discount factor is the interest rate implicit in the lease, if this is practical to determine; if not, the lessee's incremental borrowing rate should be used. *(17.12)*

Lease payments should be apportioned between the finance charge and the reduction of the outstanding liability. The finance charge should be allocated to periods during the lease term so as to produce a constant periodic rate of interest on the remaining balance of the liability for each period. *(17.17)*

A finance lease gives rise to a depreciation expense for the asset as well as a finance expense for each accounting period. The depreciation policy for leased assets should be consistent with that for depreciable assets which are owned, and the depreciation recognised should be calculated on the basis set out in IAS 16, *Property, Plant and Equipment* (see section 3.2, p. 190). If there is no reasonable certainty that the lessee will obtain ownership by the end of the lease term, the asset should be fully depreciated over the shorter of the lease term or its useful life. *(17.19)*

The depreciable amount of a leased asset is allocated to each accounting period during the period of expected use on a systematic basis consistent with the depreciation policy the lessee adopts for depreciable assets that are owned. If there is reasonable certainty that the lessee will obtain ownership by the end of the lease term, the period of expected use is the useful life of the asset; otherwise the asset is depreciated over the shorter of the lease term or its useful life. *(17.20)*

The sum of the depreciation expense for the asset and the finance expense for the period is rarely the same as the lease payments payable for the period, and it is, therefore, inappropriate simply to recognise the lease payments payable as an expense in the income statement. Accordingly, the asset and the related liability are unlikely to be equal in amount after the inception of the lease. *(17.21)*

To determine whether a leased asset has become impaired an enterprise applies the International Accounting Standard dealing with impairment of assets. *(17.22)*

Lessees should, in addition to the requirements of IAS 32, *Financial Instruments: Disclosure and Presentation* (see section 6.2, p. 370), make the following disclosures for finance leases:

(a)   for each class of asset, the net carrying amount at the balance sheet date;

(b)   a reconciliation between the total of minimum lease payments at the balance sheet date, and their present value. In addition, an enterprise should disclose the total of minimum lease payments at the balance sheet date, and their present value, for each of the following periods:

(i)   not later than one year;

(ii)   later than one year and not later than five years;

(iii)   later than five years;

(c)   contingent rents recognised in income for the period;

(d)   the total of future minimum sublease payments expected to be received under non-cancellable subleases at the balance sheet date; and

(e)   a general description of the lessee's significant leasing arrangements including, but not limited to, the following:

(i)   the basis on which contingent rent payments are determined;

(ii)   the existence and terms of renewal or purchase options and escalation clauses; and

(iii)   restrictions imposed by lease arrangements, such as those concerning dividends, additional debt, and further leasing. *(17.23)*

Operating Leases

Lease payments under an operating lease should be recognised as an expense in the income statement on a straight line basis over the lease term unless another systematic basis is representative of the time pattern of the user's benefit. *(17.25)*

Incentives or Inducements Received

In negotiating a new or renewed operating lease, the lessor may provide incentives for the lessee to enter into the agreement. All incentives for the agreement of a new or renewed operating lease (for example, an up-front cash payment to the lessee or the reimbursement or assumption by the lessor of relocation costs, leasehold improvements, etc., or initial periods of the lease term being rent-free or at a reduced rent) should be recognised as an integral part of the net consideration agreed for the use of the leased asset, irrespective of the incentive's nature or form or the timing of payments.

SIC-15, *Operating Leases – Incentives*, states that the lessee should recognise the aggregate benefit of incentives as a reduction of rental expense over the lease term, on a straight-line basis unless another systematic basis is representative of the time pattern of the lessee's benefit from the use of the leased asset. *(SIC-15)*

Disclosures

Lessees should, in addition to the requirements of IAS 32, *Financial Instruments: Disclosure and Presentation*, make the following disclosures for operating leases:

(a)   the total of future minimum lease payments under non-cancellable operating leases for each of the following periods:

(i)   not later than one year;

(ii)   later than one year and not later than five years;

(iii)   later than five years;

(b)   the total of future minimum sublease payments expected to be received under non-cancellable subleases at the balance sheet date;

(c)   lease and sublease payments recognised in income for the period, with separate amounts for minimum lease payments, contingent rents, and sublease payments;

(d)   a general description of the lessee's significant leasing arrangements including, but not limited to, the following:

    (i)   the basis on which contingent rent payments are determined;

    (ii)   the existence and terms of renewal or purchase options and escalation clauses; and

    (iii)   restrictions imposed by lease arrangements, such as those concerning dividends, additional debt, and further leasing. (17.27)

Leases in the Financial Statements of Lessors

Finance Leases

Lessors should recognise assets held under a finance lease in their balance sheets and present them as a receivable at an amount equal to the net investment in the lease. (17.28)

The recognition of finance income should be based on a pattern reflecting a constant periodic rate of return on the lessor's net investment outstanding in respect of the finance lease. (17.30)

Manufacturer or dealer lessors should recognise selling profit or loss in income for the period, in accordance with the policy followed by the enterprise for outright sales. If artificially low rates of interest are quoted, selling profit should be restricted to that which would apply if a commercial rate of interest were charged. Initial direct costs should be recognised as an expense in the income statement at the inception of the lease. (17.34)

Manufacturers or dealers often offer to customers the choice of either buying or leasing an asset. A finance lease of an asset by a manufacturer or dealer lessor gives rise to two types of income:

(a)   the profit or loss equivalent to the profit or loss resulting from an outright sale of the asset being leased, at normal selling prices, reflecting any applicable volume or trade discounts; and

(b)   the finance income over the lease term. (17.35)

Lessors should, in addition to the requirements in IAS 32, *Financial Instruments: Disclosure and Presentation*, make the following disclosures for finance leases:

(a)   a reconciliation between the total gross investment in the lease at the balance sheet date, and the present value of minimum lease payments receivable at the balance sheet date. In addition, an enterprise should disclose the total gross investment in the lease and the present value of minimum lease payments receivable at the balance sheet date, for each of the following periods:

(i)   not later than one year;

(ii)   later than one year and not later than five years;

(iii) later than five years;

(b)   unearned finance income;

(c)   the unguaranteed residual values accruing to the benefit of the lessor;

(d)   the accumulated allowance for uncollectible minimum lease payments receivable;

(e)   contingent rents recognised in income; and

(f)   a general description of the lessor's significant leasing arrangements. *(17.39)*

Operating Leases

Lessors should present assets subject to operating leases in their balance sheets according to the nature of the asset. *(17.41)*

Lease income from operating leases should be recognised in income on a straight line basis over the lease term, unless another systematic basis is more representative of the time pattern in which use benefit derived from the leased asset is diminished. *(17.42)*

Incentives and Inducements Granted

In negotiating a new or renewed operating lease, the lessor may provide incentives for the lessee to enter into the agreement. All incentives for the agreement of a new or renewed operating lease (for example, an up-front cash payment to the lessee or the reimbursement or assumption by the lessor of relocation costs, leasehold improvements, etc., or initial periods of the lease term being rent-free or at a reduced rent) should be recognised as an integral part of the net consideration agreed for the use of the leased asset, irrespective of the incentive's nature or form or the timing of payments.

SIC-15 provides that the lessor should recognise the aggregate cost of incentives as a reduction of rental income over the lease term, on a straight-line basis unless another systematic basis is representative of the time pattern over which the benefit of the leased asset is diminished. *(SIC-15)*

Depreciation and Impairment of Leased Assets

The depreciation of leased assets should be on a basis consistent with the lessor's normal depreciation policy for similar assets, and the depreciation charge should be calculated on the basis set out in IAS 16, *Property, Plant and Equipment* (see section 3.2, p. 190). *(17.45)*

To determine whether a leased asset has become impaired, that is when the expected future economic benefits from that asset are lower than its carrying amount, an enterprise applies the International Accounting Standard dealing with impairment of assets that sets out the requirements for how an enterprise should perform the review of the carrying amount of its assets, how it should determine the recoverable amount of an asset and when it should recognise, or reverse, an impairment loss. *(17.46)*

Disclosure

Lessors should, in addition to the requirements of IAS 32, *Financial Instruments: Disclosure and Presentation*, make the following disclosures for operating leases:

(a)   for each class of asset, the gross carrying amount, the accumulated depreciation and accumulated impairment losses at the balance sheet date; and

   (i)   the depreciation recognised in income for the period;

   (ii)   impairment losses recognised in income for the period;

   (iii)   impairment losses reversed in income for the period;

(b)   the future minimum lease payments under non-cancellable operating leases in the aggregate and for each of the following periods:

   (i)   not later than one year;

   (ii)   later than one year and not later than five years;

   (iii)   later than five years;

(c)   total contingent rents recognised in income; and

(d)   a general description of the lessor's significant leasing arrangements. *(17.48)*

Sale and Leaseback Transactions

A sale and leaseback transaction involves the sale of an asset by the vendor and the leasing of the same asset back to the vendor. The lease payment and the sale price are usually interdependent as they are negotiated as a package. The accounting treatment of a sale and leaseback transaction depends upon the type of lease involved. *(17.49)*

If a sale and leaseback transaction results in a finance lease, any excess of sales proceeds over the carrying amount should not be immediately recognised as income in the financial statements of a seller-lessee. Instead, it should be deferred and amortised over the lease term. *(17.50)*

If a sale and leaseback transaction results in an operating lease, and it is clear that the transaction is established at fair value, any profit or loss should be recognised immediately. If the sale price is below fair value, any profit or loss should be recognised immediately except that, if the loss is compensated by future lease payments at below market price, it should be deferred and amortised in proportion to the lease payments over the period for which the asset is expected to be used. If the sale price is above fair value, the excess over fair value should be deferred and amortised over the period for which the asset is expected to be used. *(17.52)*

For operating leases, if the fair value at the time of a sale and leaseback transaction is less than the carrying amount of the asset, a loss equal to the amount of the difference between the carrying amount and fair value should be recognised immediately. *(17.54)*

For finance leases, no such adjustment is necessary unless there has been an impairment in value, in which case the carrying amount is reduced to recoverable amount in accordance with the International Accounting Standard dealing with impairment of assets. *(17.55)*

Disclosure requirements for lessees and lessors apply equally to sale and leaseback transactions. The required description of the significant leasing arrangements leads to disclosure of unique or unusual provisions of the agreement or terms of the sale and leaseback transactions. *(17.56)*

Appendix D:

Sale and Leaseback Transactions that Result in Operating Leases

A sale and leaseback transaction that results in an operating lease may give rise to profit or a loss, the determination and treatment of which depends on the leased asset's carrying amount, fair value and selling price. The table below shows the requirements of the Standard in various circumstances.

	Carrying amount equal to fair value	Carrying amount less than fair value	Carrying amount above fair value
Sale price established at fair value (paragraph 17.52)			
Profit	no profit	recognise profit immediately	not applicable
Loss	no loss	not applicable	recognise loss immediately
Sale price below fair value (paragraph 17.52)			
Profit	no profit	recognise profit immediately	no profit (note 1)
Loss not compensated by future lease payments at below market price	recognise loss immediately	recognise loss immediately	(note 1)
Loss compensated by future lease payments at below market price	defer and amortise loss	defer and amortise loss	(note 1)
Sale price above fair value (paragraph 17.52)			
Profit	defer and amortise profit	defer and amortise profit	defer and amortise profit (note 2)
Loss	no loss	no loss	(note 1)

Figure 88

Note 1: *These parts of the table represent circumstances that would require the carrying amount of an asset to be written down to fair value where it is subject to a sale and leaseback.*

Note 2: *The profit would be the difference between fair value and sale price as the carrying amount would have been written down to fair value.*

4.4 Provisions, Contingent Liabilities and Contingent Assets

IAS 37 should be applied by all enterprises in accounting for provisions, contingent liabilities and contingent assets, except:

(a)   those resulting from financial instruments that are carried at fair value;

(b)   those resulting from executory contracts, except where the contract is onerous;

(c)   those arising in insurance enterprises from contracts with policyholders; and

(d)   those covered by another International Accounting Standard. *(37.1)*

IAS 37 uses the following terms:

- A *provision* is a liability of uncertain timing or amount.

- A *liability* is a present obligation of the enterprise arising from past events, the settlement of which is expected to result in an outflow from the enterprise of resources embodying economic benefits.

- An *obligating event* is an event that creates a legal or constructive obligation that results in an enterprise having no realistic alternative to settling that obligation.

- A *legal obligation* is an obligation that derives from:

    (a)   a contract (through its explicit or implicit terms);

    (b)   legislation; or

    (c)   other operation of law.

- A *constructive obligation* is an obligation that derives from an enterprise's actions where:

    (a)   by an established pattern of past practice, published policies or a sufficiently specific current statement, the enterprise has indicated to other parties that it will accept certain responsibilities; and

    (b)   as a result, the enterprise has created a valid expectation on the part of those other parties that it will discharge those responsibilities.

- A *contingent liability* is:

    (a)   a possible obligation that arises from past events and whose existence will be confirmed only by the occurrence or non-occurrence of one or more uncertain future events not wholly within the control of the enterprise; or

    (b)   a present obligation that arises from past events but is not recognised because:

        (i)   it is not probable that an outflow of resources embodying economic benefits will be required to settle the obligation; or

        (ii)   the amount of the obligation cannot be measured with sufficient reliability.

- A *contingent asset* is a possible asset that arises from past events and whose existence will be confirmed only by the occurrence or non-occurrence of one or more uncertain future events not wholly within the control of the enterprise.

- An *onerous contract* is a contract in which the unavoidable costs of meeting the obligations under the contract exceed the economic benefits expected to be received under it.

- A *restructuring* is a programme that is planned and controlled by management, and materially changes either:

    (a)   the scope of a business undertaken by an enterprise; or

    (b)   the manner in which that business is conducted. *(37.10)*

Provisions and Other Liabilities

Provisions can be distinguished from other liabilities such as trade payables and accruals because there is uncertainty about the timing or amount of the future expenditure required in settlement. Accruals are often reported as part of trade and other payables, whereas provisions are reported separately. *(37.11)*

Relationship between Provisions and Contingent Liabilities

In a general sense, all provisions are contingent because they are uncertain in timing or amount. However, within IAS 37 the term 'contingent' is used for liabilities and assets that are not recognised because their existence will be confirmed only by the occurrence or non-occurrence of one or more uncertain future events not wholly within the control of the enterprise. In addition, the term 'contingent liability' is used for liabilities that do not meet the recognition criteria. *(37.12)*

IAS 37 distinguishes between:

(a)   *provisions* – which are recognised as liabilities (assuming that a reliable estimate can be made) because they are present obligations and it is probable that an outflow of resources embodying economic benefits will be required to settle the obligations; and

(b)   *contingent liabilities* – which are not recognised as liabilities because they are either:

    (i)   possible obligations, as it has yet to be confirmed whether the enterprise has a present obligation that could lead to an outflow of resources embodying economic benefits; or

    (ii)   present obligations that do not meet the recognition criteria in IAS 37 (because either it is not probable that an outflow of resources embodying economic benefits will be required to settle the obligation, or a sufficiently reliable estimate of the amount of the obligation cannot be made). *(37.13)*

Recognition

Provisions

A provision should be recognised when:

(a) an enterprise has a present obligation (legal or constructive) as a result of a past event;

(b) it is probable that an outflow of resources embodying economic benefits will be required to settle the obligation; and

(c) a reliable estimate can be made of the amount of the obligation.

If these conditions are not met, no provision should be recognised. *(37.14)*

Present Obligation

In rare cases it is not clear whether there is a present obligation. In these cases, a past event is deemed to give rise to a present obligation if, taking account of all available evidence, it is more likely than not that a present obligation exists at the balance sheet date. *(37.15)*

Past Event

A past event that leads to a present obligation is called an obligating event. For an event to be an obligating event, it is necessary that the enterprise has no realistic alternative to settling the obligation created by the event. This is the case only:

(a) where the settlement of the obligation can be enforced by law; or

(b) in the case of a constructive obligation, where the event (which may be an action of the enterprise) creates valid expectations in other parties that the enterprise will discharge the obligation. *(37.17)*

Probable Outflow of Resources Embodying Economic Benefits

For a liability to qualify for recognition there must be not only a present obligation but also the probability of an outflow of resources embodying economic benefits to settle that obligation. For the purpose of IAS 37, an outflow of resources or other event is regarded as probable if the event is more likely than not to occur, i.e. the probability that the event will occur is greater than the probability that it will not. Where it is not probable that a present obligation exists, an enterprise discloses a contingent liability, unless the possibility of an outflow of resources embodying economic benefits is remote. *(37.23)*

Reliable Estimate of the Obligation

The use of estimates is an essential part of the preparation of financial statements and does not undermine their reliability. This is especially true in the case of provisions, which by their nature are more uncertain than most other balance sheet items. Except in extremely rare cases, an enterprise will be able to determine a range of possible outcomes and can therefore make an estimate of the obligation that is sufficiently reliable to use in recognising a provision. *(37.25)*

Contingent Liabilities and Contingent Assets

An enterprise should not recognise a contingent liability, or a contingent asset. (37.27, 37.31)

Measurement

Best Estimate

The amount recognised as a provision should be the best estimate of the expenditure required to settle the present obligation at the balance sheet date. (37.36)

Risks and Uncertainties

The risks and uncertainties that inevitably surround many events and circumstances should be taken into account in reaching the best estimate of a provision. (37.42)

Present Value

Where the effect of the time value of money is material, the amount of a provision should be the present value of the expenditures expected to be required to settle the obligation. (37.45)

The discount rate (or rates) should be a pre-tax rate (or rates) that reflect(s) current market assessments of the time value of money and the risks specific to the liability. The discount rate(s) should not reflect risks for which future cash flow estimates have been adjusted. (37.47)

Future Events

Future events that may affect the amount required to settle an obligation should be reflected in the amount of a provision where there is sufficient objective evidence that they will occur. (37.48)

Expected Disposal of Assets

Gains from the expected disposal of assets should not be taken into account in measuring a provision. (37.51)

Reimbursements

Where some or all of the expenditure required to settle a provision is expected to be reimbursed by another party, the reimbursement should be recognised when, and only when, it is virtually certain that reimbursement will be received if the enterprise settles the obligation. The reimbursement should be treated as a separate asset. The amount recognised for the reimbursement should not exceed the amount of the provision. (37.53)

In the income statement, the expense relating to a provision may be presented net of the amount recognised for a reimbursement. (37.54)

Changes in Provisions

Provisions should be reviewed at each balance sheet date and adjusted to reflect the current best estimate. If it is no longer probable that an outflow of resources embodying economic benefits will be required to settle the obligation, the provision should be reversed. *(37.59)*

Use of Provisions

A provision should be used only for expenditures for which the provision was originally recognised. That is, only expenditures that relate to the original provision are set against it. Setting expenditures against a provision that was originally recognised for another purpose would conceal the impact of two different events. *(37.61, 37.62)*

Application of the Recognition and Measurement Rules

Future Operating Losses

Provisions should not be recognised for future operating losses. *(37.63)*

Onerous Contracts

If an enterprise has a contract that is onerous, the present obligation under the contract should be recognised and measured as a provision. Before a separate provision for an onerous contract is established, an enterprise recognises any impairment loss that has occurred on assets dedicated to that contract (see IAS 36, *Impairment of Assets*, section 3.5, p. 214). *(37.66, 37.69)*

Restructuring

A constructive obligation to restructure arises only when an enterprise:

(a)   has a detailed formal plan for the restructuring identifying at least:

   (i)   the business or part of a business concerned;

   (ii)   the principal locations affected;

   (iii) the location, function, and approximate number of employees who will be compensated for terminating their services;

   (iv)   the expenditures that will be undertaken; and

   (v)   when the plan will be implemented;

         and

(b)   has raised a valid expectation in those affected that it will carry out the restructuring by starting to implement that plan or announcing its main features to those affected by it. *(37.72)*

No obligation arises for the sale of an operation until the enterprise is committed to the sale, i.e. there is a binding sale agreement. *(37.78)*

A restructuring provision should include only the direct expenditures arising from the restructuring, which are those that are both:

(a)   necessarily entailed by the restructuring; and

(b)   not associated with the ongoing activities of the enterprise. *(37.80)*

Disclosure

For each class of provision, an enterprise should disclose:

(a)   the carrying amount at the beginning and end of the period;

(b)   additional provisions made in the period, including increases to existing provisions;

(c)   amounts used (i.e. incurred and charged against the provision) during the period;

(d)   unused amounts reversed during the period; and

(e)   the increase during the period in the discounted amount arising from the passage of time and the effect of any change in the discount rate.

Comparative information is not required. *(37.84)*

An enterprise should disclose the following for each class of provision:

(a)   a brief description of the nature of the obligation and the expected timing of any resulting outflows of economic benefits;

(b)   an indication of the uncertainties about the amount or timing of those outflows. Where necessary to provide adequate information, an enterprise should disclose the major assumptions made concerning future events, as addressed in paragraph 37.48; and

(c)   the amount of any expected reimbursement, stating the amount of any asset that has been recognised for that expected reimbursement. *(37.85)*

Unless the possibility of any outflow in settlement is remote, an enterprise should disclose for each class of contingent liability at the balance sheet date a brief description of the nature of the contingent liability and, where practical:

(a)   an estimate of its financial effect;

(b)   an indication of the uncertainties relating to the amount or timing of any outflow; and

(c)   the possibility of any reimbursement. *(37.86)*

Where an inflow of economic benefits is probable, an enterprise should disclose a brief description of the nature of the contingent assets at the balance sheet date, and, where practical, an estimate of their financial effect. *(37.89)*

In extremely rare cases, disclosure of some or all of the information required by IAS 37 can be expected to prejudice seriously the position of the enterprise in a dispute with other parties on the subject matter of the provision, contingent liability or contingent asset. In such cases, an enterprise need not disclose the information, but should disclose the general nature of the dispute, together with the fact that, and reason why, the information has not been disclosed. *(37.92)*

Appendix E:

Tables – Provisions, Contingent Liabilities, Contingent Assets and Reimbursements

Provisions and Contingent Liabilities

Where, as a result of past events, there may be an outflow of resources embodying future economic benefits in settlement of: (a) a present obligation; or (b) a possible obligation whose existence will be confirmed only by the occurrence or non-occurrence of one or more uncertain future events not wholly within the control of the enterprise.

There is a present obligation that probably requires an outflow of resources.	There is a possible obligation or a present obligation that may, but probably will not, require an outflow of resources.	There is a possible obligation or a present obligation where the likelihood of an outflow of resources is remote.
A provision is recognised (paragraph 37.14).	No provision is recognised (paragraph 37.27).	No provision is recognised (paragraph 37.27).
Disclosures are required for the provision (paragraphs 37.84 and 37.85).	Disclosures are required for the contingent liability (paragraph 37.86).	No disclosure is required (paragraph 37.86).

Figure 89

A contingent liability also arises in the extremely rare case where there is a liability that cannot be recognised because it cannot be measured reliably. Disclosures are required for the contingent liability.

Contingent Assets

Where, as a result of past events, there is a possible asset whose existence will be confirmed only by the occurrence or non-occurrence of one or more uncertain future events not wholly within the control of the enterprise.

The inflow of economic benefits is virtually certain.	The inflow of economic benefits is probable, but not virtually certain.	The inflow is not probable.
The asset is not contingent.	No asset is recognised (paragraph 37.31). Disclosures are required (paragraph 37.89).	No asset is recognised (paragraph 37.31). No disclosure is required (paragraph 37.89).

Figure 90

Reimbursements

Some or all of the expenditure required to settle a provision is expected to be reimbursed by another party.

The enterprise has no obligation for the part of the expenditure to be reimbursed by the other party.	The obligation for the amount expected to be reimbursed remains with the enterprise and it is virtually certain that reimbursement will be received if the enterprise settles the provision.	The obligation for the amount expected to be reimbursed remains with the enterprise and the reimbursement is not virtually certain if the enterprise settles the provision.
The entity has no liability for the amount to be reimbursed.	The reimbursement is recognised as a separate asset in the balance sheet and may be offset against the expense in the income statement. The amount recognised for the expected reimbursement does not exceed the liability (paragraphs 37.53 and 37.54).	The expected reimbursement is not recognised as an asset (paragraph 37.53).
No disclosure is required.	The reimbursement is disclosed together with the amount recognised for the reimbursement (paragraph 37.85(c))	The expected reimbursement is disclosed (paragraph 37.85(c)).

Figure 91

Chapter 5

Accounting for Revenue and Expenses

IAS 18 prescribes the accounting treatment of revenue arising from certain types of transactions and events.

IAS 11 prescribes the accounting treatment of revenue and costs associated with construction contracts.

IAS 20 prescribes accounting and disclosure for government grants and other government assistance.

IAS 23 prescribes the acceptable accounting treatments for borrowing costs.

5.1 Revenue

Income is defined in the IASC Framework as increases in economic benefits during the accounting period in the form of inflows or enhancements of assets or decreases of liabilities that result in increases in equity, other than those relating to contributions from equity participants. *Income* encompasses both revenue and gains. *Revenue* is income that arises in the course of ordinary activities of an enterprise and is referred to by a variety of different names including sales, fees, interest, dividends and royalties.

The primary issue in accounting for revenue is determining when to recognise revenue. Revenue is recognised when it is probable that future economic benefits will flow to the enterprise and these benefits can be measured reliably. IAS 18 identifies the circumstances in which these criteria will be met and, therefore, revenue will be recognised. It also provides practical guidance on the application of these criteria.

IAS 18 should be applied in accounting for revenue arising from the following transactions and events:

(a)   the sale of goods;

(b)   the rendering of services; and

(c)   the use by others of enterprise assets yielding interest, royalties and dividends. *(18.1)*

Goods includes goods produced by the enterprise for the purpose of sale and goods purchased for resale, such as merchandise purchased by a retailer or land and other property held for resale. *(18.3)*

The rendering of services typically involves the performance by the enterprise of a contractually agreed task over an agreed period of time. *(18.4)*

IAS 18 uses the following terms:

- *Revenue* is the gross inflow of economic benefits during the period arising in the course of the ordinary activities of an enterprise when those inflows result in increases in equity, other than increases relating to contributions from equity participants.
- *Fair value* is the amount for which an asset could be exchanged, or a liability settled, between knowledgeable, willing parties in an arm's length transaction. *(18.7)*

Measurement of Revenue

Revenue should be measured at the fair value of the consideration received or receivable. *(18.9)*

The amount of revenue is measured at the fair value of the consideration received or receivable taking into account the amount of any trade discounts and volume rebates allowed by the enterprise. *(18.10)*

In most cases, the consideration is in the form of cash or cash equivalents and the amount of revenue is the amount of cash or cash equivalents received or receivable. However, when the inflow of cash or cash equivalents is deferred, the fair value of the consideration may be less than the nominal amount of cash received or receivable. When the arrangement effectively constitutes a financing transaction, the fair value of the consideration is determined by discounting all future receipts using an imputed rate of interest. The imputed rate of interest is the more clearly determinable of either:

(a)   the prevailing rate for a similar instrument of an issuer with a similar credit rating; or

(b)   a rate of interest that discounts the nominal amount of the instrument to the current cash sales price of the goods or services.

The difference between the fair value and the nominal amount of the consideration is recognised as interest revenue in accordance with the provisions of IAS 18 and in accordance with IAS 39, *Financial Instruments: Recognition and Measurement* (see section 6.1, p. 349). *(18.11)*

Identification of the Transaction

The recognition criteria in IAS 18 are usually applied separately to each transaction. However, in certain circumstances, it is necessary to apply the recognition criteria to the separately identifiable components of a single transaction in order to reflect the substance of the transaction. Conversely, the recognition criteria are applied to two or more transactions together when they are linked in such a way that the commercial effect cannot be understood without reference to the series of transactions as a whole. *(18.13)*

Sale of Goods

Revenue from the sale of goods should be recognised when all the following conditions have been satisfied:

(a)   the enterprise has transferred to the buyer the significant risks and rewards of ownership of the goods;

(b)   the enterprise retains neither continuing managerial involvement to the degree usually associated with ownership nor effective control over the goods sold;

(c)   the amount of revenue can be measured reliably;

(d)   it is probable that the economic benefits associated with the transaction will flow to the enterprise; and

(e)   the costs incurred or to be incurred in respect of the transaction can be measured reliably. *(18.14)*

Example – Sale of Goods

The law in different countries may mean the recognition criteria in IAS 18 are met at different times. In particular, the law may determine the point in time at which the enterprise transfers the significant risks and rewards of ownership. Therefore, the examples in this section of the Appendix need to be read in the context of the laws relating to the sale of goods in the country in which the transaction takes place.

- *'Bill and hold' sales, in which delivery is delayed at the buyer's request but the buyer takes title and accepts billing.*

   Revenue is recognised when the buyer takes title, provided:

   (a)   it is probable that delivery will be made;

   (b)   the item is on hand, identified and ready for delivery to the buyer at the time the sale is recognised;

   (c)   the buyer specifically acknowledges the deferred delivery instructions; and

   (d)   the usual payment terms apply.

   Revenue is not recognised when there is simply an intention to acquire or manufacture the goods in time for delivery.

- *Goods shipped subject to conditions.*

(a)   *installation and inspection*

   Revenue is normally recognised when the buyer accepts delivery, and installation and inspection are complete. However, revenue is recognised immediately upon the buyer's acceptance of delivery when:

   (i)   the installation process is simple in nature, for example the installation of a factory tested television receiver which only requires unpacking and connection of power and antennae; or

        (ii)   the inspection is performed only for purposes of final determination of contract prices, for example, shipments of iron ore, sugar or soya beans.

(b)   *on approval when the buyer has negotiated a limited right of return.*

If there is uncertainty about the possibility of return, revenue is recognised when the shipment has been formally accepted by the buyer or the goods have been delivered and the time period for rejection has elapsed.

(c)   *consignment sales under which the recipient (buyer) undertakes to sell the goods on behalf of the shipper (seller).*

Revenue is recognised by the shipper when the goods are sold by the recipient to a third party.

(d)   *cash on delivery sales*

Revenue is recognised when delivery is made and cash is received by the seller or its agent.

- *Lay away sales under which the goods are delivered only when the buyer makes the final payment in a series of instalments.*

Revenue from such sales is recognised when the goods are delivered. However, when experience indicates that most such sales are consummated, revenue may be recognised when a significant deposit is received provided the goods are on hand, identified and ready for delivery to the buyer.

- *Orders when payment (or partial payment) is received in advance of delivery for goods not presently held in inventory, for example, the goods are still to be manufactured or will be delivered directly to the customer from a third party.*

Revenue is recognised when the goods are delivered to the buyer.

- *Sale and repurchase agreements (other than swap transactions) under which the seller concurrently agrees to repurchase the same goods at a later date, or when the seller has a call option to repurchase, or the buyer has a put option to require the repurchase, by the seller, of the goods.*

The terms of the agreement need to be analysed to ascertain whether, in substance, the seller has transferred the risks and rewards of ownership to the buyer and hence revenue is recognised. When the seller has retained the risks and rewards of ownership, even though legal title has been transferred, the transaction is a financing arrangement and does not give rise to revenue.

- *Sales to intermediate parties, such as distributors, dealers or others for resale.*

Revenue from such sales is generally recognised when the risks and rewards of ownership have passed. However, when the buyer is acting, in substance, as an agent, the sale is treated as a consignment sale.

- *Subscriptions to publications and similar items.*

When the items involved are of similar value in each time period, revenue is recognised on a straight line basis over the period in which the items are despatched. When the items vary in value from period to period, revenue is recognised on the basis of the sales value of the item despatched in relation to the total estimated sales value of all items covered by the subscription.

- *Instalment sales, under which the consideration is receivable in instalments.*

  Revenue attributable to the sales price, exclusive of interest, is recognised at the date of sale. The sale price is the present value of the consideration, determined by discounting the instalments receivable at the imputed rate of interest. The interest element is recognised as revenue as it is earned, on a time proportion basis that takes into account the imputed rate of interest.

- *Real estate sales*

  Revenue is normally recognised when legal title passes to the buyer. However, in some jurisdictions the equitable interest in a property may vest in the buyer before legal title passes and therefore the risks and rewards of ownership have been transferred at that stage. In such cases, provided that the seller has no further substantial acts to complete under the contract, it may be appropriate to recognise revenue. In either case, if the seller is obliged to perform any significant acts after the transfer of the equitable and/or legal title, revenue is recognised as the acts are performed. An example is a building or other facility on which construction has not been completed.

  In some cases, real estate may be sold with a degree of continuing involvement by the seller such that the risks and rewards of ownership have not been transferred. Examples are sale and repurchase agreements which include put and call options, and agreements whereby the seller guarantees occupancy of the property for a specified period, or guarantees a return on the buyer's investment for a specified period. In such cases, the nature and extent of the seller's continuing involvement determines how the transaction is accounted for. It may be accounted for as a sale, or as a financing, leasing or some other profit-sharing arrangement. If it is accounted for as a sale, the continuing involvement of the seller may delay the recognition of revenue.

  A seller must also consider the means of payment and evidence of the buyer's commitment to complete payment. For example, when the aggregate of the payments received, including the buyer's initial down payment, or continuing payments by the buyer, provide insufficient evidence of the buyer's commitment to complete payment, revenue is recognised only to the extent cash is received. *(18-Appendix)*

Rendering of Services

When the outcome of a transaction involving the rendering of services can be estimated reliably, revenue associated with the transaction should be recognised by reference to the stage of completion of the transaction at the balance sheet date. The outcome of a transaction can be estimated reliably when all the following conditions are satisfied:

(a)   the amount of revenue can be measured reliably;

(b)　it is probable that the economic benefits associated with the transaction will flow to the enterprise;

(c)　the stage of completion of the transaction at the balance sheet date can be measured reliably; and

(d)　the costs incurred for the transaction and the costs to complete the transaction can be measured reliably. *(18.20)*

The recognition of revenue by reference to the stage of completion of a transaction is often referred to as the percentage of completion method. Under this method, revenue is recognised in the accounting periods in which the services are rendered. The recognition of revenue on this basis provides useful information on the extent of service activity and performance during a period. IAS 11, *Construction Contracts* (see section 5.2, p. 331), also requires the recognition of revenue on this basis. The requirements of that Standard are generally applicable to the recognition of revenue and the associated expenses for a transaction involving the rendering of services. *(18.21)*

When the outcome of the transaction involving the rendering of services cannot be estimated reliably, revenue should be recognised only to the extent of the expenses recognised that are recoverable. *(18.26)*

Examples – Rendering of Services

- *Installation fees*

  Installation fees are recognised as revenue by reference to the stage of completion of the installation, unless they are incidental to the sale of a product in which case they are recognised when the goods are sold.

- *Servicing fees included in the price of the product.*

  When the selling price of a product includes an identifiable amount for subsequent servicing (for example, after sales support and product enhancement on the sale of software), that amount is deferred and recognised as revenue over the period during which the service is performed. The amount deferred is that which will cover the expected costs of the services under the agreement, together with a reasonable profit on those services.

- *Advertising commissions*

  Media commissions are recognised when the related advertisement or commercial appears before the public. Production commissions are recognised by reference to the stage of completion of the project.

- *Insurance agency commissions*

  Insurance agency commissions received or receivable which do not require the agent to render further service are recognised as revenue by the agent on the effective commencement or renewal dates of the related policies. However, when it is probable that the agent will be required to render further services during the life of the policy, the commission, or part thereof, is deferred and recognised as revenue over the period during which the policy is in force.

- *Financial service fees*

  The recognition of revenue for financial service fees depends on the purposes for which the fees are assessed and the basis of accounting for any associated financial instrument. The description of fees for financial services may not be indicative of the nature and substance of the services provided. Therefore, it is necessary to distinguish between fees which are an integral part of the effective yield of a financial instrument, fees which are earned as services are provided, and fees which are earned on the execution of a significant act.

  (a)   *Fees which are an integral part of the effective yield of a financial instrument.*

  Such fees are generally treated as an adjustment to the effective yield. However, when the financial instrument is to be measured at fair value subsequent to its initial recognition the fees are recognised as revenue when the instrument is initially recognised.

  (i)   *Origination fees received by the enterprise relating to the creation or acquisition of a financial instrument which is held by the enterprise as an investment.*

  Such fees may include compensation for activities such as evaluating the borrower's financial condition, evaluating and recording guarantees, collateral and other security arrangements, negotiating the terms of the instrument, preparing and processing documents and closing the transaction. These fees are an integral part of generating an ongoing involvement with the resultant financial instrument and, together with the related direct costs, are deferred and recognised as an adjustment to the effective yield.

  (ii)   *Commitment fees received by the enterprise to originate or purchase a loan.*

  If it is probable that the enterprise will enter into a specific lending arrangement, the commitment fee received is regarded as compensation for an ongoing involvement with the acquisition of a financial instrument and, together with the related direct costs, is deferred and recognised as an adjustment to the effective yield. If the commitment expires without the enterprise making the loan, the fee is recognised as revenue on expiry.

  (b)   *Fees earned as services are provided.*

  (i)   *Fees charged for servicing a loan.*

  Fees charged by an enterprise for servicing a loan are recognised as revenue as the services are provided. If the enterprise sells a loan but retains the servicing of that loan at a fee which is lower than a normal fee for such services, part of the sales price of the loan is deferred and recognised as revenue as the servicing is provided.

    (ii) *Commitment fees to originate or purchase a loan.*

        If it is unlikely that a specific lending arrangement will be entered into, the commitment fee is recognised as revenue on a time proportion basis over the commitment period.

  (c) *Fees earned on the execution of a significant act, which is much more significant than any other act.*

    The fees are recognised as revenue when the significant act has been completed, as in the examples below.

    (i) *Commission on the allotment of shares to a client.*

        The commission is recognised as revenue when the shares have been allotted.

    (ii) *Placement fees for arranging a loan between a borrower and an investor.*

        The fee is recognised as revenue when the loan has been arranged.

    (iii) *Loan syndication fees*

        It is necessary to distinguish between fees earned on completion of a significant act and fees related to future performance or risk retained. A syndication fee received by an enterprise which arranges a loan and which retains no part of the loan package for itself (or retains a part at the same effective yield for comparable risk as other participants) is compensation for the service of syndication. Such a fee is recognised as revenue when the syndication has been completed. However, when a syndicator retains a portion of the loan package at an effective yield for comparable risk which is lower than that earned by other participants in the syndicate, part of the syndication fee received relates to the risk retained. The relevant portion of the fee is deferred and recognised as revenue as an adjustment to the effective yield of the investment, as in 14(a) above. Conversely, when a syndicator retains a portion of the loan package at an effective yield for comparable risk which is higher than that earned by other participants in the syndicate, part of the effective yield relates to the syndication fee. The relevant portion of the effective yield is recognised as part of the syndication fee when the syndication has been completed.

- *Admission fees*

Revenue from artistic performances, banquets and other special events is recognised when the event takes place. When a subscription to a number of events is sold, the fee is allocated to each event on a basis which reflects the extent to which services are performed at each event.

- *Tuition fees*

Revenue is recognised over the period of instruction.

- *Initiation, entrance and membership fees*

  Revenue recognition depends on the nature of the services provided. If the fee permits only membership, and all other services or products are paid for separately, or if there is a separate annual subscription, the fee is recognised as revenue when no significant uncertainty as to its collectability exists. If the fee entitles the member to services or publications to be provided during the membership period, or to purchase goods or services at prices lower than those charged to non-members, it is recognised on a basis that reflects the timing, nature and value of the benefits provided.

- *Franchise fees*

  Franchise fees may cover the supply of initial and subsequent services, equipment and other tangible assets, and know-how. Accordingly, franchise fees are recognised as revenue on a basis that reflects the purpose for which the fees were charged. The following methods of franchise fee recognition are appropriate:

  (a) *Supplies of equipment and other tangible assets.*

  The amount, based on the fair value of the assets sold, is recognised as revenue when the items are delivered or title passes.

  (b) *Supplies of initial and subsequent services.*

  Fees for the provision of continuing services, whether part of the initial fee or a separate fee are recognised as revenue as the services are rendered. When the separate fee does not cover the cost of continuing services together with a reasonable profit, part of the initial fee, sufficient to cover the costs of continuing services and to provide a reasonable profit on those services, is deferred and recognised as revenue as the services are rendered.

  The franchise agreement may provide for the franchisor to supply equipment, inventories, or other tangible assets, at a price lower than that charged to others or a price that does not provide a reasonable profit on those sales. In these circumstances, part of the initial fee, sufficient to cover estimated costs in excess of that price and to provide a reasonable profit on those sales, is deferred and recognised over the period the goods are likely to be sold to the franchisee. The balance of an initial fee is recognised as revenue when performance of all the initial services and other obligations required of the franchisor (such as assistance with site selection, staff training, financing and advertising) has been substantially accomplished.

  The initial services and other obligations under an area franchise agreement may depend on the number of individual outlets established in the area. In this case, the fees attributable to the initial services are recognised as revenue in proportion to the number of outlets for which the initial services have been substantially completed.

  If the initial fee is collectable over an extended period and there is a significant uncertainty that it will be collected in full, the fee is recognised as cash instalments are received.

(c) *Continuing Franchise Fees*

Fees charged for the use of continuing rights granted by the agreement, or for other services provided during the period of the agreement, are recognised as revenue as the services are provided or the rights used.

(d) *Agency Transactions*

Transactions may take place between the franchisor and the franchisee which, in substance, involve the franchisor acting as agent for the franchisee. For example, the franchisor may order supplies and arrange for their delivery to the franchisee at no profit. Such transactions do not give rise to revenue.

- *Fees from the development of customised software.*

Fees from the development of customised software are recognised as revenue by reference to the stage of completion of the development, including completion of services provided for post delivery service support.

Interest, Royalties and Dividends

Revenue arising from the use by others of enterprise assets yielding interest, royalties and dividends should be recognised on the bases set out in the following paragraph when:

(a) it is probable that the economic benefits associated with the transaction will flow to the enterprise; and

(b) the amount of the revenue can be measured reliably. *(18.29)*

Revenue should be recognised on the following bases:

(a) interest should be recognised on a time proportion basis that takes into account the effective yield on the asset;

(b) royalties should be recognised on an accrual basis in accordance with the substance of the relevant agreement; and

(c) dividends should be recognised when the shareholder's right to receive payment is established. *(18.30)*

The effective yield on an asset is the rate of interest required to discount the stream of future cash receipts expected over the life of the asset to equate to the initial carrying amount of the asset. Interest revenue includes the amount of amortisation of any discount, premium or other difference between the initial carrying amount of a debt security and its amount at maturity. *(18.31)*

➤ Examples - Interest, Royalties and Dividends

- *Licence fees and royalties.*

Fees and royalties paid for the use of an enterprise's assets (such as trademarks, patents, software, music copyright, record masters and motion picture films) are normally recognised in accordance with the substance of the agreement. As a practical matter, this may be on a straight line basis over the life of the agreement, for example, when a licensee has the right to use certain technology for a specified period of time.

An assignment of rights for a fixed fee or non-refundable guarantee under a non-cancellable contract which permits the licensee to exploit those rights freely and the licensor has no remaining obligations to perform is, in substance, a sale. An example is a licensing agreement for the use of software when the licensor has no obligations subsequent to delivery. Another example is the granting of rights to exhibit a motion picture film in markets where the licensor has no control over the distributor and expects to receive no further revenues from the box office receipts. In such cases, revenue is recognised at the time of sale.

In some cases, whether or not a licence fee or royalty will be received is contingent on the occurrence of a future event. In such cases, revenue is recognised only when it is probable that the fee or royalty will be received, which is normally when the event has occurred.

Disclosure

An enterprise should disclose:

(a) the accounting policies adopted for the recognition of revenue including the methods adopted to determine the stage of completion of transactions involving the rendering of services;

(b) the amount of each significant category of revenue recognised during the period including revenue arising from:

    (i) the sale of goods;

    (ii) the rendering of services;

    (iii) interest;

    (iv) royalties;

    (v) dividends; and

(c) the amount of revenue arising from exchanges of goods or services included in each significant category of revenue. *(18.35)*

| 5.2 | **Construction Contracts** |

Because of the nature of the activity undertaken in construction contracts, the date at which the contract activity is entered into and the date when the activity is completed usually fall into different accounting periods. Therefore, the primary issue in accounting for construction contracts is the allocation of contract revenue and contract costs to the accounting periods in which construction work is performed. IAS 11 uses the recognition criteria established in the Framework for the Preparation and Presentation of Financial Statements to determine when contract revenue and contract costs should be recognised as revenue and expenses in the income statement. It also provides practical guidance on the application of these criteria.

IAS 11 should be applied in accounting for construction contracts in the financial statements of contractors. *(11.1)*

IAS 11 uses the following terms with the meanings specified:

- A *construction contract* is a contract specifically negotiated for the construction of an asset or a combination of assets that are closely interrelated or interdependent in terms of their design, technology and function or their ultimate purpose or use.

- A *fixed price contract* is a construction contract in which the contractor agrees to a fixed contract price, or a fixed rate per unit of output, which in some cases is subject to cost escalation clauses.

- A *cost plus contract* is a construction contract in which the contractor is reimbursed for allowable or otherwise defined costs, plus a percentage of these costs or a fixed fee. *(11.3)*

For the purposes of IAS 11, construction contracts include:

(a)   contracts for the rendering of services which are directly related to the construction of the asset, for example, those for the services of project managers and architects; and

(b)   contracts for the destruction or restoration of assets, and the restoration of the environment following the demolition of assets. *(11.5)*

Combining and Segmenting Construction Contracts

When a contract covers a number of assets, the construction of each asset should be treated as a separate construction contract when:

(a)   separate proposals have been submitted for each asset;

(b)   each asset has been subject to separate negotiation and the contractor and customer have been able to accept or reject that part of the contract relating to each asset; and

(c)   the costs and revenues of each asset can be identified. *(11.8)*

A group of contracts, whether with a single customer or with several customers, should be treated as a single construction contract when:

(a)   the group of contracts is negotiated as a single package;

(b)   the contracts are so closely interrelated that they are, in effect, part of a single project with an overall profit margin; and

(c)   the contracts are performed concurrently or in a continuous sequence. *(11.9)*

A contract may provide for the construction of an additional asset at the option of the customer or may be amended to include the construction of an additional asset. The construction of the additional asset should be treated as a separate construction contract when:

(a)   the asset differs significantly in design, technology or function from the asset or assets covered by the original contract; or

(b)   the price of the asset is negotiated without regard to the original contract price. *(11.10)*

Contract Revenue

Contract revenue should comprise:

(a)   the initial amount of revenue agreed in the contract; and

(b)   variations in contract work, claims and incentive payments:

   (i)   to the extent that it is probable that they will result in revenue; and

   (ii)   they are capable of being reliably measured. *(11.11)*

Contract revenue is measured at the fair value of the consideration received or receivable. The measurement of contract revenue is affected by a variety of uncertainties that depend on the outcome of future events. The estimates often need to be revised as events occur and uncertainties are resolved. Therefore, the amount of contract revenue may increase or decrease from one period to the next. *(11.12)*

A variation is an instruction by the customer for a change in the scope of the work to be performed under the contract. A variation may lead to an increase or a decrease in contract revenue. *(11.13)*

A claim is an amount that the contractor seeks to collect from the customer or another party as reimbursement for costs not included in the contract price. *(11.14)*

Incentive payments are additional amounts paid to the contractor if specified performance standards are met or exceeded. *(11.15)*

Contract Costs

Contract costs should comprise:

(a)   costs that relate directly to the specific contract;

(b)   costs that are attributable to contract activity in general and can be allocated to the contract; and

(c)   such other costs as are specifically chargeable to the customer under the terms of the contract. *(11.16)*

Costs that relate directly to a specific contract include:

(a)   site labour costs, including site supervision;

(b)   costs of materials used in construction;

(c)   depreciation of plant and equipment used on the contract;

(d)   costs of moving plant, equipment and materials to and from the contract site;

(e)   costs of hiring plant and equipment;

(f)   costs of design and technical assistance that is directly related to the contract;

(g)   the estimated costs of rectification and guarantee work, including expected warranty costs; and

(h)   claims from third parties.

These costs may be reduced by any incidental income that is not included in contract revenue, for example, income from the sale of surplus materials and the disposal of plant and equipment at the end of the contract. *(11.17)*

Costs that may be attributable to contract activity in general and can be allocated to specific contracts include:

(a)   insurance;

(b)   costs of design and technical assistance that are not directly related to a specific contract; and

(c)   construction overheads.

Such costs are allocated using methods that are systematic and rational and are applied consistently to all costs having similar characteristics. The allocation is based on the normal level of construction activity. Construction overheads include costs such as the preparation and processing of construction personnel payroll. Costs that may be attributable to contract activity in general and can be allocated to specific contracts also include borrowing costs when the contractor adopts the allowed alternative treatment in IAS 23, *Borrowing Costs* (see section 5.4, p. 345). *(11.18)*

Costs that are specifically chargeable to the customer under the terms of the contract may include some general administration costs and development costs for which reimbursement is specified in the terms of the contract. *(11.19)*

Recognition of Contract Revenue and Expenses

When the outcome of a construction contract can be estimated reliably, contract revenue and contract costs associated with the construction contract should be recognised as revenue and expenses respectively by reference to the stage of completion of the contract activity at the balance sheet date. An expected loss on the construction contract should be recognised as an expense immediately in accordance with the requirements for the recognition of expected losses, discussed below. *(11.22)*

In the case of a fixed price contract, the outcome of a construction contract can be estimated reliably when all the following conditions are satisfied:

(a)   total contract revenue can be measured reliably;

(b)   it is probable that the economic benefits associated with the contract will flow to the enterprise;

(c)   both the contract costs to complete the contract and the stage of contract completion at the balance sheet date can be measured reliably; and

(d)   the contract costs attributable to the contract can be clearly identified and measured reliably so that actual contract costs incurred can be compared with prior estimates. *(11.23)*

In the case of a cost plus contract, the outcome of a construction contract can be estimated reliably when all the following conditions are satisfied:

(a)   it is probable that the economic benefits associated with the contract will flow to the enterprise; and

(b)   the contract costs attributable to the contract, whether or not specifically reimbursable, can be clearly identified and measured reliably. *(11.24)*

The recognition of revenue and expenses by reference to the stage of completion of a contract is often referred to as the percentage of completion method. *(11.25)*

A contractor may have incurred contract costs that relate to future activity on the contract. Such contract costs are recognised as an asset provided it is probable that they will be recovered. Such costs represent an amount due from the customer and are often classified as contract work in progress. *(11.27)*

The stage of completion of a contract may be determined in a variety of ways. The enterprise uses the method that measures reliably the work performed. Depending on the nature of the contract, the methods may include:

(a)   the proportion that contract costs incurred for work performed to date bear to the estimated total contract costs;

(b)   surveys of work performed; or

(c)   completion of a physical proportion of the contract work.

Progress payments and advances received from customers often do not reflect the work performed. *(11.30)*

When the stage of completion is determined by reference to the contract costs incurred to date, only those contract costs that reflect work performed are included in costs incurred to date. Examples of contract costs which are excluded are:

(a)   contract costs that relate to future activity on the contract, such as costs of materials that have been delivered to a contract site or set aside for use in a contract but not yet installed, used or applied during contract performance, unless the materials have been made specially for the contract; and

(b)   payments made to subcontractors in advance of work performed under the subcontract. *(11.31)*

When the outcome of a construction contract cannot be estimated reliably:

(a)   revenue should be recognised only to the extent of contract costs incurred that it is probable will be recoverable; and

(b)   contract costs should be recognised as an expense in the period in which they are incurred.

An expected loss on the construction contract should be recognised as an expense immediately in accordance with the requirements for the recognition of expected losses, discussed below. *(11.32)*

Contract costs that are not probable of being recovered are recognised as an expense immediately. Examples of circumstances in which the recoverability of contract costs incurred may not be probable and in which contract costs may need to be recognised as an expense immediately include contracts:

(a)   which are not fully enforceable, that is, their validity is seriously in question;

(b)   the completion of which is subject to the outcome of pending litigation or legislation;

(c)   relating to properties that are likely to be condemned or expropriated;

(d)   where the customer is unable to meet its obligations; or

(e)   where the contractor is unable to complete the contract or otherwise meet its obligations under the contract. *(11.34)*

When the uncertainties that prevented the outcome of the contract being estimated reliably no longer exist, revenue and expenses associated with the construction contract should be recognised in accordance with the requirements for the recognition of contract revenue rather than in accordance with those for expected losses. *(11.35)*

Recognition of Expected Losses

When it is probable that total contract costs will exceed total contract revenue, the expected loss should be recognised as an expense immediately. *(11.36)*

The amount of such a loss is determined irrespective of:

(a)   whether or not work has commenced on the contract;

(b)   the stage of completion of contract activity; or

(c)   the amount of profits expected to arise on other contracts which are not treated as a single construction contract. *(11.37)*

Changes in Estimates

The percentage of completion method is applied on a cumulative basis in each accounting period to the current estimates of contract revenue and contract costs. Therefore, the effect of a change in the estimate of contract revenue or contract costs, or the effect of a change in the estimate of the outcome of a contract, is accounted for as a change in accounting estimate (see IAS 8, *Net Profit or Loss for the Period*, section 2.2.2, p. 106, *Fundamental Errors and Changes in Accounting Policies*, section 2.5.4, p. 145). The changed estimates are used in the determination of the amount of revenue and expenses recognised in the income statement in the period in which the change is made and in subsequent periods. *(11.38)*

Disclosure

An enterprise should disclose:

(a)   the amount of contract revenue recognised as revenue in the period;

(b)   the methods used to determine the contract revenue recognised in the period; and

(c)   the methods used to determine the stage of completion of contracts in progress. *(11.39)*

An enterprise should disclose each of the following for contracts in progress at the balance sheet date:

(a)   the aggregate amount of costs incurred and recognised profits (less recognised losses) to date;

(b)   the amount of advances received; and

(c)   the amount of retentions. *(11.40)*

Retentions are amounts of progress billings which are not paid until the satisfaction of conditions specified in the contract for the payment of such amounts or until defects have been rectified. Progress billings are amounts billed for work performed on a contract whether or not they have been paid by the customer. Advances are amounts received by the contractor before the related work is performed. *(11.41)*

An enterprise should present:

(a)   the gross amount due from customers for contract work as an asset; and

(b)   the gross amount due to customers for contract work as a liability. *(11.42)*

The gross amount due from customers for contract work is the net amount of:

(a)   costs incurred plus recognised profits; less

(b)   the sum of recognised losses and progress billings

for all contracts in progress for which costs incurred plus recognised profits (less recognised losses) exceeds progress billings. *(11.43)*

The gross amount due to customers for contract work is the net amount of:

(a)   costs incurred plus recognised profits; less

(b)   the sum of recognised losses and progress billings

for all contracts in progress for which progress billings exceed costs incurred plus recognised profits (less recognised losses). *(11.44)*

An enterprise discloses any contingent gains and losses in accordance with IAS 10, *Contingencies and Events Occurring After the Balance Sheet Date* (see section 2.5.3, p. 142). Contingent gains and contingent losses may arise from such items as warranty costs, claims, penalties or possible losses. *(11.45)*

Appendix F:

Disclosure of Accounting Policies

The following are examples of accounting policy disclosures:

Revenue from fixed price construction contracts is recognised on the percentage of completion method, measured by reference to the percentage of labour hours incurred to date to estimated total labour hours for each contract.

Revenue from cost plus contracts is recognised by reference to the recoverable costs incurred during the period plus the fee earned, measured by the proportion that costs incurred to date bear to the estimated total costs of the contract.

The Determination of Contract Revenue and Expenses

The following example illustrates one method of determining the stage of completion of a contract and the timing of the recognition of contract revenue and expenses.

A construction contractor has a fixed price contract for 9,000 to build a bridge. The initial amount of revenue agreed in the contract is 9,000. The contractor's initial estimate of contract costs is 8,000. It will take three years to build the bridge.

By the end of Year 1, the contractor's estimate of contract costs has increased to 8,050.

In Year 2, the customer approves a variation resulting in an increase in contract revenue of 200 and estimated additional contract costs of 150. At the end of Year 2, costs incurred include 100 for standard materials stored at the site to be used in Year 3 to complete the project.

The contractor determines the stage of completion of the contract by calculating the proportion that contract costs incurred for work performed to date bear to the latest estimated total contract costs. A summary of the financial data during the construction period is as follows:

	Year 1	Year 2	Year 3
Initial amount of revenue agreed in contract	9,000	9,000	9,000
Variation	-	200	200
Total contract revenue	9,000	9,200	9,200
Contract costs incurred to date	2,093	6,168	8,200
Contract costs to complete	5,957	2,032	-
Total estimated contract costs	8,050	8,200	8,200
Estimated profit	950	1,000	1,000
Stage of completion	26%	74%	100%

Figure 92

The stage of completion for Year 2 (74%) is determined by excluding from contract costs incurred for work performed to date the 100 of standard materials stored at the site for use in Year 3.

The amounts of revenue, expenses and profit recognised in the income statement in the three years are as follows:

	To Date	Recognised in prior years	Recognised in current year
Year 1			
Revenue (9,000 x .26)	2,340		2,340
Expenses (8,050 x .26)	2,093		2,093
Profit	247		247
Year 2			
Revenue (9,200 x .74)	6,808	2,340	4,468
Expenses (8,200 x .74)	6,068	2,093	3,975
Profit	740	247	493
Year 3			
Revenue (9,200 x 1.00)	9,200	6,808	2,392
Expenses	8,200	6,068	2,132
Profit	1,000	740	260

Figure 93

Contract Disclosures

A contractor has reached the end of its first year of operations. All its contract costs incurred have been paid for in cash and all its progress billings and advances have been received in cash. Contract costs incurred for contracts B, C and E include the cost of materials that have been purchased for the contract but which have not been used in contract performance to date. For contracts B, C and E, the customers have made advances to the contractor for work not yet performed.

The status of its five contracts in progress at the end of Year 1 is shown in Figure 94 overleaf.

			Contract			
	A	B	C	D	E	Total
Contract revenue recognised	145	520	380	200	55	1,300
Contract expenses recognised	110	450	350	250	55	1,215
Expected losses recognised in accordance with paragraph 11.36	-	-	-	40	30	70
Recognised profits less recognised losses	35	70	30	(90)	(30)	15
Contract costs incurred in the period	110	510	450	250	100	1,420
Contract costs incurred recognised as contract expenses in the period	110	450	350	250	55	1,215
Contract costs that relate to future activity recognised as an asset	-	60	100	-	45	205
Contract revenue (see above)	145	520	380	200	55	1,300
Progress billings	100	520	380	180	55	1,235
Unbilled contract revenue	45	-	-	20	-	65
Advances	-	80	20	-	25	125

Contract revenue recognised as revenue in the period	1,300
Contract costs incurred and recognised profits (less recognised losses) to date	1,435
Advances received	125
Gross amount due from customers for contract work - presented as an asset	220
Gross amount due to customers for contract work - presented as a liability	(20)

Figure 94

The amounts to be disclosed in accordance with disclosure requirements in IAS 11 are calculated as follows:

	A	B	C	D	E	Total
Contract costs incurred	110	510	450	250	100	1,420
Recognised profits less recognised losses	35	70	30	(90)	(30)	15
	145	580	480	160	70	1,435
Progress billings	100	520	380	180	55	1,235
Due from customers	45	60	100	-	15	220
Due to customers	-	-	-	(20)	-	(20)

Figure 95

The amount disclosed as the aggregate amount of costs incurred and recognised profits less recognised losses to date is the same as the amount for the current period because the disclosures relate to the first year of operation.

5.3 | Accounting for Government Grants and Disclosure of Government Assistance

IAS 20 should be applied in accounting for, and in the disclosure of, government grants and in the disclosure of other forms of government assistance. *(20.1)*

IAS 20 does not deal with:

(a)   the special problems arising in accounting for government grants in financial statements reflecting the effects of changing prices or in supplementary information of a similar nature;

(b)   government assistance that is provided for an enterprise in the form of benefits that are available in determining taxable income or are determined or limited on the basis of income tax liability (such as income tax holidays, investment tax credits, accelerated depreciation allowances and reduced income tax rates); and

(c)   government participation in the ownership of the enterprise. *(20.2)*

IAS 20 uses the following terms:

• *Government* refers to government, government agencies and similar bodies whether local, national or international.

• *Government assistance* is action by government designed to provide an economic benefit specific to an enterprise or range of enterprises qualifying under certain criteria. Government assistance for the purpose of IAS 20 does not include benefits provided only indirectly through action affecting general trading conditions, such as the provision of infrastructure in development areas or the imposition of trading constraints on competitors.

• *Government grants* are assistance by government in the form of transfers of resources to an enterprise in return for past or future compliance with certain conditions relating to the operating activities of the enterprise. They exclude those forms of government assistance which cannot reasonably have a value placed upon them and transactions with government which cannot be distinguished from the normal trading transactions of the enterprise.

• *Grants related to assets* are government grants whose primary condition is that an enterprise qualifying for them should purchase, construct or otherwise acquire long-term assets. Subsidiary conditions may also be attached restricting the type or location of the assets or the periods during which they are to be acquired or held.

• *Grants related to income* are government grants other than those related to assets.

• *Forgivable loans* are loans which the lender undertakes to waive repayment of under certain prescribed conditions.

• *Fair value* is the amount for which an asset could be exchanged between a knowledgeable, willing buyer and a knowledgeable, willing seller in an arm's length transaction. *(20.3)*

Government Grants

Government grants, including non-monetary grants at fair value, should not be recognised until there is reasonable assurance that:

(a)   the enterprise will comply with the conditions attaching to them; and

(b)   the grants will be received. *(20.7)*

Government grants should be recognised as income over the periods necessary to match them with the related costs which they are intended to compensate, on a systematic basis. They should not be credited directly to shareholders' interests. *(20.12)*

In some countries government assistance to enterprises may be aimed at encouragement or long-term support of business activities either in certain regions or industry sectors. Conditions to receive such assistance may not be specifically related to the operating activities of the enterprise. Examples of such assistance are transfers of resources by governments to enterprises which:

(a)   operate in a particular industry;

(b)   continue operating in recently privatised industries; or

(c)   start or continue to run their business in underdeveloped areas.

Such government assistance meets the definition of government grants, even if there are no conditions specifically relating to the operating activities of the enterprise other than the requirement to operate in certain regions or industry sectors. Such grants should therefore not be credited directly to equity. *(SIC-10)*

A government grant that becomes receivable as compensation for expenses or losses already incurred or for the purpose of giving immediate financial support to the enterprise with no future related costs should be recognised as income of the period in which it becomes receivable, as an extraordinary item if appropriate (see IAS 8, *Net Profit or Loss for the Period*, under section 2.2.2, p. 106, *Fundamental Errors and Changes in Accounting Policies*, under section 2.5.4, p. 145). *(20.20)*

Non-monetary Government Grants

A government grant may take the form of a transfer of a non-monetary asset, such as land or other resources, for the use of the enterprise. In these circumstances it is usual to assess the fair value of the non-monetary asset and to account for both grant and asset at that fair value. An alternative course that is sometimes followed is to record both asset and grant at a nominal amount. *(20.23)*

Presentation of Grants Related to Assets

Government grants related to assets, including non-monetary grants at fair value, should be presented in the balance sheet either by setting up the grant as deferred income or by deducting the grant in arriving at the carrying amount of the asset. *(20.24)*

Presentation of Grants Related to Income

Grants related to income are sometimes presented as a credit in the income statement, either separately or under a general heading such as "Other income"; alternatively, they are deducted in reporting the related expense. *(20.29)*

Both methods are regarded as acceptable for the presentation of grants related to income. *(20.31)*

Repayment of Government Grants

A government grant that becomes repayable should be accounted for as a revision to an accounting estimate (see IAS 8, *Net Profit or Loss for the Period*, section 2.2.2, p. 106, *Fundamental Errors and Changes in Accounting Policies*, section 2.5.4, p. 145). Repayment of a grant related to income should be applied first against any unamortised deferred credit set up in respect of the grant. To the extent that the repayment exceeds any such deferred credit, or where no deferred credit exists, the repayment should be recognised immediately as an expense. Repayment of a grant related to an asset should be recorded by increasing the carrying amount of the asset or reducing the deferred income balance by the amount repayable. The cumulative additional depreciation that would have been recognised to date as an expense in the absence of the grant should be recognised immediately as an expense. *(20.32)*

Government Assistance

Excluded from the definition of government grants in paragraph 20.3 are certain forms of government assistance which cannot reasonably have a value placed upon them and transactions with government which cannot be distinguished from the normal trading transactions of the enterprise. *(20.34)*

Disclosure

The following matters should be disclosed:

(a)   the accounting policy adopted for government grants, including the methods of presentation adopted in the financial statements;

(b)   the nature and extent of government grants recognised in the financial statements and an indication of other forms of government assistance from which the enterprise has directly benefited; and

(c)   unfulfilled conditions and other contingencies attaching to government assistance that has been recognised. *(20.39)*

5.4 Borrowing Costs

IAS 23 generally requires the immediate expensing of borrowing costs. However, the Standard permits, as an allowed alternative treatment, the capitalisation of borrowing costs that are directly attributable to the acquisition, construction or production of a qualifying asset.

IAS 23 does not deal with the actual or imputed cost of equity, including preferred capital not classified as a liability. *(23.3)*

IAS 23 uses the following terms:

- *Borrowing costs* are interest and other costs incurred by an enterprise in connection with the borrowing of funds.
- A *qualifying asset* is an asset that necessarily takes a substantial period of time to get ready for its intended use or sale. *(23.4)*

Borrowing Costs - Benchmark Treatment

Recognition

Borrowing costs should be recognised as an expense in the period in which they are incurred. *(23.7)*

Disclosure

The financial statements should disclose the accounting policy adopted for borrowing costs. *(23.9)*

Borrowing Costs - Allowed Alternative Treatment

Recognition

Borrowing costs should be recognised as an expense in the period in which they are incurred, except to the extent that they are capitalised in accordance with the treatment in the following paragraph. *(23.10)*

Borrowing costs that are directly attributable to the acquisition, construction or production of a qualifying asset should be capitalised as part of the cost of that asset. The amount of borrowing costs eligible for capitalisation should be determined in accordance with IAS 23. *(23.11)*

Borrowing Costs Eligible for Capitalisation

To the extent that funds are borrowed specifically for the purpose of obtaining a qualifying asset, the amount of borrowing costs eligible for capitalisation on that asset should be determined as the actual borrowing costs incurred on that borrowing during the period less any investment income on the temporary investment of those borrowings. *(23.15)*

To the extent that funds are borrowed generally and used for the purpose of obtaining a qualifying asset, the amount of borrowing costs eligible for capitalisation should be determined by applying a capitalisation rate to the expenditures on that asset. The capitalisation rate should be the weighted average of the borrowing costs applicable to the borrowings of the enterprise that are outstanding during the period, other than borrowings made specifically for the purpose of obtaining a qualifying asset. The amount of borrowing costs capitalised during a period should not exceed the amount of borrowing costs incurred during that period. *(23.17)*

Excess of the Carrying Amount of the Qualifying Asset over Recoverable Amount

When the carrying amount or the expected ultimate cost of the qualifying asset exceeds its recoverable amount or net realisable value, the carrying amount is written down or written off in accordance with the requirements of other IAS. In certain circumstances, the amount of the write-down or write-off is written back in accordance with those Standards.*(23.19)*

Commencement of Capitalisation

The capitalisation of borrowing costs as part of the cost of a qualifying asset should commence when:

(a)   expenditures for the asset are being incurred;

(b)   borrowing costs are being incurred; and

(c)   activities that are necessary to prepare the asset for its intended use or sale are in progress. *(23.20)*

Suspension of Capitalisation

Capitalisation of borrowing costs should be suspended during extended periods in which active development is interrupted. *(23.23)*

Cessation of Capitalisation

Capitalisation of borrowing costs should cease when substantially all the activities necessary to prepare the qualifying asset for its intended use or sale are complete. *(23.25)*

When the construction of a qualifying asset is completed in parts and each part is capable of being used while construction continues on other parts, capitalisation of borrowing costs should cease when substantially all the activities necessary to prepare that part for its intended use or sale are completed. *(23.27)*

Consistent Use of Allowed Alternative Treatments

Where an enterprise adopts the Allowed Alternative treatment, that treatment should be applied consistently to all borrowing costs that are directly attributable to the acquisition, construction or production of all qualifying assets of the enterprise. *(SIC-2)*

Disclosure

The financial statements should disclose:

(a)   the accounting policy adopted for borrowing costs;

(b)   the amount of borrowing costs capitalised during the period; and

(c)   the capitalisation rate used to determine the amount of borrowing costs eligible for capitalisation. *(23.29)*

Chapter 6

Financial Instruments

There are two International Accounting Standards dealing with financial instruments. **IAS 39** establishes principles for recognising, measuring and disclosing information about financial assets and financial liabilities, while **IAS 32** prescribes the disclosure and presentation of financial instruments.

6.1 Recognition and Measurement

The objective of IAS 39, *Financial Instruments, Recognition and Measurement*, is to establish principles for recognising, measuring, and disclosing information about financial instruments in the financial statements of business enterprises.

Under IAS 39, all financial assets and financial liabilities are recognised on the balance sheet, including all derivatives. They are initially measured at cost, which is the fair value of whatever was paid or received to acquire the financial asset or liability.

IAS 39 should be applied by all enterprises to all financial instruments except:

(a) those interests in subsidiaries, associates, and joint ventures that are accounted for under IAS 27, *Consolidated Financial Statements* and *Accounting for Investments in Subsidiaries* (see section 7.2, p. 402); IAS 28, *Accounting for Investments in Associates* (see section 7.3, p. 407); and IAS 31, *Financial Reporting of Interests in Joint Ventures* (see section 7.4, p. 411);

(b) rights and obligations under leases, to which IAS 17, *Leases* (see section 4.3, p. 300), applies; however, (i) lease receivables recognised on a lessor's balance sheet are subject to the derecognition provisions of IAS 39 and (ii) IAS 39 does apply to derivatives that are embedded in leases;

(c) employers' assets and liabilities under employee benefit plans, to which IAS 19, *Employee Benefits* (see section 4.2, p. 277), applies;

(d) rights and obligations under insurance contracts as defined in IAS 32, but IAS 39 does apply to derivatives that are embedded in insurance contracts;

(e) equity instruments issued by the reporting enterprise including options, warrants, and other financial instruments that are classified as shareholders' equity of the reporting enterprise (however, the holder of such instruments is required to apply IAS 39 to those instruments);

(f)   financial guarantee contracts, including letters of credit, that provide for payments to be made if the debtor fails to make payment when due (IAS 37, *Provisions, Contingent Liabilities and Contingent Assets* (see section 4.4, p. 311), provides guidance for recognising and measuring financial guarantees, warranty obligations, and other similar instruments). In contrast, financial guarantee contracts are subject to IAS 39 if they provide for payments to be made in response to changes in a specified interest rate, security price, commodity price, credit rating, foreign exchange rate, index of prices or rates, or other variable (sometimes called the 'underlying'). Also, IAS 39 does require recognition of financial guarantees incurred or retained as a result of the derecognition standards;

(g)   contracts for contingent consideration in a business combination; and

(h)   contracts that require a payment based on climatic, geological, or other physical variables, but IAS 39 does apply to other types of derivatives that are embedded in such contracts. *(39.1)*

IAS 39 should be applied to commodity-based contracts that give either party the right to settle in cash or some other financial instrument, with the exception of commodity contracts that (a) were entered into and continue to meet the enterprise's expected purchase, sale, or usage requirements, (b) were designated for that purpose at their inception, and (c) are expected to be settled by delivery. *(39.6)*

Definitions

IAS 32 and IAS 39 use the following terms with the meanings specified:

- A *financial instrument* is any contract that gives rise to both a financial asset of one enterprise and a financial liability or equity instrument of another enterprise.

  Commodity-based contracts that give either party the right to settle in cash or some other financial instrument should be accounted for as if they were financial instruments, with the exception of commodity contracts that (a) were entered into and continue to meet the enterprise's expected purchase, sale, or usage requirements, (b) were designated for that purpose at their inception, and (c) are expected to be settled by delivery.

- A *financial asset* is any asset that is:

    (a)   cash;

    (b)   a contractual right to receive cash or another financial asset from another enterprise;

    (c)   a contractual right to exchange financial instruments with another enterprise under conditions that are potentially favourable; or

    (d)   an equity instrument of another enterprise.

- A *financial asset or liability held for trading* is one that was acquired or incurred principally for the purpose of generating a profit from short-term fluctuations in price or dealer's margin. A financial asset should be classified as held for trading if, regardless of why it was acquired, it is part of a portfolio for which there is evidence of a recent actual pattern of short-term profit-taking. Derivative financial assets and derivative financial liabilities are always deemed held for trading unless they are designated and effective hedging instruments.

- *Held-to-maturity investments* are financial assets with fixed or determinable payments and fixed maturity that an enterprise has the positive intent and ability to hold to maturity other than loans and receivables originated by the enterprise.

- *Loans and receivables originated by the enterprise* are financial assets that are created by the enterprise by providing money, goods, or services directly to a debtor, other than those that are originated with the intent to be sold immediately or in the short term, which should be classified as held for trading. Loans and receivables originated by the enterprise are not included in held-to-maturity investments but, rather, are classified separately under this Standard.

- *Available-for-sale financial assets* are those financial assets that are not (a) loans and receivables originated by the enterprise, (b) held-to-maturity investments, or (c) financial assets held for trading.

- A *financial liability* is any liability that is a contractual obligation:

    (a)   to deliver cash or another financial asset to another enterprise; or

    (b)   to exchange financial instruments with another enterprise under conditions that are potentially unfavourable.

    An enterprise may have a contractual obligation that it can settle either by payment of financial assets or by payment in the form of its own equity securities. In such a case, if the number of equity securities required to settle the obligation varies with changes in their fair value so that the total fair value of the equity securities paid always equals the amount of the contractual obligation, the holder of the obligation is not exposed to gain or loss from fluctuations in the price of its equity securities. Such an obligation should be accounted for as a financial liability of the enterprise.

- An *equity instrument* is any contract that evidences a residual interest in the assets of an enterprise after deducting all of its liabilities.

- *Monetary* financial assets and financial liabilities (also referred to as monetary financial instruments) are financial assets and financial liabilities to be received or paid in fixed or determinable amounts of money.

- *Fair value* is the amount for which an asset could be exchanged, or a liability settled, between knowledgeable, willing parties in an arm's length transaction.

- *Market value* is the amount obtainable from the sale, or payable on the acquisition, of a financial instrument in an active market.

Definition of a Derivative

- A *derivative* is a financial instrument:

(a)   whose value changes in response to the change in a specified interest rate, security price, commodity price, foreign exchange rate, index of prices or rates, a credit rating or credit index, or similar variable (sometimes called the 'underlying');

(b)   that requires no initial net investment or little initial net investment relative to other types of contracts that have a similar response to changes in market conditions; and

(c)   that is settled at a future date.

Definitions Relating to Recognition and Measurement

- *Amortised cost of a financial asset or financial liability* is the amount at which the financial asset or liability was measured at initial recognition minus principal repayments, plus or minus the cumulative amortisation of any difference between that initial amount and the maturity amount, and minus any write-down (directly or through the use of an allowance account) for impairment or uncollectability.

- The *effective interest method* is a method of calculating amortisation using the effective interest rate of a financial asset or financial liability. The effective interest rate is the rate that exactly discounts the expected stream of future cash payments through maturity or the next market-based repricing date to the current net carrying amount of the financial asset or financial liability. That computation should include all fees and points paid or received between parties to the contract. The effective interest rate is sometimes termed the level yield to maturity or to the next repricing date, and is the internal rate of return of the financial asset or financial liability for that period.

- *Transaction costs* are incremental costs that are directly attributable to the acquisition or disposal of a financial asset or liability.

- A *firm commitment* is a binding agreement for the exchange of a specified quantity of resources at a specified price on a specified future date or dates.

- *Control* of an asset is the power to obtain the future economic benefits that flow from the asset.

- *Derecognise* means remove a financial asset or liability, or a portion of a financial asset or liability, from an enterprise's balance sheet.

Definitions Relating to Hedge Accounting

- *Hedging*, for accounting purposes, means designating one or more hedging instruments so that their change in fair value is an offset, in whole or in part, to the change in fair value or cash flows of a hedged item.

- A *hedged item* is an asset, liability, firm commitment, or forecasted future transaction that (a) exposes the enterprise to risk of changes in fair value or changes in future cash flows and that (b) for hedge accounting purposes, is designated as being hedged.

- A *hedging instrument*, for hedge accounting purposes, is a designated derivative or (in limited circumstances) another financial asset or liability whose fair value or cash flows are expected to offset changes in the fair value or cash flows of a designated hedged item. Under IAS 39, a non-derivative financial asset or liability may be designated as a hedging instrument for hedge accounting purposes only if it hedges the risk of changes in foreign currency exchange rates.

- *Hedge effectiveness* is the degree to which offsetting changes in fair value or cash flows attributable to a hedged risk are achieved by the hedging instrument.

Other Definitions

- *Securitisation* is the process by which financial assets are transformed into securities.
- A *repurchase agreement* is an agreement to transfer a financial asset to another party in exchange for cash or other consideration and a concurrent obligation to reacquire the financial asset at a future date for an amount equal to the cash or other consideration exchanged plus interest. *(32.5, 39.10)*

Elaboration on the Definitions

Equity Instrument

An enterprise may have a contractual obligation that it can settle either by payment of financial assets or by payment in the form of its own equity securities. In such a case, if the number of equity securities required to settle the obligation varies with changes in their fair value so that the total fair value of the equity securities paid always equals the amount of the contractual obligation, the holder of the obligation is not exposed to gain or loss from fluctuations in the price of the equity securities. Such an obligation should be accounted for as a financial liability of the enterprise and, therefore, is not excluded from the scope of IAS 39, notwithstanding the general scope exclusion of equity instruments. *(39.11)*

Derivatives

Typical examples of derivatives are futures and forward, swap, and option contracts. A derivative usually has a notional amount, which is an amount of currency, a number of shares, a number of units of weight or volume, or other units specified in the contract. However, a derivative instrument does not require the holder or writer to invest or receive the notional amount at the inception of the contract. Alternatively, a derivative could require a fixed payment as a result of some future event that is unrelated to a notional amount. For example, a contract may require a fixed payment of 1,000 if six-month LIBOR increases by 100 basis points. In this example, a notional amount is not specified. *(39.13)*

One of the defining conditions of a derivative is that it requires little initial net investment relative to other contracts that have a similar response to market conditions. An option contract meets that definition because the premium is significantly less than the investment that would be required to obtain the underlying financial instrument to which the option is linked. *(39.15)*

Transaction Costs

Transaction costs include fees and commissions paid to agents, advisers, brokers, and dealers; levies by regulatory agencies and securities exchanges; and transfer taxes and duties. Transaction costs do not include debt premium or discount, financing costs, or allocations of internal administrative or holding costs. *(39.17)*

Liability Held for Trading

Liabilities held for trading include (a) derivative liabilities that are not hedging instruments and (b) the obligation to deliver securities borrowed by a short seller (an enterprise that sells securities that it does not yet own). The fact that a liability is used to fund trading activities does not make that liability one held for trading. *(39.18)*

Loans and Receivables Originated by the Enterprise

A loan acquired by an enterprise as a participation in a loan from another lender is considered to be originated by the enterprise provided it is funded by the enterprise on the date that the loan is originated by the other lender. However, the acquisition of an interest in a pool of loans or receivables, for example, in connection with a securitisation, is a purchase, not an origination, because the enterprise did not provide money, goods, or services directly to the underlying debtors nor acquire its interest through a participation with another lender on the date the underlying loans or receivables were originated. Also, a transaction that is, in substance, a purchase of a loan that was previously originated – for example, a loan to an unconsolidated special purpose entity that is made to provide funding for its purchases of loans originated by others – is not a loan originated by the enterprise. A loan acquired by an enterprise in a business combination is considered to be originated by the acquiring enterprise provided that it was similarly classified by the acquired enterprise. The loan is measured at acquisition under IAS 22, *Business Combinations* (see section 7.1, p. 389). A loan acquired through a syndication is an originated loan because each lender shares in the origination of the loan and provides money directly to the debtor. (39.19)

Available-for-Sale Financial Assets

A financial asset is classified as available for sale if it does not properly belong in one of the three other categories of financial assets – held for trading, held to maturity, and loans and receivables originated by the enterprise. A financial asset is classified as held for trading, rather than available for sale, if it is part of a portfolio of similar assets for which there is a pattern of trading for the purpose of generating a profit from short-term fluctuations in price or dealer's margin. *(39.21)*

Embedded Derivatives

An embedded derivative should be separated from the host contract and accounted for as a derivative under IAS 39 if all of the following conditions are met:

(a)   the economic characteristics and risks of the embedded derivative are not closely related to the economic characteristics and risks of the host contract;

(b)   a separate instrument with the same terms as the embedded derivative would meet the definition of a derivative; and

(c)   the hybrid (combined) instrument is not measured at fair value with changes in fair value reported in net profit or loss.

If an embedded derivative is separated, the host contract itself should be accounted for (a) under IAS 39 if it is, itself, a financial instrument and (b) in accordance with other appropriate International Accounting Standards if it is not a financial instrument. *(39.23)*

If an enterprise is required by IAS 39 to separate an embedded derivative from its host contract but is unable to separately measure the embedded derivative either at acquisition or at a subsequent financial reporting date, it should treat the entire combined contract as a financial instrument held for trading. *(39.26)*

Recognition

Initial Recognition

An enterprise should recognise a financial asset or financial liability on its balance sheet when, and only when, it becomes a party to the contractual provisions of the instrument. *(39.27)*

Trade Date vs. Settlement Date

A 'regular way' purchase of financial assets should be recognised using trade date accounting or settlement date accounting described in the Standard. The method used should be applied consistently for each of the four categories of financial assets described in the definitions. A 'regular way' sale of financial assets should be recognised using settlement date accounting. *(39.30)*

Derecognition

Derecognition of a Financial Asset

An enterprise should derecognise a financial asset or a portion of a financial asset when, and only when, the enterprise loses control of the contractual rights that comprise the financial asset (or a portion of the financial asset). An enterprise loses such control if it realises the rights to benefits specified in the contract, the rights expire, or the enterprise surrenders those rights. *(39.35)*

Determining whether an enterprise has lost control of a financial asset depends both on the enterprise's position and that of the transferee. Consequently, if the position of either enterprise indicates that the transferor has retained control, the transferor should not remove the asset from its balance sheet. *(39.37)*

On derecognition, the difference between (a) the carrying amount of an asset (or portion of an asset) transferred to another party and (b) the sum of (i) the proceeds received or receivable and (ii) any prior adjustment to reflect the fair value of that asset that had been reported in equity should be included in net profit or loss for the period. *(39.43)*

Accounting for Collateral

If a debtor delivers collateral to the creditor and the creditor is permitted to sell or repledge the collateral without constraints, then:

(a) the debtor should disclose the collateral separately from other assets not used as collateral; and

(b) the creditor should recognise the collateral in its balance sheet as an asset, measured initially at its fair value, and should also recognise its obligation to return the collateral as a liability. *(39.44)*

►Illustration

A transfers and delivers certain securities to B but the transaction does not qualify for derecognition on A's books, and B takes possession of the collateral and is free to sell or pledge it, the following journal entries would be made to reflect the collateral:

A's Books (the 'borrower'):	Debit	Credit
Securities given as collateral	xx	
Securities		xx
To separate the collateralised asset from unrestricted assets.		
Cash	xx	
Liability		xx
To record the collateralised borrowing.		

B's Books (the 'lender'):	Debit	Credit
Securities held as collateral	xx	
Obligation to return securities		xx
To reflect B's control of the asset and its obligation to return them to A.		
Receivable	xx	
Cash		xx
To record the collateralised lending.		

Figure 96

Derecognition of Part of a Financial Asset

If an enterprise transfers a part of a financial asset to others while retaining a part, the carrying amount of the financial asset should be allocated between the part retained and the part sold based on their relative fair values on the date of sale. A gain or loss should be recognised based on the proceeds for the portion sold. In the rare circumstance that the fair value of the part of the asset that is retained cannot be measured reliably, then that asset should be recorded at zero. The entire carrying amount of the financial asset should be attributed to the portion sold, and a gain or loss should be recognised equal to the difference between (a) the proceeds and (b) the previous carrying amount of the financial asset plus or minus any prior adjustment that had been reported in equity to reflect the fair value of that asset (a 'cost recovery' approach). *(39.47)*

➤ Examples:

(a)   separating the principal and interest cash flows of a bond and selling some of them to another party while retaining the rest; and

(b)   selling a portfolio of receivables while retaining the right to service the receivables profitably for a fee, resulting in an asset for the servicing right. *(39.48)*

➤ Illustration

Assume receivables with a carrying amount of 100 are sold for 90. The selling enterprise retains the right to service those receivables for a fee that is expected to exceed the cost of servicing, but the fair value of the servicing right cannot be measured reliably. In that case, a loss of 10 would be recognised and the servicing right would be recorded at zero. (39.49)

Figure 97

➤ Illustration – Servicing is retained

An enterprise originates 1,000 of loans that yield 10 per cent interest for their estimated lives of 9 years. The enterprise sells the 1,000 principal plus the right to receive interest income of 8 per cent to another enterprise for 1,000. The transferor will continue to service the loans, and the contract stipulates that its compensation for performing the servicing is the right to receive half of the interest income not sold (that is, 100 of the 200 basis points). The remaining half of the interest income not sold is considered an interest-only strip receivable. At the date of the transfer, the fair value of the loans, including servicing, is 1,100, of which the fair value of the servicing asset is 40 and the fair value of the interest-only strip receivable is 60. Allocation of the 1,000 carrying amount of the loan is computed as follows:

	Fair Value	Percentage of Total Fair Value	Allocated Carrying Amount
Loans sold	1,000	91.0%	910
Servicing asset	40	3.6	36
Interest-only strip receivable	60	5.4	54
Total	1,100	100.0%	1,000

The transferor will recognise a gain of 90 on the sale of the loan – the difference between the net proceeds of 1,000 and the allocated carrying amount of 910. Its balance sheet will also report a servicing asset of 36 and an interest-only strip receivable of 54. The servicing asset is an intangible asset subject to the provisions of IAS 38, *Intangible Assets* (see section 3.4, p. 204). (39.50)

Figure 98

Asset Derecognition Coupled with a New Financial Asset or Liability

If an enterprise transfers control of an entire financial asset but, in doing so, creates a new financial asset or assumes a new financial liability, the enterprise should recognise the new financial asset or financial liability at fair value and should recognise a gain or loss on the transaction based on the difference between:

(a)   the proceeds; and

(b)   the carrying amount of the financial asset sold plus the fair value of any new financial liability assumed, minus the fair value of any new financial asset acquired, and plus or minus any adjustment that had previously been reported in equity to reflect the fair value of that asset. *(39.51)*

➤ **Examples:**

(a)   selling a portfolio of receivables while assuming an obligation to compensate the purchaser of the receivables if collections are below a specified level; and

(b)   selling a portfolio of receivables while retaining the right to service the receivables for a fee, and the fee to be received is less than the costs of servicing, thereby resulting in a liability for the servicing obligation. *(39.52)*

➤ **Illustration:**

A transfers certain receivables to *B* for a single, fixed cash payment. *A* is not obligated to make future payments of interest on the cash it has received from *B*. However, *A* guarantees *B* against default loss on the receivables up to a specified amount. Actual losses in excess of the amount guaranteed will be borne by *B*. As a result of the transaction, *A* has lost control over the receivables and *B* has obtained control. *B* now has the contractual right to receive cash inherent in the receivables as well as a guarantee from *A*. Under IAS 39:

(a)   *B* recognises the receivables on its balance sheet, and *A* removes the receivables from its balance sheet because they were sold to *B*; and

(b)   the guarantee is treated as a separate financial instrument, created as a result of the transfer, to be recognised as a financial liability by *A* and a financial asset by *B*. For practical purposes, *B* might include the guarantee asset with the receivables. (39.53)

Figure 99

In the rare circumstance that the fair value of the new financial asset or new financial liability cannot be measured reliably, then:

(a)   if a new financial asset is created but cannot be measured reliably, its initial carrying amount should be zero, and a gain or loss should be recognised equal to the difference between (i) the proceeds and (ii) the previous carrying amount of the derecognised financial asset plus or minus any prior adjustment that had been reported in equity to reflect the fair value of that asset; and

(b)   if a new financial liability is assumed but cannot be measured reliably, its initial carrying amount should be such that no gain is recognised on the transaction and, if IAS 37, *Provisions, Contingent Liabilities and Contingent Assets* (see section 4.4, p. 311), requires recognition of a provision, a loss should be recognised. *(39.54)*

To illustrate subparagraph (b), above the excess of the proceeds over the carrying amount is not recognised in net profit or loss. Instead it is recorded as a liability in the balance sheet. *(39.55)*

If a guarantee is recognised as a liability under IAS 39, it continues to be recognised as a liability of the guarantor, measured at its fair value (or at the greater of its original recorded amount and any provision required by IAS 37, if fair value cannot be reliably measured), until it expires. If the guarantee involves a large population of items, the guarantee should be measured by weighting all possible outcomes by their associated probabilities. *(39.56)*

Derecognition of a Financial Liability

An enterprise should remove a financial liability (or a part of a financial liability) from its balance sheet when, and only when, it is extinguished – that is, when the obligation specified in the contract is discharged, cancelled, or expires. *(39.57)*

This condition is met when either:

(a)   the debtor discharges the liability by paying the creditor, normally with cash, other financial assets, goods, or services; or

(b)   the debtor is legally released from primary responsibility for the liability (or part thereof) either by process of law or by the creditor (the fact that the debtor may have given a guarantee does not necessarily mean that this condition is not met). *(39.58)*

An exchange between an existing borrower and lender of debt instruments with substantially different terms is an extinguishment of the old debt that should result in derecognition of that debt and recognition of a new debt instrument. Similarly, a substantial modification of the terms of an existing debt instrument (whether or not due to the financial difficulty of the debtor) should be accounted for as an extinguishment of the old debt. *(39.61)*

The difference between the carrying amount of a liability (or part of a liability) extinguished or transferred to another party, including related unamortised costs, and the amount paid for it should be included in net profit or loss for the period. *(39.63)*

Derecognition of Part of a Financial Liability or Coupled with a New Financial Asset or Liability

If an enterprise transfers a part of a financial liability to others while retaining a part, or if an enterprise transfers an entire financial liability and in so doing creates a new financial asset or assumes a new financial liability, the enterprise should account for the transaction using the general requirements for accounting for asset derecognition coupled with a new financial asset or liability, above. *(39.65)*

Measurement

Initial Measurement of Financial Assets and Financial Liabilities

When a financial asset or financial liability is recognised initially, an enterprise should measure it at its cost, which is the fair value of the consideration given (in the case of an asset) or received (in the case of a liability) for it. Transaction costs are included in the initial measurement of all financial assets and liabilities. *(39.66)*

Subsequent Measurement of Financial Assets

After initial recognition, an enterprise should measure financial assets, including derivatives that are assets, at their fair values, without any deduction for transaction costs that it may incur on sale or other disposal, except for the following categories of financial assets, which should be measured under the provisions of the following paragraph:

(a)   loans and receivables originated by the enterprise and not held for trading;

(b)   held-to-maturity investments; and

(c)   any financial asset that does not have a quoted market price in an active market and whose fair value cannot be reliably measured.

Financial assets that are designated as hedged items are subject to measurement under the hedge accounting provisions. *(39.69)*

Those financial assets that are excluded from fair valuation under the preceding paragraph and that have a fixed maturity should be measured at amortised cost using the effective interest rate method. Those that do not have a fixed maturity should be measured at cost. All financial assets are subject to review for impairment as set out on page 364 in the section "Impairment and Uncollectability of Financial Assets". *(39.73)*

There is a presumption that fair value can be reliably determined for most financial assets classified as available for sale or held for trading. However, that presumption can be overcome for an investment in an equity instrument (including an investment that is in substance an equity instrument) that does not have a quoted market price in an active market and for which other methods of reasonably estimating fair value are clearly inappropriate or unworkable. The presumption can also be overcome for a derivative that is linked to and that must be settled by delivery of such an unquoted equity instrument. *(39.70)*

Held-to-Maturity Investments

An enterprise does not have the positive intent to hold to maturity an investment in a financial asset with a fixed maturity if any one of the following conditions is met:

(a)   the enterprise has the intent to hold the financial asset for only an undefined period;

(b) the enterprise stands ready to sell the financial asset (other than if a situation arises that is non-recurring and could not have been reasonably anticipated by the enterprise) in response to changes in market interest rates or risks, liquidity needs, changes in the availability of and the yield on alternative investments, changes in financing sources and terms, or changes in foreign currency risk; or

(c) the issuer has a right to settle the financial asset at an amount significantly below its amortised cost. (39.79)

An enterprise should not classify any financial assets as held-to-maturity if the enterprise has, during the current financial year or during the two preceding financial years, sold, transferred, or exercised a put option on more than an insignificant amount of held-to-maturity investments before maturity (more than insignificant in relation to the total held-to-maturity portfolio) other than by:

(a) sales close enough to maturity or exercised call date so that changes in the market rate of interest did not have a significant effect on the financial asset's fair value;

(b) sales after the enterprise has already collected substantially all of the financial asset's original principal through scheduled payments or prepayments; or

(c) sales due to an isolated event that is beyond the enterprise's control and that is non-recurring and could not have been reasonably anticipated by the enterprise.

Reclassifications between fair value and amortised cost are discussed below. *(39.83)*

An enterprise does not have a demonstrated ability to hold to maturity an investment in a financial asset with a fixed maturity if either one of the following conditions is met:

(a) it does not have the financial resources available to continue to finance the investment until maturity; or

(b) it is subject to an existing legal or other constraint that could frustrate its intention to hold the financial asset to maturity (however, an issuer's call option does not necessarily frustrate an enterprise's intent to hold a financial asset to maturity). *(39.87)*

Reclassification

If, due to a change of intent or ability, it is no longer appropriate to carry a held-to-maturity investment at amortised cost, it should be remeasured at fair value, and the difference between its carrying amount and fair value should be accounted for in accordance with the general requirements for gains and losses on remeasurement to fair value (see overleaf). *(39.90)*

Similarly, if a reliable measure becomes available for a financial asset for which such a measure previously was not available, the asset should be remeasured at fair value, and the difference between its carrying amount and fair value should be accounted for in accordance with (see previous). *(39.91)*

If, due to a change of intent or ability or in the rare circumstance that a reliable measure of fair value is no longer available or because the 'two preceding financial years' have now passed, it becomes appropriate to carry a financial asset at amortised cost rather than at fair value, the fair value carrying amount of the financial asset on that date becomes its new amortised cost. Any previous gain or loss on that asset that has been recognised directly in equity should be accounted for as follows:

(a)   in the case of a financial asset with a fixed maturity, a previous gain or loss on that asset that has been recognised directly in equity should be amortised over the remaining life of the held-to-maturity investment. Any difference between the new amortised cost and maturity amount should be amortised over the remaining life of the financial asset as an adjustment of yield, similar to amortisation of premium and discount; and

(b)   in the case of a financial asset that does not have a fixed maturity, a previous gain or loss on that asset that has been recognised directly in equity should be left in equity until the financial asset has been sold or otherwise disposed of, at which time it should enter into the determination of net profit or loss. *(39.92)*

Subsequent Measurement of Financial Liabilities

After initial recognition, an enterprise should measure all financial liabilities, other than liabilities held for trading and derivatives that are liabilities, at amortised cost. After initial recognition, an enterprise should measure liabilities held for trading and derivatives that are liabilities at fair value, except for a derivative liability that is linked to and that must be settled by delivery of an unquoted equity instrument whose fair value cannot be reliably measured, which should be measured at cost. Financial liabilities that are designated as hedged items are subject to measurement under the hedge accounting provisions. *(39.93)*

Fair Value Measurement Considerations

The fair value of a financial instrument is reliably measurable if (a) the variability in the range of reasonable fair value estimates is not significant for that instrument or (b) if the probabilities of the various estimates within the range can be reasonably assessed and used in estimating fair value. Often, an enterprise will be able to make an estimate of the fair value of a financial instrument that is sufficiently reliable to use in financial statements. Occasionally, the variability in the range of reasonable fair value estimates is so great and the probabilities of the various outcomes are so difficult to assess that the usefulness of a single estimate of fair value is negated. *(39.95)*

Situations in which fair value is reliably measurable include (a) a financial instrument for which there is a published price quotation in an active public securities market for that instrument, (b) a debt instrument that has been rated by an independent rating agency and whose cash flows can be reasonably estimated, and (c) a financial instrument for which there is an appropriate valuation model and for which the data inputs to that model can be measured reliably because the data come from active markets. *(39.96)*

Gains and Losses on Remeasurement to Fair Value

A recognised gain or loss arising from a change in the fair value of a financial asset or financial liability that is not part of a hedging relationship should be reported as follows:

(a)   a gain or loss on a financial asset or liability held for trading should be included in net profit or loss for the period in which it arises (in this regard, a derivative should always be considered to be held for trading unless it is a designated hedging instrument);

(b)   a gain or loss on an available-for-sale financial asset should be either:

  (i)   included in net profit or loss for the period in which it arises; or

  (ii) recognised directly in equity, through the statement of changes in equity, until the financial asset is sold, collected, or otherwise disposed of, or until the financial asset is determined to be impaired, at which time the cumulative gain or loss previously recognised in equity should be included in net profit or loss for the period. *(39.103)*

An enterprise should choose either subparagraph (b)(i) or subparagraph (b)(ii) as its accounting policy and should apply that policy to all of its available-for-sale financial assets (except for hedges – see 'Hedging' p. 365). *(39.104)*

If an enterprise recognises purchases of financial assets using settlement date accounting (see paragraph 39.30, p. 355), any change in the fair value of the asset to be received during the period between the trade date and the settlement date is not recognised for assets carried at cost or amortised cost (other than impairment losses). For assets remeasured to fair value, however, the change in fair value should be recognised in net profit or loss or in equity, as appropriate under the accounting policy chosen. *(39.106)*

Because the designation of a financial asset as held for trading is based on the objective for initially acquiring it, an enterprise should not reclassify its financial assets that are being remeasured to fair value out of the trading category while they are held. An enterprise should reclassify a financial asset into the trading category only if there is evidence of a recent actual pattern of short-term profit taking that justifies such reclassification. *(39.107)*

Gains and Losses on Financial Assets and Liabilities Not Remeasured to Fair Value

For those financial assets and financial liabilities carried at amortised cost, a gain or loss is recognised in net profit or loss when the financial asset or liability is derecognised or impaired, as well as through the amortisation process. However, if there is a hedging relationship between those financial assets or liabilities (the items being hedged) and a hedging instrument as described in 'Hedging' on page 365, accounting for the gain or loss should follow that for fair value hedges or cash flow hedges, as appropriate. *(39.108)*

Impairment and Uncollectability of Financial Assets

A financial asset is impaired if its carrying amount is greater than its estimated recoverable amount. An enterprise should assess at each balance sheet date whether there is any objective evidence that a financial asset or group of assets may be impaired. If any such evidence exists, the enterprise should estimate the recoverable amount of that asset or group of assets and recognise any impairment loss in accordance with the requirements discussed below for financial assets carried at amortised cost or for financial assets remeasured to fair value, as appropriate. *(39.109)*

Financial Assets Carried at Amortised Cost

If it is probable that an enterprise will not be able to collect all amounts due (principal and interest) according to the contractual terms of loans, receivables, or held-to-maturity investments carried at amortised cost, an impairment or bad debt loss has occurred. The amount of the loss is the difference between the asset's carrying amount and the present value of expected future cash flows discounted at the financial instrument's original effective interest rate (recoverable amount). Cash flows relating to short-term receivables generally are not discounted. The carrying amount of the asset should be reduced to its estimated recoverable amount either directly or through use of an allowance account. The amount of the loss should be included in net profit or loss for the period. *(39.111)*

If, in a subsequent period, the amount of the impairment or bad debt loss decreases and the decrease can be objectively related to an event occurring after the write-down (such as an improvement in the debtor's credit rating), the write-down of the financial asset should be reversed either directly or by adjusting an allowance account. The reversal should not result in a carrying amount of the financial asset that exceeds what amortised cost would have been, had the impairment not been recognised, at the date the write-down of the financial asset is reversed. The amount of the reversal should be included in net profit or loss for the period. *(39.114)*

The carrying amount of any financial asset that is not carried at fair value because its fair value cannot be reliably measured should be reviewed for an indication of impairment at each balance sheet date based on an analysis of expected net cash inflows. If there is an indication of impairment, the amount of the impairment loss of such a financial asset is the difference between its carrying amount and the present value of expected future cash flows discounted at the current market rate of interest for a similar financial asset (recoverable amount). *(39.115)*

Interest Income After Impairment Recognition

Once a financial asset has been written down to its estimated recoverable amount, interest income is thereafter recognised based on the rate of interest that was used to discount the future cash flows for the purpose of measuring the recoverable amount. Additionally, after initially recognising an impairment loss, the enterprise will review this asset for further impairment at subsequent financial reporting dates. Paragraph 18.30 provides guidance for recognising interest income on unimpaired financial assets. *(39.116)*

Financial Assets Remeasured to Fair Value

If a loss on a financial asset carried at fair value (recoverable amount is below original acquisition cost) has been recognised directly in equity and there is objective evidence that the asset is impaired, the cumulative net loss that had been recognised directly in equity should be removed from equity and recognised in net profit or loss for the period even though the financial asset has not been derecognised. *(39.117)*

The amount of the loss that should be removed from equity and reported in net profit or loss is the difference between its acquisition cost (net of any principal repayment and amortisation) and current fair value (for equity instruments) or recoverable amount (for debt instruments), less any impairment loss on that asset previously recognised in net profit or loss. The recoverable amount of a debt instrument remeasured to fair value is the present value of expected future cash flows discounted at the current market rate of interest for a similar financial asset. *(39.118)*

If, in a subsequent period, the fair value or recoverable amount of the financial asset carried at fair value increases and the increase can be objectively related to an event occurring after the loss was recognised in net profit or loss, the loss should be reversed, with the amount of the reversal included in net profit or loss for the period. *(39.119)*

Fair Value Accounting in Certain Financial Services Industries

In some countries, either based on national law or accepted industry practice, enterprises in certain financial services industries measure substantially all financial assets at fair value. Examples of such industries include, in certain countries, mutual funds, unit trusts, securities brokers and dealers, and insurance companies. Under IAS 39, such an enterprise will be able to continue to measure its financial assets at fair value if its financial assets are classified as either available for sale or held for trading. *(39.120)*

Hedging

If there is a hedging relationship between a hedging instrument and a related item being hedged as described in the following paragraphs, accounting for the gain or loss should follow the requirements for fair value hedges or cash flow hedges, as appropriate. *(39.121)*

Hedging Instruments

Hedging involves a proportionate income offset between changes in fair value of, or cash flows attributable to, the hedging instrument and the hedged item. The potential loss on an option that an enterprise writes could be significantly greater than the potential gain in value of a related hedged item. That is, a written option is not effective in reducing the exposure on net profit or loss. Therefore, a written option is not a hedging instrument unless it is designated as an offset to a purchased option, including one that is embedded in another financial instrument, for example, a written option used to hedge callable debt. In contrast, a purchased option has potential gains equal to or greater than losses and, therefore, has the potential to reduce profit or loss exposure from changes in fair values or cash flows. Accordingly, it can qualify as a hedging instrument. *(39.124)*

Hedged Items

A hedged item can be a recognised asset or liability, an unrecognised firm commitment, or an uncommitted but highly probable anticipated future transaction ('forecasted transaction'). The hedged item can be (a) a single asset, liability, firm commitment, or forecasted transaction or (b) a group of assets, liabilities, firm commitments, or forecasted transactions with similar risk characteristics. Unlike originated loans and receivables, a held-to-maturity investment cannot be a hedged item with respect to interest-rate risk because designation of an investment as held-to-maturity involves not accounting for associated changes in interest rates. However, a held-to-maturity investment can be a hedged item with respect to risks from changes in foreign currency exchange rates and credit risk. *(39.127)*

If the hedged item is a non-financial asset or liability, it should be designated as a hedged item either (a) for foreign currency risks or (b) in its entirety for all risks, because of the difficulty of isolating and measuring the appropriate portion of the cash flows or fair value changes attributable to specific risks other than foreign currency risks. *(39.129)*

Hedge Accounting

Hedging relationships are of three types:

(a) **fair value hedge**: a hedge of the exposure to changes in the fair value of a recognised asset or liability, or an identified portion of such an asset or liability, that is attributable to a particular risk and that will affect reported net income;

(b) **cash flow hedge**: a hedge of the exposure to variability in cash flows that (i) is attributable to a particular risk associated with a recognised asset or liability (such as all or some future interest payments on variable rate debt) or a forecasted transaction (such as an anticipated purchase or sale) and that (ii) will affect reported net profit or loss. A hedge of an unrecognised firm commitment to buy or sell an asset at a fixed price in the enterprise's reporting currency is accounted for as a cash flow hedge even though it has a fair value exposure; and

(c) **hedge of a net investment in a foreign entity** as defined in IAS 21, *The Effects of Changes in Foreign Exchange Rates* (see section 2.5.1, p. 135). *(39.137)*

Under IAS 39, a hedging relationship qualifies for special hedge accounting under the Standard if, and only if, all of the following conditions are met:

(a) at the inception of the hedge there is formal documentation of the hedging relationship and the enterprise's risk management objective and strategy for undertaking the hedge. That documentation should include identification of the hedging instrument, the related hedged item or transaction, the nature of the risk being hedged, and how the enterprise will assess the hedging instrument's effectiveness in offsetting the exposure to changes in the hedged item's fair value or the hedged transaction's cash flows that is attributable to the hedged risk;

(b)   the hedge is expected to be highly effective in achieving offsetting changes in fair value or cash flows attributable to the hedged risk, consistent with the originally documented risk management strategy for that particular hedging relationship;

(c)   for cash flow hedges, a forecasted transaction that is the subject of the hedge must be highly probable and must present an exposure to variations in cash flows that could ultimately affect reported net profit or loss;

(d)   the effectiveness of the hedge can be reliably measured, that is, the fair value or cash flows of the hedged item and the fair value of the hedging instrument can be reliably measured; and

(e)   the hedge was assessed on an ongoing basis and determined actually to have been highly effective throughout the financial reporting period. *(39.142)*

Assessing Hedge Effectiveness

A hedge is normally regarded as highly effective if, at inception and throughout the life of the hedge, the enterprise can expect changes in the fair value or cash flows of the hedged item to be almost fully offset by the changes in the fair value or cash flows of the hedging instrument, and actual results are within a range of 80 per cent to 125 per cent. For example, if the loss on the hedging instrument is 120 and the gain on the cash instrument is 100, offset can be measured by 120/100, which is 120 per cent, or by 100/120, which is 83 per cent. The enterprise will conclude that the hedge is highly effective. *(39.146)*

In assessing the effectiveness of a hedge, an enterprise will generally need to consider the time value of money. The fixed rate on a hedged item need not exactly match the fixed rate on a swap designated as a fair value hedge. Nor does the variable rate on an interest-bearing asset or liability need to be the same as the variable rate on a swap designated as a cash flow hedge. A swap's fair value comes from its net settlements. The fixed and variable rates on a swap can be changed without affecting the net settlement if both are changed by the same amount. *(39.152)*

Fair Value Hedges

If a fair value hedge meets the necessary conditions for the special hedge accounting under IAS 39 during the financial reporting period, it should be accounted for as follows:

(a)   the gain or loss from remeasuring the hedging instrument at fair value should be recognised immediately in net profit or loss; and

(b)   the gain or loss on the hedged item attributable to the hedged risk should adjust the carrying amount of the hedged item and be recognised immediately in net profit or loss. This applies even if a hedged item is otherwise measured at fair value with changes in fair value recognised directly in equity. It also applies if the hedged item is otherwise measured at cost. *(39.153)*

The following illustrates how this paragraph applies to a hedge of exposure to changes in the fair value of an investment in fixed rate debt as a result of changes in interest rates. This example is presented from the perspective of the holder.

In Year 1 an investor purchases for 100 a debt security that is classified as available for sale. At the end of Year 1, current fair value is 110. Therefore, the 10 increase is reported in equity (assuming the investor has elected this method), and the carrying amount is increased to 110 in the balance sheet. To protect the 110 value, the holder enters into a hedge by acquiring a derivative. By the end of Year 2, the derivative has a gain of 5, and the debt security has a corresponding decline in fair value.

Investor's Books Year 1:	**Debit**	**Credit**
Investment in debt security	100	
Cash		100
To reflect the purchase of the security		
Investment in debt security	10	
Increase in fair value (included in equity)		10
To reflect the increase in fair value of the security		

Investor's Books Year 2:	**Debit**	**Credit**
Derivative asset	5	
Gain (included in net profit or loss)		5
To reflect the increase in fair value of the derivative		
Loss (included in net profit or loss)	5	
Investment in debt security		5
To reflect the decrease in fair value of the debt security		

The carrying amount of the debt security is 105 at the end of Year 2, and the carrying amount of the derivative is 5. The gain of 10 is reported in equity until the debt security is sold, and it is subject to amortisation. *(39.154)*

Figure 100

An enterprise should discontinue prospectively the hedge accounting specified above if any one of the following occurs:

(a)   the hedging instrument expires or is sold, terminated, or exercised (for this purpose, the replacement or a rollover of a hedging instrument into another hedging instrument is not considered an expiration or termination if such replacement or rollover is part of the enterprise's documented hedging strategy); or

(b)   the hedge no longer meets the criteria for qualification for hedge accounting. *(39.156)*

An adjustment to the carrying amount of a hedged interest-bearing financial instrument should be amortised to net profit or loss. Amortisation should begin no later than when the hedged item ceases to be adjusted for changes in its fair value attributable to the risk being hedged. The adjustment should be fully amortised by maturity. *(39.157)*

Cash Flow Hedges

If a cash flow hedge meets the necessary conditions for special hedge accounting under IAS 39 during the financial reporting period, it should be accounted for as follows:

(a) the portion of the gain or loss on the hedging instrument that is determined to be an effective hedge should be recognised directly in equity through the statement of changes in equity; and

(b) the ineffective portion should be reported:

   (i) immediately in net profit or loss if the hedging instrument is a derivative; or

   (ii) in the limited circumstances in which the hedging instrument is not a derivative, either in net profit or loss or directly in equity as permitted by the Standard. *(39.158)*

If the hedged firm commitment or forecasted transaction results in the recognition of an asset or a liability, then at the time the asset or liability is recognised the associated gains or losses that were recognised directly in equity in accordance with subparagraph b(ii) above should be removed from equity and should enter into the initial measurement of the acquisition cost or other carrying amount of the asset or liability. *(39.160)*

For all cash flow hedges other than those covered by the preceding paragraph, amounts that had been recognised directly in equity should be included in net profit or loss in the same period or periods during which the hedged firm commitment or forecasted transaction affects net profit or loss (for example, when a forecasted sale actually occurs). *(39.162)*

An enterprise should discontinue prospectively the hedge accounting specified above if any one of the following occurs:

(a) the hedging instrument expires or is sold, terminated, or exercised (for this purpose, the replacement or a rollover of a hedging instrument into another hedging instrument is not considered an expiration or termination if such replacement or rollover is part of the enterprise's documented hedging strategy). In this case, the cumulative gain or loss on the hedging instrument that initially had been reported directly in equity when the hedge was effective should remain separately in equity until the forecasted transaction occurs. When the transaction occurs the general principles described above apply;

(b) the hedge no longer meets the criteria for qualification for hedge accounting. In this case, the cumulative gain or loss on the hedging instrument that initially had been reported directly in equity when the hedge was effective should remain separately in equity until the committed or forecasted transaction occurs. When the transaction occurs, the general principles described above apply; or

(c) the committed or forecasted transaction is no longer expected to occur, in which case any related net cumulative gain or loss that has been reported directly in equity should be reported in net profit or loss for the period. *(39.163)*

Hedges of a Net Investment in a Foreign Entity

Hedges of a net investment in a foreign entity (see IAS 21, *The Effects of Changes in Foreign Exchange Rates,* under section 2.5.1, p. 135) should be accounted for similarly to cash flow hedges:

(a)   the portion of the gain or loss on the hedging instrument that is determined to be an effective hedge should be recognised directly in equity through the statement of changes in equity; and

(b)   the ineffective portion should be reported:

    (i)   immediately in net profit or loss if the hedging instrument is a derivative; or

    (ii)   in accordance with IAS 21, in the limited circumstances in which the hedging instrument is not a derivative.

The gain or loss on the hedging instrument relating to the effective portion of the hedge should be classified in the same manner as the foreign currency translation gain or loss. *(39.164)*

6.2 | Disclosure and Presentation

The dynamic nature of international financial markets has resulted in the widespread use of a variety of financial instruments ranging from traditional primary instruments, such as bonds, to various forms of derivative instruments, such as interest rate swaps. IAS 32 enhances financial statement users' understanding of the significance of on-balance-sheet and off-balance-sheet financial instruments to an enterprise's financial position, performance and cash flows.

IAS 32 includes a prescription of certain requirements for presentation of on-balance-sheet financial instruments and identifies the information that should be disclosed about both on-balance-sheet (recognised) and off-balance-sheet (unrecognised) financial instruments. The presentation standards deal with the classification of financial instruments between liabilities and equity, the classification of related interest, dividends, losses and gains, and the circumstances in which financial assets and financial liabilities should be offset. The disclosure standards deal with information about factors that affect the amount, timing and certainty of an enterprise's future cash flows relating to financial instruments and the accounting policies applied to the instruments. In addition, the Standard encourages disclosure of information about the nature and extent of an enterprise's use of financial instruments, the business purposes that they serve, the risks associated with them and management's policies for controlling those risks.

IAS 32 should be applied in presenting and disclosing information about all types of financial instruments, both recognised and unrecognised, other than:

(a)   interests in subsidiaries;

(b)   interests in associates;

(c)   interests in joint ventures;

(d)   employers' and plans' obligations for post–employment benefits of all types, including employee benefit plans;

(e)   employers' obligations under employee stock option and stock purchase plans; and

(f)   obligations arising under insurance contracts. *(32.1)*

For purposes of IAS 32, an insurance contract is a contract that exposes the insurer to identified risks of loss from events or circumstances occurring or discovered within a specified period, including death (in the case of an annuity, the survival of the annuitant), sickness, disability, property damage, injury to others and business interruption. However, the provisions of IAS 32 apply when a financial instrument takes the form of an insurance contract but principally involves the transfer of financial risks (see paragraph 32.43, p. 373), for example, some types of financial reinsurance and guaranteed investment contracts issued by insurance and other enterprises. Enterprises that have obligations under insurance contracts are encouraged to consider the appropriateness of applying the provisions of IAS 32 in presenting and disclosing information about such obligations. *(32.3)*

Presentation

Liabilities and Equity

The issuer of a financial instrument should classify the instrument, or its component parts, as a liability or as equity in accordance with the substance of the contractual arrangement on initial recognition and the definitions of a financial liability and an equity instrument. (32.18)

Where the rights and obligations regarding the manner of settlement of a financial instrument depend on the occurrence or non-occurrence of uncertain future events or on the outcome of uncertain circumstances that are beyond the control of both the issuer and the holder, the financial instrument should be classified as a liability except that where the possibility of the issuer being required to settle in cash or another financial asset is remote at the time of issuance, the contingent settlement provision should be ignored and the instrument should be classified as equity.

The critical feature in differentiating a financial liability from an equity instrument is the existence of a contractual obligation on one party to the financial instrument (the issuer) either to deliver cash or another financial asset to the other party (the holder) or to exchange another financial instrument with the holder under conditions that are potentially unfavourable to the issuer. When such a contractual obligation exists, that instrument meets the definition of a financial liability regardless of the manner in which the contractual obligation will be settled. A restriction on the ability of the issuer to satisfy an obligation, such as lack of access to foreign currency or the need to obtain approval for payment from a regulatory authority, does not negate the issuer's obligation or the holder's right under the instrument. *(32.20)*

When a financial instrument does not give rise to a contractual obligation on the part of the issuer to deliver cash or another financial asset or to exchange another financial instrument under conditions that are potentially unfavourable, it is an equity instrument. Although the holder of an equity instrument may be entitled to receive a pro rata share of any dividends or other distributions out of equity, the issuer does not have a contractual obligation to make such distributions. *(32.21)*

Reacquired Own Equity Instruments ('Treasury Shares')

An enterprise may hold its own equity instruments, often referred to as "treasury shares". Depending on the jurisdiction, such treasury shares may be acquired and held by the issuing enterprise itself or by its subsidiaries. Where treasury shares are:

(a)   classified as equity under IAS 32;

(b)   acquired and held by the issuing enterprise itself or by its consolidated subsidiaries; and

(c)   legally available for reissue or resale, even if the enterprise intends to cancel them.

they should be presented in the balance sheet as a deduction from equity. The acquisition of treasury shares should be presented in the financial statements as a change in equity. No gain or loss should be recognised in the income statement on the sale, issuance, or cancellation of treasury shares. Consideration should be presented in the financial statements as a change in equity. *(SIC-16)*

Classification of Compound Instruments by the Issuer

The issuer of a financial instrument that contains both a liability and an equity element should classify the instrument's component parts separately in accordance with paragraph 32.18. *(32.23)*

Interest, Dividends, Losses and Gains

Interest, dividends, losses and gains relating to a financial instrument, or a component part, classified as a financial liability should be reported in the income statement as expense or income. Distributions to holders of a financial instrument classified as an equity instrument should be debited by the issuer directly to equity. *(32.30)*

The classification of a financial instrument in the balance sheet determines whether interest, dividends, losses and gains relating to that instrument are classified as expenses or income and reported in the income statement. Thus, dividend payments on shares classified as liabilities are classified as expenses in the same way as interest on a bond and reported in the income statement. Similarly, gains and losses associated with redemptions or refinancings of instruments classified as liabilities are reported in the income statement, while redemptions or refinancings of instruments classified as equity of the issuer are reported as movements in equity. *(32.31)*

Offsetting of a Financial Asset and a Financial Liability

A financial asset and a financial liability should be offset and the net amount reported in the balance sheet when an enterprise:

(a) has a legally enforceable right to set off the recognised amounts; and

(b) intends either to settle on a net basis, or to realise the asset and settle the liability simultaneously. (32.33)

Disclosure

Transactions in financial instruments may result in an enterprise's assuming or transferring to another party one or more of the financial risks described below. The required disclosures provide information that assists users of financial statements in assessing the extent of risk related to both recognised and unrecognised financial instruments.

(a) *Price risk* — There are three types of price risk: *currency risk*, *interest rate risk* and *market risk*.

   (i)   *Currency risk* is the risk that the value of a financial instrument will fluctuate due to changes in foreign exchange rates.

   (ii) *Interest rate risk* is the risk that the value of a financial instrument will fluctuate due to changes in market interest rates.

   (iii) *Market risk* is the risk that the value of a financial instrument will fluctuate as a result of changes in market prices whether those changes are caused by factors specific to the individual security or its issuer or factors affecting all securities traded in the market.

   The term "price risk" embodies not only the potential for loss but also the potential for gain.

(b) *Credit risk* is the risk that one party to a financial instrument will fail to discharge an obligation and cause the other party to incur a financial loss.

(c) *Liquidity risk*, also referred to as funding risk, is the risk that an enterprise will encounter difficulty in raising funds to meet commitments associated with financial instruments. Liquidity risk may result from an inability to sell a financial asset quickly at close to its fair value.

(d) *Cash flow risk* is the risk that future cash flows associated with a monetary financial instrument will fluctuate in amount. In the case of a floating rate debt instrument, for example, such fluctuations result in a change in the effective interest rate of the financial instrument, usually without a corresponding change in its fair value. *(32.43)*

Disclosure of Risk Management Policies

An enterprise should describe its financial risk management objectives and policies, including its policy for hedging each major type of forecasted transaction for which hedge accounting is used. *(32.43A)*

Terms, Conditions and Accounting Policies

For each class of financial asset, financial liability and equity instrument, both recognised and unrecognised, an enterprise should disclose:

(a)   information about the extent and nature of the financial instruments, including significant terms and conditions that may affect the amount, timing and certainty of future cash flows; and

(b)   the accounting policies and methods adopted, including the criteria for recognition and the basis of measurement applied, including;

    (i)   the methods and significant assumptions applied in estimating fair values of financial assets and financial liabilities that are carried at fair value, separately for significant classes of financial assets;

    (ii)   whether gains and losses arising from changes in the fair value of those available-for-sale financial assets that are measured at fair value subsequent to initial recognition are included in net profit or loss for the period or are recognised directly in equity until the financial asset is disposed of; and

    (iii) for each of the four categories of financial assets defined in paragraph 39.10, whether 'regular way' purchases of financial assets are accounted for at trade date or settlement date. *(32.47; 39.167)*

Interest Rate Risk

For each class of financial asset and financial liability, both recognised and unrecognised, an enterprise should disclose information about its exposure to interest rate risk, including:

(a)   contractual repricing or maturity dates, whichever dates are earlier; and

(b)   effective interest rates, when applicable. *(32.56)*

Information about maturity dates, or repricing dates when they are earlier, indicates the length of time for which interest rates are fixed and information about effective interest rates indicates the levels at which they are fixed. Disclosure of this information provides financial statement users with a basis for evaluating the interest rate price risk to which an enterprise is exposed and thus the potential for gain or loss. For instruments that reprice to a market rate of interest before maturity, disclosure of the period until the next repricing is more important than disclosure of the period to maturity. *(32.58)*

An enterprise indicates which of its financial assets and financial liabilities are:

(a)   exposed to interest rate price risk, such as monetary financial assets and financial liabilities with a fixed interest rate;

(b)   exposed to interest rate cash flow risk, such as monetary financial assets and financial liabilities with a floating interest rate that is reset as market rates change; and

(c)   not exposed to interest rate risk, such as some investments in equity securities. *(32.60)*

The nature of an enterprise's business and the extent of its activity in financial instruments will determine whether information about interest rate risk is presented in narrative form, in tables, or by using a combination of the two. When an enterprise has a significant number of financial instruments exposed to interest rate price or cash flow risks, it may adopt one or more of the following approaches to presenting information.

(a)   The carrying amounts of financial instruments exposed to interest rate price risk may be presented in tabular form, grouped by those that are contracted to mature or be repriced:

   (i)   within one year of the balance sheet date;

   (ii)   more than one year and less than five years from the balance sheet date; and

   (iii)   five years or more from the balance sheet date.

(b)   When the performance of an enterprise is significantly affected by the level of its exposure to interest rate price risk or changes in that exposure, more detailed information is desirable. An enterprise such as a bank may disclose, for example, separate groupings of the carrying amounts of financial instruments contracted to mature or be repriced:

   (i)   within one month of the balance sheet date;

   (ii)   more than one and less than three months from the balance sheet date; and

   (iii)   more than three and less than twelve months from the balance sheet date.

(c)   Similarly, an enterprise may indicate its exposure to interest rate cash flow risk through a table indicating the aggregate carrying amount of groups of floating rate financial assets and financial liabilities maturing within various future time periods.

(d)   Interest rate information may be disclosed for individual financial instruments or weighted average rates or a range of rates may be presented for each class of financial instrument. An enterprise groups instruments denominated in different currencies or having substantially different credit risks into separate classes when these factors result in instruments having substantially different effective interest rates. *(32.64)*

Credit Risk

For each class of financial asset, both recognised and unrecognised, an enterprise should disclose information about its exposure to credit risk, including:

(a)   the amount that best represents its maximum credit risk exposure at the balance sheet date, without taking account of the fair value of any collateral, in the event other parties fail to perform their obligations under financial instruments; and

(b)   significant concentrations of credit risk. *(32.66)*

The purposes of disclosing amounts exposed to credit risk without regard to potential recoveries from realisation of collateral ("an enterprise's maximum credit risk exposure") are:

(a)   to provide users of financial statements with a consistent measure of the amount exposed to credit risk for both recognised and unrecognised financial assets; and

(b)   to take into account the possibility that the maximum exposure to loss may differ from the carrying amount of a recognised financial asset or the fair value of an unrecognised financial asset that is otherwise disclosed in the financial statements. (32.68)

An enterprise may have entered into one or more master netting arrangements that serve to mitigate its exposure to credit loss but do not meet the criteria for offsetting. When a master netting arrangement significantly reduces the credit risk associated with financial assets not offset against financial liabilities with the same counterparty, an enterprise provides additional information concerning the effect of the arrangement. Such disclosure indicates that:

(a)   the credit risk associated with financial assets subject to a master netting arrangement is eliminated only to the extent that financial liabilities due to the same counterparty will be settled after the assets are realised; and

(b)   the extent to which an enterprise's overall exposure to credit risk is reduced through a master netting arrangement may change substantially within a short period following the balance sheet date because the exposure is affected by each transaction subject to the arrangement.

It is also desirable for an enterprise to disclose the terms of its master netting arrangements that determine the extent of the reduction in its credit risk. *(32.71)*

Fair Value

For each class of financial asset and financial liability, both recognised and unrecognised, an enterprise should disclose information about fair value. When it is not practical within constraints of timeliness or cost to determine the fair value of a financial asset or financial liability with sufficient reliability, that fact should be disclosed together with information about the principal characteristics of the underlying financial instrument that are pertinent to its fair value. *(32.77)*

Financial Assets Carried at an Amount in Excess of Fair Value

When an enterprise carries one or more financial assets at an amount in excess of their fair value, the enterprise should disclose:

(a)   the carrying amount and the fair value of either the individual assets or appropriate groupings of those individual assets; and

(b)   the reasons for not reducing the carrying amount, including the nature of the evidence that provides the basis for management's belief that the carrying amount will be recovered. *(32.88)*

Hedges of Anticipated Future Transactions

When an enterprise has accounted for a financial instrument as a hedge of risks associated with anticipated future transactions, it should disclose:

(a)   a description of the anticipated transactions, including the period of time until they are expected to occur;

(b)   a description of the hedging instruments; and

(c)   the amount of any deferred or unrecognised gain or loss and the expected timing of recognition as income or expense. *(32.91)*

(d)   describe the enterprise's financial risk management objectives and policies, including its policy for hedging each major type of forecasted transaction;

For example, in the case of hedges of risks relating to future sales, that description indicates the nature of the risks being hedged, approximately how many months or years of expected future sales have been hedged, and the approximate percentage of sales in those future months or years;

(e)   disclose the following separately for designated fair value hedges, cash flow hedges, and hedges of a net investment in a foreign entity:

(i)   a description of the hedge;

(ii)   a description of the financial instruments designated as hedging instruments for the hedge and their fair values at the balance sheet date;

(iii)   the nature of the risks being hedged; and

(iv)   for hedges of forecasted transactions, the periods in which the forecasted transactions are expected to occur, when they are expected to enter into the determination of net profit or loss, and a description of any forecasted transaction for which hedge accounting had previously been used but that is no longer expected to occur; and

(f)   if a gain or loss on derivative and non-derivative financial assets and liabilities designated as hedging instruments in cash flow hedges has been recognised directly in equity, through the statement of changes in equity, disclose:

(i)   the amount that was so recognised in equity during the current period;

(ii)   the amount that was removed from equity and reported in net profit or loss for the period; and

(iii)   the amount that was removed from equity and added to the initial measurement of the acquisition cost or other carrying amount of the asset or liability in a hedged forecasted transaction during the current period (see paragraph 39.160 p. 369). *(39.169)*

Treasury Shares

The amounts of reductions to equity for treasury shares held should be disclosed separately either on the face of the balance sheet or in the notes. *(SIC-16)*

Other Disclosures

Additional disclosures are encouraged when they are likely to enhance financial statement users' understanding of financial instruments. It may be desirable to disclose such information as:

(a)   the total amount of the change in the fair value of financial assets and financial liabilities that has been recognised as income or expense for the period;

(b)   the total amount of deferred or unrecognised gain or loss on hedging instruments other than those relating to hedges of anticipated future transactions; and

(c)   the average aggregate carrying amount during the year of recognised financial assets and financial liabilities, the average aggregate principal, stated, notional or other similar amount during the year of unrecognised financial assets and financial liabilities and the average aggregate fair value during the year of all financial assets and financial liabilities, particularly when the amounts on hand at the balance sheet date are unrepresentative of amounts on hand during the year. (32.94)

(d)   if a gain or loss from remeasuring available-for-sale financial assets to fair value (other than assets relating to hedges) has been recognised directly in equity, through the statement of changes in equity, disclose:

    (i)   the amount that was so recognised in equity during the current period; and

    (ii)   the amount that was removed from equity and reported in net profit or loss for the period;

(e)   if the presumption that fair value can be reliably measured for all financial assets that are available for sale or held for trading has been overcome and the enterprise is, therefore, measuring any such financial assets at amortised cost, disclose that fact together with a description of the financial assets, their carrying amount, an explanation of why fair value cannot be reliably measured, and, if possible, the range of estimates within which fair value is highly likely to lie. Further, if financial assets whose fair value previously could not be measured reliably are sold, that fact, the carrying amount of such financial assets at the time of sale, and the amount of gain or loss recognised should be disclosed;

(f)   disclose significant items of income, expense, and gains and losses resulting from financial assets and financial liabilities, whether included in net profit or loss or as a separate component of equity. For this purpose:

    (i)   total interest income and total interest expense (both on a historical cost basis) should be disclosed separately;

    (ii)   with respect to available-for-sale financial assets that are adjusted to fair value after initial acquisition, total gains and losses from derecognition of such financial assets included in net profit or loss for the period should be reported separately from total gains and losses from fair value adjustments of recognised assets and liabilities included in net profit or loss for the period (a similar split of 'realised' versus 'unrealised' gains and losses with respect to financial assets and liabilities held for trading is not required);

(iii) the enterprise should disclose the amount of interest income that has been accrued on impaired loans pursuant to IAS 39 and that has not yet been received in cash;

(g) if the enterprise has entered into a securitisation or repurchase agreement, disclose, separately for such transactions occurring in the current financial reporting period and for remaining retained interests from transactions occurring in prior financial reporting periods:

(i) the nature and extent of such transactions, including a description of any collateral and quantitative information about the key assumptions used in calculating the fair values of new and retained interests;

(ii) whether the financial assets have been derecognised;

(h) if the enterprise has reclassified a financial asset as one required to be reported at amortised cost rather than at fair value (see paragraph 39.92, p. 362), disclose the reason for that reclassification; and

(i) disclose the nature and amount of any impairment loss or reversal of an impairment loss recognised for a financial asset, separately for each significant class of financial asset. *(39.170)*

Appendix G:

Examples of the Application of the Standard

Definitions

Common Types of Financial Instruments, Financial Assets and Financial Liabilities

1. Currency (cash) is a financial asset because it represents the medium of exchange and is therefore the basis on which all transactions are measured and reported in financial statements. A deposit of cash with a bank or similar financial institution is a financial asset because it represents the contractual right of the depositor to obtain cash from the institution or to draw a cheque or similar instrument against the balance in favour of a creditor in payment of a financial liability.

2. Common examples of financial assets representing a contractual right to receive cash in the future and corresponding financial liabilities representing a contractual obligation to deliver cash in the future are:

    (a)   trade accounts receivable and payable;

    (b)   notes receivable and payable;

    (c)   loans receivable and payable; and

    (d)   bonds receivable and payable.

    In each case, one party's contractual right to receive (or obligation to pay) cash is matched by the other party's corresponding obligation to pay (or right to receive).

3. Another type of financial instrument is one for which the economic benefit to be received or given up is a financial asset other than cash. For example, a note payable in government bonds gives the holder the contractual right to receive and the issuer the contractual obligation to deliver government bonds, not cash. The bonds are financial assets because they represent obligations of the issuing government to pay cash. The note is, therefore, a financial asset of the note holder and a financial liability of the note issuer.

4. Under IAS 17, *Leases* (see section 4.3, p. 300), a finance lease is accounted for as a sale with delayed payment terms. The lease contract is considered to be primarily an entitlement of the lessor to receive, and an obligation of the lessee to pay, a stream of payments that are substantially the same as blended payments of principal and interest under a loan agreement. The lessor accounts

for its investment in the amount receivable under the lease contract rather than the leased asset itself. An operating lease, on the other hand, is considered to be primarily an uncompleted contract committing the lessor to provide the use of an asset in future periods in exchange for consideration similar to a fee for a service. The lessor continues to account for the leased asset itself rather than any amount receivable in the future under the contract. Accordingly, a finance lease is considered to be a financial instrument and an operating lease is considered not to be a financial instrument (except as regards individual payments currently due and payable).

Equity Instruments

5. Examples of equity instruments include common shares, certain types of preferred shares, and warrants or options to subscribe for or purchase common shares in the issuing enterprise. An enterprise's obligation to issue its own equity instruments in exchange for financial assets of another party is not potentially unfavourable since it results in an increase in equity and cannot result in a loss to the enterprise. The possibility that existing holders of an equity interest in the enterprise may find the fair value of their interest reduced as a result of the obligation does not make the obligation unfavourable to the enterprise itself.

6. An option or other similar instrument acquired by an enterprise that gives it the right to reacquire its own equity instruments is not a financial asset of the enterprise. The enterprise will not receive cash or any other financial asset through exercise of the option. Exercise of the option is not potentially favourable to the enterprise since it results in a reduction in equity and an outflow of assets. Any change in equity recorded by the enterprise from reacquiring and cancelling its own equity instruments represents a transfer between those holders of equity instruments who have given up their equity interest and those who continue to hold an equity interest, rather than a gain or loss by the enterprise.

Derivative Financial Instruments

7. On inception, derivative financial instruments give one party a contractual right to exchange financial assets with another party under conditions that are potentially favourable, or a contractual obligation to exchange financial assets with another party under conditions that are potentially unfavourable. Some instruments embody both a right and an obligation to make an exchange. Since the terms of the exchange are determined on inception of the derivative instrument, as prices in financial markets change, those terms may become either favourable or unfavourable.

8. A put or call option to exchange financial instruments gives the holder a right to obtain potential future economic benefits associated with changes in the fair value of the financial instrument underlying the contract. Conversely, the writer of an option assumes an obligation to forego potential future economic benefits or bear potential losses of economic benefits associated with changes in the fair value of the underlying financial instrument. The contractual right of the holder and obligation of the writer meet the definition of a financial asset and a

financial liability respectively. The financial instrument underlying an option contract may be any financial asset, including shares and interest-bearing instruments. An option may require the writer to issue a debt instrument, rather than transfer a financial asset, but the instrument underlying the option would still constitute a financial asset of the holder if the option were exercised. The option-holder's right to exchange the assets under potentially favourable conditions and the writer's obligation to exchange the assets under potentially unfavourable conditions are distinct from the underlying assets to be exchanged upon exercise of the option. The nature of the holder's right and the writer's obligation is not affected by the likelihood that the option will be exercised. An option to buy or sell an asset other than a financial asset (such as a commodity) does not give rise to a financial asset or financial liability because it does not fit the requirements of the definitions for the receipt or delivery of financial assets or exchange of financial instruments.

9.   Another example of a derivative financial instrument is a forward contract to be settled in six months' time in which one party (the purchaser) promises to deliver 1,000,000 cash in exchange for 1,000,000 face amount of fixed rate government bonds, and the other party (the seller) promises to deliver 1,000,000 face amount of fixed rate government bonds in exchange for 1,000,000 cash. During the six months, both parties have a contractual right and a contractual obligation to exchange financial instruments. If the market price of the government bonds rises above 1,000,000, the conditions will be favourable to the purchaser and unfavourable to the seller; if the market price falls below 1,000,000, the effect will be the opposite. The purchaser has both a contractual right (a financial asset) similar to the right under a call option held and a contractual obligation (a financial liability) similar to the obligation under a put option written; the seller has a contractual right (a financial asset) similar to the right under a put option held and a contractual obligation (a financial liability) similar to the obligation under a call option written. As with options, these contractual rights and obligations constitute financial assets and financial liabilities separate and distinct from the underlying financial instruments (the bonds and cash to be exchanged). The significant difference between a forward contract and an option contract is that both parties to a forward contract have an obligation to perform at the agreed time, whereas performance under an option contract occurs only if and when the holder of the option chooses to exercise it.

10.   Many other types of derivative instruments embody a right or obligation to make a future exchange, including interest rate and currency swaps, interest rate caps, collars and floors, loan commitments, note issuance facilities and letters of credit. An interest rate swap contract may be viewed as a variation of a forward contract in which the parties agree to make a series of future exchanges of cash amounts, one amount calculated with reference to a floating interest rate and the other with reference to a fixed interest rate. Futures contracts are another variation of forward contracts, differing primarily in that the contracts are standardised and traded on an exchange.

Commodity Contracts and Commodity-linked Financial Instruments

11.   Contracts that provide for settlement by receipt or delivery of a physical asset only (for example, an option, futures or forward contract on silver) are not

financial instruments. Many commodity contracts are of this type. Some are standardised in form and traded on organised markets in much the same fashion as some derivative financial instruments. For example, a commodity futures contract may be readily bought and sold for cash because it is listed for trading on an exchange and may change hands many times. However, the parties buying and selling the contract are, in effect, trading the underlying commodity. The ability to buy or sell a commodity contract for cash, the ease with which it may be bought or sold and the possibility of negotiating a cash settlement of the obligation to receive or deliver the commodity do not alter the fundamental character of the contract in a way that creates a financial instrument.

12.   A contract that involves receipt or delivery of physical assets does not give rise to a financial asset of one party and a financial liability of the other party unless any corresponding payment is deferred past the date on which the physical assets are transferred. Such is the case with the purchase or sale of goods on trade credit.

13.   Some contracts are commodity-linked but do not involve settlement through physical receipt or delivery of a commodity. They specify settlement through cash payments that are determined according to a formula in the contract, rather than through payment of fixed amounts. For example, the principal amount of a bond may be calculated by applying the market price of oil prevailing at the maturity of the bond to a fixed quantity of oil. The principal is indexed by reference to a commodity price but is settled only in cash. Such a contract constitutes a financial instrument.

14.   The definition of a financial instrument encompasses also a contract that gives rise to a non-financial asset or liability in addition to a financial asset or liability. Such financial instruments often give one party an option to exchange a financial asset for a non-financial asset. For example, an oil-linked bond may give the holder the right to receive a stream of fixed periodic interest payments and a fixed amount of cash on maturity, with the option to exchange the principal amount for a fixed quantity of oil. The desirability of exercising this option will vary from time to time based on the fair value of oil relative to the exchange ratio of cash for oil (the exchange price) inherent in the bond. The intentions of the bondholder concerning the exercise of the option do not affect the substance of the component assets. The financial asset of the holder and the financial liability of the issuer make the bond a financial instrument, regardless of the other types of assets and liabilities also created.

15.   Although IAS 32 was not developed to apply to commodity or other contracts that do not satisfy the definition of a financial instrument, enterprises may consider whether it is appropriate to apply the relevant portions of the disclosure standards to such contracts.

Liabilities and Equity

16.   It is relatively easy for issuers to classify certain types of financial instruments as liabilities or equity. Examples of equity instruments include common (ordinary) shares and options that, if exercised, would require the writer of the option to issue common shares. Common shares do not oblige the issuer to transfer assets

to shareholders, except when the issuer formally acts to make a distribution and becomes legally obligated to the shareholders to do so. This may be the case following declaration of a dividend or when the enterprise is being wound up and any assets remaining after the satisfaction of liabilities become distributable to shareholders.

"Perpetual" debt instruments

17.   "Perpetual" debt instruments, such as perpetual bonds, debentures and capital notes, normally provide the holder with the contractual right to receive payments on account of interest at fixed dates extending into the indefinite future, either with no right to receive a return of principal or a right to a return of principal under terms that make it very unlikely or very far in the future. For example, an enterprise may issue a financial instrument requiring it to make annual payments in perpetuity equal to a stated interest rate of 8% applied to a stated par or principal amount of 1,000. Assuming 8% to be the market rate of interest for the instrument when issued, the issuer assumes a contractual obligation to make a stream of future interest payments having a fair value (present value) of 1,000. The holder and issuer of the instrument have a financial asset and financial liability, respectively, of 1,000 and corresponding interest income and expense of 80 each year in perpetuity.

Preferred Shares

18.   Preferred (or preference) shares may be issued with various rights. In classifying a preferred share as a liability or equity, an enterprise assesses the particular rights attaching to the share to determine whether it exhibits the fundamental characteristic of a financial liability. For example, a preferred share that provides for redemption on a specific date or at the option of the holder meets the definition of a financial liability if the issuer has an obligation to transfer financial assets to the holder of the share. The inability of an issuer to satisfy an obligation to redeem a preferred share when contractually required to do so, whether due to a lack of funds or a statutory restriction, does not negate the obligation. An option of the issuer to redeem the shares does not satisfy the definition of a financial liability because the issuer does not have a present obligation to transfer financial assets to the shareholders. Redemption of the shares is solely at the discretion of the issuer. An obligation may arise, however, when the issuer of the shares exercises its option, usually by formally notifying the shareholders of an intention to redeem the shares.

19.   When preferred shares are non-redeemable, the appropriate classification is determined by the other rights that may attach to them. When distributions to holders of the preferred shares whether, cumulative or non-cumulative, are at the discretion of the issuer, the shares are equity instruments.

Compound Financial Instruments

20.   The requirement in IAS 32 to bifurcate certain financial instruments applies only to a limited group of compound instruments for the purpose of having the issuers present liability and equity components separately on their balance

sheets. The requirements do not deal with compound instruments from the perspective of holders.

21.   A common form of compound financial instrument is a debt security with an embedded conversion option, such as a bond convertible into common shares of the issuer. IAS 32 requires the issuer of such a financial instrument to present the liability component and the equity component separately on the balance sheet from their initial recognition.

(a)   The issuer's obligation to make scheduled payments of interest and principal constitutes a financial liability which exists as long as the instrument is not converted. On inception, the fair value of the liability component is the present value of the contractually determined stream of future cash flows discounted at the rate of interest applied by the market at that time to instruments of comparable credit status and providing substantially the same cash flows, on the same terms, but without the conversion option.

(b)   The equity instrument is an embedded option to convert the liability into equity of the issuer. The fair value of the option comprises its time value and its intrinsic value, if any. The intrinsic value of an option or other derivative financial instrument is the excess, if any, of the fair value of the underlying financial instrument over the contractual price at which the underlying instrument is to be acquired, issued, sold or exchanged. The time value of a derivative instrument is its fair value less its intrinsic value. The time value is associated with the length of the remaining term to maturity or expiry of the derivative instrument. It reflects the income foregone by the holder of the derivative instrument from not holding the underlying instrument, the cost avoided by the holder of the derivative instrument from not having to finance the underlying instrument and the value placed on the probability that the intrinsic value of the derivative instrument will increase prior to its maturity or expiry due to future volatility in the fair value of the underlying instrument. It is uncommon for the embedded option in a convertible bond or similar instrument to have any intrinsic value on issuance.

22.   The components of a compound financial instrument may be valued on initial recognition. The following example illustrates in greater detail how such valuations may be made.

An enterprise issues 2,000 convertible bonds at the start of Year 1. The bonds have a three-year term, and are issued at par with a face value of 1,000 per bond, giving total proceeds of 2,000,000. Interest is payable annually in arrears at a nominal annual interest rate of 6%. Each bond is convertible at any time up to maturity into 250 common shares.

When the bonds are issued, the prevailing market interest rate for similar debt without conversion options is 9%. At the issue date, the market price of one common share is 3. The dividends expected over the three-year term of the bonds amount to 0.14 per share at the end of each year. The risk-free annual interest rate for a three-year term is 5%.

Residual valuation of equity component

Under this approach, the liability component is valued first, and the difference

Present value of principal – 2,000,000 payable at the end of three years	1,544,367
Present value of the interest – 120,000 payable annually in arrears for three years	303,755
Total liability component	1,848,122
Equity component (by deduction)	151,878
Proceeds of the bond issue	2,000,000

Figure 101

between the proceeds of the bond issue and the fair value of the liability is assigned to the equity component. The present value of the liability component is calculated using a discount rate of 9%, the market interest rate for similar bonds having no conversion rights, as shown.

Option pricing model valuation of equity component

Option pricing models may be used to determine the fair value of conversion options directly rather than by deduction as illustrated above. Option pricing models are often used by financial institutions for pricing day-to-day transactions. There are a number of models available, of which the Black–Scholes model is one of the most well-known, and each has a number of variants. The following example illustrates the application of a version of the Black–Scholes model that utilises tables available in finance textbooks and other sources. The steps in applying this version of the model are set out below.

This model first requires the calculation of two amounts that are used in the option valuation tables:

(i)   Standard deviation of proportionate changes in the fair value of the asset underlying the option multiplied by the square root of the time to expiry of the option.

This amount relates to the potential for favourable (and unfavourable) changes in the price of the asset underlying the option, in this case the common shares of the enterprise issuing the convertible bonds. The volatility of the returns on the underlying asset are estimated by the standard deviation of the returns. The higher the standard deviation, the greater the fair value of the option. In this example, the standard deviation of the annual returns on the shares is assumed to be 30%. The time to expiry of the conversion rights is three years. The standard deviation of proportionate changes in fair value of the shares multiplied by the square root of the time to expiry of the option is thus determined as:

$$0.3 \times \sqrt{3} = 0.5196$$

(ii)   Ratio of the fair value of the asset underlying the option to the present value of the option exercise price.

This amount relates the present value of the asset underlying the option to the cost that the option holder must pay to obtain that asset, and is associated with the intrinsic value of the option. The higher this amount, the greater the fair value of a call option. In this example, the market value of each share on issuance of the bonds is 3. The present value of the expected dividends over the term of the option is deducted from the market price, since the payment of dividends reduces the fair value of the shares and thus the fair value of the option. The present value of a dividend of 0.14 per share at the end of each year, discounted at the risk-free rate of 5%, is 0.3813. The present value of the asset underlying the option is therefore:

$$3 - 0.3813 = 2.6187 \text{ per share}$$

The present value of the exercise price is 4 per share discounted at the risk-free rate of 5% over three years, assuming that the bonds are converted at maturity, or 3.4554. The ratio is thus determined as:

$$2.6187 \div 3.4554 = \underline{0.7579}$$

The bond conversion option is a form of call option. The call option valuation table indicates that, for the two amounts calculated above (i.e. 0.5196 and 0.7579), the fair value of the option is approximately 11.05% of the fair value of the underlying asset.

The valuation of the conversion options can therefore be calculated as:

$$0.1105 \times 2.6187 \text{ per share} \times 250 \text{ shares per bond} \times 2,000 \text{ bonds} = \underline{144,683}$$

The fair value of the debt component of the compound instrument calculated above by the present value method plus the fair value of the option calculated by the Black–Scholes option pricing model does not equal the 2,000,000 proceeds from issuance of the convertible bonds (i.e. 1,848,122 + 144,683 = 1,992,805). The small difference can be prorated over the fair values of the two components to produce a fair value for the liability of 1,854,794 and a fair value for the option of 145,206.

Offsetting of a Financial Asset and a Financial Liability

23.   IAS 32 does not provide special treatment for so–called "synthetic instruments", which are groupings of separate financial instruments acquired and held to emulate the characteristics of another instrument. For example, a floating rate long-term debt combined with an interest rate swap that involves receiving floating payments and making fixed payments synthesises a fixed rate long-term debt. Each of the separate components of a synthetic instrument represents a contractual right or obligation with its own terms and conditions and each may be transferred or settled separately. Each component is exposed to risks that may differ from the risks to which other components are exposed.

Accordingly, when one component of a synthetic instrument is an asset and another is a liability, they are not offset and presented on an enterprise's balance sheet on a net basis unless they meet the criteria for offsetting. Such is often not the case. Disclosures are provided about the significant terms and conditions of each financial instrument constituting a component of a synthetic instrument without regard to the existence of the synthetic instrument, although an enterprise may indicate in addition the nature of the relationship between the components.

Chapter 7

Corporate Groups

IAS 22 prescribes the accounting treatment for business combinations. The Standard covers both an acquisition of one enterprise by another and also the rare situation of a uniting of interests when an acquirer cannot be identified.

IAS 27 should be applied in the preparation and presentation of consolidated financial statements, that is, reporting the financial position, results of operations and cash flows of a group of enterprises under the control of a parent.

IAS 28 deals with the accounting for investments in associates

IAS 31 comprises the financial reporting of interests *in* joint ventures. At present, there is no IAS specifically addressing financial reporting *by* joint ventures.

7.1	**Business Combinations**

Business combinations are classified by IAS 22 as either acquisitions or unitings of interest. Most business combinations are acquisitions. Accounting for an acquisition involves determination of the cost of the acquisition, allocation of the cost over the identifiable assets and liabilities of the enterprise being acquired and accounting for the resulting goodwill or negative goodwill, both at acquisition and subsequently. Other accounting issues include the determination of the minority interest amount, accounting for acquisitions which occur over a period of time, subsequent changes in the cost of acquisition or in the identification of assets and liabilities, and the disclosures required.

However, in rare circumstances, it will not be possible to identify an acquirer. In such cases, the combination is treated as a uniting of interests.

IAS 22 should be applied in accounting for business combinations. *(22.1)*

A business combination may give rise to a legal merger. While the requirements for legal mergers differ among countries, a legal merger is usually a merger between two companies in which either:

(a) the assets and liabilities of one company are transferred to the other company and the first company is dissolved; or

(b) the assets and liabilities of both companies are transferred to a new company and both the original companies are dissolved.

Many legal mergers arise as part of the restructuring or reorganisation of a group and are not dealt with in IAS 22 because they are transactions among enterprises under common control. However, any business combination that resulted in the two companies becoming members of the same group is dealt with as an acquisition or as a uniting of interests in consolidated financial statements under the requirements of IAS 22. (22.5)

IAS 22 does not deal with:

(a)   transactions among enterprises under common control; and

(b)   interests in joint ventures (see IAS 31, *Financial Reporting of Interests in Joint Ventures*, section 7.4, p. 411) and the financial statements of joint ventures. (22.7)

IAS 22 uses the following terms:

- A *business combination* is the bringing together of separate enterprises into one economic entity as a result of one enterprise uniting with or obtaining control over the net assets and operations of another enterprise.

- An *acquisition* is a business combination in which one of the enterprises, *the acquirer*, obtains control over the net assets and operations of another enterprise, *the acquiree*, in exchange for the transfer of assets, incurrence of a liability or issue of equity.

- A *uniting of interests* is a business combination in which the shareholders of the combining enterprises combine control over the whole, or effectively the whole, of their net assets and operations to achieve a continuing mutual sharing in the risks and benefits attaching to the combined entity such that neither party can be identified as the acquirer.

- *Control* is the power to govern the financial and operating policies of an enterprise so as to obtain benefits from its activities.

- A *parent* is an enterprise that has one or more subsidiaries.

- A *subsidiary* is an enterprise that is controlled by another enterprise (known as the parent).

- *Minority interest* is that part of the net results of operations and of net assets of a subsidiary attributable to interests which are not owned, directly or indirectly through subsidiaries, by the parent.

- *Fair value* is the amount for which an asset could be exchanged or a liability settled between knowledgeable, willing parties in an arm's length transaction.

- *Monetary assets* are money held and assets to be received in fixed or determinable amounts of money.

- *Date of acquisition* is the date on which control of the net assets and operations of the acquiree is effectively transferred to the acquirer. (22.8)

Nature of a Business Combination

In accounting for a business combination, an acquisition is in substance different from a uniting of interests and the substance of the transaction needs to be reflected in the financial statements. Accordingly, a different accounting method is prescribed for each. *(22.9)*

Acquisitions

In virtually all business combinations one of the combining enterprises obtains control over the other combining enterprise, thereby enabling an acquirer to be identified. Control is presumed to be obtained when one of the combining enterprises acquires more than one half of the voting rights of the other combining enterprise unless, in exceptional circumstances, it can be clearly demonstrated that such ownership does not constitute control. Even when one of the combining enterprises does not acquire more than one half of the voting rights of the other combining enterprise, it may still be possible to identify an acquirer when one of the combining enterprises, as a result of the business combination, acquires:

(a) power over more than one half of the voting rights of the other enterprise by virtue of an agreement with other investors;

(b) power to govern the financial and operating policies of the other enterprise under a statute or an agreement;

(c) power to appoint or remove the majority of the members of the board of directors or equivalent governing body of the other enterprise; or

(d) power to cast the majority of votes at meetings of the board of directors or equivalent governing body of the other enterprise. *(22.10)*

Reverse Acquisitions

Occasionally an enterprise obtains ownership of the shares of another enterprise but as part of the exchange transaction issues enough voting shares, as consideration, such that control of the combined enterprise passes to the owners of the enterprise whose shares have been acquired. This situation is described as a reverse acquisition. *(22.12)*

Unitings of Interests

In exceptional circumstances, it may not be possible to identify an acquirer. Instead of a dominant party emerging, the shareholders of the combining enterprises join in a substantially equal arrangement to share control over the whole, or effectively the whole, of their net assets and operations. In addition, the management of the combining enterprises participate in the management of the combined entity. As a result, the shareholders of the combining enterprises share mutually in the risks and benefits of the combined entity. Such a business combination is accounted for as a uniting of interests. *(22.13)*
In order to achieve a mutual sharing of the risks and benefits of the combined entity:

(a) the substantial majority, if not all, of the voting common shares of the combining enterprises are exchanged or pooled;

(b)   the fair value of one enterprise is not significantly different from that of the other enterprise; and

(c)   the shareholders of each enterprise maintain substantially the same voting rights and interest in the combined entity, relative to each other, after the combination as before. *(22.15)*

These sub-paragraphs describe the essential characteristics of a uniting of interests. An enterprise should classify a business combination as an acquisition, unless all of these three characteristics are present. Even if all of the three characteristics are present, an enterprise should classify a business combination as a uniting of interests only if the enterprise can demonstrate that an acquirer cannot be identified. *(SIC-9)*

The mutual sharing of the risks and benefits of the combined entity diminishes and the likelihood that an acquirer can be identified increases when:

(a)   the relative equality in fair values of the combining enterprises is reduced and the percentage of voting common shares exchanged decreases;

(b)   financial arrangements provide a relative advantage to one group of shareholders over the other shareholders. Such arrangements may take effect either prior to or after the business combination; and

(c)   one party's share of the equity in the combined entity depends on how the business which it previously controlled performs subsequent to the business combination. *(22.16)*

The classification of a business combination should be based on an overall evaluation of all relevant facts and circumstances of the particular transaction. The guidance given in IAS 22 provides examples of important factors to be considered, not a comprehensive set of conditions to be met. Single characteristics of a combined enterprise such as voting power or relative fair values of the combining enterprises should not be evaluated in isolation in order to determine how a business combination should be accounted for. *(SIC-9)*

Acquisitions

Accounting for Acquisitions

A business combination which is an acquisition should be accounted for by use of the purchase method of accounting. *(22.17)*

Date of Acquisition

As from the date of acquisition, an acquirer should:

(a)   incorporate into the income statement the results of operations of the acquiree; and

(b)   recognise in the balance sheet the identifiable assets and liabilities of the acquiree and any goodwill or negative goodwill arising on the acquisition. *(22.19)*

Cost of Acquisition

An acquisition should be accounted for at its cost, being the amount of cash or cash equivalents paid or the fair value, at the date of exchange, of the other purchase consideration given by the acquirer in exchange for control over the net assets of the other enterprise, plus any costs directly attributable to the acquisition. *(22.21)*

Recognition of Identifiable Assets and Liabilities

The identifiable assets and liabilities acquired that are recognised at the date of acquisition should be those of the acquiree that existed at that date together with any liabilities recognised in accordance with IAS 22. They should be recognised separately as at the date of acquisition if, and only if:

(a)   it is probable that any associated future economic benefits will flow to, or resources embodying economic benefits will flow from, the acquirer; and

(b)   a reliable measure is available of their cost or fair value. *(22.26)*

Subject to the conditions described in the following paragraph, liabilities should not be recognised at the date of acquisition if they result from the acquirer's intentions or actions. Liabilities should also not be recognised for future losses or other costs expected to be incurred as a result of the acquisition, whether they relate to the acquirer or the acquiree. *(22.29)*

At the date of acquisition, the acquirer should recognise a provision that was not a liability of the acquiree at that date if, and only if, the acquirer has:

(a)   at, or before, the date of acquisition, developed the main features of a plan that involves terminating or reducing the activities of the acquiree and that relates to:

(i)   compensating employees of the acquiree for termination of their employment;

(ii)   closing facilities of the acquiree;

(iii)   eliminating product lines of the acquiree; or

(iv)   terminating contracts of the acquiree that have become onerous because the acquirer has communicated to the other party at, or before, the date of acquisition that the contract will be terminated;

(b)   by announcing the main features of the plan at, or before, the date of acquisition, raised a valid expectation in those affected by the plan that it will implement the plan; and

(c)   by the earlier of three months after the date of acquisition and the date when the annual financial statements are approved, developed those main features into a detailed formal plan identifying at least:

(i)   the business or part of a business concerned;

(ii)   the principal locations affected;

(iii)   the location, function, and approximate number of employees who will be compensated for terminating their services;

(iv)   the expenditures that will be undertaken; and

(v)   when the plan will be implemented.

Any provision recognised under this paragraph should cover only the costs of the items listed in (a)(i) to (iv) above. *(22.31)*

Allocation of Cost of Acquisition

Benchmark Treatment

The identifiable assets and liabilities recognised on the date of acquisition should be measured at the aggregate of:

(a)   the fair value of the identifiable assets and liabilities acquired as at the date of the exchange transaction to the extent of the acquirer's interest obtained in the exchange transaction; and

(b)   the minority's proportion of the pre-acquisition carrying amounts of the identifiable assets and liabilities of the subsidiary.

Any goodwill or negative goodwill should be accounted for in accordance with the provisions of IAS 22 discussed below. *(22.32)*

Allowed Alternative Treatment

The identifiable assets and liabilities recognised under paragraph 22.26 should be measured at their fair values as at the date of acquisition. Any goodwill or negative goodwill should be accounted for under IAS 22. Any minority interest should be stated at the minority's proportion of the fair values of the identifiable assets and liabilities recognised. *(22.34)*

Successive Share Purchases

An acquisition may involve more than one exchange transaction as, for example, when it is achieved in stages by successive purchases on a stock exchange. When this occurs, each significant transaction is treated separately for the purpose of determining the fair values of the identifiable assets and liabilities acquired and for determining the amount of any goodwill or negative goodwill on that transaction. This results in a step-by-step comparison of the cost of the individual investments with the acquirer's percentage interest in the fair values of the identifiable assets and liabilities acquired at each significant step. *(22.36)*

Determining the Fair Values of Identifiable Assets and Liabilities Acquired

General guidelines for arriving at the fair values of identifiable assets and liabilities acquired are as follows:

(a)   marketable securities at their current market values;

(b)   non-marketable securities at estimated values that take into consideration features such as price earnings ratios, dividend yields and expected growth rates of comparable securities of enterprises with similar characteristics;

(c)   receivables at the present values of the amounts to be received, determined at appropriate current interest rates, less allowances for uncollectability and collection costs, if necessary. However, discounting is not required for short-term receivables when the difference between the nominal amount of the receivable and the discounted amount is not material;

(d)   inventories:

   (i)   finished goods and merchandise at selling prices less the sum of (a) the costs of disposal and (b) a reasonable profit allowance for the selling effort of the acquirer based on profit for similar finished goods and merchandise;

   (ii)   work in progress at selling prices of finished goods less the sum of (a) costs to complete, (b) costs of disposal and (c) a reasonable profit allowance for the completing and selling effort based on profit for similar finished goods; and

   (iii)   raw materials at current replacement costs;

(e)   land and buildings at their market value;

(f)   plant and equipment at market value, normally determined by appraisal. When there is no evidence of market value because of the specialised nature of the plant and equipment or because the items are rarely sold, except as part of a continuing business, they are valued at their depreciated replacement cost;

(g)   intangible assets, as defined in IAS 38, *Intangible Assets* (see section 3.4, p. 204), at fair value determined:

   (i)   by reference to an active market as defined in IAS 38; and

   (ii)   if no active market exists, on a basis that reflects the amount that the enterprise would have paid for the asset in an arm's length transaction between knowledgeable willing parties, based on the best information available (see IAS 38 for further guidance on determining the fair value of an intangible asset acquired in a business combination);

(h)   net employee benefit assets or liabilities for defined benefit plans at the present value of the defined benefit obligation less the fair value of any plan assets. However, an asset is only recognised to the extent that it is probable that it will be available to the enterprise in the form of refunds from the plan or a reduction in future contributions;

(i)   tax assets and liabilities at the amount of the tax benefit arising from tax losses or the taxes payable in respect of the net profit or loss, assessed from the perspective of the combined entity or group resulting from the acquisition. The tax asset or liability is determined after allowing for the tax effect of restating identifiable assets and liabilities to their fair values and is not discounted. The tax assets include any deferred tax asset of the acquirer that was not recognised prior to the business combination, but which, as a consequence of the business combination, now satisfies the recognition criteria in IAS 12, *Income Taxes* (see section 4.1, p. 247);

(j)   accounts and notes payable, long-term debt, liabilities, accruals and other claims payable at the present values of amounts to be disbursed in meeting the liability determined at appropriate current interest rates. However, discounting is not required for short-term liabilities when the difference between the nominal amount of the liability and the discounted amount is not material;

(k)   onerous contracts and other identifiable liabilities of the acquiree at the present values of amounts to be disbursed in meeting the obligation determined at appropriate current interest rates; and

(l)   provisions for terminating or reducing activities of the acquiree that are recognised under paragraph 22.31, at an amount determined under IAS 37, *Provisions, Contingent Liabilities and Contingent Assets* (see section 4.4, p. 311).

Certain of the guidelines above assume that fair values will be determined by the use of discounting. When the guidelines do not refer to the use of discounting, discounting may or may not be used in determining the fair values of identifiable assets and liabilities. *(22.39)*

If the fair value of an intangible asset cannot be measured by reference to an active market (as defined in IAS 38, *Intangible Assets*), the amount recognised for that intangible asset at the date of the acquisition should be limited to an amount that does not create or increase negative goodwill that arises on the acquisition (see "Negative Goodwill Arising on Acquisition – Recognition and Measurement", on page 397). *(22.40)*

Goodwill Arising on Acquisition

Recognition and Measurement

Any excess of the cost of the acquisition over the acquirer's interest in the fair value of the identifiable assets and liabilities acquired as at the date of the exchange transaction should be described as goodwill and recognised as an asset. *(22.41)*

Goodwill should be carried at cost less any accumulated amortisation and any accumulated impairment losses. *(22.43)*

Amortisation

Goodwill should be amortised on a systematic basis over its useful life. The amortisation period should reflect the best estimate of the period during which future economic benefits are expected to flow to the enterprise. There is a rebuttable presumption that the useful life of goodwill will not exceed twenty years from initial recognition. *(22.44)*

The amortisation method used should reflect the pattern in which the future economic benefits arising from goodwill are expected to be consumed. The straight-line method should be adopted unless there is persuasive evidence that another method is more appropriate in the circumstances. *(22.45)*

The amortisation for each period should be recognised as an expense. *(22.46)*

The amortisation period and the amortisation method should be reviewed at least at each financial year end. If the expected useful life of goodwill is significantly different from previous estimates, the amortisation period should be changed accordingly. If there has been a significant change in the expected pattern of economic benefits from goodwill, the method should be changed to reflect the changed pattern. Such changes should be accounted for as changes in accounting estimates under IAS 8, *Net Profit or Loss for the Period* (see section 2.2.2, p. 106), *Fundamental Errors and Changes in Accounting Policies* (see section 2.5.4, p. 145), by adjusting the amortisation charge for the current and future periods. *(22.54)*

Recoverability of the Carrying Amount - Impairment Losses

In addition to following the requirements included in IAS 36, *Impairment of Assets* (see section 3.5, p. 214), an enterprise should, at least at each financial year end, estimate in accordance with IAS 36 the recoverable amount of goodwill that is amortised over a period exceeding twenty years from initial recognition, even if there is no indication that it is impaired. *(22.56)*

Negative Goodwill Arising on Acquisition

Recognition and Measurement

Any excess, as at the date of the exchange transaction, of the acquirer's interest in the fair values of the identifiable assets and liabilities acquired over the cost of the acquisition, should be recognised as negative goodwill. *(22.59)*

To the extent that negative goodwill relates to expectations of future losses and expenses that are identified in the acquirer's plan for the acquisition and can be measured reliably, but which do not represent identifiable liabilities at the date of acquisition, that portion of negative goodwill should be recognised as income in the income statement when the future losses and expenses are recognised. If these identifiable future losses and expenses are not recognised in the expected period, negative goodwill should be treated under paragraph 22.62 (a) and (b). *(22.61)*

To the extent that negative goodwill does not relate to identifiable expected future losses and expenses that can be measured reliably at the date of acquisition, negative goodwill should be recognised as income in the income statement as follows:

(a)   the amount of negative goodwill not exceeding the fair values of acquired identifiable non-monetary assets should be recognised as income on a systematic basis over the remaining weighted average useful life of the identifiable acquired depreciable/amortisable assets; and

(b)   the amount of negative goodwill in excess of the fair values of acquired identifiable non-monetary assets should be recognised as income immediately. *(22.62)*

Presentation

Negative goodwill should be presented as a deduction from the assets of the reporting enterprise, in the same balance sheet classification as goodwill. *(22.64)*

Adjustments to Purchase Consideration Contingent on Future Events

When the acquisition agreement provides for an adjustment to the purchase consideration contingent on one or more future events, the amount of the adjustment should be included in the cost of the acquisition as at the date of acquisition if the adjustment is probable and the amount can be measured reliably. *(22.65)*

Subsequent Changes in Cost of Acquisition

The cost of the acquisition should be adjusted when a contingency affecting the amount of the purchase consideration is resolved subsequent to the date of the acquisition, so that payment of the amount is probable and a reliable estimate of the amount can be made. *(22.68)*

Subsequent Identification or Changes in Value of Identifiable Assets and Liabilities

Identifiable assets and liabilities, which are acquired but which do not satisfy the criteria in the Standard for separate recognition when the acquisition is initially accounted for, should be recognised subsequently as and when they satisfy the criteria. The carrying amounts of identifiable assets and liabilities acquired should be adjusted when, subsequent to acquisition, additional evidence becomes available to assist with the estimation of the amounts assigned to those identifiable assets and liabilities when the acquisition was initially accounted for. The amount assigned to goodwill or negative goodwill should also be adjusted, when necessary, to the extent that:

(a)   the adjustment does not increase the carrying amount of goodwill above its recoverable amount, as defined in IAS 36, *Impairment of Assets*; and

(b)   such adjustment is made by the end of the first annual accounting period commencing after acquisition (except for the recognition of an identifiable liability under IAS 22 paragraph 22.31 (see p. 393), for which the time-frame in IAS 22 paragraph 31(c) applies);

otherwise the adjustments to the identifiable assets and liabilities should be recognised as income or expense. *(22.71)*

SIC-22, *Business Combinations – Subsequent Adjustment of Fair Values and Goodwill Initially Recorded* states that an adjustment to the carrying amount of identifiable assets and liabilities acquired, made in the limited circumstances described in IAS 22, paragraph 71, should be calculated as if the adjusted fair values had been applied from the date of acquisition. As a result, the adjustment should include both the effect of the change to the fair values initially assigned and the effect of depreciation and other changes which would have resulted if the adjusted fair values had been applied from the date of acquisition. *[SIC-22]*

If provisions for terminating or reducing activities of the acquiree were recognised under paragraph 31, these provisions should be reversed if, and only if:

(a)   the outflow of economic benefits is no longer probable; or

(b) the detailed formal plan is not implemented:

   (i)   in the manner set out in the detailed formal plan; or

   (ii) within the time established in the detailed formal plan.

Such a reversal should be reflected as an adjustment to goodwill or negative goodwill (and minority interests, if appropriate), so that no income or expense is recognised in respect of it. The adjusted amount of goodwill should be amortised prospectively over its remaining useful life. There are special requirements for the adjusted amount of negative growth.

Unitings of Interests

Accounting for Unitings of Interests

A uniting of interests should be accounted for by use of the pooling of interests method. *(22.77)*

In applying the pooling of interests method, the financial statement items of the combining enterprises for the period in which the combination occurs and for any comparative periods disclosed should be included in the financial statements of the combined enterprises as if they had been combined from the beginning of the earliest period presented. The financial statements of an enterprise should not incorporate a uniting of interests to which the enterprise is a party if the date of the uniting of interests is after the date of the most recent balance sheet included in the financial statements. *(22.78)*

Any difference between the amount recorded as share capital issued plus any additional consideration in the form of cash or other assets and the amount recorded for the share capital acquired should be adjusted against equity. *(22.79)*

Expenditures incurred in relation to a uniting of interests should be recognised as expenses in the period in which they are incurred. *(22.83)*

All Business Combinations

Taxes on Income

In some countries, the accounting treatment for a business combination may differ from that applied under their respective income tax laws. Any resulting deferred tax liabilities and deferred tax assets are recognised under IAS 12, *Income Taxes* (see section 4.1, p. 247). *(22.84)*

The potential benefit of income tax loss carryforwards, or other deferred tax assets, of an acquired enterprise, which were not recognised as an identifiable asset by the acquirer at the date of acquisition, may subsequently be realised. When this occurs, the acquirer recognises the benefit as income under IAS 12, *Income Taxes*. In addition, the acquirer:

(a)   adjusts the gross carrying amount of the goodwill and the related accumulated amortisation to the amounts that would have been recorded if the deferred tax asset had been recognised as an identifiable asset at the date of the business combination; and

(b)   recognises the reduction in the net carrying amount of the goodwill as an expense.

However, this procedure does not create negative goodwill, nor does it increase the carrying amount of negative goodwill. *(22.85)*

Disclosure

For all business combinations, the following disclosures should be made in the financial statements for the period during which the combination has taken place:

(a)   the names and descriptions of the combining enterprises;

(b)   the method of accounting for the combination;

(c)   the effective date of the combination for accounting purposes; and

(d)   any operations resulting from the business combination which the enterprise has decided to dispose of. *(22.86)*

For a business combination which is an acquisition, the following additional disclosures should be made in the financial statements for the period during which the acquisition has taken place:

(a)   the percentage of voting shares acquired; and

(b)   the cost of acquisition and a description of the purchase consideration paid or contingently payable. *(22.87)*

For goodwill, the financial statements should disclose:

(a)   the amortisation period(s) adopted;

(b)   if goodwill is amortised over more than twenty years, the reasons why the presumption that the useful life of goodwill will not exceed twenty years from initial recognition is rebutted. In giving these reasons, the enterprise should describe the factor(s) that played a significant role in determining the useful life of the goodwill ;

(c)   if goodwill is not amortised on the straight-line basis, the basis used and reason why that basis is more appropriate than the straight-line basis;

(d)   the line item(s) of the income statement in which the amortisation of goodwill is included; and

(e)   a reconciliation of the carrying amount of goodwill at the beginning and end of the period showing:

    (i)   the gross amount and the accumulated amortisation (aggregated with accumulated impairment losses), at the beginning of the period;

(ii)   any additional goodwill recognised during the period;

(iii) any adjustments resulting from subsequent identification or changes in value of identifiable assets and liabilities;

(iv)   any goodwill derecognised on the disposal of all or part of the business to which it relates during the period;

(v)   amortisation recognised during the period;

(vi)   impairment losses recognised during the period under IAS 36, *Impairment of Assets* (see section 3.5, p. 214) (if any);

(vii) impairment losses reversed during the period under IAS 36 (if any);

(viii) other changes in the carrying amount during the period (if any); and

(ix)   the gross amount and the accumulated amortisation (aggregated with accumulated impairment losses), at the end of the period.

Comparative information is not required. *(22.88)*

For negative goodwill, the financial statements should disclose:

(a)   to the extent that negative goodwill is treated under IAS 22 paragraph 22.61, a description, the amount and the timing of the expected future losses and expenses;

(b)   the period(s) over which negative goodwill is recognised as income;

(c)   the line item(s) of the income statement in which negative goodwill is recognised as income; and

(d)   a reconciliation of the carrying amount of negative goodwill at the beginning and end of the period showing:

(i)   the gross amount of negative goodwill and the accumulated amount of negative goodwill already recognised as income, at the beginning of the period;

(ii)   any additional negative goodwill recognised during the period;

(iii) any adjustments resulting from subsequent identification or changes in value of identifiable assets and liabilities;

(iv)   any negative goodwill derecognised on the disposal of all or part of the business to which it relates during the period;

(v)   negative goodwill recognised as income during the period, showing separately the portion of negative goodwill recognised as income under IAS 22 paragraph 22.61 (if any);

(vi)   other changes in the carrying amount during the period (if any); and

(vii) the gross amount of negative goodwill and the accumulated amount of negative goodwill already recognised as income, at the end of the period.

Comparative information is not required. *(22.91)*

The disclosure requirements of IAS 37, *Provisions, Contingent Liabilities and Contingent Assets*, apply to provisions recognised under paragraph 22.31 for terminating or reducing the activities of an acquiree. These provisions should be treated as a separate class of provisions for the purpose of disclosure under IAS 37. In addition, the aggregate carrying amount of these provisions should be disclosed for each individual business combination. *(22.92)*

In an acquisition, if the fair values of the identifiable assets and liabilities or the purchase consideration can only be determined on a provisional basis at the end of the period in which the acquisition took place, this should be stated and reasons given. When there are subsequent adjustments to such provisional fair values, those adjustments should be disclosed and explained in the financial statements of the period concerned. *(22.93)*

For a business combination which is a uniting of interests, the following additional disclosures should be made in the financial statements for the period during which the uniting of interests has taken place:

(a)   description and number of shares issued, together with the percentage of each enterprise's voting shares exchanged to effect the uniting of interests;

(b)   amounts of assets and liabilities contributed by each enterprise; and

(c)   sales revenue, other operating revenues, extraordinary items and the net profit or loss of each enterprise prior to the date of the combination that are included in the net profit or loss shown by the combined enterprise's financial statements. *(22.94)*

Certain additional disclosures are required for business combinations effected after the balance sheet date. If it is impractical to disclose any of the required information, this fact should be disclosed. *(22.96)*

7.2 Consolidated Financial Statement and Accounting for Investments in Subsidiaries

IAS 27 should be applied in the preparation and presentation of consolidated financial statements for a group of enterprises under the control of a parent. *(27.1)*

IAS 27 should also be applied in accounting for investments in subsidiaries in a parent's separate financial statements. *(27.2)*

IAS 27 uses the following terms:

- *Control* (for the purpose of IAS 27) is the power to govern the financial and operating policies of an enterprise so as to obtain benefits from its activities.

- A *subsidiary* is an enterprise that is controlled by another enterprise (known as the parent).

- A *parent* is an enterprise that has one or more subsidiaries.

- A *group* is a parent and all its subsidiaries.

- *Consolidated financial statements* are the financial statements of a group presented as those of a single enterprise.

- *Minority interest* is that part of the net results of operations and of net assets of a subsidiary attributable to interests which are not owned, directly or indirectly through subsidiaries, by the parent. *(27.6)*

Presentation of Consolidated Financial Statements

A parent, other than a parent mentioned in the following paragraph, should present consolidated financial statements. *(27.7)*

A parent that is a wholly owned subsidiary, or is virtually wholly owned, need not present consolidated financial statements provided, in the case of one that is virtually wholly owned, the parent obtains the approval of the owners of the minority interest. Such a parent should disclose the reasons why consolidated financial statements have not been presented together with the bases on which subsidiaries are accounted for in its separate financial statements. The name and registered office of its parent that publishes consolidated financial statements should also be disclosed. *(27.8)*

Scope of Consolidated Financial Statements

A parent which issues consolidated financial statements should consolidate all subsidiaries, foreign and domestic, other than those which are required to be excluded from consolidation, as discussed below. *(27.11)*

The consolidated financial statements include all enterprises that are controlled by the parent. Control is presumed to exist when the parent owns, directly or indirectly through subsidiaries, more than one half of the voting power of an enterprise unless, in exceptional circumstances, it can be clearly demonstrated that such ownership does not constitute control. Control also exists even when the parent owns one half or less of the voting power of an enterprise when there is:

(a)   power over more than one half of the voting rights by virtue of an agreement with other investors;

(b)   power to govern the financial and operating policies of the enterprise under a statute or an agreement;

(c)   power to appoint or remove the majority of the members of the board of directors or equivalent governing body; or

(d)   power to cast the majority of votes at meetings of the board of directors or equivalent governing body. *(27.12)*

Special Purpose Entities

Sometimes, an entity is created to accomplish a narrow and well-defined objective (e.g. to effect a lease, research and development activities or a securitisation of financial assets). Such a special purpose entity ("SPE") may take the form of a corporation, trust, partnership or unincorporated entity. SPEs often are created with legal arrangements that impose strict and sometimes permanent limits on the decision-making powers of their governing board, trustee or management over the operations of the SPE. The sponsor (or enterprise on whose behalf the SPE was created) frequently transfers assets to the SPE, obtains the right to use assets held by the SPE or performs services for the SPE, while other parties ("capital providers") may provide the funding to the SPE. An enterprise that engages in transactions with an SPE (frequently the creator or sponsor) may in substance control the SPE. In most cases, the creator or sponsor (or the enterprise on whose behalf the SPE was created) retains a significant beneficial interest in the SPE's activities, even though it may own little or none of the SPE's equity.

SIC-12 states that an enterprise should consolidate an SPE when the substance of the relationship between an enterprise and the SPE indicates that the SPE is controlled by that enterprise. In the context of an SPE, control may arise through the predetermination of the activities of the SPE (operating on "autopilot") or otherwise. SIC-12 provides examples of circumstances which may indicate that the enterprise controls the SPE. That guidance is in addition to the situations described in the previous sub-section. *(SIC-12)*

Exclusions from Consolidation

A subsidiary should be excluded from consolidation when:

(a)   control is intended to be temporary because the subsidiary is acquired and held exclusively with a view to its subsequent disposal in the near future; or

(b)   it operates under severe long-term restrictions which significantly impair its ability to transfer funds to the parent.

Such subsidiaries should be accounted for as if they are investments in accordance with IAS 39, *Financial Instruments: Recognition and Measurement* (see section 6.1, p. 349). *(27.13)*

Sometimes a subsidiary is excluded from consolidation when its business activities are dissimilar from those of the other enterprises within the group. Exclusion on these grounds is not justified because better information is provided by consolidating such subsidiaries and disclosing additional information in the consolidated financial statements about the different business activities of subsidiaries. For example, the disclosures required by IAS 14, *Segment Reporting* (see section 2.3, p. 119), help to explain the significance of different business activities within the group. *(27.14)*

Consolidation Procedures

In preparing consolidated financial statements, the financial statements of the parent and its subsidiaries are combined on a line-by-line basis by adding together like items of assets, liabilities, equity, income and expenses. In order that the consolidated financial statements present financial information about the group as that of a single enterprise, the following steps are then taken:

(a) the carrying amount of the parent's investment in each subsidiary and the parent's portion of equity of each subsidiary are eliminated (see IAS 22 (revised 1998), *Business Combinations* (section 7.1, p. 389), which also describes the treatment of any resultant goodwill);

(b) minority interests in the net income of consolidated subsidiaries for the reporting period are identified and adjusted against the income of the group in order to arrive at the net income attributable to the owners of the parent; and

(c) minority interests in the net assets of consolidated subsidiaries are identified and presented in the consolidated balance sheet separately from liabilities and the parent shareholders' equity. Minority interests in the net assets consist of:

    (i) the amount at the date of the original combination calculated in accordance with IAS 22 (revised 1998), *Business Combinations*; and

    (ii) the minority's share of movements in equity since the date of the combination. *(27.15)*

Intragroup balances and intragroup transactions and resulting unrealised profits should be eliminated in full. Unrealised losses resulting from intragroup transactions should also be eliminated unless cost cannot be recovered. *(27.17)*

When the financial statements used in the consolidation are drawn up to different reporting dates, adjustments should be made for the effects of significant transactions or other events that occur between those dates and the date of the parent's financial statements. In any case the difference between reporting dates should be no more than three months. *(27.19)*

Consolidated financial statements should be prepared using uniform accounting policies for like transactions and other events in similar circumstances. If it is not practical to use uniform accounting policies in preparing the consolidated financial statements, that fact should be disclosed together with the proportions of the items in the consolidated financial statements to which the different accounting policies have been applied. *(27.21)*

An investment in an enterprise should be accounted for in accordance with IAS 39, *Financial Instruments: Recognition and Measurement*, from the date that it ceases to fall within the definition of a subsidiary and does not become an associate as defined in IAS 28, *Accounting for Investments in Associates* (see section 7.3, p. 407). *(27.24)*

The carrying amount of the investment at the date that it ceases to be a subsidiary is regarded as cost thereafter. *(27.25)*

Minority interests should be presented in the consolidated balance sheet separately from liabilities and the parent shareholders' equity. Minority interests in the income of the group should also be presented separately. *(27.26)*

Accounting for Investments in Subsidiaries in a Parent's Separate Financial Statements

In a parent's separate financial statements, investments in subsidiaries that are included in the consolidated financial statements should be either:

(a)   carried at cost;

(b)   accounted for using the equity method as described in IAS 28; or

(c)   accounted for as available-for-sale financial assets as described in IAS 39. *(27.29)*

Investments in subsidiaries that are excluded from consolidated financial statements should be either:

(a)   carried at cost;

(b)   accounted for using the equity method as described in IAS 28, *Accounting for Investments in Associates*; or

(c)   accounted for as available-for-sale financial assets as described in IAS 39, *Financial Instruments: Recognition and Measurement*. *(27.30)*

Disclosure

In addition to those disclosures required by specific paragraphs and discussed above, the following disclosures should be made:

(a)   in consolidated financial statements a listing of significant subsidiaries including the name, country of incorporation or residence, proportion of ownership interest and, if different, proportion of voting power held;

(b)   in consolidated financial statements, where applicable:

   (i)   the reasons for not consolidating a subsidiary;

   (ii)   the nature of the relationship between the parent and a subsidiary of which the parent does not own, directly or indirectly through subsidiaries, more than one half of the voting power;

   (iii)   the name of an enterprise in which more than one half of the voting power is owned, directly or indirectly through subsidiaries, but which, because of the absence of control, is not a subsidiary; and

   (iv)   the effect of the acquisition and disposal of subsidiaries on the financial position at the reporting date, the results for the reporting period and on the corresponding amounts for the preceding period; and

(c)   in the parent's separate financial statements, a description of the method used to account for subsidiaries. *(27.32)*

| 7.3 | **Accounting for Investments in Associates** |

IAS 28 should be applied in accounting by an investor for investments in associates. *(28.1)*

The following terms are used with the meanings specified:

- *An associate* is an enterprise in which the investor has significant influence and which is neither a subsidiary nor a joint venture of the investor.

- *Significant influence* is the power to participate in the financial and operating policy decisions of the investee but is not control over those policies.

- *Control* (for the purpose of IAS 28) is the power to govern the financial and operating policies of an enterprise so as to obtain benefits from its activities.

- A *subsidiary* is an enterprise that is controlled by another enterprise (known as the parent).

- The *equity method* is a method of accounting whereby the investment is initially recorded at cost and adjusted thereafter for the post acquisition change in the investor's share of net assets of the investee. The income statement reflects the investor's share of the results of operations of the investee.

- The *cost method* is a method of accounting whereby the investment is recorded at cost. The income statement reflects income from the investment only to the extent that the investor receives distributions from accumulated net profits of the investee arising subsequent to the date of acquisition. *(28.3)*

Significant Influence

If an investor holds, directly or indirectly through subsidiaries, 20% or more of the voting power of the investee, it is presumed that the investor has significant influence, unless it can be clearly demonstrated that this is not the case. Conversely, if the investor holds, directly or indirectly through subsidiaries, less than 20% of the voting power of the investee, it is presumed that the investor does not have significant influence, unless such influence can be clearly demonstrated. A substantial or majority ownership by another investor does not necessarily preclude an investor from having significant influence. *(28.4)*

The existence of significant influence by an investor is usually evidenced in one or more of the following ways:

(a) representation on the board of directors or equivalent governing body of the investee;

(b) participation in policy-making processes;

(c) material transactions between the investor and the investee;

(d) interchange of managerial personnel; or

(e) provision of essential technical information. *(28.5)*

Consolidated Financial Statements

An investment in an associate should be accounted for in consolidated financial statements under the equity method except when the investment is acquired and held exclusively with a view to its disposal in the near future, in which case it should be accounted for under the cost method. *(28.8)*

An investor should discontinue the use of the equity method from the date that:

(a)   it ceases to have significant influence in an associate but retains, either in whole or in part, its investment; or

(b)   the use of the equity method is no longer appropriate because the associate operates under severe long-term restrictions that significantly impair its ability to transfer funds to the investor.

The carrying amount of the investment at that date should be regarded as cost thereafter. *(28.11)*

Equity Method

Under the equity method, the investment is initially recorded at cost and the carrying amount is increased or decreased to recognise the investor's share of the profits or losses of the investee after the date of acquisition. Distributions received from an investee reduce the carrying amount of the investment. Adjustments to the carrying amount may also be necessary for alterations in the investor's proportionate interest in the investee arising from changes in the investee's equity that have not been included in the income statement. Such changes include those arising from the revaluation of property, plant, equipment and investments, from foreign exchange translation differences and from the adjustment of differences arising on business combinations. *(28.6)*

Cost Method

Under the cost method, an investor records its investment in the investee at cost. The investor recognises income only to the extent that it receives distributions from the accumulated net profits of the investee arising subsequent to the date of acquisition by the investor. Distributions received in excess of such profits are considered a recovery of investment and are recorded as a reduction of the cost of the investment. *(28.7)*

Separate Financial Statements of the Investor

An investment in an associate that is included in the separate financial statements of an investor that issues consolidated financial statements and that is not held exclusively with a view to its disposal in the near future should be either:

(a)   carried at cost;

(b)   accounted for using the equity method as described in this Standard; or

(c) accounted for as an available-for-sale financial asset as described in IAS 39, *Financial Instruments: Recognition and Measurement* (see section 6.1. p 349). *(28.12)*

An investment in an associate that is included in the financial statements of an investor that does not issue consolidated financial statements should be either:

(a) carried at cost;

(b) accounted for using the equity method as described in IAS 28 if the equity method would be appropriate for the associate if the investor issued consolidated financial statements; or

(c) accounted for under IAS 39, *Financial Instruments: Recognition and Measurement*, as an available-for-sale financial asset or a financial asset held for trading based on the definitions in IAS 39. *(28.14)*

Application of the Equity Method

Many of the procedures appropriate for the application of the equity method are similar to the consolidation procedures set out in IAS 27, *Consolidated Financial Statements and Accounting for Investments in Subsidiaries* (see section 7.2, p. 402). Furthermore, the broad concepts underlying the consolidation procedures used in the acquisition of a subsidiary are adopted on the acquisition of an investment in an associate. *(28.16)*

An investment in an associate is accounted for under the equity method from the date on which it falls within the definition of an associate. On acquisition of the investment any difference (whether positive or negative) between the cost of acquisition and the investor's share of the fair values of the net identifiable assets of the associate is accounted for in accordance with IAS 22, *Business Combinations* (see section 7.1, p. 389). Appropriate adjustments to the investor's share of the profits or losses after acquisition are made to account for:

(a) depreciation of the depreciable assets, based on their fair values; and

(b) amortisation of the difference between the cost of the investment and the investor's share of the fair values of the net identifiable assets. *(28.17)*

Unrealised Profits and Losses

IAS 27 does not give explicit guidance on the elimination of unrealised profits and losses resulting from "upstream" or "downstream" transactions between an investor (or its consolidated subsidiaries) and associates. "Upstream" transactions are, for example, sales of assets from an associate to the investor (or its consolidated subsidiaries). "Downstream" transactions are, for example, sales of assets from the investor (or its consolidated subsidiaries) to an associate.

SIC-3, *Elimination of Unrealised Profits and Losses on Transactions with Associates*, states that where an associate is accounted for using the equity method, unrealised profits and losses resulting from "upstream" and "downstream" transactions between an investor (or its consolidated subsidiaries) and associates should be eliminated to the extent of the investor's interest in the associate. However, unrealised losses should not be eliminated to the extent that the transaction provides evidence of an impairment of the asset transferred. *(SIC-3)*

Recognition of Losses

IAS 28 indicates that in applying the equity method, once the investor's share of losses of an associate equals or exceeds the carrying amount of the investment, the investor normally discontinues including its share of further losses in its income statement. However, additional losses are provided for to the extent that the investor has incurred obligations or made payments on behalf of the associate to satisfy obligations of the associate that the investor has guaranteed or otherwise committed.

SIC-20 states that while financial interests which are accounted for under the equity method of accounting may be described in a variety of ways (for example, some interests are described as ordinary shares or as preferred shares) for the purpose of applying IAS 28, the carrying amount of the investment should include only instruments which provide unlimited rights of participation in earnings or losses and a residual equity interest in the investee. If the investor's share of losses exceeds the carrying amount of the investment, the carrying amount of the investment is reduced to nil and recognition of further losses should be discontinued, unless the investor has incurred obligations to the investee or to satisfy obligations of the investee that the investor has guaranteed or otherwise committed, whether funded or not. To the extent that the investor has incurred such obligations, the investor continues to recognise its share of losses of the investee. Financial interests in an investee which are not included in the carrying amount of the investment are accounted for in accordance with IAS 39.

Continuing losses of an investee should be considered objective evidence that financial interests in that investee may be impaired. Impairment of the carrying amount of a financial interest is determined based on the carrying amount after any adjustment for equity method losses.

If the investor has guaranteed or otherwise committed to obligations to the investee or to satisfying obligations of the investee, in addition to continuing to recognise its share of losses of the investee, the investor should determine whether a provision should be recognised in accordance with IAS 37. *(SIC-20)*

Impairment Losses

If there is an indication that an investment in an associate may be impaired, an enterprise applies IAS 36, *Impairment of Assets* (see section 3.5, p. 214). In determining the value in use of the investment, an enterprise estimates:

(a)   its share of the present value of the estimated future cash flows expected to be generated by the investee as a whole, including the cash flows from the operations of the investee and the proceeds on the ultimate disposal of the investment; or

(b)   the present value of the estimated future cash flows expected to arise from dividends to be received from the investment and from its ultimate disposal.

Under appropriate assumptions, both methods give the same result. Any resulting impairment loss for the investment is allocated in accordance with IAS 36. Therefore, it is allocated first to any remaining goodwill. *(28.23)*

The recoverable amount of an investment in an associate is assessed for each individual associate, unless an individual associate does not generate cash inflows from continuing use that are largely independent of those from other assets of the reporting enterprise. *(28.24)*

Contingent Liabilities

In accordance with IAS 37, *Provisions, Contingent Liabilities and Contingent Assets* the investor discloses:

(a)   its share of the contingent liabilities and capital commitments of an associate for which it is also contingently liable; and

(b)   those contingent liabilities that arise because the investor is severally liable for all the liabilities of the associate. *(28.26)*

Disclosure

In addition to the disclosure required by specific paragraphs of IAS 28, the following disclosures should be made:

(a)   an appropriate listing and description of significant associates including the proportion of ownership interest and, if different, the proportion of voting power held; and

(b)   the methods used to account for such investments. *(28.27)*

Investments in associates accounted for using the equity method should be classified as long-term assets and disclosed as a separate item in the balance sheet. The investor's share of the profits or losses of such investments should be disclosed as a separate item in the income statement. The investor's share of any extraordinary or prior period items should also be separately disclosed. *(28.28)*

7.4	**Financial Reporting of Interests in Joint Ventures**

IAS 31 should be applied in accounting for interests in joint ventures and the reporting of joint venture assets, liabilities, income and expenses in the financial statements of venturers and investors, regardless of the structures or forms under which the joint venture activities take place. *(31.1)*

IAS 31 does not apply to financial reporting by joint ventures.

IAS 31 uses the following terms:

- A *joint venture* is a contractual arrangement whereby two or more parties undertake an economic activity which is subject to joint control.
- *Control* is the power to govern the financial and operating policies of an economic activity so as to obtain benefits from it.
- *Joint control* is the contractually agreed sharing of control over an economic activity.
- *Significant influence* is the power to participate in the financial and operating policy decisions of an economic activity but is not control or joint control over those policies.
- A *venturer* is a party to a joint venture and has joint control over that joint venture.
- An *investor* in a joint venture is a party to a joint venture and does not have joint control over that joint venture.
- *Proportionate consolidation* is a method of accounting and reporting whereby a venturer's share of each of the assets, liabilities, income and expenses of a jointly-controlled entity is combined on a line-by-line basis with similar items in the venturer's financial statements or reported as separate line items in the venturer's financial statements.
- *The equity method* is a method of accounting and reporting whereby an interest in a jointly-controlled entity is initially recorded at cost and adjusted thereafter for the post-acquisition change in the venturer's share of net assets of the jointly-controlled entity. The income statement reflects the venturer's share of the results of operations of the jointly-controlled entity. *(31.2)*

Forms of Joint Venture

Joint ventures take many different forms and structures. IAS 31 identifies three broad types – jointly-controlled operations, jointly-controlled assets and jointly-controlled entities – which are commonly described as, and meet the definition of, joint ventures. The following characteristics are common to all joint ventures:

(a)   two or more venturers are bound by a contractual arrangement; and

(b)   the contractual arrangement establishes joint control. *(31.3)*

Contractual Arrangement

The existence of a contractual arrangement distinguishes interests which involve joint control from investments in associates in which the investor has significant influence (see IAS 28, *Accounting for Investments in Associates*, under section 7.3, p. 407). Activities which have no contractual arrangement to establish joint control are not joint ventures for the purposes of IAS 31. *(31.4)*

The contractual arrangement may be evidenced in a number of ways, for example, by a contract between the venturers or minutes of discussions between the venturers. In some cases, the arrangement is incorporated in the articles or other by-laws of the joint venture. Whatever its form, the contractual arrangement is usually in writing and deals with such matters as:

(a)   the activity, duration and reporting obligations of the joint venture;

(b)   the appointment of the board of directors or equivalent governing body of the joint venture and the voting rights of the venturers;

(c)   capital contributions by the venturers; and

(d)   the sharing by the venturers of the output, income, expenses or results of the joint venture. *(31.5)*

Jointly-Controlled Operations

The operation of some joint ventures involves the use of the assets and other resources of the venturers rather than the establishment of a corporation, partnership or other entity, or a financial structure that is separate from the venturers themselves. Each venturer uses its own property, plant and equipment and carries its own inventories. It also incurs its own expenses and liabilities and raises its own finance, which represent its own obligations. The joint venture activities may be carried out by the venturer's employees alongside the venturer's similar activities. The joint venture agreement usually provides a means by which the revenue from the sale of the joint product and any expenses incurred in common are shared among the venturers. *(31.8)*

In respect of its interests in jointly-controlled operations, a venturer should recognise in its separate financial statements and consequently in its consolidated financial statements:

(a)   the assets that it controls and the liabilities that it incurs; and

(b)   the expenses that it incurs and its share of the income that it earns from the sale of goods or services by the joint venture. *(31.10)*

Jointly-Controlled Assets

Some joint ventures involve the joint control, and often the joint ownership, by the venturers of one or more assets contributed to, or acquired for the purpose of, the joint venture and dedicated to the purposes of the joint venture. The assets are used to obtain benefits for the venturers. Each venturer may take a share of the output from the assets and each bears an agreed share of the expenses incurred. *(31.13)*

These joint ventures do not involve the establishment of a corporation, partnership or other entity, or a financial structure that is separate from the venturers themselves. Each venturer has control over its share of future economic benefits through its share in the jointly-controlled asset. *(31.14)*

In respect of its interest in jointly-controlled assets, a venturer should recognise in its separate financial statements and consequently in its consolidated financial statements:

(a)   its share of the jointly-controlled assets, classified according to the nature of the assets;

(b)   any liabilities which it has incurred;

(c)   its share of any liabilities incurred jointly with the other venturers in relation to the joint venture;

(d)   any income from the sale or use of its share of the output of the joint venture, together with its share of any expenses incurred by the joint venture; and

(e)   any expenses which it has incurred in respect of its interest in the joint venture. *(31.16)*

Jointly-Controlled Entities

A jointly-controlled entity is a joint venture which involves the establishment of a corporation, partnership or other entity in which each venturer has an interest. The entity operates in the same way as other enterprises, except that a contractual arrangement between the venturers establishes joint control over the economic activity of the entity. *(31.19)*

A jointly-controlled entity controls the assets of the joint venture, incurs liabilities and expenses and earns income. It may enter into contracts in its own name and raise finance for the purposes of the joint venture activity. Each venturer is entitled to a share of the results of the jointly-controlled entity, although some jointly-controlled entities also involve a sharing of the output of the joint venture. *(31.20)*

A jointly-controlled entity maintains its own accounting records and prepares and presents financial statements in the same way as other enterprises in conformity with the appropriate national requirements and International Accounting Standards. *(31.23)*

Each venturer usually contributes cash or other resources to the jointly-controlled entity. These contributions are included in the accounting records of the venturer and recognised in its separate financial statements as an investment in the jointly-controlled entity. *(31.24)*

Consolidated Financial Statements of a Venturer

Benchmark Treatment - Proportionate Consolidation

In its consolidated financial statements, a venturer should report its interest in a jointly-controlled entity using one of the two reporting formats for proportionate consolidation. *(31.25)*

A venturer should discontinue the use of proportionate consolidation from the date on which it ceases to have joint control over a jointly-controlled entity. *(31.30)*

Allowed Alternative Treatment - Equity Method

In its consolidated financial statements, a venturer should report its interest in a jointly-controlled entity using the equity method. *(31.32)*

A venturer should discontinue the use of the equity method from the date on which it ceases to have joint control over, or have significant influence in, a jointly-controlled entity. *(31.34)*

Exceptions to Benchmark and Allowed Alternative Treatments

A venturer should account for the following interests as if they are investments either at cost or in accordance with IAS 39 (*see* p. 349)*:*

(a)   an interest in a jointly-controlled entity which is acquired and held exclusively with a view to its subsequent disposal in the near future; and

(b)   an interest in a jointly-controlled entity which operates under severe long-term restrictions that significantly impair its ability to transfer funds to the venturer. *(31.35)*

From the date on which a jointly-controlled entity becomes a subsidiary of a venturer, the venturer accounts for its interest in accordance with IAS 27 (see section 7.2, p. 402). *(31.37)*

Transactions between a Venturer and a Joint Venture

When a venturer contributes or sells assets to a joint venture, recognition of any portion of a gain or loss from the transaction should reflect the substance of the transaction. While the assets are retained by the joint venture, and provided the venturer has transferred the significant risks and rewards of ownership, the venturer should recognise only that portion of the gain or loss which is attributable to the interests of the other venturers. The venturer should recognise the full amount of any loss when the contribution or sale provides evidence of a reduction in the net realisable value of current assets or an impairment loss. *(31.39)*

Non-Monetary Contributions to a Jointly-Controlled Entity

There is no explicit guidance in IAS 31 on the recognition of gains and losses resulting from contributions of non-monetary assets to jointly-controlled entities. Such contributions may take various forms: they may be made simultaneously by the venturers either upon establishing the jointly-controlled entity or subsequently. The consideration received by the venturer(s) in exchange for assets contributed to the jointly-controlled entity may also include cash or other consideration that does not depend on future cash flows of the jointly-controlled entity ("additional consideration").

SIC-13, *Jointly-Controlled Entities – Non-Monetary Contributions by Venturers*, states that, in applying IAS 31 to non-monetary contributions to a jointly-controlled entity in exchange for an equity interest in the jointly-controlled entity, a venturer should recognise in the income statement for the period the portion of a gain or loss attributable to the equity interests of the other venturers except when:

• the significant risks and rewards of ownership of the contributed non-monetary asset(s) have not been transferred to the jointly-controlled entity;

• the gain or loss on the non-monetary contribution cannot be measured reliably; or

• the non-monetary assets contributed are similar to those contributed by the other venturers. Non-monetary assets are similar to those contributed by other venturers when they have a similar nature, a similar use in the same line of business and a similar fair value. A contribution meets the similarity test only if all of the significant component assets thereof are similar to those contributed by the other venturers.

Where any of the above exceptions applies, the gain or loss would be considered unrealised and would therefore not be recognised in the income statement unless the following paragraph also applies.

If, in addition to receiving an equity interest in the jointly-controlled entity, a venturer receives monetary or non-monetary assets dissimilar to those it contributed, an appropriate portion of gain or loss on the transaction should be recognised by the venturer in the income statement.

Unrealised gains or losses on non-monetary assets contributed to jointly-controlled entities should be eliminated against the underlying assets under the proportionate consolidation method or against the investment under the equity method. Such unrealised gains or losses should not be presented as deferred gains or losses in the venturer's consolidated balance sheet. *(SIC-13)*

Other Transactions Between a Venturer and a Joint Venture

When a venturer purchases assets from a joint venture, the venturer should not recognise its share of the profits of the joint venture from the transaction until it resells the assets to an independent party. A venturer should recognise its share of the losses resulting from these transactions in the same way as profits except that losses should be recognised immediately when they represent a reduction in the net realisable value of current assets or an impairment loss. *(31.40)*

To assess whether a transaction between a venturer and a joint venture provides evidence of impairment of an asset, the venturer determines the recoverable amount of the asset under IAS 36, *Impairment of Assets*. In determining value in use, future cash flows from the asset are estimated based on continuing use of the asset and its ultimate disposal by the joint venture. *(31.41)*

Reporting Interests in Joint Ventures in the Financial Statements of an Investor

An investor in a joint venture, which does not have joint control, should report its interest in a joint venture in its consolidated financial statements in accordance with IAS 39, *Financial Instruments: Recognition and Measurement*, or, if it has significant influence in the joint venture, in accordance with IAS 28, *Accounting for Investments in Associates*. In the separate financial statements of an investor that issues consolidated financial statements, it may also report the investment at cost. *(31.42)*

Operators of Joint Ventures

Operators or managers of a joint venture should account for any fees in accordance with IAS 18, *Revenue* (see section 5.1, p. 321). *(31.43)*

Disclosure

In accordance with IAS 10, *Contingencies and Events Occurring After the Balance Sheet Date* (see section 2.5.3, p. 142), a venturer should disclose the aggregate amount of the following contingencies, unless the probability of loss is remote, separately from the amount of other contingencies:

(a) any contingencies that the venturer has incurred in relation to its interests in joint ventures and its share in each of the contingencies which have been incurred jointly with other venturers;

(b) its share of the contingencies of the joint ventures themselves for which it is contingently liable; and

(c) those contingencies that arise because the venturer is contingently liable for the liabilities of the other venturers of a joint venture. *(31.45)*

A venturer should disclose the aggregate amount of the following commitments in respect of its interests in joint ventures separately from other commitments:

(a) any capital commitments of the venturer in relation to its interests in joint ventures and its share in the capital commitments that have been incurred jointly with other venturers; and

(b) its share of the capital commitments of the joint ventures themselves. *(31.46)*

A venturer should disclose a listing and description of interests in significant joint ventures and the proportion of ownership interest held in jointly-controlled entities. A venturer which reports its interests in jointly-controlled entities using the line-by-line reporting format for proportionate consolidation or the equity method should disclose the aggregate amounts of each of current assets, long-term assets, current liabilities, long-term liabilities, income and expenses related to its interests in joint ventures. *(31.47)*

A venturer which does not issue consolidated financial statements, because it does not have subsidiaries, should disclose additional information specified in the Standard. *(31.48)*

Paragraphs 31.39, 31.40 and 31.41 become operative when IAS 36 (see section 3.5, p. 214) becomes operative – i.e. for annual financial statements covering periods beginning on or after 1 July 1999, unless IAS 36 is applied for earlier periods. *(31.51)*

Glossary

accounting policies
The specific principles, bases, conventions, rules and practices adopted by an enterprise in preparing and presenting financial statements.

accounting profit
The net profit or loss for a period before deducting tax expense.

accrual basis of accounting
The effects of transactions and other events are recognised when they occur (and not as cash or its equivalent is received or paid) and they are recorded in the accounting records and reported in the financial statements of the periods to which they relate.

accumulating compensated absences
Compensated absences that are carried forward and can be used in future periods if the current period's entitlement is not used in full.

acquisition
A business combination in which one of the enterprises, the acquirer, obtains control over the net assets and operations of another enterprise, the acquiree, in exchange for the transfer of assets, incurrence of a liability or issue of equity.

active market
A market where all the following conditions exist:
  (a) the items traded within the market are homogeneous;
  (b) willing buyers and sellers can normally be found at any time; and
  (c) prices are available to the public.

actuarial assumptions
An enterprise's unbiased and mutually compatible best estimates of the demographic and financial variables that will determine the ultimate cost of providing post-employment benefits.

actuarial gains and losses
Actuarial gains and losses comprise:
  (a) experience adjustments (the effects of differences between the previous actuarial assumptions and what has actually occurred); and
  (b) the effects of changes in actuarial assumptions.

actuarial present value of promised retirement benefits
The present value of the expected payments by a retirement benefit plan to existing and past employees, attributable to the service already rendered.

adjusting event after the balance sheet date
see events after the balance sheet date.

amortisation
The systematic allocation of the depreciable amount of an asset over its useful life. In the case of an intangible asset or goodwill, the term 'amortisation' is generally used instead of 'depreciation'. Both terms have the same meaning.

amortised cost of a financial asset or financial liability
The amount at which the financial asset or liability was measured at initial recognition minus principal repayments, plus or minus the cumulative amortisation of any difference between that initial amount and the maturity amount, and minus any write-down (directly or through the use of an allowance account) for impairment or uncollectibility.

asset
A resource controlled by an enterprise as a result of past events and from which future economic benefits are expected to flow to the enterprise.

associate
An enterprise in which an investor has significant influence and which is neither a subsidiary nor a joint venture of the investor.

available-for-sale financial assets
Those financial assets that are not (a) loans and receivables originated by the enterprise, (b) held-to-maturity investments, or (c) financial assets held for trading.

bank
A financial institution one of whose principal activities is to take deposits and borrow with the objective of lending and investing and which is within the scope of banking or similar legislation.

basic earnings per share
The amount of net profit for the period that is attributable to ordinary shareholders divided by the weighted average number of ordinary shares outstanding during the period.

borrowing costs
Interest and other costs incurred by an enterprise in connection with the borrowing of funds.

business combination

The bringing together of separate enterprises into one economic entity as a result of one enterprise uniting with or obtaining control over the net assets and operations of another enterprise.

business segment

A distinguishable component of an enterprise that is engaged in providing an individual product or service or a group of related products or services and that is subject to risks and returns that are different from those of other business segments.

capital

Under a financial concept of capital, such as invested money or invested purchasing power, the net assets or equity of the enterprise. The financial concept of capital is adopted by most enterprises.

Under a physical concept of capital, such as operating capability, the productive capacity of the enterprise is based on, for example, units of output per day.

capitalisation

Recognising a cost as part of the cost of an asset.

carrying amount

The amount at which an asset is recognised in the balance sheet after deducting any accumulated depreciation (amortisation) and accumulated impairment losses thereon.

cash

Cash on hand and demand deposits.

cash equivalents

Short-term, highly liquid investments that are readily convertible to known amounts of cash and which are subject to an insignificant risk of changes in value.

cash flow risk

The risk that future cash flows associated with a monetary financial instrument will fluctuate in amount.

cash flows

Inflows and outflows of cash and cash equivalents.

cash generating unit

The smallest identifiable group of assets that generates cash inflows from continuing use that is largely independent of the cash inflows from other assets or groups of assets.

class of assets
Grouping of assets of a similar nature and use in an enterprise's operations.

closing rate
The spot exchange rate of two currencies at the balance sheet date.

compound instrument
A financial instrument that, from the issuer's perspective, contains both a liability and an equity element.

consolidated financial statements
The financial statements of a group presented as those of a single enterprise.

construction contract
A contract specifically negotiated for the construction of an asset or a combination of assets that are closely interrelated or interdependent in terms of their design, technology and function or their ultimate purpose or use.

constructive obligation
An obligation that derives from an enterprise's actions where:
(a) by an established pattern of past practice, published policies or a sufficiently specific current statement, the enterprise has indicated to other parties that it will accept certain responsibilities; and
(b) as a result, the enterprise has created a valid expectation on the part of those other parties that it will discharge those responsibilities.

contingent asset
A possible asset that arises from past events and whose existence will be confirmed only by the occurrence or non-occurrence of one or more uncertain future events not wholly within the control of the enterprise.

contingent liability
(a) A possible obligation that arises from past events and whose existence will be confirmed only by the occurrence or non-occurrence of one or more uncertain future events not wholly within the control of the enterprise; or
(b) a present obligation that arises from past events but is not recognised because:
  (i)   it is not probable that an outflow of resources embodying economic benefits will be required to settle the obligation; or
  (ii) the amount of the obligation cannot be measured with sufficient reliability.

contingent rent
That portion of the lease payments that is not fixed in amount but is based on a factor other than just the passage of time (e.g. percentage of sales, amount of usage, price indices, market rates of interest).

contract
An agreement between two or more parties that has clear economic consequences that the parties have little, if any, discretion to avoid, usually because the agreement is enforceable at law. Contracts may take a variety of forms and need not be in writing.

control (of an asset)
The power to obtain the future economic benefits that flow from the asset.

control (of an enterprise)
The power to govern the financial and operating policies of an enterprise so as to obtain benefits from its activities.

corporate assets
Assets other than goodwill that contribute to the future cash flows of both the cash-generating unit under review and other cash-generating units.

corridor
A range around an enterprise's best estimate of post-employment benefit obligations. Outside that range, it is not reasonable to assume that actuarial gains or losses will be offset in future years.

cost
The amount of cash or cash equivalents paid or the fair value of the other consideration given to acquire an asset at the time of its acquisition or construction.

cost method
A method of accounting for investments whereby the investment is recorded at cost. The income statement reflects income from the investment only to the extent that the investor receives distributions from accumulated net profits of the investee arising subsequent to the date of acquisition.

cost of an acquisition
The amount of cash or cash equivalents paid or the fair value, at the date of exchange, of the other purchase consideration given by the acquirer in exchange for control over the net assets of the other enterprise, plus any costs directly attributable to the acquisition.

cost of an asset acquired in exchange or part exchange for dissimilar asset
The fair value of the asset received, which is equivalent to the fair value of the consideration given adjusted by the amount of any cash or cash equivalents received or paid.

cost of an asset acquired in exchange or part exchange for similar asset
The carrying amount of the asset given up. However, the fair value of the asset received may provide evidence of an impairment in the asset given up. Under these circumstances the asset given up is written down and this written down value assigned to the new asset.

cost of an investment

The cost includes acquisition charges such as brokerages, fees, duties and bank fees.

If an investment is acquired, or partly acquired, by the issue of shares or other securities, the acquisition cost is the fair value of the securities issued and not their nominal or par value.

cost of conversion

Costs directly related to the units of production, such as direct labour together with a systematic allocation of fixed and variable production overheads that are incurred in converting materials into finished goods.

cost of inventories

All costs of purchase, costs of conversion and other costs incurred in bringing the inventories to their present location and condition.

cost of purchase

All of the purchase price, import duties and other taxes (other than those subsequently recoverable by the enterprise from the taxing authorities), and transport, handling and other costs directly attributable to the acquisition of the item. Trade discounts, rebates and other similar items are deducted in determining the costs of purchase.

cost plus contract

A construction contract in which the contractor is reimbursed for allowable or otherwise defined costs, plus a percentage of these costs or a fixed fee.

cost plus method

A pricing method which seeks to add an appropriate mark-up to the supplier's cost.

costs of disposal

Incremental costs directly attributable to the disposal of an asset, excluding finance costs and income tax expense.

credit risk

The risk that one party to a financial instrument will fail to discharge an obligation and cause the other party to incur a financial loss.

currency risk

A price risk – The risk that the value of a financial instrument will fluctuate due to changes in foreign exchange rates.

current asset

An asset that:

(a) is expected to be realised in, or is held for sale or consumption in, the normal course of the enterprise's operating cycle; or

(b) is held primarily for trading purposes or for the short-term and expected to be realised within twelve months of the balance sheet date; or

(c) is cash or a cash equivalent asset which is not restricted in its use.

current cost

The amount of cash or cash equivalents that would have to be paid if the same or an equivalent asset was acquired currently.

The undiscounted amount of cash or cash equivalents that would be required to settle an obligation currently.

current cost approach

In general, methods which use replacement cost as the primary measurement basis. If, however, replacement cost is higher than both net realisable value and present value, the higher of net realisable value and present value is usually used as the measurement basis.

current investment

An investment that is by its nature readily realisable and is intended to be held for not more than one year.

current liabilities

A liability that:

(a) is expected to be settled in the normal course of the enterprise's operating cycle; or

(b) is due to be settled within twelve months of the balance sheet date.

current service cost

The increase in the present value of the defined benefit obligation resulting from employee service in the current period.

current tax

The amount of income taxes payable (recoverable) in respect of the taxable profit (tax loss) for a period.

curtailment

A curtailment occurs when an enterprise either:

(a) is demonstrably committed to make a material reduction in the number of employees covered by a plan; or

(b) amends the terms of a defined benefit plan such that a material element of future service by current employees will no longer qualify for benefits, or will qualify only for reduced benefits.

date of acquisition

The date on which control of the net assets and operations of the acquirer is effectively transferred to the acquirer.

dealing securities
Marketable securities that are acquired and held with the intention of reselling them in the short term.

deductible temporary difference
A temporary difference that will result in amounts that are deductible in determining taxable profit (tax loss) of future periods when the carrying amount of the asset or liability is recovered or settled.

deferred tax assets
The amounts of income taxes recoverable in future periods in respect of:
 (a) deductible temporary differences;
 (b) the carryforward of unused tax losses; and
 (c) the carryforward of unused tax credits.

deferred tax liabilities
The amounts of income taxes payable in future periods in respect of taxable temporary differences.

defined benefit liability
The net total of the following amounts:
 (a) the present value of the defined benefit obligation at the balance sheet date;
 (b) plus any actuarial gains (less any actuarial losses) not recognised;
 (c) minus any past service cost not yet recognised;
 (d) minus the fair value at the balance sheet date of plan assets (if any) out of which the obligations are to be settled directly.

defined benefit obligation (present value of)
The present value, without deducting any plan assets, of expected future payments required to settle the obligation resulting from employee service in the current and prior periods.

defined benefit plans
Post-employment benefit plans other than defined contribution plans.

defined contribution plans
Post-employment benefit plans under which an enterprise pays fixed contributions into a separate entity (a fund) and will have no legal or constructive obligation to pay further contributions if the fund does not hold sufficient assets to pay all employee benefits relating to employee service in the current and prior periods.

demonstrably committed
An enterprise is demonstrably committed to pay termination benefits when, and only when, an enterprise has a detailed formal plan for the termination and is without realistic possibility of withdrawal. The detailed plan should include, as a minimum:
 (a) the location, function, and approximate number of employees whose services are to be terminated;

(b) the termination benefits for each job classification or function; and

(c) the time at which the plan will be implemented. Implementation should begin as soon as possible and the period of time to complete implementation should be such that material changes to the plan are not likely.

depreciable amount
The cost of an asset, or other amount substituted for cost in the financial statements, less its residual value.

depreciable assets
Assets which:

(a) are expected to be used during more than one accounting period;

(b) have a limited useful life; and

(c) are held by an enterprise for use in the production or supply of goods and services, for rental to others, or for administrative purposes.

depreciation
The systematic allocation of the depreciable amount of an asset over its useful life.

derecognise (a financial instrument)
Remove a financial asset or liability, or a portion of a financial asset or liability, from an enterprise's balance sheet.

derivative
A financial instrument:

(a) whose value changes in response to the change in a specified interest rate, security price, commodity price, foreign exchange rate, index of prices or rates, a credit rating or credit index, or similar variable (sometimes called the 'underlying');

(b) that requires no initial net investment or little initial net investment relative to other types of contracts that have a similar response to changes in market conditions; and

(c) that is settled at a future date.

derivative financial instruments
Financial instruments, such as financial options, futures and forwards, interest rate swaps and currency swaps, which create rights and obligations that have the effect of transferring between the parties to the instrument one or more of the financial risks inherent in an underlying primary financial instrument. Derivative instruments do not result in a transfer of the underlying primary financial instrument on inception of the contract and such a transfer does not necessarily take place on maturity of the contract.

development
The application of research findings or other knowledge to a plan or design for the production of new or substantially improved materials, devices, products, processes, systems or services prior to the commencement of commercial production or use.

diluted earnings per share

The amount of net profit for the period that is attributable to ordinary shareholders divided by the weighted average number of ordinary shares outstanding during the period, both adjusted for the effects of all dilutive potential ordinary shares.

dilutive potential ordinary shares

Potential ordinary shares whose conversion to ordinary shares would decrease net profit per share from continuing ordinary operations or increase loss per share from continuing ordinary operations.

direct method of reporting cash flows from operating activities

A method which discloses major classes of gross cash receipts and gross cash payments.

discontinuing operation

A component of an enterprise:

   (a) that the enterprise, pursuant to a single plan, is:

      (i)   disposing of substantially in its entirety, such as by selling the component in a single transaction, by demerger or spin-off of ownership of the component to the enterprise's shareholders;

      (ii) disposing of piecemeal, such as by selling off the component's assets and settling its liabilities individually; or

      (iii) terminating through abandonment;

   (b) that represents a separate major line of business or geographical area of operations; and

   (c) that can be distinguished operationally and for financial reporting purposes.

dividends

Distributions of profits to holders of equity investments in proportion to their holdings of a particular class of capital.

downstream transactions

For example, sales of assets from an investor (or its consolidated subsidiaries) to an associate.

economic life

The period over which an asset is expected to be economically usable by one or more users or the number of production or similar units expected to be obtained from the asset by one or more users.

effective interest method

A method of calculating amortisation using the effective interest rate of a financial asset or financial liability. The effective interest rate is the rate that exactly discounts the expected stream of future cash payments through maturity or the next market-based repricing date to the current net carrying amount of the financial asset or financial liability. That computation should include all fees and points paid or received between parties to the contract. The effective interest rate is sometimes termed the level yield to maturity or to the next repricing date, and is the internal rate of return of the financial asset or financial liability for that period.

embedded derivative

A derivative that is a component of a hybrid (combined) financial instrument that includes both the derivative and a host contract – with the effect that some of the cash flows of the combined instrument vary in a similar way to a stand-alone derivative.

employee benefits

All forms of consideration given by an enterprise in exchange for service rendered by employees.

equity

The residual interest in the assets of the enterprise after deducting all its liabilities.

equity compensation benefits

Employee benefits under which either:

   (a) employees are entitled to receive equity financial instruments issued by the enterprise (or its parent); or

   (b) the amount of the enterprise's obligation to employees depends on the future price of equity financial instruments issued by the enterprise.

equity compensation plans

Formal or informal arrangements under which an enterprise provides equity compensation benefits for one or more employees.

equity instrument

Any contract that evidences a residual interest in the assets of an enterprise after deducting all of its liabilities.

equity method

A method of accounting whereby the investment (an interest in a jointly-controlled entity) is initially recorded at cost and adjusted thereafter for the post-acquisition change in the investor's (the venturer's) share of net assets of the investee (the jointly-controlled entity). The income statement reflects the investor's (the venturer's) share of the results of operations of the investee (the jointly-controlled entity).

events after the balance sheet date

Events after the balance sheet date are those events, both favourable and unfavourable, that occur between the balance sheet date and the date when the financial statements are authorised for issue. Two types of events can be identified:

   (a) those that provide evidence of conditions that existed at the balance sheet date (adjusting events after the balance sheet date); and

(b) those that are indicative of conditions that arose after the balance sheet date (non-adjusting events after the balance sheet date).

exchange difference
The difference resulting from reporting the same number of units of a foreign currency in the reporting currency at different exchange rates.

exchange rate
The ratio for exchange of two currencies.

expenses
Decreases in economic benefits during the accounting period in the form of outflows or depletions of assets or incurrences of liabilities that result in decreases in equity, other than those relating to distributions to equity participants.

experience adjustments
The effect of differences between previous actuarial assumptions and what has actually occurred.

extraordinary items
Income or expenses that arise from events or transactions that are clearly distinct from the ordinary activities of the enterprise and therefore are not expected to recur frequently or regularly.

fair value
The amount for which an asset could be exchanged, or a liability settled, between knowledgeable, willing parties in an arm's length transaction.

FIFO (first-in, first-out)
The assumption that the items of inventory which were purchased first are sold first, and consequently the items remaining in inventory at the end of the period are those most recently purchased or produced.

finance lease
A lease that transfers substantially all the risks and rewards incident to ownership of an asset. Title may or may not eventually be transferred.

financial asset
Any asset that is:
(a) cash;
(b) a contractual right to receive cash or another financial asset from another enterprise;
(c) a contractual right to exchange financial instruments with another enterprise under conditions that are potentially favourable; or
(d) an equity instrument of another enterprise.

financial asset or liability held for trading

A financial asset or liability that was acquired or incurred principally for the purpose of generating a profit from short-term fluctuations in price or dealer's margin. A financial asset should be classified as held for trading if, regardless of why it was acquired, it is part of a portfolio for which there is evidence of a recent actual pattern of short-term profit-taking. Derivative financial assets and derivative financial liabilities are always deemed held for trading unless they are designated and effective hedging instruments.

financial instrument

Any contract that gives rise to both a financial asset of one enterprise and a financial liability or equity instrument of another enterprise.

financial liability

Any liability that is a contractual obligation:

(a) to deliver cash or another financial asset to another enterprise; or

(b) to exchange financial instruments with another enterprise under conditions that are potentially unfavourable.

financial position

The relationship of the assets, liabilities, and equities of an enterprise, as reported in the balance sheet.

financial statements

A complete set of financial statements includes the following components:

(a) balance sheet;

(b) income statement;

(c) a statement showing either:

(i)   all changes in equity; or

(ii)   changes in equity other than those arising from capital transactions with owners and distributions to owners;

(d) cash flow statement; and

(e) accounting policies and explanatory notes.

financing activities

Activities that result in changes in the size and composition of the equity capital and borrowings of the enterprise.

firm commitment

A binding agreement for the exchange of a specified quantity of resources at a specified price on a specified future date or dates.

fixed price contract

A contract in which the contractor agrees to a fixed contract price, or a fixed rate per unit of output, which in some cases is subject to cost escalation clauses.

fixed production overheads
Those indirect costs of production that remain relatively constant regardless of the volume of production, such as depreciation and maintenance of factory buildings and equipment, and the cost of factory management and administration.

foreign currency
A currency other than the reporting currency of an enterprise.

foreign currency transaction
A transaction which is denominated in or requires settlement in a foreign currency.

foreign entity
A foreign operation, the activities of which are not an integral part of those of the reporting enterprise.

foreign operation
A subsidiary, associate, joint venture or branch of the reporting enterprise, the activities of which are based or conducted in a country other than the country of the reporting enterprise.

forgivable loans
Loans which the lender undertakes to waive repayment of under certain prescribed conditions.

fundamental errors
Errors discovered in the current period that are of such significance that the financial statements of one or more prior periods can no longer be considered to have been reliable at the date of their issue.

funding
Contributions by an enterprise, and sometimes its employees, into an entity, or fund, that is legally separate from the reporting enterprise and from which the employee benefits are paid.

future economic benefit
The potential to contribute, directly or indirectly, to the flow of cash and cash equivalents to the enterprise. The potential may be a productive one that is part of the operating activities of the enterprise. It may also take the form of convertibility into cash or cash equivalents or a capability to reduce cash outflows, such as when an alternative manufacturing process lowers the costs of production.

gains
Increases in economic benefits and as such are no different in nature from revenue.

general purchasing power approach
The restatement of some or all of the items in the financial statements for changes in the general price level.

geographical segments
A distinguishable component of an enterprise that is engaged in providing products or services within a particular economic environment and that is subject to risks and returns that are different from those of components operating in other economic environments.

going concern
The enterprise is normally viewed as a going concern, that is, as continuing in operation for the foreseeable future. It is assumed that the enterprise has neither the intention nor the necessity of liquidation or of curtailing materially the scale of its operations.

goodwill
Any excess of the cost of the acquisition over the acquirer's interest in the fair value of the identifiable assets and liabilities acquired as at the date of the exchange transaction.

government
Government, government agencies and similar bodies whether local, national or international.

government assistance
Action by government designed to provide an economic benefit specific to an enterprise or range of enterprises qualifying under certain criteria.

government grants
Assistance by government in the form of transfers of resources to an enterprise in return for past or future compliance with certain conditions relating to the operating activities of the enterprise. They exclude those forms of government assistance which cannot reasonably have a value placed upon them and transactions with government which cannot be distinguished from the normal trading transactions of the enterprise.

grants related to assets
Government grants whose primary condition is that an enterprise qualifying for them should purchase, construct or otherwise acquire long-term assets. Subsidiary conditions may also be attached restricting the type or location of the assets or the periods during which they are to be acquired or held.

grants related to income
Government grants other than those related to assets.

gross investment in the lease
The aggregate of the minimum lease payments under a finance lease from the standpoint of the lessor and any unguaranteed residual value accruing to the lessor.

group
A parent and all its subsidiaries.

group administration (employee benefit) plans
An aggregation of single employer plans combined to allow participating employers to pool their assets for investment purposes and reduce investment management and administration costs, but the claims of different employers are segregated for the sole benefit of their own employees.

guaranteed residual value
In the case of the lessee, that part of the residual value which is guaranteed by the lessee or by a party related to the lessee (the amount of the guarantee being the maximum amount that could, in any event, become payable); and in the case of the lessor, that part of the residual value which is guaranteed by the lessee or by a third party unrelated to the lessor who is financially capable of discharging the obligations under the guarantee.

hedge effectiveness
The degree to which offsetting changes in fair value or cash flows attributable to a hedged risk are achieved by the hedging instrument.

hedged item
An asset, liability, firm commitment, or forecasted future transaction that (a) exposes the enterprise to risk of changes in fair value or changes in future cash flows and that (b) for hedge accounting purposes, is designated as being hedged.

hedging
Designating one or more hedging instruments so that their change in fair value is an offset, in whole or in part, to the change in fair value or cash flows of a hedged item.

hedging instrument
A designated derivative or (in limited circumstances) another financial asset or liability whose fair value or cash flows are expected to offset changes in the fair value or cash flows of a designated hedged item. A non-derivative financial asset or liability may be designated as a hedging instrument for hedge accounting purposes only if it hedges the risk of changes in foreign currency exchange rates.

held-to-maturity investment
Financial assets with fixed or determinable payments and fixed maturity that an enterprise has the positive intent and ability to hold to maturity other than loans and receivables originated by the enterprise.

hire-purchase contract
The definition of a lease includes contracts for the hire of an asset which contain a provision giving the hirer an option to acquire title to the asset upon the fulfilment of agreed conditions. These contracts are sometimes known as hire purchase contracts.

historical cost

Assets are recorded at the amount of cash or cash equivalents paid or the fair value of the consideration given to acquire them at the time of their acquisition. Liabilities are recorded at the amount of proceeds received in exchange for the obligation, or in some circumstances (for example, income taxes), at the amounts of cash or cash equivalents expected to be paid to satisfy the liability in the normal course of business.

hyperinflation

Loss of purchasing power of money at such a rate that comparison of amounts from transactions and other events that have occurred at different times, even within the same accounting period, is misleading.

Hyperinflation is indicated by characteristics of the economic environment of a country which include, but are not limited to, the following:

(a) the general population prefers to keep its wealth in nonmonetary assets or in a relatively stable foreign currency. Amounts of local currency held are immediately invested to maintain purchasing power;

(b) the general population regards monetary amounts not in terms of the local currency but in terms of a relatively stable foreign currency. Prices may be quoted in that currency;

(c) sales and purchases on credit take place at prices that compensate for the expected loss of purchasing power during the credit period, even if the period is short;

(d) interest rates, wages and prices are linked to a price index; and

(e) the cumulative inflation rate over three years is approaching, or exceeds, 100%.

impairment

When recoverable amount declines below carrying amount.

impairment loss

The amount by which the carrying amount of an asset exceeds its recoverable amount.

imputed rate of interest

The more clearly determinable of either:

(a)   the prevailing rate for a similar instrument of an issuer with a similar credit rating; or

(b)   a rate of interest that discounts the nominal amount of the instrument to the current cash sales price of the goods or services.

inception of a lease

The earlier of the date of the lease agreement or of a commitment by the parties to the principal provisions of the lease.

income

Increases in economic benefits during the accounting period in the form of inflows or enhancements of assets or decreases of liabilities that result in increases in equity, other than those relating to contributions from equity participants.

incremental borrowing rate of interest (lessee's)

The rate of interest the lessee would have to pay on a similar lease or, if that is not determinable, the rate that, at the inception of the lease, the lessee would incur to borrow over a similar term, and with a similar security, the funds necessary to purchase the asset.

indirect method of reporting cash flows from operating activities

Under this method, net profit or loss is adjusted for the effects of transactions of a non-cash nature, any deferrals or accruals of past or future operating cash receipts or payments, and items of income or expense associated with investing or financing cash flows.

initial disclosure event (for a discontinuing operation)

The occurrence of one of the following, whichever occurs earlier:

(a)   the enterprise has entered into a binding sale agreement for substantially all of the assets attributable to the discontinuing operation; or

(b)   the enterprise's board of directors or similar governing body has both (i) approved a detailed, formal plan for the discontinuance and (ii) made an announcement of the plan.

intangible asset

An identifiable non-monetary asset without physical substance held for use in the production or supply of goods or services, for rental to others, or for administrative purposes.

interest cost (for an employee benefit plan)

The increase during a period in the present value of a defined benefit obligation which arises because the benefits are one period closer to settlement.

interest rate implicit in a lease

The discount rate that, at the inception of the lease, causes the aggregate present value of:

(a)   the minimum lease payments; and

(b)   the unguaranteed residual value

to be equal to the fair value of the leased asset.

interest rate risk
  A price risk – The risk that the value of a financial instrument will fluctuate due to changes in market interest rates.

interim financial report
  A financial report containing either a complete set of financial statements (as described in IAS 1) or a set of condensed financial statements (as described in IAS 34) for an interim period.

interim period
  A financial reporting period shorter than a full financial year.

inventories
  Assets:

  (a) held for sale in the ordinary course of business;
  (b) in the process of production for such sale; or
  (c) in the form of materials or supplies to be consumed in the production process or in the rendering of services.

  Inventories encompass goods purchased and held for resale including, for example, merchandise purchased by a retailer and held for resale, or land and other property held for resale. Inventories also encompass finished goods produced, or work in progress being produced, by the enterprise and include materials and supplies awaiting use in the production process. In the case of a service provider, inventories include the costs of the service for which the enterprise has not yet recognised the related revenue.

investing activities
  The acquisition and disposal of long-term assets and other investments not included in cash equivalents.

investment
  An asset held by an enterprise for the accretion of wealth through distribution (such as interest, royalties, dividends and rentals), for capital appreciation or for other benefits to the investing enterprise such as those obtained through trading relationships.

investment property
  An investment in land or buildings that are not occupied substantially for use by, or in the operations of, the investing enterprise or another enterprise in the same group as the investing enterprise.

investment securities
  Securities acquired and held for yield or capital growth purposes, usually held to maturity.

investor in a joint venture
  A party to a joint venture that does not have joint control over that joint venture.

joint control

The contractually agreed sharing of control over an economic activity.

joint venture

A contractual arrangement whereby two or more parties undertake an economic activity which is subject to joint control.

jointly-controlled entity

A joint venture which involves the establishment of a corporation, partnership or other entity in which each venturer has an interest. The entity operates in the same way as other enterprises, except that a contractual arrangement between the venturers establishes joint control over the economic activity of the entity.

lease

An agreement whereby the lessor conveys to the lessee in return for a payment or series of payments the right to use an asset for an agreed period of time.

lease term

The non-cancellable period for which the lessee has contracted to lease the asset together with any further terms for which the lessee has the option to continue to lease the asset, with or without further payment, which option at the inception of the lease it is reasonably certain that the lessee will exercise.

legal merger

Usually a merger between two companies in which either:

(a) the assets and liabilities of one company are transferred to the other company and the first company is dissolved; or

(b) the assets and liabilities of both companies are transferred to a new company and both the original companies are dissolved.

legal obligation

An obligation that derives from:

(a) a contract (through its explicit or implicit terms);

(b) legislation; or

(c) other operation of law.

liability

A present obligation of the enterprise arising from past events, the settlement of which is expected to result in an outflow from the enterprise of resources embodying economic benefits.

LIFO (last-in, first-out)
The assumption that the items of inventory which were purchased or produced last are sold first, and consequently the items remaining in inventory at the end of the period are those first purchased or produced.

liquidity
The availability of sufficient funds to meet deposit withdrawals and other financial commitments as they fall due.

liquidity risk
The risk that an enterprise will encounter difficulty in raising funds to meet commitments associated with financial instruments. Liquidity risk may result from an inability to sell a financial asset quickly at close to its fair value.

loans and receivables originated by the enterprise
Financial assets that are created by the enterprise by providing money, goods, or services directly to a debtor other than those that are originated with the intent to be sold immediately or in the short term, which should be classified as held for trading.

long-term investment
An investment other than a current investment.

losses
Decreases in economic benefits and as such they are no different in nature from other expenses.

market risk
A price risk – The risk that the value of a financial instrument will fluctuate as a result of changes in market prices whether those changes are caused by factors specific to the individual security or its issuer, or factors affecting all securities traded in the market.

market value
The amount obtainable from the sale, or payable on the acquisition, of a (financial) instrument in an active market.

marketable
There is an active market from which a market value (or some indicator that enables a market value to be calculated) is available.

master netting arrangement
An arrangement providing for an enterprise that undertakes a number of financial instrument transactions with a single counterparty to make a single net settlement of all financial instruments covered by the agreement in the event of default on, or termination of, any one contract.

matching of costs with revenues

Expenses are recognised in the income statement on the basis of a direct association between the costs incurred and the earning of specific items of income. This process involves the simultaneous or combined recognition of revenues and expenses that result directly and jointly from the same transactions or other events. However, the application of the matching concept does not allow the recognition of items in the balance sheet which do not meet the definition of assets or liabilities.

materiality

Information is material if its non-disclosure could influence the economic decisions of users taken on the basis of the financial statements.

measurement

The process of determining the monetary amounts at which the elements of the financial statements are to be recognised and carried in the balance sheet and income statement.

minimum lease payments

The payments over the lease term that the lessee is or can be required to make (excluding costs for services and taxes to be paid by and be reimbursable to the lessor) together with:

(a) in the case of the lessee, any amounts guaranteed by the lessee or by a party related to the lessee; or

(b) in the case of the lessor, any residual value guaranteed to the lessor by either:

    (i)   the lessee;

    (ii) a party related to the lessee; or

    (iii) an independent third party financially capable of meeting this guarantee.

However, if the lessee has the option to purchase the asset at a price which is expected to be sufficiently lower than the fair value at the date the option becomes exercisable that, at the inception of the lease, it is reasonably certain that the option will be exercised, the minimum lease payments comprise the minimum rentals payable over the lease term and payment required to exercise this purchase option.

minority interest

That part of the net results of operations and of net assets of a subsidiary attributable to interests which are not owned, directly or indirectly through subsidiaries, by the parent.

monetary items (monetary assets; monetary financial assets and financial liabilities; monetary financial instruments)

Money held and assets (financial assets) and liabilities (financial liabilities) to be received or paid in fixed or determinable amounts of money.

multi-employer (benefit) plans

Defined contribution plans (other than state plans) or defined benefit plans (other than state plans) that:

(a) pool the assets contributed by various enterprises that are not under common control; and

(b) use those assets to provide benefits to employees of more than one enterprise, on the basis that contribution and benefit levels are determined without regard to the identity of the enterprise that employs the employees concerned.

negative goodwill
Any (remaining) excess, as at the date of the exchange transaction, of the acquirer's interest in the fair values of the identifiable assets and liabilities acquired over the cost of the acquisition.

net assets available for benefits
The assets of a plan less liabilities other than the actuarial present value of promised retirement benefits.

net investment in a foreign entity
The reporting enterprise's share in the net assets of that entity.

net investment in a lease
The gross investment in the lease less unearned finance income.

net profit or loss
Comprises the following components:
(a) profit or loss from ordinary activities; and
(b) extraordinary items.

net realisable value
The estimated selling price in the ordinary course of business less the estimated costs of completion and the estimated costs necessary to make the sale.

net selling price
The amount obtainable from the sale of an asset in an arm's length transaction between knowledgeable, willing parties, less the costs of disposal.

neutrality
Freedom from bias of the information contained in financial statements.

non-adjusting events after the balance sheet date
see events after the balance sheet date.

non-cancellable lease
A lease that is cancellable only:
(a) upon the occurrence of some remote contingency;
(b) with the permission of the lessor;
(c) if the lessee enters into a new lease for the same or an equivalent asset with the same lessor; or

(d) upon payment by the lessee of an additional amount such that, at inception, continuation of the lease is reasonably certain.

normal capacity of production facilities
The production expected to be achieved on average over a number of periods or seasons under normal circumstances, taking into account the loss of capacity resulting from planned maintenance.

obligating event
An event that creates a legal or constructive obligation that results in an enterprise having no realistic alternative to settling that obligation.

obligation
A duty or responsibility to act or perform in a certain way. Obligations may be legally enforceable as a consequence of a binding contract or statutory requirement. Obligations also arise, however, from normal business practice, custom and a desire to maintain good business relations or act in an equitable manner.

offsetting
See set-off, legal right of

onerous contract
A contract in which the unavoidable costs of meeting the obligations under the contract exceed the economic benefits expected to be received under it.

operating activities
The principal revenue-producing activities of an enterprise and other activities that are not investing or financing activities.

operating cycle
The time between the acquisition of materials entering into a process and its realisation in cash or an instrument that is readily convertible into cash.

operating lease
A lease other than a finance lease.

option
A financial instrument that gives the holder the right to purchase ordinary shares.

ordinary activities
Any activities which are undertaken by an enterprise as part of its business and such related activities in which the enterprise engages in furtherance of, incidental to, or arising from these activities.

ordinary share
An equity instrument that is subordinate to all other classes of equity instruments.

originated loans and receivables
see loans and receivables originated by the enterprise.

other long-term employee benefits
Employee benefits (other than post-employment benefits, termination benefits and equity compensation benefits) which do not fall due wholly within twelve months after the end of the period in which the employees render the related service.

parent
An enterprise that has one or more subsidiaries.

participants
The members of a retirement benefit plan and others who are entitled to benefits under the plan.

past service cost
The increase in the present value of the defined benefit obligation for employee service in prior periods, resulting in the current period from the introduction of, or changes to, post-employment benefits or other long-term employee benefits. Past service cost may be either positive (where benefits are introduced or improved) or negative (where existing benefits are reduced).

percentage of completion method
A method by which contract revenue is matched with the contract costs incurred in reaching the stage of completion, resulting in the reporting of revenue, expenses and profit which can be attributed to the proportion of work completed.

performance
The relationship of the income and expenses of an enterprise, as reported in the income statement.

plan assets (of an employee benefit plan)
Assets (other than non-transferable financial instruments issued by the reporting enterprise) held by an entity (a fund) that satisfies all of the following conditions:

(a) the entity is legally separate from the reporting enterprise;

(b) the assets of the fund are to be used only to settle the employee benefit obligations, are not available to the enterprise's own creditors and cannot be returned to the enterprise (or can be returned to the enterprise only if the remaining assets of the fund are sufficient to meet the plan's obligations); and

(c) to the extent that sufficient assets are in the fund, the enterprise will have no legal or constructive obligation to pay the related employee benefits directly.

post-employment benefit plans
Formal or informal arrangements under which an enterprise provides post-employment benefits for one or more employees.

post-employment benefits

Employee benefits (other than termination benefits and equity compensation benefits) which are payable after the completion of employment.

potential ordinary share

A financial instrument or other contract that may entitle its holder to ordinary shares.

present value

A current estimate of the present discounted value of the future net cash flows in the normal course of business.

present value of a defined benefit obligation

see defined benefit obligation (present value of).

price risk

There are three types of price risk: currency risk, interest rate risk and market risk. The term "price risk" embodies not only the potential for loss but also the potential for gain.

primary financial instruments

Financial instruments such as receivables, payables and equity securities, that are not derivative financial instruments.

profit

The residual amount that remains after expenses (including capital maintenance adjustments, where appropriate) have been deducted from income. Any amount over and above that required to maintain the capital at the beginning of the period is profit.

projected unit credit method

An actuarial valuation method that sees each period of service as giving rise to an additional unit of benefit entitlement and measures each unit separately to build up the final obligation (sometimes known as the accrued benefit method pro-rated on service or as the benefit/years of service method).

property, plant and equipment

Tangible assets that:

(a) are held by an enterprise for use in the production or supply of goods or services, for rental to others, or for administrative purposes; and

(b) are expected to be used during more than one period.

proportionate consolidation

A method of accounting and reporting whereby a venturer's share of each of the assets, liabilities, income and expenses of a jointly-controlled entity is combined on a line-by-line basis with similar items in the venturer's financial statements or reported as separate line items in the venturer's financial statements.

prospective application
Application of a new accounting policy to the events and transactions occurring after the date of the change.

provision
A liability of uncertain timing or amount.

prudence
The inclusion of a degree of caution in the exercise of the judgements needed in making the estimates required under conditions of uncertainty, such that assets or income are not overstated and liabilities or expenses are not understated.

realisable value
The amount of cash or cash equivalents that could currently be obtained by selling an asset in an orderly disposal.

recognition
The process of incorporating in the balance sheet or income statement an item that meets the definition of an element and satisfies the following criteria for recognition:
   (a) it is probable that any future economic benefit associated with the item will flow to or from the enterprise; and
   (b) the item has a cost or value that can be measured with reliability.

recoverable amount
The higher of an asset's net selling price and its value in use.

regular way contract
A contract for the purchase or sale of financial assets that requires delivery of the assets within the time-frame generally established by regulation or convention in the market place concerned.

related parties
Parties are considered to be related if one party has the ability to control the other party or exercise significant influence over the other party in making financial and operating decisions.

related party transaction
A transfer of resources or obligations between related parties, regardless of whether a price is charged.

relevance
Information has the quality of relevance when it influences the economic decisions of users by helping them evaluate past, present or future events or confirming, or correcting, their past evaluations.

reliability
Information has the quality of reliability when it is free from material error and bias and can be depended upon by users to represent faithfully that which it either purports to represent or could reasonably be expected to represent.

replacement cost of an asset
Normally derived from the current acquisition cost of a similar asset, new or used, or of an equivalent productive capacity or service potential.

reportable segment
A business segment or a geographical segment for which segment information is required to be disclosed.

reporting currency
The currency used in presenting the financial statements.

reporting enterprise
An enterprise for which there are users who rely on the financial statements as their major source of financial information about the enterprise.

repurchase agreement
An agreement to transfer a financial asset to another party in exchange for cash or other consideration and a concurrent obligation to reacquire the financial asset at a future date for an amount equal to the cash or other consideration exchanged plus interest.

research
Original and planned investigation undertaken with the prospect of gaining new scientific or technical knowledge and understanding.

residual value
The net amount which an enterprise expects to obtain for an asset at the end of its useful life after deducting the expected costs of disposal.

restructuring
A programme that is planned and controlled by management, and materially changes either:
(a) the scope of a business undertaken by an enterprise; or
(b) the manner in which that business is conducted.

retirement benefit plans
Arrangements whereby an enterprise provides benefits for its employees on or after termination of service (either in the form of an annual income or as a lump sum) when such benefits, or the employer's contributions towards them, can be determined or estimated in advance of retirement from the provisions of a document or from the enterprise's practices.
see also post-employment benefit plans.

retrospective application
Application of a new accounting policy to events and transactions as if the new accounting policy had always been in use.

return on plan assets (of an employee benefit plan)
Interest, dividends and other revenue derived from the plan assets, together with realised and unrealised gains or losses on the plan assets, less any costs of administering the plan and less any tax payable by the plan itself.

revaluation
Restatement of assets and liabilities.

revalued amount of an asset
The fair value of an asset at the date of a revaluation less any subsequent accumulated depreciation.

revenue
The gross inflow of economic benefits during the period arising in the course of the ordinary activities of an enterprise when those inflows result in increases in equity, other than increases relating to contributions from equity participants.

reverse acquisition
An acquisition when an enterprise obtains ownership of the shares of another enterprise but as part of the exchange transaction issues enough voting shares, as consideration, such that control of the combined enterprise passes to the owners of the enterprise whose shares have been acquired.

rewards associated with a leased asset
The expectation of profitable operation over the asset's economic life and of gain from appreciation in value or realisation of a residual value.

risks associated with a leased asset
Possibilities of losses from idle capacity or technological obsolescence and of variations in return due to changing economic conditions.

sale and leaseback transaction
The sale of an asset by the vendor and the leasing of the same asset back to the vendor. The rentals and the sale price are usually interdependent as they are negotiated as a package and need not represent fair values.

securitisation
The process by which financial assets are transformed into securities.

segment assets
Those operating assets that are employed by a segment in its operating activities and that either are directly attributable to the segment or can be allocated to the segment on a reasonable basis.

segment expense
Expense resulting from the operating activities of a segment that is directly attributable to the segment and the relevant portion of an expense that can be allocated on a reasonable basis to the segment, including expenses relating to sales to external customers and expenses relating to transactions with other segments of the same enterprise.

segment result
Segment revenue less segment expense. Segment result is determined before any adjustments for minority interest.

segment revenue
Revenue reported in the enterprise's income statement that is directly attributable to a segment and the relevant portion of enterprise revenue that can be allocated on a reasonable basis to a segment, whether from sales to external customers or from transactions with other segments of the same enterprise.

set-off, legal right of
A debtor's legal right, by contract or otherwise, to settle or otherwise eliminate all or a portion of an amount due to a creditor by applying against that amount an amount due from the creditor.

settle net
To make a cash payment based on the change in fair value of two offsetting derivatives.

settlement (of employee benefit obligations)
A transaction that eliminates all further legal or constructive obligation for part or all of the benefits provided under a defined benefit plan, for example, when a lump-sum cash payment is made to, or on behalf of, plan participants in exchange for their rights to receive specified post-employment benefits.

settlement date
The date that a financial asset is delivered to the enterprise that purchased it.

settlement value
The undiscounted amounts of cash or cash equivalents expected to be paid to satisfy the liabilities in the normal course of business.

short seller
An enterprise that sells securities that it does not yet own.

short-term employee benefits

Employee benefits (other than termination benefits and equity compensation benefits) which fall due wholly within twelve months after the end of the period in which the employees render the related service.

significant influence

The power to participate in the financial and operating policy decisions of an economic activity but not control or joint control over those policies.

solvency

The availability of cash over the longer term to meet financial commitments as they fall due.

state (employee benefit) plan

Employee benefit plans established by legislation to cover all enterprises (or all enterprises in a particular category, for example, a specific industry) and operated by national or local government or by another body (for example, an autonomous agency created specifically for this purpose) which is not subject to control or influence by the reporting enterprise.

subsidiary

An enterprise that is controlled by another enterprise (known as the parent).

substance over form

The principle that transactions and other events are accounted for and presented in accordance with their substance and economic reality and not merely their legal form.

tax base of an asset or liability

The amount attributed to that asset or liability for tax purposes.

tax expense (tax income)

The aggregate amount included in the determination of net profit or loss for the period in respect of current tax and deferred tax. Tax expense (tax income) comprises current tax expense (current tax income) and deferred tax expense (deferred tax income).

taxable profit (tax loss)

The profit (loss) for a period, determined in accordance with the rules established by the taxation authorities, upon which income taxes are payable (recoverable).

taxable temporary difference
A temporary difference that will result in taxable amounts in determining taxable profit (tax loss) of future periods when the carrying amount of the asset or liability is recovered or settled.

temporary difference
A difference between the carrying amount of an asset or liability in the balance sheet and its tax base. A temporary difference may be either:

(a) a taxable temporary difference; or

(b) a deductible temporary difference.

termination benefits
Employee benefits payable as a result of either:

(a) an enterprise's decision to terminate an employee's employment before the normal retirement date; or

(b) an employee's decision to accept voluntary redundancy in exchange for those benefits.

trade date
The date that an enterprise commits to purchase a financial asset.

trading – financial asset or liability held for trading
see financial asset or liability held for trading.

transaction costs (financial instruments)
Incremental costs that are directly attributable to the acquisition or disposal of a financial asset or liability.

transitional liability (defined benefit plans)
The following total:

(a) the present value of the obligation at the date of adopting IAS 19 (revised);

(b) minus the fair value, at the date of adoption, of plan assets (if any) out of which the obligations are to be settled directly;

(c) minus any past service cost that should be recognised in later periods.

treasury shares
Equity instruments re-acquired and held by the issuing enterprise itself or by its subsidiaries.

understandability
Information provided in financial statements has the quality of understandability when is comprehensible to users who have a reasonable knowledge of business and economic activities and accounting and a willingness to study the information with reasonable diligence.

unearned finance income
The difference between:

(a) the aggregate of the minimum lease payments under a finance lease from the standpoint of the lessor and any unguaranteed residual value accruing to the lessor; and

(b) the present value of (a) above, at the interest rate implicit in the lease.

unguaranteed residual value
That portion of the residual value of the leased asset, the realisation of which by the lessor is not assured or is guaranteed solely by a party related to the lessor.

uniting of interests
A business combination in which the shareholders of the combining enterprises combine control over the whole, or effectively the whole, of their net assets and operations to achieve a continuing mutual sharing in the risks and benefits attaching to the combined entity such that neither party can be identified as the acquirer.

upstream transactions
For example, sales of assets from an associate to the investor (or its consolidated subsidiaries).

useful life
Either:

(a) the period over which a depreciable asset is expected to be used by the enterprise; or

(b) the number of production or similar units expected to be obtained from the asset by the enterprise.

value in use
The present value of estimated future cash flows expected to arise from the continuing use of an asset and from its disposal at the end of its useful life.

variable production overheads
Those indirect costs of production that vary directly, or nearly directly, with the volume of production, such as indirect materials and indirect labour.

venturer
A party to a joint venture that has joint control over that joint venture.

vested employee benefits
Employee benefits that are not conditional on future employment.

warrant
A financial instrument that gives the holder the right to purchase ordinary shares.

weighted average cost method
Under this method, the cost of each item is determined from the weighted average of the cost of similar items at the beginning of a period and the cost of similar items purchased or produced during the period. The average may be calculated on a periodic basis, or as each additional shipment is received, depending upon the circumstances of the enterprise.

weighted average number of ordinary shares outstanding during the period
Number of ordinary shares outstanding at the beginning of the period, adjusted by the number of ordinary shares cancelled, bought back or issued during the period multiplied by a time-weighting factor.

Index